**Simulating
Regional Economic
Development**

Simulating Regional Economic Development

An Interindustry Analysis of
the West Virginia Economy

William H. Miernyk
Kenneth L. Shellhammer
Douglas M. Brown
Ronald L. Coccari
Charles J. Gallagher
Wesley H. Wineman

Heath Lexington Books
D. C. Heath and Company
Lexington, Massachusetts

To Wassily Leontief

Contents

Tables

Tables (continued)

Tables (continued)

Figures

Matrix Tables

Introduction

This book discusses the use of an input-output model to simulate the process of regional economic development. The data relate to a specific state, but the emphasis is on method. Thus the book is addressed to a wider audience than those who might have an interest in a given area. Some results have been published in preliminary reports and articles.[a] All tables in the present volume have been revised, however, including the basic (1965) transactions table.

In a widely reprinted article, which first appeared in 1957, the late Charles Tiebout was critical of the use of input-output models at the regional level.[b] Tiebout was particularly critical of the fixed production coefficient assumption, and concluded that if the use of fixed coefficients "at the national level is at all dubious, even more is left to be desired at the regional level."[c] He pointed out that trade patterns vary from region to region, and that it is risky to assume the stability of trade coefficients. Finally, he argued that the use of average national coefficients to estimate regional coefficients is bound to lead to substantial error because of differences in industry and product-mix between a region and the nation.

How does the present study deal with the problems which Tiebout raised? First, we agree with his criticism of the short-cut methods used to construct regional input-output tables more than a decade ago. We feel, however, that these problems have been avoided in this study.

1. The West Virginia transactions table was not derived indirectly by using national technical coefficients and state control totals. It was constructed from data obtained by personal interviews with a representative sample of establishments in the state. Random sampling techniques were used to select survey establishments, and tests of significance were made to check the reliability of the data.

2. When making forecasts, of both the static and dynamic variety, we did not assume fixed input coefficients or fixed trade coefficients. These coefficients were projected using a "best practice" establishment technique. Subsamples of technologically advanced establishments were selected in each sector. The assumption was made that these would be representative of average establishments in the target year, and projected coefficients were computed from the subsamples.

[a]John H. Chapman, Jr., and Kenneth L. Shellhammer, *The Structure of the West Virginia Economy, 1965: A Preliminary Report* (November 1967); William H. Miernyk and Kenneth L. Shellhammer, *The Structure of the West Virginia Economy in 1975: A Preliminary Forecast* (May 1968); *Simulating Regional Economic Development with an Input-Output Model* (July 1968), Morgantown, W. Va.: Regional Research Institute, West Virginia University. Roy W. Bahl and Kenneth L. Shellhammer, "Evaluating the State Business Tax Structure: An Application of Input-Output Analysis," *National Tax Journal* XXII, No. 2 (1969); Miernyk, "Sampling Techniques in Making Regional Industry Forecasts," in *Applications of Input-Output Analysis* (Amsterdam: North-Holland Publishing Company, 1970); The Dynamic Model," *Growth and Change* I, No. 2 (1970).

[b]Charles M. Tiebout, "Regional and Interregional Input-Output Models: An Appraisal," *The Southern Economic Journal* (November 1957), pp. 140-47. For another critical analysis of the use of constant production and interareal input coefficients in regional input-output forecasts see Walter Isard, *Methods of Regional Analysis: An Introduction to Regional Science* (Cambridge, Mass.: The M.I.T. Press, 1960), pp. 327-371.

[c]Tiebout, "Input-Output Models," p. 143.

3. A dynamic model was developed so that capital requirements are generated by the system rather than being projected exogenously. Separate matrices of expansion and replacement coefficients were constructed which permitted *all* capital transactions to be treated endogenously.

4. We have not assumed that the structure of the regional economy will remain constant. No attempt was made to forecast the exact direction of structural change, but several economically feasible new activities were simulated to show the effects that such changes would have on the static and dynamic forecasts.

5. Finally, the projections of the West Virginia economy are not limited to output. Employment projections have also been made, and for both the base and target years employment is given not only by sector but by occupational group. The influence of technological change is thus not limited to production coefficients. The impact of technology on the occupational distribution of the labor force is also taken into account.

We did not attempt to project price changes in West Virginia during the period of the forecast. All projections of output, capital sales, and capital requirements are in 1965 prices. Similarly, data on costs and sales in the simulated sectors are expressed in 1965 prices, although the assumption is made that these will not be in operation until 1975. It might have been an interesting exercise to assume some average price increase, and this would have resulted in substantially larger output projections. We know, however, that even during a period of general price increases, there is wide variation in the rates at which different prices rise. Thus the assumption of an average price increase could have distorted the structural relationships.

Why was all this done? The first and rather obvious answer is that if regional input-output studies are to be conducted they should avoid the assumptions which Tiebout, Isard, and others have criticized. It would be unduly immodest to suggest that we have solved all the problems that Tiebout and Isard have discussed. We would like to believe, however, that we have made some progress in the application of the input-output model to regional analysis.

A second and even more important reason for devoting four years to the study reported in these pages is that we hoped to develop an analytical tool that would be useful to those responsible for the planning and execution of regional development programs. Wassily Leontief, the founder of input-output economics, has said: "The input-output table is not merely a device for displaying or storing information; *it is above all an analytical tool.*"[d] This is how we view the present study. We hope that it will be useful to public officials concerned with economic development in West Virginia. But we hope its usefulness will extend beyond the region analyzed, and that it will be helpful to others who are concerned with the strategy of regional development. The last chapter is concerned primarily with this important issue.

A central focus of the study is the use of an input-output model to "simulate" certain aspects of economic development. The term simulation is

[d]*Input-Output Economics* (New York: Oxford University Press, 1966), p. 43, emphasis added.

used here in a general sense. What we have done is to measure the impacts of economic activities not now represented in the region on gross output and employment. While this appears to be a legitimate use of the term, it should be clear that we have not used the technique of *system simulation* employed by operations researchers and industrial engineers. The systems that the latter use typically include stochastic variables and frequently employ the Monte Carlo method. Also, the West Virginia model is not of the "feedback" variety which has been used by economists in a number of regional applications.[e] While we are not aware of earlier uses of the input-output method in precisely this way at the regional level, the basic model is ideally suited to the analysis of development.[f]

To simulate the impact of new activities on the regional economy, columns of input coefficients were developed for each of the simulated sectors. Data for these sectors were obtained by field interviews with operating establishments outside the region, or from the records of pilot plants in the cases dealing with technologically advanced activities not yet in the production stage. To permit direct comparison of the relative impact of each type of simulated activity, the final sales of each were assumed to be $100 million. The analysis shows the differential impact on the region of each of the simulated sectors. It is the primary basis for tentative conclusions about the strategy of regional development.

It would be pretentious to suggest that this study has resulted in a complete development strategy. We hope it has made a modest contribution to the evolution of such a strategy, however, by developing a method for measuring the payoff of alternative types of new investments in a region.

A word is required to explain the numbering of tables in the report. All matrix tables, which include the transactions tables and others derived from them, are identified by Roman numerals and presented at the end of the report because of their size. Other tables interspersed throughout the text are identified by the conventional double numbering system, with the first number referring to the chapter and the second to the specific table in that chapter.

All students of input-output analysis owe an intellectual debt to Professor Wassily Leontief of Harvard University, the founder of this branch of economics. In our case the debt is specific since it was he who suggested the feasibility of

[e]For a discussion of system simulation see Abe Schuchman, *Scientific Decision Making in Business* (New York: Holt, Rinehart & Winston, Inc. 1963), pp. 396-434. For a concise review of a number of feedback models see John F. Kain and John R. Meyer, "Computer Simulations, Physio-Economic Systems, and Intraregional Models," *American Economic Review* (May 1968), pp. 171-181.

[f]The input-output model has been used, of course, to analyze development at the *national* level. As one of many references that could be cited, see Wassily Leontief, "The Structure of Development," *Scientific American* (September 1963), pp. 148-66.

conducting a dynamic analysis at the regional level. We are pleased to dedicate this book to Professor Leontief.

It is also a pleasure to acknowledge the cooperation of the West Virginia businessmen who provided the basic information for the 1965 transactions table. They must remain anonymous, since the detailed information provided was given on a confidential basis. It will be apparent to readers that without their participation this work could not have been done. Dozens of state officials were involved in the collection and evaluation of data used in the study. Many of them are unknown to us, but their efforts are gratefully acknowledged. Because of their special contributions we must mention Angus Peyton, former Commissioner of Commerce in West Virginia; Thomas Battles, former Tax Commissioner of West Virginia; William Rader, Chief of Data Processing, West Virginia Tax Commission; Ralph Halstead, Supervisor of Research and Statistics, West Virginia Department of Employment Security; and Fielding Lewis, West Virginia Department of Commerce. Sidney Katell and James Eckerd, U. S. Bureau of Mines, Morgantown Research Center, provided valuable assistance during the simulation study. We also wish to acknowledge the assistance provided by the entire staff of the Economic Research Service, U.S. Department of Agriculture, West Virginia University.

The following present and former staff members of the Regional Research Institute participated in the study:

Research Associates: Kenneth L. Shellhammer, Assistant Professor of Economics and Research Associate, RRI; Dr. John H. Chapman, Jr., Professor of Economics, Coe College.

Graduate Research Assistants: Douglas M. Brown, Ronald L. Coccari, Charles J. Gallagher, and Wesley H. Wineman. Graduate assistants who participated in earlier phases of the study include Frank Pellegrini, Dietrick Schaupp, Richard H. Smith, and Paul Stein.

Interviewers: John Aluise, William Courtney, Francis Gallela, Virgil Hackett, Mrs. Christy Kleber, Thomas Rosenberger, and Frederick Schaupp.

Programming and Systems Analysis: Mrs. Carol Fuller, Jimmie Davis, and Jeremiah Hague.

Clerical Staff: Anita Arble, Judith Cobb, Alvin Emch, Joseph Gilmore, James Green, Shirley Marsh, Patricia Nichols, Jane Nottingham, Judith Olexa, and Patricia Panarella.

Secretaries: Mrs. Judith DeFazio, Dixie Shafer, Louise Rich, Kathryn Feather, and Patricia Oleksa.

The initial phase of the study was financed by the Regional Research Institute of West Virginia University, but the simulation study, development of the dynamic model, and the study of manpower requirements derived their primary support from the Economic Development Administration, U.S. Department of Commerce. This support is gratefully acknowledged.

William H. Miernyk

January, 1970

**Simulating
Regional Economic
Development**

1

The 1965 Transactions Table

The basis of an input-output analysis is the transactions table, which simultaneously shows all sales and purchases in the economy that it represents. The 1965 transactions table for West Virginia is of the conventional open variety, with relatively little disaggregation of the final demand sectors. A preliminary version was published in 1967.[1] The table included in this study as Table I has been substantially revised, however, and the preliminary table is now considered obsolete.

In all transactions tables, total gross output equals total gross outlay for each processing sector. The individual row and column totals in the final demand and final payment sectors do not balance, although total final demand must equal total final payments. In the preliminary West Virginia table, all rows and columns balanced. This was accomplished by adding a "gross savings" row, which included depreciation and retained profits in addition to other forms of saving. Negative entries in this row represented *net inflows* into the state. Some readers of the preliminary report appear to have misinterpreted the negative entries in the "southeast corner" of the table, and the final version shows actual row and column totals for each final demand and final payments sector. This represents an accounting change only, but it makes the West Virginia transactions table comparable with other regional tables.

The second revision involved a substantive change. In the preliminary table, transportation charges in the coal mining, oil and gas, and chemicals sectors were not imputed to the appropriate transportation sector as is the customary practice. The reasons for this were given in an interim report, and will not be repeated here.[2] In the revised table of this report transportation charges from these sectors have been imputed to the appropriate transportation sector, eliminating an upward bias in current outputs in these sectors. Additional information collected on capital purchases also led to revision of the "southeast corner" of the final table. The preliminary table understated capital imports in 1965 by about $120 million primarily in chemicals, electric systems, and primary metals. In the process of making these changes, the entire table was carefully checked but no reason was found to make further changes.

The remaining differences between the West Virginia transactions table and most other published tables is in the treatment of inventories. Like the 1958 national table, the West Virginia table shows *net* inventory change as a column, but beginning inventory for each sector is also given, although this row has been placed outside the table. It is thus possible to compute gross inventory change for each sector. More important, however, a detailed breakdown of inventory by type was maintained during the adjustment of output for inventory change. This has resulted in improved estimates of transactions in the base year, and hence in more accurate technical coefficients. The details of the adjustment procedure are discussed in the concluding section of this chapter.

Sectoring the West Virginia Economy

The basic criterion for sectoring the West Virginia economy was product or service homogeneity. The objectives were to obtain as much disaggregation as possible without violating disclosure rules, and to maintain a balance between the size of sectors and the degree of disaggregation. A preliminary sectoring was based on information on the number of firms by size and standard industrial classification from *County Business Patterns, 1964.*

As lists of the names of establishments were compiled for subsequent sampling, some of the preliminary sectors had to be aggregated. It was not possible to maintain a distinction among all activities primarily because many establishments produced a range of products which crossed the preliminary sector boundaries. Letters were sent to several hundred West Virginia business-men inquiring about product-mix, and whether or not accounting practices distinguished among product lines. The response rate was encouraging, but the message of the response was not. Some of the preliminary sectors had to be combined as a result of this survey. A few of the sectors had to be aggregated after all survey work was completed to avoid disclosure. Finally, the agriculture sector was constructed from secondary sources by the staff of the Economic Research Service, U. S. Department of Agriculture at West Virginia University.

There is an abundance of information on agricultural transactions, but the relatively small size of this sector in West Virginia suggested that further disaggregation would not have added meaningful detail. The 48 sectors in Table I represent the maximum degree of feasible disaggregation of the West Virginia economy in 1965.

The West Virginia sectors follow the standard industrial classification, and the relationship between these sectors and those of the 1958 national table is given in Table 1.1. There is more disaggregation in the West Virginia table in coal mining, food and kindred products, and in some of the trade and service sectors. On the other hand, there is much more aggregation in some of the manufacturing sectors, as indicated by the relatively large number of national activities that are wholly included in the West Virginia sectors. As a result of the approach followed in the West Virginia study some of the sectors are at the two-digit level, but others are at the three-or four-digit level. The right-hand column of Table 1.1 shows the composition of the West Virginia sectors in terms of the actual standard industrial classifications employed.

It is customary in input-output analysis to treat all levels of government as exogenous sectors, and it is a frequent practice to combine all levels of government into a single sector. In the West Virginia table, state and local activities have been separated from federal activities. All educational activities, public and private, have been included in sector 40, however, and municipal utilities are included in sectors 46 and 48. This was done partly to relate capital investment to the appropriate activity, but also because inputs to these sectors are similar whether they are publicly or privately owned.

The Sample Survey

After the West Virginia sectors had been defined, the next step was to obtain data on interindustry transactions, sales to final demand, payments to primary sectors, and capital purchases. The interindustry flow data were obtained by means of a sample survey in all sectors except agriculture.

Lists of all establishments operating in each sector were compiled from a master list of the 29,692 nonagricultural establishments operating in West Virginia in 1965.[3]

The next step was to array all establishments in each sector in terms of employment. Only establishments employing four or more workers were to be included in the sample survey. After deleting establishments with three or fewer employees, a total of 12,402 establishments remained. These comprised the population from which samples were selected.

In some sectors simple random sampling was employed. In other sectors such as coal mining, where there are a few large establishments and a relatively large number of small establishments, stratified random sampling procedures were followed. The size of sectoral samples varied substantially, but in sectors such as coal mining, chemicals, and primary metals, stratified sampling ensured that both large and small establishments would be represented.

The results of the sample survey are summarized in Table 1.2. The total sample of 406 establishments comprised 3.3% of all establishments in the test population. But the size of sectoral samples ranged from 0.2 to 33.3%. After the survey was completed, a second random sample, identical in size to the first, was selected for each sector for testing purposes. The only statistic that could be used for the tests was annual average earnings for all establishments listed with the West Virginia Department of Employment Security.

The results of the tests are given in the two right-hand columns of Table 1.2. Both in terms of the t and F tests, differences between the two sets of samples are not significant in most cases. The West Virginia establishments included in the survey to obtain interindustry flow data are evidently a representative cross section of establishments in most sectors.

There were two reasons for limiting the test population and the sample survey to establishments employing four or more persons. First, these are the only establishments for which comparable data could be obtained for both the firms interviewed and those included in the test samples. Second, the assumption was

Table 1.1 West Virginia and National
Sectors

West Virginia Sectors	National Sectors[a]
1. Agriculture	1, 2, 3, 4
2. Coal mining (underground)	(7)
3. Coal mining (strip and auger)	(7)
4. Petroleum and natural gas	8
5. All other mining	5, 6, 9, 10
6. General contractors (building)	(11), (12)
7. General contractors (nonbuilding)	(11), (12)
8. Special trades contractors	(11), (12)
9. Food and kindred products (n. e. c.)	(14)
10. Food and kindred products (dairies)	(14)
11. Food and kindred products (bakeries)	(14)
12. Food and kindred products (beverages)	(14)
13. Apparel and accessories	18, (19)
14. Logging and sawmills	20
15. Furniture and other wood fabrication	21, 22, 23
16. Printing and publishing	26
17. Chemicals	27, 28, 29, 30
18. Petroleum	31
19. Glass	35

Standard Industrial Classification
0133, 0139, 0143, 0132, 011, 012
0142, 0144, 019, 07, 08, 09
121
121
13
10, 14
15
16
17
201, 203, 204, 209
202
2051
208
23
241, 242
243, 244, 249, 25
27
28
29
321, 322

Table 1.1 (continued)

West Virginia Sectors	National Sectors[a]
20. Stone and clay products	36
21. Primary metal products	37, 38
22. Fabricated metal products	39, 40, 41, 42
23. Machinery (except electrical)	43, 44, 45, 46, 47 48, 49, 50, 51, 52
24. Electrical machinery and apparatus	53, 54, 55, 56, 57 58
25. Transportation equipment	59, 60, 61
26. Instruments and related products	62, 63
27. All other manufacturing	13, 15, 16, 17, (19) (32), 64, (36), 24 25, 33, 34
28. Eating and drinking establishments	(69)
29. Wholesale trade	(69)
30. Retail food stores	(69)
31. Retail gasoline service stations	(69)
32. All other retail	(69)
33. Banking	(70)
34. Other finance	(70)
35. Insurance agents and brokers	(70)

Standard Industrial Classification
32 (excluding 321, 322 and 329)
33
34
35
36
37
38
21, 22, 30, 329, 39, 19, 26, 31
58
50
54
5541
53, 55, (except 5541), 56, 57, 59
60
61
64

Table 1.1 (continued)

West Virginia Sectors	National Sectors[a]
36. Real estate	71, (73)
37. All other FIRE	(70)
38. Hotels and other lodging places	(72)
39. Medical and legal services	(77)
40. Educational services	(77), 74
41. All other services	(72), (73), 75, (76) (77)
42. Railroads	(65)
43. Trucking and warehousing	(65)
44. All other transportation	(65)
45. Communications	66, 67
46. Electric companies and systems	(68)
47. Gas companies and systems	(68)
48. Water and sanitary services	(68)

Standard Industrial Classification
65
62, 63, 66, 67
70
80, 81
82 (including 9182, 9282, 9382)
72, 73, 75, 76, 79, 86, 89
40
42
44, 41, 45, 46, 47
48
491
492
494, 495, 496 (including 9249, 9349)

[a]U.S. Sectors from *Survey of current Business* (September 1965), p. 33. Numbers without parentheses in the first column indicate that all of the activities included in the national sector are included in the West Virginia sector. Numbers with parentheses indicate that only part of the activities in the national sector are included in the West Virginia sector.

Table 1.2 Sample Sizes and Tests of
Significance[a]

	Test Population (1)	Sample (2)	(2) as % of (1) (3)
1. Agriculture	–	–	–
2. Coal mines (underground)	1,311	8	0.6%
3. Coal mines (strip and auger)	272	10	3.7
4. Petroleum and natural gas	305	4	1.3
5. All other mining	43	3	7.0
6. Building construction	556	8	1.4
7. Nonbuilding construction	288	5	1.7
8. Special construction	854	12	1.4
9. Food products (n. e. c.)	51	4	7.8
10. Food products (dairies)	38	3	7.9
11. Food products (bakeries)	40	6	15.0
12. Food products (beverages)	58	5	8.6
13. Apparel and accessories	37	4	10.8
14. Logging and sawmills	362	18	5.0
15. Furniture and wood fabrication	73	13	17.8
16. Printing and publication	104	19	18.3
17. Chemicals	53	11	20.8
18. Petroleum	15	4	26.7
19. Glass	43	9	20.9

	t (4)		F (5)
	–		–
x	1.29	x	1.53
	*		*
x	0.62	x	4.29
	*		*
x	1.30	x	1.11
x	0.87	z	7.44
x	1.31	x	2.01
x	0.09	x	3.72
	*		*
x	0.16	x	2.90
	*		*
	*		*
	(4.38)	x	1.01
z	2.45	x	1.15
x	0.13	x	1.50
x	1.07	z	7.34
	*		*
z	2.38	x	1.94

Table 1.2 (continued)

	Test Population (1)	Sample (2)	(2) as % of (1) (3)
20. Stone and clay products	94	17	18.1
21. Primary metals	35	10	28.6
22. Fabricated metals	73	12	16.4
23. Machinery (except electric)	98	10	10.2
24. Electrical machinery	18	5	27.8
25. Transportation equipment	11	3	27.3
26. Instruments and related products	10	3	30.0
27. All other manufacturing	69	14	20.3
28. Eating and drinking establishments	826	2	0.2
29. Wholesale trade	569	31	5.5
30. Retail food stores	442	3	0.7
31. Retail gasoline stations	266	9	3.4
32. All other retail	2,036	37	1.8
33. Banking	181	9	5.0
34. Other finance	187	3	1.6
35. Insurance agents and brokers	116	3	2.6
36. Real estate	193	9	4.7
37. All other FIRE	171	3	1.8

	t (4)		F (5)
z	2.18	x	2.64
x	1.21	x	1.02
x	0.83	x	1.75
x	0.81	x	1.79
	*		*
	*		*
	*		*
z	2.80	x	2.45
	*		*
z	0.25		(7.19)
	*		*
x	1.58	x	2.30
z	2.07	x	1.43
x	1.35	x	1.76
	*		*
	*		*
z	2.84		(183.61)
	*		*

Table 1.2 (continued)

	Test Population (1)	Sample (2)	(2) as % of (1) (3)
38. Hotels and lodgings	173	5	2.9
39. Medical and legal services	257	19	7.4
40. Educational services	22	3	2.5
41. All other services	1,354	14	1.0
42. Railroads	17	2	11.8
43. Trucking and warehousing	370	4	0.5
44. All other transportation	128	8	3.7
45. Communications	100	7	7.0
46. Electric companies and systems	21	7	33.3
47. Gas companies and systems	31	7	22.6
48. Water and sanitary services	31	1	3.3
49. Total	12,402	406	3.3

	t (4)		F (5)
x	1.26		(63.51)
z	2.43		(3.99)
	*		*
x	0.76		(8.29)
	*		*
x	0.11	x	1.83
x	1.18	x	1.14
x	0.59	x	1.63
x	1.40	x	1.43
x	1.45	x	1.17
	*		*

[a]Asterisk indicates test not made because of insufficient number of degrees of freedom. 1% level; numbers in parentheses not sig cant at 1% level.

x = significant at 5% level; z = significant at

made that more could be learned about sales from small to large establishments from the purchasers than from the sellers. Small restaurants, drugstores, filling stations, and family-type retail stores can rarely provide information about their customers. Large establishments, however, are able to provide information about the total amounts they spend in each of these sectors. The assumption about the reliability of the direction of information flow from small to large establishments was largely borne out by the experience of the survey. Most of the excluded establishments were of the "all other retail" or "all other services" variety. These sectors cover such conglomerate activity that even perfect information would fail to produce meaningful coefficients.

All interviews were conducted during the summer of 1966 by a team of seven graduate research assistants. A two-week training session was conducted during which the interviewers were given instruction in the rudiments of input-output analysis, and in the interpretation of business accounts on an input-output basis. Pilot interviews were conducted with local establishments, and each of these was followed by a critique. Interviewers were then assigned a specific area of the state, with each area containing about one-seventh of the sample establishments.

The interviewers did not have to arrange their own contacts. Letters were sent to the manager of each sample establishment explaining the nature of the project and requesting the firm's cooperation. The response rate was high. There were, of course, some establishments that did not respond to the letter or which refused to cooperate. Replacement establishments in each sector were selected on a random basis. In some cases it was necessary to obtain approval from corporate headquarters, particularly those based outside the state. In all such cases permission to interview local managers, their purchasing officers, and representatives of the sales department was granted. The statistical test of the samples and the virtual absence of a nonresponse problem — with complete cooperation in all of the major sectors — suggest that the data on interindustry transactions are highly reliable.

The questionnaire used in the sample survey is included as Appendix A. The first section is concerned with sales, inventories, purchases of raw materials, resale merchandise; and manufacturing, administrative, selling and general expenses. Information concerning taxes and profits is also included in this part of the questionnaire. The second section is concerned primarily with sectoral and with in-state and out-of-state breakdowns of sales, expenses, raw materials or resales merchandise purchases, taxes, and final payments. The third portion of the questionnaire is concerned with in-state and out-of-state breakdowns of capital purchases by sector. The latter information was required to construct the gross private investment column of the transactions table, and the table of capital coefficients to be discussed in Chapter 3.

A careful examination of the questionnaire will indicate that even large organizations could provide only estimates in answering some of the questions. The interviewers were instructed to begin with the questions for which specific data could be provided, and to raise questions where estimates were acceptable later in the interview. This proved to be a successful strategy since earlier experience had indicated that if the respondent felt that estimates were acceptable in answering all questions, the interview generally produced poor results. Interviews with small establishments could be completed in about three hours. Interviews with large establishments, particularly those involving several departments, were conducted over a period of two to three days.

The Recapitulation Sheet

Each completed interview scheduled was edited and checked for internal consistency prior to transfer to a recapitulation sheet. This is a device that had been used in earlier studies to facilitate the preparation of data for computation.[4] The recapitulation sheet is divided into 80 columns, corresponding to the number of columns on an IBM card, and 84 rows. Each row on the sheet is keypunched as a single IBM card. All data were transferred from the edited questionnaires to the recapitulation sheets, which could be interpreted directly by keypunch operators.

The Development of Control Totals

There were three major sources of control totals for the West Virginia sectors. The primary source was a set of highly detailed business and occupations tax data obtained from the West Virginia State Tax Commission. The classification system used by the state of West Virginia does not follow the sectors in the West Virginia input-output table. But data for all establishments are available on a four-digit standard industrial classification, and the Tax Commission reclassified and recomputed totals on the basis of the West Virginia input-output sectors. Supplementary data on employment and earnings were obtained from the West Virginia Department of Employment Security.

The business and occupations tax — a gross receipts tax — would be an ideal source of data for estimating control totals if the tax rates were effectively uniform on all establishments. But accounting practices vary particularly between multiplant firms with out-of-state headquarters and firms that operate entirely within the state. Thus the control totals originally estimated from tax data were adjusted, generally in an upward direction, on the basis of wage and employment data. A second round of adjustments, to be discussed in the next section, were made following completion of the survey when data on in-state and out-of-state sales were available on a sample basis.

Constructing the Transactions Table

When the sample data had been compiled, they were expanded by control totals to obtain dollar transactions. Five separate categories of transactions were maintained throughout the data handling procedure: (1) sales of capital goods; (2) sales of current inputs and final deliveries, including all exports; (3) purchases of capital goods, including capital imports; (4) purchases of raw materials and resale merchandise, including imports of raw materials and resale merchandise; and (5) current expenses, including imported expense items and final payments. In preparation for reconciliation, the sales data, (1) and (2), were transferred to "rows only" tables, and the purchase data, (3), (4), and (5), were transferred to "columns only" tables.

Reconciliation is necessary to eliminate discrepancies between the estimates of industry i's sales to industry j, and the estimates of industry j's purchases from industry i. With perfect information the two numbers would be equal. In practice this rarely occurs, and a judgment must be made as to which is the more reliable estimate. To assist in making the judgment, a "reliability quotient" was calculated for each sector. The "reliability quotients" were based upon: (1) the proportion of total sales accounted for by the sample, (2) reliability of the sector control total, (3) homogeneity of output within the sector (the "all other" sectors, for example, are generally considered to be not highly reliable), (4) the representativeness of the sample as determined by the t and F tests, and (5) the judgment of interviewers. The latter were asked to give their opinions of the reliability of each interview.

Spot checks indicated that, in general, cells with high reliability quotients for both sales and purchases had smaller relative discrepancies than those with low reliability quotients. The reliability quotients were used as a guide to reconciliation. By proceeding from the cell with the highest reliability quotients to the cell with the lowest, the range of possible entries in the least reliable cells was systematically narrowed. This proved to be an excellent tactic, and in most sectors more than 90% of interindustry transactions were locked in before using data of questionable reliability. While this by no means eliminated judgmental adjustments, the use of judgment was minimized.

Sales on capital account were reconciled with capital purchases, and the resulting matrix summed to form the gross private state investment vector. The same matrix later formed the basis of the analysis of capital requirements which is discussed in Chapter 3. Sales on current account were reconciled with the "columns only" tables of raw materials and resale merchandise purchases, and current expenses. The separation between expense items and resale merchandise or raw materials purchases was continued throughout the reconciliation process in order to make appropriate adjustments for inventory changes, and to margin the trade sectors.

By maintaining the separation between the different types of purchases, each type of purchase could be adjusted for each type of inventory change. For example, expenses in the trade sectors are for the most part associated with selling and were accordingly not adjusted for changes in resale merchandise inventories. Only resale merchandise purchases were adjusted. Similarly, in manufacturing industries, adjustments were made in raw materials purchases for changes in raw materials inventories. Both expenses and adjusted raw materials purchases were, in effect, adjusted for changes in goods-in-process and finished goods inventories by including these "net additions to inventories" in total gross output.

This method of handling inventory change is an improvement over that followed in earlier input-output studies in that it leads to a more precise measure of the technical coefficients of production. The conventional approach has included gross inventory depletions in total outlays and gross inventory additions in total gross outputs. Technical flow coefficients are then calculated by first subtracting inventory depletions from total gross output and dividing each column entry of the transactions table by this *adjusted* gross output figure. All purchases are therefore proportionately adjusted for inventory changes.

The separation of resale merchandise purchases and expenses in the trade sectors was also useful in margining the trade sectors. Margining is the process of "rerouting" resale merchandise from producer to buyer. Total sales by trade sectors are reduced to reflect only the markup on sales. The markup equals selling expenses plus profit. By keeping resale merchandise transactions separate from selling expenses, we were able to avoid the use of national average markups.

The accounting procedures just described required the ordering of a large body of data, and careful attention to detail at each stage of the calculations. But they simplified the difficult task of reconciling the independently derived row and column entries in the transactions table, and minimized the use of judgment. They also led to a more accurate statement of the technical relationship between inputs and outputs represented by the input coefficients than would have resulted from gross inventory adjustments, and the use of national average trade margins.

2

Comparative Static Projections to 1975

During the early days of input-output analysis there was frequent criticism of the assumption of fixed technical coefficients, or of linearity and proportionality in the static input-output model. But as Evans and Hoffenberg pointed out in their classic paper on the 1947 U.S. model, ". . . the question as to proportionality, linearity, or nonlinearity is not properly conceptual, but rather a subject for empirical investigation and an appeal to facts."[1] Their point was well taken, and several empirical studies of the behavior of technical coefficients have been made.

Pilot studies of the tin can and ball and roller bearings industries in the United States were made by Anne Carter, and Per Sevaldson studied the behavior of input coefficients in the cork and mechanical woodpulp industries of Norway.[2] The results of these pilot studies were interesting and suggestive, but they could only point the way toward more comprehensive research, which would examine the effects of changing technology on the structure of an entire economy. Studies of this kind could be made only when more than one input-output table was available for a given economy.

After publication of the 1958 table for the United States, Dr. Carter made a detailed analysis of the structural changes resulting from technological advancements between 1947 and 1958.[3] She found that "the many substitutions, technological developments, and innovations introduced between 1947 and 1958 result in definite changes in input-output patterns . . . [but] even in this period of rapid technical advance . . . broad changes in the structure of production were moderate."[4] Not all sectors of the economy are equally affected by technological change. Dr. Carter, however, found a relative increase in what she calls "general" inputs, which are those used by all or almost all sectors. Some of these are electric energy, communications, maintenance construction, business services, printing and publishing, finance, insurance, and real estate. She also found an "increasing diversification of the bill of materials consumed by each industry."[5]

The evidence is clear that changing technology affects the pattern of inputs in an industrialized economy. The changes in direct input coefficients might be relatively small, but these are magnified when the table of direct coefficients is inverted to obtain a general solution and the inverse is multiplied by relatively large final demand entries. For short-term forecasts of one or two years it is no doubt safe to work with fixed technical coefficients. For long-term forecasts of five years or more the assumption of constant technology is not tenable.

The Effects of Changing Technology and
Trade Patterns on a Regional Economy

The problem of making long-range regional interindustry forecasts becomes somewhat more complex than that of making national projections, particularly if the national economy is relatively closed. Regional input coefficients can change over time not only because of changing technology, but also because of changes in interregional trade patterns.[6] Indeed, in some sectors trade pattern changes can be substantially larger than those resulting from changes in technology. When using a regional input-output model to make long-range forecasts it is not always possible to distinguish between the effects of changes in technology and those resulting from changes in trade patterns on the basis of available data. It is necessary, therefore, to utilize a forecasting technique that will take into account both types of changes simultaneously. The method used to project input coefficients in this study is a refinement of a technique used earlier in making long-range forecasts of the six subbasins that comprise the Colorado River Basin.[7]

The method is quite simple, provided appropriate data have been collected for the construction of the regional table. It consists of the selection of a subsample of "best practice" establishments in each sector. The assumption is that these establishments are more technologically advanced than the average establishment in each sector, and that their input structures will represent those of average establishments at some future time.

Selection of the "Best Practice" Establishments

Four different ratios were used to identify the "best practice" establishments in the West Virginia sample. In each case the denominator is total gross output (TGO), and the numerators are employment, wages, profits, and depreciation. The first two ratios measure the relative labor intensity of the establishment. Ideally, man-hours should have been used in computing this set of ratios, but man-hour data were not available for all establishments in the sample. *A priori,* the best practice establishments were expected to have low ratios of employment to TGO compared with the average ratio for each sector.

The second ratio (wages/TGO) is somewhat ambiguous. A highly efficient firm in a given industry could have a relatively high ratio if the firm followed the practice of paying above-average wages to attract superior workers. At the same time, a highly efficient firm could have a low ratio if it were more capital intensive than the average firm in the industry.

The profit ratio also requires rather careful interpretation. One would expect on *a priori* grounds that profits and efficiency are positively correlated, other things being equal. But it is possible for a new establishment of the latest design, and incorporating the most recent technological developments, to operate for some time before showing a profit. Similarly, relatively inefficient establishments can report high profits if they operate in a sheltered environment. A local monopsonist in the labor market would be a case in point of the latter. In the final ratio, depreciation was used as a proxy for investment. This again might be satisfactory if all establishments in the sector follow the same depreciation policy, but this is a rather questionable assumption.

If the ratio of depreciation to TGO is considered as a proxy for the *total capital input,* a relatively low ratio indicates a best practice establishment. For example, if one dollar's worth of depreciation resulted in two dollars of output in establishment *A,* and one dollar's worth of depreciation resulted in four dollars of output in establishment *B* (other things being equal), *B* is getting more for its investment than *A,* and we would conclude that *B* is more technologically advanced than *A.* The major problem is that there is no way of knowing whether other things are indeed equal.

None of the ratios by itself could be used as a reliable guide to the selection of best practice establishments in each sector. However, used *in combination,* the ratios identify the establishments in each sector which are more efficient than the average. For example, a low employment and high wage ratio coupled with a relatively high depreciation ratio would suggest more investment per worker in an establishment than in the sector as a whole. If the profit ratio of the establishment also happened to be relatively high, it would qualify as one of the best practice establishments in the sector. On the other hand, high employment and profit ratios associated with low wage and depreciation ratios, relative to the average for the sector, would suggest that the establishment is not as technologically advanced as the average, but that its favorable profit position is due to circumstances peculiar to that establishment.

This type of evaluation was made, establishment by establishment, to identify the best practice establishments in each sector. Because of the aggregation problem, the size of establishment and type of product were also taken into consideration when the four ratios were evaluated.

The number of best practice establishments selected in each sector and the sectoral subsamples as a percent of the original sample are given in Table 2.1. The total subsample amounted to 43% of the original sample. The range was from 25% in sectors 8 (special trades contractors) and 13 (apparel and accessories) to 67% in several sectors. (The relatively large size of some of the subsamples led one member of the staff to comment, not entirely in jest, that what we had actually done was to eliminate the "worst practice" establishments from the sectors.)

The next step was to construct a new table of input coefficients from the subsample in each sector. These were then compared, cell by cell, with the 1965 a_{ij}'s. In general, the differences were not expected to be large, and differences that were out of line with expectations were carefully examined. Where the influence

Table 2.1 Sub-sample of Best Practice Establishments

		Original Sample (1)	Best–Practice Sub-sample (2)	(2) as % of (1) (3)
1.	Agriculture	–	–	–
2.	Coal mining (underground)	8	3	38%
3.	Coal mining (strip and auger)	10	4	40
4.	Petroleum and natural gas	4	2	50
5.	All other mining	3	2	67
6.	General contractors (building)	8	4	50
7.	General contractors (non–building)	5	3	60
8.	Special trades contractors	12	3	25
9.	Food and kindred products (n. e. c.)	4	2	50
10.	Food and kindred products (dairies)	3	2	67
11.	Food and kindred products (bakeries)	6	3	50
12.	Food and kindred products (beverages)	5	2	40
13.	Apparel and accessories	4	1	25
14.	Logging and sawmills	18	7	39
15.	Furniture and other wood fabrications	13	6	46
16.	Printing and publishing	19	6	32
17.	Chemicals	11	5	45
18.	Petroleum	4	2	50
19.	Glass	9	4	45
20.	Stone and clay products	17	7	41

Table 2.1 (continued)

		Original Sample (1)	Best–Practice Sub–sample (2)	(2) as % of (1) (3)
21.	Primary metal products	10	4	40
22.	Fabricated metal products	12	5	42
23.	Machinery (except electric)	10	3	30
24.	Electrical machinery and apparatus	5	3	60
25.	Transportation equipment	3	2	67
26.	Instrument and related product	3	2	67
27.	All other manufacturing	14	5	36
28.	Eating and drinking establishments	2	1	50
29.	Wholesale trade	31	13	42
30.	Retail food stores	3	2	67
31.	Retail gasoline service stations	9	4	45
32.	All other retail	37	15	41
33.	Banking	9	5	55
34.	Other finance	3	2	67
35.	Insurance agents and brokerage	3	2	67
36.	Real estate	9	3	33
37.	All other FIRE	3	2	67
38.	Hotels and other lodging places	5	2	40
39.	Medical and legal services	19	5	26

Table 2.1 (continued)

		Original Sample (1)	Best–Practice Sub–sample (2)	(2) as % of (1) (3)
40.	Educational services	3	2	67
41.	All other services	14	6	43
42.	Railroads	2	1	50
43.	Trucking and warehousing	4	2	50
44.	All other transportation	8	5	62
45.	Communications	7	4	57
46.	Electric companies and systems	7	4	57
47.	Gas companies and systems	7	3	43
48.	Water and sanitary services	1	–	–
49.	Total	406	175	43

of technological change could be isolated, trends in the regional coefficients were compared with trends in national coefficients.[8] While there was a presumption that national and regional coefficients would be different, primarily because of differences in industry and product-mix between the region and the nation, there should be less difference in the *rate of change* between national and regional coefficients than in the coefficients themselves.

It is apparent upon examination that some of the coefficients were affected more by changes in trade patterns than technology. Fortunately, trade pattern changes could be checked because excellent data were available on out-of-state purchases by all sample establishments. While we know relatively little about the stability of interregional trade patterns in the industrial detail required for a regional input-output model, the assumption was made that the trade patterns of best practice establishments in 1965 would be representative of the average trade patterns in each sector in the target year.

When the table of direct input coefficients was finished, it was a relatively simple matter to complete the "comparative static" interindustry projections to 1975. Final demand for each sector was projected, by methods described later in this chapter, and these were applied to the Leontief inverse matrix derived from the table of projected coefficients to obtain the target year forecasts of interindustry transactions in West Virginia. There was one problem involved in the projection of the input coefficients, however, and this was the determination of the time interval that would be required for the best practice coefficients to become future average coefficients.

One method of determining this time interval is to compare the rates of change in one or more "general" national coefficients, as Anne Carter has called them, with the rates of change in regional coefficients as "projected" by the method described earlier.[9] There is no reason to expect these rates of change to be identical, but they should be reasonably close. Only rough comparison can be made between national coefficients and regional coefficients, however, because of differences in sectoral definitions.

The coefficient chosen for making this comparison was electrical energy inputs. Unfortunately, in the national table for 1958, and the projection of this table to 1970, electrical energy is combined with gas, water, and sanitary services. In the West Virginia table electrical energy is a separate sector. A considerable amount of time and effort was devoted to a comparison of trends in the national and regional coefficients, but the results were largely inconclusive. They helped somewhat, however, in making the final decisions, which were largely judgmental. In most cases we assumed it would require about 10 years for the best practice establishments of 1965 to become average establishments. In some cases, however, the best practice establishments were estimated to be about five years ahead of the average, and linear extrapolations were made to 1975. Admittedly, this is an arbitrary decision, and where reasonably good comparisons can be made, as in the petroleum and natural gas sector, for example, the projections of the West Virginia coefficients appear to be on the conservative side. We preferred to err in this direction if necessary rather than to overstate the rate of technological progress in the region.

Comparison of the 1965 and 1975 Coefficients

The direct coefficients computed from the 1965 transactions table are given in Table II and the projected coefficients to 1975 are given in Table IV. It is possible to compare the effects of changes in technology and trade patterns by relating these two sets of direct coefficients to a common final demand vector. The results of such a comparison, using 1965 final demand, are given in table 2.2.

There are some differences between this comparison and that given in "Sampling Techniques in Making Regional Industry Forecasts." The data in the earlier paper were preliminary, while those in Table 2.2 are the final results of the comparison. Table 2.2 can best be interpreted by considering the answer to the question: What would have happened to West Virginia output in 1965 on the basis of 1975 technology and trade patterns? Gross output would have been about $277 million or 3.1% higher than it was in 1965. There would have been an increase in interindustry transactions of 3.6% on the basis of the 1975 coefficients, and a substantial increase of 15.8% in direct requirements per dollar of sales to final demand. There would also have been increases in "general" inputs such as electrical energy, communications, printing and publishing, finance, insurance, and real estate. These shifts are consistent with those found by Anne Carter in her comparison of the effects of changing technology on national coefficients (see the references to her work in the first section of this chapter.) The sectoral effects are far from uniform, however. Most of the declines in direct inputs are in relatively minor sectors. The one exception is the electrical energy sector, and this is explained by the substantial reduction in coal inputs per kilowatt hour of output when the 1975 coefficients are used.

The modest decline in imports indicated by Table 2.2 is due in part to increased interdependence *within* the state economy and in part to changes in trade patterns. One of the largest reductions is in sector 41, "all other services," which would have imported $32 million less on the basis of 1975 coefficients than it did in 1965. Other sectors that would have had significant declines in imports include strip and auger coal mining (sector 3), glass (sector 19), stone and clay products (sector 20), and restaurants and bars (sector 28).

The largest increase in relative terms is found in apparel and accessories (sector 13), a relatively minor sector in the West Virginia economy. The electrical energy sector (46) would also have imported substantially more than it did in 1965 on the basis of 1975 coefficients. This reflects in part a sharp reduction in coal inputs per unit of output, but it also indicates a greater degree of reliance on out-of-state services, particularly financial services.

The final column in Table 2.2 shows a modest increase in "all other final payments" which offsets the decline in imports. The small difference between the two totals is due to rounding error.

Table 2.2 Effects of Projecting 1965 Coefficients to 1975[a]

Sectors	TGO (thousands of $)		Total Direct and Indirect Requirements[b]	
1. Agriculture	$ 4,963	3.9%	$ 0.015856	1.2%
2. Coal mines (undgd.)	− 31	−0.0	0.019889	1.8
3. Coal (strip and auger)	−2,227	−4.1	0.119983	7.1
4. Pet. and nat. gas	2,748	4.7	0.148622	11.6
5. All other mining	−3,936	−5.5	0.101350	8.5
6. Bldg. const.	2,246	1.3	0.088690	4.8
7. Nonbldg. const.	3,104	1.8	0.112348	7.0
8. Spec. const.	13,000	9.1	0.083058	6.5
9. Food prod. (n. e. c.)	1,705	3.3	0.079789	5.3
10. Dairies	2,854	3.6	0.090115	6.3
11. Bakeries	1,351	2.8	0.071371	5.9
12. Beverages	1,266	4.2	0.050989	4.4
13. Apparel and acc.	2,138	9.1	0.053195	4.9
14. Logging and sawmills	9,498	15.2	0.161273	11.2
15. Furn. and wood fab.	2,331	9.0	−0.032194	−2.4
16. Print. and pub.	39,093	63.6	0.003490	0.2
17. Chemicals	−2,204	−0.2	0.002005	0.1
18. Pet. prod.	6,879	9.9	0.035300	2.5
19. Glass	5,120	1.9	0.100842	8.2
20. Stone and clay prod.	6,378	4.8	0.141426	10.9

Direct Inputs (thousands of $)		Imports (thousands of $)		All Other Final Payments (thousands of $)	
$ 1,601	4.9%	$ 1,575	4.3%	$ 1,786	3.1%
10,333	14.7	−6,627	−2.7	−3,775	−1.0
2,060	7.8	−2,248	−28.7	−2,038	−10.2
7,062	54.5	− 877	−12.1	−3,437	− 8.9
4,123	38.1	−4,460	−13.4	−3,600	−13.2
6,336	5.7	−2,192	−16.0	−1,899	− 3.9
11,663	14.3	−3,140	−14.5	−5,422	− 7.6
11,452	35.7	−1,683	− 6.2	3,231	3.9
4,218	21.3	−2,199	− 9.6	− 314	− 3.3
5,885	22.7	−3,162	− 9.4	131	0.7
2,669	31.4	−1,663	− 7.3	342	2.1
1,262	33.3	− 127	− 1.2	132	0.8
1,242	82.4	787	132.7	109	0.5
8,797	43.6	− 591	− 6.8	1,290	3.8
− 474	−7.7	1,265	13.8	1,537	14.7
14,675	65.8	4,251	47.8	20,167	66.7
−3,047	−0.8	2,110	0.4	−1,274	− 0.3
3,046	12.9	1,869	7.0	1,964	10.3
20,506	40.8	−11,806	−19.3	−3,579	− 2.3
14,986	45.8	10,630	30.4	2,019	3.1

Table 2.2 (continued)

Sectors	TGO (thousands of $)		Total Direct and Indirect Requirements[b]	
21. Primary metals	11,308	1.2	0.004363	0.4
22. Fab. metals	9,751	8.1	0.026031	2.2
23. Mach. (ex. elec.)	2,993	2.7	−0.003157	−0.3
24. Elec. mach.	3,547	3.0	0.010357	0.8
25. Transp. equip.	− 45	−0.0	0.002908	0.3
26. Ins. and prod.	− 275	−3.2	0.029008	2.6
27. All other mfg.	11,097	8.8	0.012839	1.1
28. Rest. and bars	2,018	1.7	0.106545	8.3
29. Wholesale trade	1,871	0.6	0.032150	2.8
30. Retail food	− 9	−0.0	0.021558	1.7
31. Auto serv. sta.	4,839	12.5	−0.016322	−1.3
32. All other retail	8,521	2.2	0.089591	7.2
33. Banking	7,166	7.2	0.023092	2.1
34. Other fin.	2,687	4.8	0.016272	1.4
35. Ins. agents	12,776	4.7	−0.011361	−1.0
36. Real estate	1,439	2.4	0.038702	2.8
37. All other FIRE	486	1.0	0.027378	1.7
38. Hotels and lodging	2,246	5.9	0.024341	1.6

Direct Inputs (thousands of $)		Imports (thousands of $)		All Other Final Payments (thousands of $)	
1,841	2.0	5,142	0.9	4,324	1.3
4,382	22.7	4,771	9.2	600	1.2
- 537	-3.0	1,573	3.2	1,957	4.3
1,361	3.6	2,885	9.7	- 697	- 1.4
254	1.1	553	0.6	- 855	- 1.3
149	21.0	30	0.7	- 455	-12.5
1,686	10.4	7,614	10.7	1,797	4.6
8,563	33.8	-5,070	-15.3	-1,474	- 2.6
7,590	18.1	797	6.4	-4,925	- 1.9
1,799	7.2	-234	-1.9	-1,573	- 1.9
21	0.2	611	19.8	4,208	15.7
25,932	34.7	-8,607	-13.2	-8,801	- 3.5
1,752	18.5	1,832	19.4	3,581	4.4
833	11.0	-145	- 1.8	1,999	4.9
-1,407	-5.0	12,617	7.0	1,568	2.4
1,367	8.3	425	10.6	-353	- 0.9
416	1.8	789	12.2	-719	- 3.8
1,159	8.0	561	11.6	527	2.8

32

Table 2.2 (continued)

Sectors	TGO (thousands of $)		Total Direct and Indirect Requirements[b]	
39. Med. and legal serv.	10,118	5.7	0.043824	3.6
40. Ed. serv.	1,777	0.8	0.112972	8.7
41. All other serv.	15,094	3.4	0.137978	12.0
42. Railroads	−16,401	−7.7	0.002931	0.3
43. Truck and warehsg.	13,226	7.1	0.085553	7.4
44. All other transp.	5,115	9.6	0.040061	3.2
45. Communications	13,755	11.5	0.013342	1.2
46. Elec. systems	38,905	24.7	−0.094723	−6.6
47. Gas systems	15,379	4.1	0.034313	2.9
48. Water and san. serv.	1,296	4.3	0.011941	0.8
49. Total	$276,955	3.1%	$2.269884	3.7%

Direct Inputs (thousands of $)		Imports (thousands of $)		All Other Final Payments (thousands of $)	
6,057	20.1	−2,288	−10.2	6,351	5.1
16,051	38.2	−2,726	−12.6	−11,997	− 7.9
47,892	88.6	−32,119	−22.4	−681	− 0.3
−2,505	−8.5	−1,939	− 4.1	−11,957	− 8.8
13,440	57.7	148	0.3	−361	− 0.3
2,354	21.4	749	3.7	2,012	9.1
2,078	19.7	1,831	9.4	9,847	11.1
−1,938	−3.7	7,973	36.1	32,869	39.4
7,181	13.3	8,711	3.5	−513	− 0.7
334	3.6	485	6.4	476	3.5
$276,954	15.8%	−$34,168	− 1.2%	$34,127	0.8%

[a]Differences between input-output components shown using 1965 and 1975 input coefficients and 1965 final demand.

[b]Assuming each sector adds one dollar of sales to the final demand.

The best practice approach to the projection of direct input coefficients is far from foolproof. The changes in West Virginia are consistent with national trends in technical coefficients, however, after taking into account the added influence of changing trade patterns on a regional economy. The projected coefficients together with the projections of final demand provide the basis for the "comparative static" forecast to 1975.

Projecting Final Demand

The final demand vectors in the 1965 table were estimated in part from data used to develop control totals, and in part from the survey data. A variety of secondary sources provided data for estimating the original components of final demand and also served as cross checks.[10] The individual components were built up from data on personal income, personal and business taxes; state, local and federal government receipts and expenditures. Secondary sources were supplemented by primary data from the survey on capital sales, and on exports and inventory change. There is nothing new, however, about the way in which the initial final demand data were estimated for the West Virginia study. The most difficult problems, as is true in any regional input-output study, were encountered in estimating the "southeast corner" entries, where the final demand columns and final payment rows intersect. Conventional methods again were followed in making these estimates and the necessary reconciliations.

The projections of final demand by sector to 1975 were obtained by the following steps:

1 A first approximation of final demand for each sector in the target year was estimated by time-series analysis and comparisons with national trends.

2 The resources that would be required to sustain the projected levels of demand were estimated.

3 Initial demand forecasts were adjusted to eliminate inconsistencies between resource requirements and resource availability.

4 The final forecasts were compared with national trends and adjusted for significant departures from these trends.

Initially, an aggregate projection of final demand was made on the basis of a straightforward time-series analysis of total income, population, and expenditures by state, local, and federal government. This provided nothing more than a reasonably accurate control total.

Fortunately, a major study on changes in final demand in the nation was published while the West Virginia study was in progress.[11] The growth rates of final demand, by sector, in the nation provided useful benchmarks for West Virginia growth rates. Because of differences in sectoral definitions between the national and West Virginia tables, it was necessary to develop a common set of sectors. This was done following the classification scheme given in Table 1-1 and involved weighting growth rates to adjust for differences in the degree of aggregation. The national growth rates were weighted on the basis of West Virginia output in 1965.

Two independent projections of final demand were made for West Virginia although both relied heavily on national growth rates. The initial projection was of *total* final demand by sector, and was based on the assumption that West Virginia would maintain a constant share of national final demand. This was treated as a first approximation, and was used primarily to compare the effects of changing technology and trade patterns discussed in the foregoing. In the second round of projections the constant share assumption was dropped, and total final demand was disaggregated into its components. Final demand for households and the three levels of government (local, state, and federal), was projected by modifying the constant share assumption. Separate projections were also made of gross private investment and exports.

The rate of change in final demand by households was modified by adjusting for differences in changes in income and consumption between West Virginia and the nation. Per capita income in West Virginia is growing at a slower rate than the national average, but because the average level of income is lower in West Virginia than in the nation as a whole the marginal propensity to consume is higher. Thus the rate of change in household final demand was adjusted to allow for both the income effect and the consumption effect.

Time-series analysis was also used in projecting the government components of final demand. Comparable data are available on a national and regional basis on local, state, and federal expenditures. These were not projected by simple extrapolation, however, but were related to the forecasts of national final demand in *Projections 1970*. The net effect was to adjust for shifts in the region's share of any single component.

There are no data for the independent projections of gross private investment. For this vector the national growth rates given in *Projections 1970* were used as first approximations. In a number of cases — particularly in the trade and service sectors — this was essentially the final forecast for the comparative static model because of the complete absence of data on capital sales at the state level. In most cases, however, the initial projections were adjusted on the basis of survey data, and after consultation with a number of experts both in private industry and state government.

The remaining component of final demand is the export vector. Again, time series are not available which would permit approximations of the trend in export sales. The survey provided information on the industries purchasing West Virginia exports, most of which are raw materials (such as coal) or intermediate products (such as steel and industrial chemicals). National growth rates of output in the purchasing sectors were then applied to the state's exports. The rate of change in export sales to other nations was estimated in the same way.

The results of the final demand projections are given in Table 2.3. They were used to make the comparative static projections of output discussed in the next section, as well as in the dynamic model discussed in Chapter 3.

Table 2.3 Annual Growth Rates in Final Demand, by Sector, West Virginia and United States[a]

		Households		Local Government	
		W.Va.	U.S.	W.Va.	U.S.
1.	Agriculture	0.43	0.39	9.82	12.35
2.	Coal Mines (undgd.)	−0.26	−0.48	0	7.19
3.	Coal (strip and auger)	−0.26	−0.48	0	7.19
4.	Pet. and nat. gas	0	0	0	0
5.	All other mining	0.61	3.80	2.12	0
6.	Bldg. const.	0	0	8.60	5.49
7.	Nonbldg. const.	0.95	0	3.08	5.49
8.	Spec. const.	0	0	2.33	5.49
9.	Food prod. (n. e. c.)	1.71	2.91	0	8.15
10.	Dairies	1.71	2.91	0	8.15
11.	Bakeries	1.71	2.91	0	8.15
12.	Beverages	1.71	2.91	0	8.15
13.	Apparel and acc.	2.65	4.17	0	7.78
14.	Logging and sawmills	3.11	5.30	0	0
15.	Furn. and wood fab.	2.50	6.33	0	5.70
16.	Print. and pub.	2.30	3.91	7.03	10.91
17.	Chemicals	3.08	7.53	2.38	7.71
18.	Pet. prod.	2.61	4.44	5.17	8.31
19.	Glass	2.72	4.62	0	0
20.	Stone and clay prod.	2.61	4.44	4.84	7.87

State Government		Federal Government		Gross Private Investment	Export	Total Final Demand	
W.Va.	U.S.	W.Va.	U.S.	W.Va.	W.Va.	W.Va.	U.S.
9.85	12.35	-0.24	1.59	0	-0.41	0.21	0.95
5.86	7.19	1.22	-2.20	4.94	3.49	3.47	4.15
0	7.19	0	-2.70	0	4.20	3.99	4.15
0	0	0	0	0	27.35	27.35	5.52
2.12	0	0	-4.39	3.45	3.43	2.19	1.00
6.16	5.49	3.57	3.67	3.53	3.78	3.65	4.25
3.08	5.49	3.49	3.67	1.57	4.22	2.95	4.25
3.08	5.49	3.66	3.67	1.85	5.17	1.96	4.25
0	8.15	4.14	4.14	0	3.00	2.00	2.92
5.07	8.15	0	4.14	2.92	3.00	1.91	2.92
0	8.15	0	4.14	0	3.00	2.26	2.92
0	8.15	0	4.14	1.54	2.96	2.10	2.92
0	7.78	0	2.26	0	4.20	3.84	3.96
0	0	2.00	-3.25	1.35	3.37	3.66	6.10
2.53	5.70	0	1.81	2.86	3.11	2.51	5.99
6.73	10.91	1.46	1.74	0	4.32	4.18	4.28
2.36	7.71	10.13	-2.34	0	4.15	4.12	5.94
2.95	8.31	4.16	1.56	0	6.36	4.59	4.25
0	0	0	3.66	0	3.64	3.59	3.91
4.84	7.87	4.75	-0.39	3.46	5.06	4.92	4.04

Table 2.3 (continued)

		Households		Local Government	
		W. Va.	U.S.	W. Va.	U.S.
21.	Primary metals	2.53	4.03	0	5.20
22.	Fab. metals	2.47	5.90	0	6.65
23.	Mach. (ex. elec.)	2.29	6.62	0	4.04
24.	Elec. mach.	4.56	9.04	0	7.83
25.	Transp. equip.	0	5.88	0	7.11
26.	Ins. and prod.	3.52	6.18	0	6.12
27.	All other mfg.	2.45	4.35	0	7.19
28.	Rest. and bars	2.56	4.36	3.34	7.99
29.	Wholesale trade	2.56	4.36	2.09	7.99
30.	Retail food	2.56	4.36	0	7.99
31.	Auto serv. sta.	2.56	4.36	0.65	7.99
32.	All other retail	2.56	4.36	2.77	7.99
33.	Banking	3.08	5.24	1.89	9.59
34.	Other fin.	3.08	5.24	2.11	9.59
35.	Ins. agents	3.08	5.24	1.27	9.59
36.	Real estate	3.44	5.11	3.55	7.22
37.	All other FIRE	3.08	5.24	1.15	9.59
38.	Hotels and lodging	2.34	3.99	3.75	28.58
39.	Med. and legal serv.	1.92	5.33	4.72	7.96

State Government		Federal Government		Gross Private Investment	Export	Total Final Demand	
W. Va.	U.S.	W. Va.	U.S.	W. Va.	W.Va.	W. Va.	U.S.
0	5.20	0	1.26	1.15	3.27	3.36	5.27
0	6.55	1.29	.87	4.00	4.16	4.06	5.01
0	4.04	0	1.97	5.75	2.70	4.22	6.72
0	7.83	0.39	−0.34	5.18	3.59	3.63	6.00
2.92	7.11	3.85	−0.49	6.78	1.90	2.75	4.65
0	6.12	1.34	2.43	4.02	5.27	4.90	5.43
0	7.19	0	1.49	3.30	3.60	3.35	3.99
3.73	7.99	0	1.49	6.84	4.47	2.93	4.53
0.91	7.99	1.49	1.49	6.84	4.55	3.38	4.53
0	7.99	0	1.49	6.84	4.50	2.67	4.53
2.16	7.99	1.34	1.49	6.83	3.81	2.67	4.53
0.35	7.99	5.24	1.49	6.84	4.33	2.99	4.53
0.77	9.59	5.49	5.49	0	3.71	3.51	5.33
1.98	9.59	4.94	5.49	0	1.70	3.02	5.33
1.91	9.59	0	5.49	0	4.16	3.10	5.33
3.64	7.22	0.71	0.74	1.30	5.55	3.61	4.98
1.30	9.59	0	5.49	0	5.04	3.85	5.33
5.67	28.59	2.54	2.58	0	4.05	3.24	4.11
5.22	7.96	2.99	7.13	0	5.43	3.43	5.41

Table 2.3 (continued)

		Households		Local Government	
		W. Va.	U.S.	W. Va.	U.S.
40.	Ed. serv.	6.77	5.33	7.47	7.96
41.	All other serv.	2.38	4.71	1.95	9.41
42.	Railroads	2.46	4.18	5.60	9.00
43.	Truck and warehsg.	2.46	4.18	5.24	9.00
44.	All other transp.	2.46	4.18	5.61	9.00
45.	Communications	2.05	6.97	2.43	7.84
46.	Elec. systems	5.04	5.60	0.62	8.69
47.	Gas systems	3.29	5.60	1.79	8.69
48.	Water and san. serv.	3.29	5.60	3.00	8.69

State Government		Federal Government		Gross Private Investment	Export	Total Final Demand	
W. Va.	U.S.	W. Va.	U.S.	W. Va.	W. Va.	W. Va.	U.S.
6.40	7.96	7.69	5.51	0	7.18	7.18	5.35
1.95	9.41	3.44	3.31	0	4.54	2.53	4.76
4.87	9.00	1.54	−0.99	0	4.30	4.08	3.99
5.60	9.00	0.47	−0.99	6.19	4.27	3.71	3.99
5.60	9.00	3.52	−0.99	0	4.20	2.86	3.99
2.44	7.84	2.04	2.26	0	6.70	3.41	6.61
0.77	8.69	0.53	1.21	0	37.47	17.66	5.58
1.05	8.69	3.58	1.21	0	5.28	5.10	5.58
2.98	8.69	2.26	1.21	0	5.46	3.35	5.58

[a] U.S. growth rates computed from *Projections 1970*, USDL, BLS, Bulletin No. 1536 (December 1966).

The Comparative Static Forecasts to 1975

The comparative static forecast discussed in this section was a preliminary interindustry forecast of the West Virginia economy to 1975. It was obtained by solving the system

$$X_{it} = (I\text{-}A_t)^{-1} Y_{it},$$

where X_{it} is the output of the ith sector in 1975, $(I - A_t)^{-1}$ is the Leontief inverse matrix with technical coefficients projected to 1975, and Y_{it} is final demand in the i th sector in 1975.

Because of the preliminary nature of the comparative static projections, the interindustry details have not been included as a transactions table. A single transactions table for 1975 was developed, and this is based on the dynamic model discussed in the next chapter.

The comparative static model takes into account the effects of technical change on input coefficients, and in this respect the basic parameters of the model change over time. Investment requirements, however, are handled in the same way as other components of final demand. In the dynamic model, investment requirements are determined by the capital coefficients of the system rather than being projected exogenously.

The aggregate results of the comparative static projections are given in Table 2.4.

Gross state product is expected to grow at an average annual rate of 4.9%, and to reach $6.9 billion by 1975. Personal income is expected to rise at a slightly lower rate (4.7%), and per capita income at the even slower rate of 3.1%. West Virginia's population, which has been declining since 1950, is expected to increase between 1965 and 1975 with all of the growth occurring after 1970. Over the entire period this yields a low annual growth rate of 1.2%. The labor force is expected to increase at a rate of 4%, representing a moderate increase in the labor force participation rate. Total employment should rise at the rate of 1.8% per year, and unemployment is expected to decline at the rate of 2.9%. The projected unemployment rate of 4.3% in 1975 will still be above the national average, if national projections are realized.

One of the interesting features of this forecast is the projection of an increase in population by 1975. A number of projections have been made, using standard demographic techniques, which indicate a continued decline in West Virginia's population during the coming decade. But these projections are based on the cohort-survival method, or some variant of this technique, and are essentially extrapolations. Such methods have built into them a continuation of recent trends, and it follows that if they are applied to the period 1965–1975 they will project a continued decline in population. This approach views population essentially as a supply phenomenon.

An extrapolation technique was not used in the present study. The first step in the West Virginia forecast was to project output and the labor inputs required to achieve this level of output. Labor requirements were used to project labor force and employment levels in 1975. The long-run trend in average family size

Table 2.4 Aggregate Projections of the West Virginia Economy to 1975

	1965	1975	Average Annual Rate of Growth
Gross state product[a]	$4.6	$6.9	4.9%
Personal income[a]	$3.7	$5.4	4.7
Per capita income	$2,030	$2,664	3.1
Population	1,812,000	2,035,000	1.2
Labor force	628,000	712,700	4.0
Employment	477,600	563,000	1.8
Unemployment	42,500	30,400	-2.9
Labor force participation rate	47.8%	52.2%	—
Unemployment rate	6.8%	4.3%	—

[a]Billions of dollars in 1965 prices.

Table 2.5 The Projection of Output to 1975

	Producing Industry	Sales (millions of dollars) Intermediate		
		1965	1975	Percent Change
1.	Agriculture	$43	$59	37%
2.	Coal mining (underground)	71	123	73
3.	Coal mining (strip and auger)	30	52	73
4.	Petroleum and natural gas	58	95	64
5.	All other mining	45	60	33
6.	General contractors (bldg.)	27	51	89
7.	General contractors (other)	25	43	72
8.	Special trades contractors	83	139	67
9.	Food products (n.e.c.)	16	24	50
10.	Food products (dairies)	6	12	100
11.	Food products (bakeries)	4	7	75
12.	Food products (beverages)	2	4	100
13.	Apparel and accessories	1	4	300
14.	Logging and sawmills	22	44	100
15.	Furniture and other wood fab.	6	12	100
16.	Printing and publishing	44	119	170
17.	Chemicals	213	287	35
18.	Petroleum	41	70	71
19.	Glass	12	23	92

	Final			Total	
1965	1975	Percent Change	1965	1975	Percent Change
$84	$86	2%	$127	$145	14%
631	887	41	702	1,010	44
24	36	50	54	88	63
1	9	800	59	104	76
26	32	23	71	92	30
146	209	43	173	260	50
150	201	34	175	244	39
59	72	22	142	211	49
36	44	22	52	68	31
72	87	21	78	99	27
44	55	25	48	62	29
28	35	25	30	39	30
23	33	43	24	37	54
41	58	41	63	102	62
20	25	25	26	37	42
17	26	53	61	145	138
1,078	1,614	50	1,291	1,901	47
28	45	61	69	115	67
257	366	42	269	389	45

Table 2.5 (continued)

	Producing Industry	Sales (millions of dollars) Intermediate		
		1965	1975	Percent Change
20.	Stone and clay products	38	65	71
21.	Primary metal products	66	111	68
22.	Fabricated metal products	35	66	89
23.	Machinery (except electric)	7	14	100
24.	Electric mach. and apparatus	4	11	175
25.	Transportation equipment	2	2	0
26.	Instruments and related prod.	4	5	25
27.	All other manufacturing	41	73	78
28.	Eating and drinking est.	4	9	125
29.	Wholesale trade	96	140	46
30.	Retail food stores	1	1	0
31.	Retail gasoline stations	9	19	111
32.	All other retail	28	53	89
33.	Banking	26	48	85
34.	Other finance	5	11	120
35.	Insurance agents and brokers	67	111	66
36.	Real estate	29	43	48

Final			Total		
1965	1975	Percent Change	1965	1975	Percent Change
94	152	62	132	217	64
903	1,257	39	969	1,368	41
85	127	49	121	193	60
106	160	51	113	174	54
115	164	43	119	175	47
176	231	31	178	233	31
5	8	60	9	13	44
85	119	40	126	192	52
112	149	33	116	158	36
214	298	39	310	438	41
118	154	31	119	155	30
30	39	30	39	58	49
366	492	34	394	545	38
73	104	42	100	152	52
51	68	33	56	79	41
208	282	36	274	393	43
31	45	45	61	88	44

Table 2.5 (continued)

| Producing Industry | Sales (millions of dollars) | | |
| | Intermediate | | |
	1965	1975	Percent Change
37. All other FIRE	32	46	44
38. Hotels and other lodgings	4	10	150
39. Medical and legal services	40	73	83
40. Educational services	2	6	200
41. All other services	111	179	61
42. Railroads	53	56	6
43. Trucking and warehousing	61	112	84
44. All other transportation	30	36	20
45. Communications	44	83	89
46. Electric companies and systems	87	195	124
47. Gas companies and systems	59	109	85
48. Water and sanitary services	16	25	56
49. Households	2,861	4,099	43
50. Out-of-state (imports)	2,903	4,161	43
51. All other final payments	1,298	2,088	61
52. Total	$8,812	$13,229	50%

Final			Total		
1965	1975	Percent Change	1965	1975	Percent Change
17	24	41	48	70	46
34	46	35	38	56	47
136	191	40	177	264	49
216	431	100	217	437	101
335	429	28	446	608	36
160	239	49	213	295	38
126	181	44	187	293	57
23	30	27	53	66	25
75	105	40	119	188	58
70	356	409	158	551	249
320	526	64	379	635	68
14	20	43	30	45	50
905	1,451	60	3,766	5,550	47
1,832	2,834	55	4,735	6,995	48
686	1,257	83	1,983	3,345	69
$10,486	$15,889	52%	$19,299	$29,032	50%

was applied to the projected labor force to obtain the population projection given in the text. Thus the population projection is a residual resulting from a projection of the *demand* for labor. Demographers might look askance at this approach to the projection of population, but it is obvious that if the output projections are realized there will be a substantial increase in West Virginia's labor force, and it is difficult to envisage the latter without an increase in population. Further details on labor force projections are given in Chapter 4.

Sectoral Forecasts in Output

A summary of the projection of output by sector to 1975 is given in Table 2.5. The column headed "Intermediate Sales" summarizes interindustry transactions by sector in West Virginia in 1965 and 1975, and shows the relative changes. The next column shows composite final demand for both years, and the relative change. The final column shows total sales in both years, and the percent changes.

Every sector of the West Virginia economy is expected to grow, but growth will be at widely varying rates. Agriculture will show relatively little growth, for example, while educational services (public and private) are expected to more than double during this 10-year span. The most rapid growth — and this will occur in one of the state's major sectors — is projected for electric utilities. This is largely because of the projected expansion of "mine-mouth" generating facilities. Much of the additional energy generated will be exported.

West Virginia's total gross output is expected to increase by slightly more than 50% between 1965 and 1975, and in the aggregate there is relatively little difference in the growth rates of intermediate and final sales.

The comparative static projections were useful in a number of ways. They provided a set of benchmarks against which to compare and evaluate the initial dynamic projections. They were also used to test the feasibility of simulating new activities in the West Virginia economy. Finally, in many sectors there is relatively little difference between the static and dynamic forecasts. The largest differences, as expected, appeared in the sectors that provide capital inputs to others. But these are important differences, and the successful implementation of a dynamic regional model undoubtedly improved the accuracy of the final forecasts, which are presented in the next chapter.

3

Final Forecast to 1975

The projections given in the last chapter take into account the effects of technological change, and changing trade patterns over time. But the result is a discrete jump from 1965 to 1975. A comparative static forecast tells nothing about the process by which the economy moves from one level of output to another. Information on how the economic system replaces its worn-out parts and adds the capacity required to meet increasing production levels is missing from this framework.

The comparative static model was modified to permit the simultaneous determination of capital requirements for replacement and expansion, which converted it to a dynamic system. In a dynamic forecast capital requirements are determined by the system instead of being projected independently as one of the components of final demand. By closing the model with respect to investment, the internal consistency of projected capital sales and purchases is ensured.

Dynamic interindustry analysis is still somewhat experimental, although there have been a number of significant developments in recent years. The theory of dynamic analysis was formulated by Wassily Leontief, the founder of input-output economics, more than 15 years ago.[1] It is not uncommon for theoretical developments to move ahead of empirical implementation, and there was a substantial lag between Leontief's theoretical work and the appearance of the first national forecast based on a dynamic model.[2]

The basic balance equation of a general dynamic model is

$$X_i - \sum_{j=1}^{n} X_{ij} - \sum_{j=1}^{n} D_{ij} - \sum_{j=1}^{n} \dot{S}_{ij} = Y_i \quad (i=1, 2, \ldots, n). \tag{3.1}$$

In this equation, X_i is the total output of industry i; X_{ij} is the total current input requirement by industry j from industry i; D_{ij} is the capital required by industry j from industry i to maintain capital stocks at current levels; $\dot{S}_{ij}$ is the expansion in the stock of capital goods produced by industry i and held by industry j; and Y_i is the final deliveries by industry i.

Sales by industry i to industry j on current account are proportional to the output of industry j, as in the static model. That is,

$$X_{ij} = a_{ij} X_j. \tag{3.2}$$

Sales of replacement capital by industry i to industry j depend upon the output of industry j.

$$D_{ij} = d_{ij}X_j. \tag{3.3}$$

Changes in the stock of industry i's capital output held by industry j depend upon changes in the rate of output of industry j.

$$\dot{S}_{ij} = b_{ij}\dot{X}_j. \tag{3.4}$$

Substituting the relationships of (2), (3), and (4) into Equation (1), we obtain the dynamic input-output equation:

$$X_i - \sum_{j=1}^{n} a_{ij}X_j - \sum_{j=1}^{n} d_{ij}X_j - \sum_{j=1}^{n} b_{ij}\dot{X}_j = Y_i \quad (i=1, 2, \ldots, n). \tag{3.5}$$

In matrix notation this becomes

$$X - AX - DX - B\dot{X} = Y. \tag{3.6}$$

The major reason for the lag between the theoretical development and empirical implementation of dynamic models was the absence of reliable capital coefficients, and in particular of expansion capital coefficients. An expansion capital coefficient has been defined as the addition to capital stocks (or net investment) required per unit increase in capacity. The reasons for relating changes in capital stocks to changes in capacity rather than changes in output levels as specified in the theoretical formulation of the dynamic model are discussed in a later section of this chapter. Capital sales and purchase information, estimates of plant and equipment used up, and data on capacity changes must be obtained for each sector to construct a table of capital coefficients.

Early efforts to develop capital coefficients were made by the Harvard Economic Research Project and the Interindustry Analysis Branch of the U. S. Bureau of Mines. The Harvard group's work dates back to at least 1948, and is continuing at present. The Bureau of Mines curtailed its work in 1953. Both the Harvard and Bureau groups have made estimates of incremental capital coefficients for many sectors.[3]

We are not aware of earlier efforts to construct a dynamic regional model. The theoretical framework of a regional model is the same as that given earlier, but there is one important difference in the empirical system. The regional model is much more open; there is much more reliance on imported capital in a region than in a national economy such as that of the United States.

Some Conceptual and Empirical Problems of Measuring the Dynamic Structure of a Regional Economy

Several problems were encountered in the measurement of parameters for the dynamic input-output model of West Virginia. These problems are outlined in this section and in the three sections that follow. First, however, a few summary words will help place these problems in proper perspective.

A large number of test runs were made of the West Virginia model, each incorporating new adjustments. In no case were the overall forecasts significantly affected since capital transactions at the regional level are dwarfed by current transactions. At the national level, gross private domestic investment is over 10% of total final demand, with a very small percentage of that originating outside the country. In West Virginia, gross investment is less than 6% of total final demand, and more than half of capital inputs originate outside the state. The relatively small magnitudes should not obscure the importance of capital transactions, however. Investment is a strategic variable in the economic development of a region and as such deserves careful attention. Also, in a few sectors capital sales account for a substantial proportion of total transactions.

The Concept and Measurement of Capacity

Two problems relating to capacity complicate the measurement of the dynamic structure of industry. First, if existing plants have excess general capacity, measurement of the relationship between changes in capital stocks and changes in annual output might understate actual capital requirement in the long run. The second problem — which also leads to an understatement of capital requirements — is that some departments in existing plants might have excess capacity. In this case, output can be increased with *unbalanced* additions to capital stocks. Without the partial excess capacity it would have been possible to increase output only with larger balanced additions to capital stocks. If capital coefficients are used to make long-run projections, they ought to show balanced or general additions to capital stocks, since these express the true engineering relationships. At the same time, it would be helpful to know both the amounts of general and partial excess capacity at the beginning of the projection period to avoid overstating capital requirements.[4]

The problems of measurement are complicated by the fact that in many sectors capacity is at best a vague concept. To derive meaningful first approximations of capital coefficients for all sectors, it was necessary to eliminate the effects of excess capacity even where the latter is difficult to measure.

From an engineering standpoint, the capacity of a plant is the maximum physical output per unit of time constrained only by technical considerations such as safety or wear and tear. In practice, few activities operate at this rate of production because of economic considerations. The net returns to variable inputs decline as they are added to the fixed quantity of capital before the physical limits of capacity are reached. Figure 3.1 illustrates this well-known condition, assuming a constant price for the firm's product.

The firm can operate profitably within the range B-D, with maximum profit at C. Output at A would just cover fixed costs, and this is the minimum economically feasible level of production. Point E is the maximum level of production representing engineering capacity. Technically, capacity can be at any point between A and E. If we assume rational behavior, however, capacity utilization will remain within the profitable boundaries B–D. The more restricted assumption of conventional economics is that output will be at the level of maximum profit, or point C. If the objective of the firm is not to maximize profit, but to maximize sales subject to some minimum profit constraint, the level of capacity utilization would fall somewhere between C and D.[5]

The model just sketched defines capacity in abstract terms. This is the framework that lies behind much of the theory of capital. But it is a static model which conveys no information about how changes in production levels affect capacity over time. Finally, it is concerned only with the concept of *general* capacity. It does not deal with the difficult problem of *partial* excess capacity mentioned earlier. It has been mentioned to emphasize the difference between the engineering and economic concepts of capacity, not because it is a useful guide to capacity measurement.

Three methods have been used in efforts to measure industry capacity, and changes in industry capacity in relation to net investment. Two of these bypass the firm completely, and use information at the industry level. These are the use of (a) capital stock benchmarks, and (b) cyclical peaks of output.[6] The third method – which is the one used in the present study – determines industry capacity by aggregating information obtained through interviews with plant managers.

The capital stock method of capacity measurement has been used by the National Industrial Conference Board (NICB) and the Federal Reserve Board (FRB).[7] Capital stock data are obtained from *Statistics of Income* (Internal

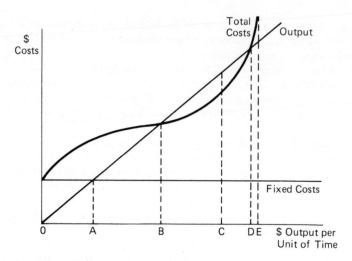

Figure 3-1 Costs, output and capacity

Revenue Service) and adjusted for depreciation and price changes. An alternative is to build up capital stocks by accumulating gross investment expenditures minus retirements, given an estimate of the capital stock at the beginning of the time period. This method cannot be used for West Virginia, since none of the data exist except gross investment, and that only for the manufacturing sectors. Output is defined as gross operating receipts adjusted for cyclical peaks and for price and inventory changes. With the capital stock and output data, one then finds the capital-output ratio for a benchmark period which is defined as a time when independent evidence indicates that capacity was being fully utilized.[8] Output in the benchmark year is defined as capacity output. Until a new benchmark is established, one can identify excess capacity by comparing the capital/output ratio for any year with the benchmark ratio.

A second and related method of estimating capacity is the peak-output approach. A time series of output is plotted, and the peak outputs are connected by straight lines. The slopes of the line segments represent changes in capacity over time. Excess capacity is estimated by taking differences between the line segments and the plotted points represented by the cross-hatched areas of Figure 3.2.[9]

The peak output method is easy to apply. But neither this method nor the capital stock method could be used in the West Virginia study because of the lack of time-series data on capital stocks for all sectors. (Time-series data are available for sectors under the jurisdiction of the state Public Service Commission, which include electricity, gas, water, sewage, miscellaneous transportation, and telephone services.) Instead, primary data on capital stocks – defined as the net depreciated book value of all plant and equipment –

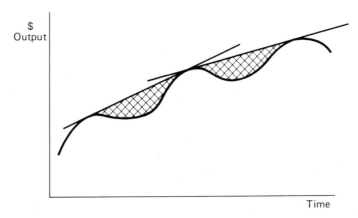

Figure 3-2 Peak-output estimate of capacity

were collected in the 1965 survey. These data were used to compute preliminary average sectoral capital coefficients.

Capacity data were collected from establishments in the form of *potential* output estimates. One of the drawbacks of this approach is that the respondent must make his own interpretation of potential output. Respondents in the trade and service sectors, in particular, found it difficult to estimate potential output. In a supermarket, for example, there are rush hours when queues form at the cash registers, but there are slack periods when the store is virtually empty. Potential capacity output was typically overstated in such cases, since the store manager felt that if buyers would change their shopping habits, total output could be increased substantially without additional plant and equipment. The estimates obtained by interviewers had to be scaled down when the preliminary capital coefficients were revised. At the other extreme, excellent estimates of capacity were obtained for electric generating plants and manufacturing activities where the production function appears to be clearly defined.

Constructing the Table of Capital Coefficients

Expansion capital coefficients, b_{ij}, have been defined as the capital requirements by sector j from sector i per unit increase of capacity in j. The first step in calculating West Virginia coefficients was to compile a table of the production of capital goods in West Virginia.[10] Sales to purchasing sectors were assigned to the appropriate column of a table of capital transactions. Sales on capital account by trade sectors (29, 30, 31, and 32) were margined, and the differences assigned to the sector of product origin. Capital sales and purchases were balanced by adding a row of capital purchases from out of state. The resulting capital transactions table is rectangular since all sectors purchased capital in 1965, but only 17 produced capital goods. The addition of the import row — with relatively large entries for most sectors — resulted in an 18 by 48 capital transactions table.

The rows of the capital transactions table were summed to obtain aggregate capital sales by sector i to each sector j, designated as I_{ij}. The latter were compared with the preliminary gross private domestic investment (GPDI) entries of the comparative static model, and adjusted upward or downward to achieve consistency. In a few cases the preliminary estimates of GPDI were adjusted after the detailed estimates of capital transactions had been completed.

The next step was to split capital transactions into those used for expansion (I_e), and replacement capital purchases (I_r). In the preliminary version of the dynamic model, replacement purchases were transferred to final demand, and only the expansion capital transactions were used to construct capital coefficients.

Before the capital coefficients could be computed, it was necessary to estimate the change in capacity in each sector, ΔK_j. The preliminary estimates were made by blowing up the sample data on capacity, and a preliminary set of expansion capital coefficients was computed from the relationship $b_{ij} = I_{e_{ij}} / \Delta K_j$. These were used to make the dynamic projections given in the interim report.[11]

After the initial projections were made, the entire table of capital coefficients was reevaluated. Reference to the survey data indicated that a small number of establishments included asset transfers in their capital transactions, and these were eliminated. A second revision followed reappraisal of the split of capital transactions into expansion and replacement purchases. The expansion coefficients were adjusted on the basis of this reappraisal, and the decision was made to modify the model to include a matrix of replacement capital coefficients, thus closing the model with respect to all capital transactions.

Replacement Capital Expenditures

All dynamic input-output models treat expansion capital as an endogenous variable, but the conventional method has assigned replacement capital expenditures to final demand. In the process of revising the West Virginia expansion capital coefficients, it became apparent that a complementary table of replacement capital coefficients could be constructed with little additional effort.

A first approximation of the expected life of capital goods in each sector was obtained by dividing the total incremental capital coefficient by the ratio of depreciation to output in that sector. The results were compared with national life expectancy figures published by the Internal Revenue Service.[12] Where differences were significant, and in most cases they were, since accounting practices are designed for tax purposes, the national life expectancy was used. Since no information was available on the age distribution of existing capital stocks, we assumed an equal distribution over the expected life in each sector. With this assumption, $d_{ij} = \dfrac{b_{ij}}{e_{ij}}$, where e_{ij} is the expected life of a unit of the ith good held by sector j.

A distinction was made between capital produced by construction sectors and that produced by equipment manufacturers, since the latter have a much shorter life expectancy. The d_{ij} are based upon the life expectancies shown in Table 3.1. Rows 5, 6, 7, and 21 of the B matrix were divided by the life expectancy figures relating to plant, and all others were divided by the figures relating to equipment.

The Stability of Capital Coefficients

A critical assumption in the West Virginia dynamic model is that the capital coefficients, both expansion and replacement, will be relatively stable during the projection period. Anne Carter has suggested that capital coefficients might be more variable than the technical coefficients of the A matrix.[13] This is because of their dependence on technical change and their incremental nature. It is easier for a firm to add to the stock of capital by buying one machine, for example, than to build a complete new process, but the new machine is not likely to be a duplicate of existing machines. Ideally, a dynamic model should be able to allow for the influence of technical change on capital coefficients as well as for process substitution.[14] But this can be done only if there is some basis for projecting changes in the coefficients. The cross-section data collected for West Virginia do not permit such projections. Thus the only sets of parameters in the West Virginia model which do not change over time are the expansion and replacement capital coefficients.

Solution of the Dynamic Model

Before the dynamic model can be solved, the rate of change in output over time, $(\dot{X})$, must be estimated. There are several ways to approximate $\dfrac{dx}{dt}$.[15] The one used here is to assume that $\dot{X} = X_t - X_{t-1}$. (A different approximation is used in the simulation model of Chapter 5, where $\dot{X} = X_{t+1} - X_t$, although the difference in solutions is very small. This formulation is difficult to use in forecasting because of the need to specify terminal year conditions. If we assume

Table 3.1 Useful Lives of Plant and Equipment (years)

	Sector	Plant	Equipment
1.	Agriculture	25	10
2.	Coal mines (underground)	45	10
3.	Coal mines (strip and auger)	45	10
4.	Petroleum and natural gas	45	14
5.	All other mining	45	10
6.	Building contractors	45	5
7.	Nonbuilding contractors	45	12
8.	Special contractors	45	12
9.	Food products (n. e. c.)	60	12
10.	Food products (dairies)	60	12
11.	Food products (bakeries)	60	12
12.	Food products (beverages)	60	12
13.	Apparel and accessories	45	9
14.	Logging and sawmills	10	6
15.	Furniture and wood fabrication	45	10
16.	Printing and publishing	45	11
17.	Chemicals	45	11
18.	Petroleum products	45	16
19.	Glass	45	14
20.	Stone and clay products	45	15

Table 3.1 (continued)

	Sector	Plant	Equipment
21.	Primary metals	45	16
22.	Fabricated metals	45	12
23.	Machinery (except electric)	45	12
24.	Electric machinery	45	12
25.	Transportation equipment	45	6
26.	Instruments and products	45	–
27.	All other manufacturing	45	12
28.	Restaurants and bars	40	10
29.	Wholesale trade	60	10
30.	Retail food stores	50	10
31.	Auto service stations	50	10
32.	All other retail	50	10
33.	Banking	50	10
34.	Other finance	50	10
35.	Insurance agents	45	10
36.	Real estate	45	10
37.	All other FIRE	45	10
38.	Hotels and lodgings	40	10
39.	Medical and legal services	45	10
40.	Educational services	45	10

Table 3.1 (continued)

	Sector	Plant	Equipment
41.	All other services	45	10
42.	Railroads	45	14
43.	Trucking and warehousing	60	8
44.	All other transportation	60	15
45.	Communications	45	–
46.	Electrical systems	45	29
47.	Gas systems	45	30
48.	Water and sanitary services	45	50

Source: Internal Revenue Service,
Depreciation Guidelines (Revised, August
1964).

that $\dot{X} = X_t - X_{t-1}$, however, there is no need to specify terminal year conditions.) Equation (3.6) can now be rewritten as

$$X_t - AX_t - DX_t - B(X_t - X_{t-1}) = Y_t. \tag{3.7}$$

To account for changes in the A matrix as the result of technological change and changing trade patterns, the best practice projections were used. As in the static model, the technical coefficients are assumed to represent the average in the terminal year. In the dynamic model, however, we assumed that annual changes in A can be represented by linear interpolation. Equation (3.7) can then be written as

$$X_t - A_t X_t - DX_t - B(X_t - X_{t-1}) = Y_t. \tag{3.8}$$

All sales to gross private state investment have been eliminated from the annual projections of final demand, Y_t. The dynamic model is solved by the following procedure. Equation (3.8) is rewritten as

$$(I - A_t - D - B) X_t + BX_{t-1} = Y_t. \tag{3.9}$$

Solving for X_t, we obtain

$$X_t = (I - A_t - D - B)^{-1} (Y_t - BX_{t-1}). \tag{3.10}$$

Since total output is known for 1965, output for 1966 is obtained by solving

$$X_{66} = (I - A_{66} - D - B)^{-1} (Y_{66} - BX_{65}).$$

Output for 1967 is obtained from

$$X_{67} = (I - A_{67} - D - B)^{-1} (Y_{67} - BX_{66}),$$

and this recursive process is followed to obtain the final projections to 1975.

Expansion capital sales and purchases for the 10-year period are calculated from $B_{ij}\hat{X}$, where $\hat{X}$ is a diagonal matrix of the *changes in output* between 1965 and 1975, or $(X_{75} - X_{65})$. To obtain capital sales by sector we sum across the rows of the resulting matrix. To obtain capital purchases by sector we sum down the columns.

Replacement capital sales and purchases for each year are obtained from $D_{ij}\hat{X}_t$ (t = 1966,..., 1975), where $\hat{X}$ is a diagonal matrix of output. To obtain replacement capital sales we sum the rows of the resulting matrix; to obtain purchases we sum the columns. Total replacement capital sales and purchases for the 10-year period are obtained by adding the annual results.

Table 3.2 shows the total expansion capital requirements per dollar of addition to capacity by sector. Total expansion capital requirements are divided into in-state purchases and imports. They range from a low of 10 cents for insurance agents and brokers, where we would expect capital requirements to be small, to a high of $3.93 in educational services. In 21 of the 48 sectors, imports make up a larger share of the total than in-state purchases. Imports range from 7% of the total (in retail gasoline service stations and banking) to 86% in "other" finance. There are relatively high import capital requirements in educational services, communications, electric systems, and water and sanitary services.

Replacement capital requirements per dollar of output are summarized in Table 3.3. Because some of the numbers are quite small they have been carried to an additional decimal place. The replacement requirements tend to follow the pattern of expansion requirements, but there are a few exceptions. The educational services sector, for example, has the largest expansion capital requirements, but this sector's replacement requirements, while still large relative to others, ranks in fourth place. One must remember, however, that expansion capital requirements are related to changes in capacity, while replacement capital requirements depend upon the level of output. The actual amounts of expansion and replacement investment projected for the decade covered by this study are given in Table 3.8.

The capital coefficients in Tables 3.2 and 3.3 are the *total* coefficients for each sector. The detailed coefficients − the b_{ij} and d_{ij} of the dynamic model − are given in Table VII. They are the parameters that must be estimated before the dynamic system can be solved to obtain interindustry projections.

Comparison of the Static and Dynamic Forecasts

The comparative static and dynamic projections to 1975 are compared in Table 3.4 in terms of output by sector. In the aggregate, the difference is small − only about 1%. A difference of this magnitude would scarcely warrant the time and effort required to construct and implement a dynamic model. But the differences in individual sectors are relatively large in some cases, particularly for general and special trades contractors. Other sectors that have sales on capital account are identified by asterisks, and in some of these the dynamic model has projected significantly larger outputs than the comparative static model. This is because the dynamic model takes into account the interindustry effects of capital transactions as well as the interindustry effects of sales on current account. In general, the differences are in the direction one would expect on *a priori* grounds. In only one sector − nonelectrical machinery − was the dynamic projection lower than that obtained from the static model. This is due to an overstatement of capital sales in the comparative static projection.

Table 3.4 gives only the projections of total output by sector. The detailed

Table 3.2 Summary of Expansion Capital Requirements per Dollar of
Addition to Capacity, West Virginia

Sectors	Expansion Capital Requirements per dollar of Addition to Capacity	In–state	Imported	Imports as percent of total
1. Agriculture	$0.80	$0.49	$0.31	39%
2. Coal mining (underground)	0.69	0.25	0.44	64
3. Coal mining (strip and auger)	0.56	0.14	0.42	75
4. Petroleum and natural gas	0.51	0.28	0.23	45
5. All other mining	0.35	0.30	0.05	14
6. General contractors (building)	0.15	0.11	0.04	27
7. General contractors (nonbuilding)	0.35	0.20	0.15	43
8. Special trades contractors	0.41	0.29	0.12	29
9. Food and kindred products (n.e.c.)	0.32	0.17	0.15	47
10. Food and kindred products (dairies)	0.32	0.22	0.10	31
11. Food and kindred products (bakeries)	0.32	0.21	0.11	34
12. Food and kindred products (beverages)	0.65	0.27	0.38	58
13. Apparel and accessories	0.57	0.28	0.29	51
14. Logging and sawmills	0.52	0.26	0.26	50
15. Furniture and other wood fabrication	0.51	0.28	0.23	45
16. Printing and publishing	1.03	0.48	0.55	53
17. Chemicals	0.75	0.57	0.18	24

Table 3.2 (continued)

Sectors	Expansion Capital Requirements per dollar of Addition to Capacity	In-State	Imported	Imports as percent of total
18. Petroleum	0.81	0.39	0.42	52
19. Glass	0.42	0.27	0.15	36
20. Stone and clay products	0.79	0.27	0.52	66
21. Primary metal products	0.69	0.43	0.26	38
22. Fabricated metal products	0.31	0.10	0.21	68
23. Machinery (except electrical)	0.23	0.18	0.05	22
24. Electrical machinery and apparatus	0.33	0.19	0.14	42
25. Transportation equipment	0.52	0.28	0.24	46
26. Instrument and related products	0.25	0.11	0.14	56
27. All other manufacturing	0.31	0.19	0.12	39
28. Eating and drinking establishments	0.20	0.08	0.12	60
29. Wholesale trade	0.29	0.09	0.20	69
30. Retail food stores	0.28	0.14	0.14	50
31. Retail gasoline service stations	0.28	0.26	0.02	7
32. All other retail	0.25	0.17	0.08	32
33. Banking	0.41	0.38	0.03	7
34. Other finance	0.50	0.07	0.43	86

Table 3.2 (continued)

Sectors	Expansion Capital Requirements per dollar of Addition to Capacity	In-State	Imported	Imports as percent of total
35. Insurance agents and brokerage	0.10	0.06	0.04	40
36. Real estate	0.32	0.22	0.10	31
37. All other FIRE	0.12	0.04	0.08	67
38. Hotels and other lodging places	1.40	1.07	0.33	24
39. Medical and legal services	0.89	0.62	0.27	30
40. Educational services	3.93	2.63	1.30	33
41. All other services	0.51	0.17	0.34	67
42. Railroads	0.80	0.41	0.39	49
43.Trucking and warehousing	1.09	0.39	0.70	64
44. All other transportation	0.71	0.43	0.28	39
45. Communications	3.10	0.58	2.52	81
46. Electric companies and systems	1.75	0.67	1.08	62
47. Gas companies and systems	1.19	0.56	0.63	53
48. Water and sanitary services	2.49	1.18	1.31	53

Table 3.3 Summary of Replacement
Capital Requirements per Dollar of
Output

Sectors	Replacement Capital Requirements per Dollar of Output	In–state	Imported	Imports as percent of total
1. Agriculture	0.061	0.030	0.031	51%
2. Coal mines (underground)	0.034	0.012	0.022	65
3. Coal mines (strip and auger)	0.053	0.011	0.042	79
4. Petroleum and natural gas	0.032	0.015	0.017	53
5. All other mining	0.028	0.023	0.005	18
6. Building contractors	0.021	0.014	0.007	33
7. Nonbuilding contractors	0.025	0.013	0.012	48
8. Special contractors	0.021	0.011	0.010	48
9. Food products (n. e. c.)	0.018	0.006	0.012	67
10. Food products (dairies)	0.015	0.007	0.008	53
11. Food products (bakeries)	0.017	0.008	0.009	53
12. Food products (beverages)	0.048	0.016	0.032	67
13. Apparel and accessories	0.053	0.021	0.032	60
14. Logging and sawmills	0.082	0.039	0.043	52
15. Furniture and wood fabrication	0.038	0.015	0.023	61
16. Printing and publishing	0.068	0.018	0.050	74
17. Chemicals	0.036	0.021	0.015	42

Table 3.3 (continued)

Sector	Replacement Capital Requirements per Dollar of Output	In-State	Imported	Imports as percent of total
18. Petroleum products	0.043	0.017	0.026	60
19. Glass	0.019	0.008	0.011	58
20. Stone and clay products	0.048	0.013	0.035	73
21. Primary metals	0.038	0.016	0.022	58
22. Fabricated metals	0.024	0.003	0.021	88
23. Machinery (except electric)	0.011	0.007	0.004	36
24. Electric machinery	0.018	0.006	0.012	67
25. Transportation equipment	0.063	0.023	0.040	64
26. Instruments and products	0.023	0.005	0.018	78
27. All other manufacturing	0.021	0.011	0.010	48
28. Restaurants and bars	0.015	0.003	0.012	80
29. Wholesale trade	0.025	0.005	0.020	80
30. Retail food stores	0.024	0.010	0.014	58
31. Auto service stations	0.018	0.016	0.002	11
32. All other retail	0.017	0.009	0.008	47
33. Banking	0.018	0.015	0.003	17
34. Other finance	0.045	0.002	0.043	96
35. Insurance agents	0.008	0.004	0.004	50

Table 3.3 (continued)

Sector	Replacement Capital Requirements per Dollar of Output	In-State	Imported	Imports as percent of total
36. Real estate	0.016	0.006	0.010	63
37. All other FIRE	0.010	0.002	0.008	80
38. Hotels and lodgings	0.078	0.045	0.033	42
39. Medical and legal services	0.048	0.021	0.027	56
40. Educational services	0.070	0.031	0.039	56
41. All other services	0.026	0.009	0.017	65
42. Railroads	0.038	0.010	0.028	74
43. Trucking and warehousing	0.084	0.025	0.059	70
44. All other transportation	0.030	0.011	0.019	63
45. Communications	0.172	0.019	0.153	89
46. Electrical systems	0.054	0.017	0.037	69
47. Gas systems	0.037	0.016	0.021	57
48. Water and sanitary services	0.052	0.026	0.026	50

Table 3.4 Alternative Projections of
Output to 1975 (thousands of
dollars)[a]

	Comparative Static Model (1)	Dynamic Model (2)	Ratio (2) (1)
1. Agriculture	$145,430	$145,745	1.002
2. Coal mining (underground)	1,017,555	1,016,067	0.999
3. Coal mining (strip and auger)	88,226	88,345	1.001
4. Petroleum and natural gas	105,533	105,782	1.002
*5. All other mining	91,918	91,348	0.994
*6. General contractors (building)	260,452	295,261	1.134
*7. General contractors (nonbuilding)	244,457	256,296	1.048
*8. Special trades contractors	211,801	238,330	1.125
9. Food and kindred products (n. e. c.)	68,213	68,283	1.001
10. Food and kindred products (dairies)	99,201	99,208	1.000
11. Food and kindred products (bakeries)	62,008	62,019	1.000
12. Food and kindred products (beverages)	39,294	39,156	0.996
13. Apparel and accessories	37,323	37,338	1.000
*14. Logging and sawmills	101,774	107,608	1.057
*15. Furniture and other wood fabrication	37,410	42,286	1.130
16. Printing and publishing	145,634	147,035	1.010
17. Chemicals	1,928,965	1,929,913	1.000

Table 3.4 (continued)

	Comparative Static Model (1)	Dynamic Model (2)	Ratio (2) (1)
18. Petroleum	114,829	117,197	1.021
19. Glass	389,351	389,639	1.001
*20. Stone and clay products	216,720	223,139	1.030
*21. Primary metal products	1,368,196	1,372,656	1.003
*22. Fabricated metal products	193,292	202,930	1.050
*23. Machinery (except electric)	174,159	169,072	0.971
*24. Electric machinery and apparatus	174,983	182,743	1.044
*25. Transportation equipment	233,218	234,967	1.008
*26. Instruments and related products	13,032	13,559	1.040
*27. All other manufacturing	192,911	197,798	1.025
28. Eating and drinking establishments	158,334	158,375	1.000
*29. Wholesale trade	438,430	447,526	1.021
30. Retail food stores	155,390	155,293	0.999
31. Retail gasoline service stations	58,405	58,526	1.002
*32. All other retail	545,544	560,002	1.026
33. Banking	152,407	153,409	1.007
34. Other finance	79,195	79,369	1.002
35. Insurance agents and brokerage	393,807	395,318	1.004

Table 3.4 (continued)

	Comparative Static Model (1)	Dynamic Model (2)	Ratio (2) (1)
36. Real estate	88,372	86,291	0.976
37. All other FIRE	69,870	70,173	1.004
38. Hotels and other lodging places	56,134	56,290	1.003
39. Medical and legal services	264,155	264,799	1.002
40. Educational services	437,232	437,279	1.000
41. All other services	609,134	611,527	1.004
42. Railroads	295,094	295,447	1.001
43. Trucking and warehousing	293,510	293,959	1.002
44. All other transportation	83,508	84,000	1.006
45. Communications	188,716	189,703	1.005
46. Electric companies and systems	551,809	553,323	1.003
47. Gas companies and systems	635,453	635,953	1.001
48. Water and sanitary services	44,924	46,409	1.033
49. Total	$13,355,308	$13,506,691	1.011

[a]Asterisks indicate sectors with sales on capital account.

interindustry projections, in the form of a transactions table, are given in Table VII. Only one projected transactions table is given in the report, and it is the one based on the dynamic model. The preliminary projections have been included for comparative purposes only. All of the analysis reported in the remaining chapters is based on the final projections of Table VII.

Changes in output by sector between 1965 and 1975 are summarized in Table 3.5. The differences between the static and dynamic projections of changes in output naturally follow the pattern of Table 3.4. Because smaller numbers are involved, the relative differences stand out more sharply in Table 3.5.

Finally, relative changes in output by sector from 1965 to 1975 are given in Table 3.6. This table adds no new information, but the percentage changes show how much each sector is expected to grow during the decade, on the basis of the alternative projections. Since the projection period is 10 years, the average annual growth rates are one-tenth of the numbers given in Table 3.6.

The Consistency of Investment Projections

As indicated earlier, capital requirements in the comparative static model were projected as exogenous variables. The dynamic model generates capital requirements on the basis of the matrices of capital coefficients and projected output. Expansion capital requirements, as projected for the comparative static model, and those generated by the dynamic model are compared in Table 3.7. In the aggregate there is a difference of only 0.3%. But for specific sectors — particularly those with substantial sales on capital account — the differences are large. The static model overstates expansion capital requirements in some sectors but understates them in others.

The dynamic model permits comparison of projected capital sales and requirements. Such a comparison is given in Table 3.8 for both expansion and replacement capital. To bring the sales and requirements columns into balance, capital imports have been added to in-state sales. In both instances, the sales and requirements totals differ by only a negligible rounding error. The internal consistency of capital sales and purchases is guaranteed by the dynamic model. This provides an additional check on the reliability of the capital projections which cannot be made in the static model where all capital transactions are treated as part of final demand.

Table 3.5 Changes in Output,
1965 to 1975, Based on Alternative
Models (thousands of dollars)

	Comparative Static Model (1)	Dynamic Model (2)	Ratio (2) (1)
1. Agriculture	$17,976	$18,291	1.02
2. Coal mining (underground)	315,213	313,725	1.00
3. Coal mining (strip and auger)	33,926	34,045	1.00
4. Petroleum and natural gas	46,609	46,858	1.01
5. All other mining	20,744	20,174	0.97
6. General contractors (building)	87,645	122,484	1.40
7. General contractors (nonbuilding)	69,595	81,434	1.17
8. Special trades contractors	69,523	96,052	1.38
9. Food and kindred products (n. e. c.)	15,868	15,938	1.00
10. Food and kindred products (dairies)	20,973	20,980	1.00
11. Food and kindred products (bakeries)	14,247	14,258	1.00
12. Food and kindred products (beverages)	9,137	8,999	0.98
13. Apparel and accessories	13,752	13,767	1.00
14. Logging and sawmills	39,261	45,455	1.16
15. Furniture and other wood fabrication	11,605	16,481	1.42
16. Printing and publishing	84,108	85,581	1.02
17. Chemicals	637,731	638,679	1.00

Table 3.5 (continued)

	Comparative Static Model (1)	Dynamic Model (2)	Ratio (2)/(1)
18. Petroleum	45,385	47,753	1.05
19. Glass	120,604	120,892	1.00
20. Stone and clay products	84,425	90,844	1.08
21. Primary metal products	398,915	403,375	1.01
22. Fabricated metal products	72,619	82,257	1.13
23. Machinery (except electrical)	61,365	56,278	0.92
24. Electrical machinery and apparatus	55,989	63,749	1.14
25. Transportation equipment	55,686	57,435	1.03
26. Instrument and related products	4,306	4,833	1.12
27. All other manufacturing	66,453	71,340	1.07
28. Eating and drinking establishments	42,599	42,640	1.00
29. Wholesale trade	128,802	137,898	1.07
30. Retail food stores	36,069	35,972	1.00
31. Retail gasoline service stations	19,555	19,676	1.01
32. All other retail	151,492	165,950	1.10
33. Banking	52,573	53,575	1.02
34. Other finance	23,194	23,368	1.01
35. Insurance agents and brokerage	119,405	120,916	1.01

Table 3.5 (continued)

	Comparative Static Model (1)	Dynamic Model (2)	Ratio (2) (1)
36. Real estate	27,625	25,543	0.92
37. All other FIRE	21,471	21,774	1.01
38. Hotels and other lodging places	18,151	18,307	1.01
39. Medical and legal services	87,324	87,968	1.01
40. Educational services	219,907	219,954	1.00
41. All other services	163,517	165,910	1.01
42. Railroads	81,968	82,321	1.00
43. Trucking and warehousing	106,760	107,209	1.00
44. All other transportation	30,345	30,837	1.02
45. Communications	69,614	70,601	1.01
46. Electric companies and systems	394,017	395,531	1.00
47. Gas companies and systems	256,209	256,709	1.00
48. Water and sanitary services	14,638	16,123	1.10
49. Total	$4,538,895	$4,690,739	1.03

Table 3.6 Relative Changes in Output,
1965 to 1975, Based on Alternative
Models

Sector	Comparative Static Model	Percent Changes
1. Agriculture	14%	14%
2. Coal mining (underground)	45	45
3. Coal mining (strip and auger)	62	63
4. Petroleum and natural gas	79	80
5. All other mining	29	28
6. General contractors (building)	51	71
7. General contractors (nonbuilding)	40	47
8. Special trades contractors	49	68
9. Food and kindred products (n. e. c.)	30	30
10. Food and kindred products (dairies)	27	27
11. Food and kindred products (bakeries)	30	30
12. Food and kindred products (beverages)	30	30
13. Apparel and accessories	58	58
14. Logging and sawmills	63	73
15. Furniture and other wood fabrication	45	64
16. Printing and publishing	137	139
17. Chemicals	49	49
18. Petroleum	65	69

Table 3.6 (continued)

	Sector	Comparative Static Model	Percent Changes
19.	Glass	45	45
20.	Stone and clay products	64	69
21.	Primary metal products	41	42
22.	Fabricated metal products	60	68
23.	Machinery (except electrical)	54	50
24.	Electrical machinery and apparatus	47	53
25.	Transportation equipment	31	32
26.	Instrument and related products	49	55
27.	All other manufacturing	53	56
28.	Eating and drinking establishments	37	37
29.	Wholesale trade	42	45
30.	Retail food stores	30	30
31.	Retail gasoline service stations	50	51
32.	All other retail	38	42
33.	Banking	53	54
34.	Other finance	41	42
35.	Insurance agents and brokerage	44	44
36.	Real estate	45	42
37.	All other FIRE	44	45

Table 3.6 (continued)

Sector	Comparative Static Model	Percent Changes
38. Hotels and other lodging places	48	48
39. Medical and legal services	49	50
40. Educational services	101	101
41. All other services	37	37
42. Railroads	38	39
43. Trucking and warehousing	57	57
44. All other transportation	57	58
45. Communications	58	59
46. Electric companies and systems	250	251
47. Gas companies and systems	68	68
48. Water and sanitary services	48	53

Table 3.7 Alternative Projections of
Expansion Capital Requirements,
1965–1975 (thousands of dollars)

	Comparative Static Model (1)	Dynamic Model (2)	Ratio (2) (1)
1. Agriculture	$14,386	$83,202	5.78
2. Coal mines (underground)	212,114	292,577	1.38
3. Coal mines (strip and auger)	18,926	37,862	2.00
4. Petroleum and natural gas	23,235	25,998	1.12
5. All other mining	7,204	22,317	3.10
6. Building contractors	13,143	47,167	3.59
7. Nonbuilding contractors	24,339	53,071	2.18
8. Special contractors	28,372	39,358	1.39
9. Food products (n. e. c.)	5,068	11,219	2.21
10. Food products (dairies)	6,710	13,578	2.02
11. Food products (bakeries)	4,558	9,380	2.06
12. Food products (beverages)	5,939	16,853	2.84
13. Apparel and accessories	7,836	16,184	2.07
14. Logging and sawmills	20,368	70,822	3.48
15. Furniture and wood fabrication	5,882	13,284	2.26
16. Printing and publishing	86,544	71,057	0.82
17. Chemicals	457,685	589,811	1.29

Table 3.7 (continued)

	Comparative Static Model (1)	Dynamic Model (2)	Ratio (2) (1)
18. Petroleum products	36,578	39,790	1.09
19. Glass	50,645	62,091	1.23
20. Stone and clay products	66,628	85,912	1.29
21. Primary metals	274,990	452,100	1.64
22. Fabricated metals	22,414	38,604	1.72
23. Machinery (except electric)	14,091	14,995	1.06
24. Electric machinery	18,464	27,907	1.51
25. Transportation equipment	28,955	130,918	4.52
26. Instruments and products	1,063	2,651	2.49
27. All other manufacturing	20,448	34,118	1.67
28. Restaurants and bars	8,516	21,274	2.50
29. Wholesale trade	37,151	95,525	2.57
30. Retail food stores	10,099	32,656	3.23
31. Auto service stations	5,454	8,981	1.65
32. All other retail	37,834	82,998	2.19
33. Banking	21,473	22,416	1.04
34. Other finance	11,579	30,884	2.67
35. Insurance agents	11,895	26,364	2.22

83

Table 3.7 (continued)

	Comparative Static Model (1)	Dynamic Model (2)	Ratio (2) (1)
36. Real estate	2,825	11,841	4.19
37. All other FIRE	2,565	5,749	2.24
38. Hotels and lodgings	25,361	36,739	1.45
39. Medical and legal services	77,551	106,620	1.37
40. Educational services	864,207	227,366	0.26
41. All other services	82,973	136,073	1.64
42. Railroads	65,415	98,304	1.50
43. Trucking and warehousing	115,853	202,302	1.74
44. All other transportation	9,240	20,655	2.24
45. Communications	214,942	266,909	1.24
46. Electrical systems	688,256	177,922	0.26
47. Gas systems	304,235	189,308	0.62
48. Water and sanitary services	36,329	19,747	0.54
49. Total	$4,110,338	$4,123,459	1.003

Table 3.8 Capital Sales and Requirements Generated by Dynamic Model,
1965—1975 (thousands of dollars)

	Replacement Capital		Expansion Capital	
	Sales	Purchases	Sales	Purchases
1. Agriculture		$83,202		$14,558
2. Coal mines (underground)		292,577		215,394
3. Coal mines (strip and auger)		37,862		18,918
4. Petroleum and natural gas		25,998		23,812
5. All other mining	$2,911	22,317	$5,536	7,138
6. Building contractors	363,004	47,167	1,228,495	18,336
7. Nonbuilding contractors	105,140	53,071	229,813	28,388
8. Special contractors	130,490	39,358	81,859	39,279
9. Food products (n. e. c.)		11,219		5,073
10. Food products (dairies)		13,578		6,685
11. Food products (bakeries)		9,380		4,540
12. Food products (beverages)		16,853		5,799
13. Apparel and accessories		16,184		7,791
14. Logging and sawmills	23,827	70,822	11,493	23,265
15. Furniture and wood fabrication	47,509	13,284	20,824	8,359
16. Printing and publishing		71,057		87,817
17. Chemicals		589,811		478,544
18. Petroleum products		39,790		38,396

Table 3.8 (continued)

| | Expansion Capital | | Expansion Capital | |
	Sales	Purchases	Sales	Purchases
19. Glass		62,091		50,652
20. Stone and clay products	23,911	85,912	43,713	71,246
21. Primary metals	60,039	452,100	117,540	277,803
22. Fabricated metals	43,730	38,604	20,559	25,313
23. Machinery (except electric)	469,916	14,995	264,001	12,920
24. Electric machinery	83,248	27,907	44,021	20,947
25. Transportation equipment	13,174	130,918	5,975	29,699
26. Instruments and products	7,243	2,651	3,517	1,201
27. All other manufacturing	30,266	34,118	13,776	21,953
28. Restaurants and bars		21,274		8,476
29. Wholesale trade	83,173	95,525	62,139	39,733
30. Retail food stores		32,656		10,007
31. Auto service stations		8,981		5,479
32. All other retail	175,699	82,998	81,801	40,659
33. Banking		22,416		21,956
34. Other finance		30,884		11,600
35. Insurance agents		26,364		12,012
36. Real estate		11,841		8,210
37. All other FIRE		5,749		2,595

Table 3.8 (continued)

	Expansion Capital		Expansion Capital	
	Sales	Purchases	Sales	Purchases
38. Hotels and lodgings		36,739		25,557
39. Medical and legal services		106,620		78,147
40. Educational services		227,366		865,322
41. All other services		136,073		84,031
42. Railroads		98,304		58,165
43. Trucking and warehousing		202,302		117,107
44. All other transportation		20,655		21,883
45. Communications		266,909		217,412
46. Electrical systems		177,922		692,687
47. Gas systems		189,308		306,410
48. Water and sanitary services		19,747		40,110
49. Imports	2,460,175		1,976,319	
50. Total	$4,123,455	$4,123,459	$4,211,381	$4,211,384

4

Projecting Labor Requirements

This chapter presents employment projections by sector and occupation to 1975. The employment projections are based on a matrix of labor coefficients which represent man-hours per dollar of output for each sector in the West Virginia economy. The labor coefficients show the interrelationships among all sectors in terms of employment rather than value.

In computing employment for a given bill of goods, one assumes that the production of a specified quantity of any particular good or service requires a definite amount of direct labor combined with certain amounts of the products of other industries.[1] With given technology, there is one and only one combination of outputs which makes the total output of each industry large enough to satisfy final demand, and at the same time meet the requirements of all other industries.[2] Once this output has been computed, the corresponding labor input can be easily determined. The amount of labor services absorbed by an industry is related to that industry's total output and expressed in terms of a labor input coefficient.[3] Thus if E_i stands for the quantity of labor used by sector i, and X_i that sector's output, $L_i = E_i/X_i$ is the labor input coefficient which measures the labor requirements of that sector per unit of output. Man-hour data, rather than employment, were used to calculate the West Virginia labor coefficients.

The L Matrix and Its Projection

The first step in constructing a table of labor coefficients for 1965 was to obtain man-hour data for the 48 West Virginia sectors from various sources.[4] Data on man-hours could not be collected on a consistent basis, and data for some West Virginia sectors were more complete than others. Average weekly hours on an annual basis were available for some sectors, while for others monthly average weekly hours could be obtained. Monthly data were used when available to estimate annual full-time employment expressed in man-hours. State data were not available for some sectors, and national data had to be used. Finally, in some of the key sectors such as coal, chemicals, and steel, data were obtained by direct interview. The sources of data by sector are presented in Table 4.1.

The second step was to convert the raw data to average man-hours per employee in each sector. We assumed an average of 50 weeks worked per year instead of using the standard or scheduled hours of work for which pay is received, which is usually 52 weeks.[5] The assumption of 50 weeks should be more representative of the actual man-hours worked, allowing for paid holidays, vacations, and sick leave.

Multiplying average weekly hours by 50 gave the annual number of man-hours worked per employee. To arrive at total man-hours per year for each sector, average man-hours were multiplied by employment. Employment data by sector were obtained from the West Virginia Department of Employment Security. To convert man-hours into labor coefficients, the number of total man-hours in each sector was divided by that sector's output. The result represents primary purchases of labor from households only. The conversion of average weekly hours into primary labor coefficients for 1965 is summarized in Table 4.2.

The primary labor coefficients measure only part of the labor inputs associated with the production of one dollar's worth of output. It is necessary to add to this the amounts of labor embodied in intermediate transactions. This was accomplished by multiplying a diagonalized matrix of *primary* man-hours (L) by Table II, the A matrix of input coefficients. The result is a matrix of intermediate man-hour requirements per dollar of output. These must be added to the primary purchases of labor to obtain the total direct labor coefficients. Thus for each sector, primary labor inputs were added to intermediate labor purchases to obtain the 1965 matrix of total labor input coefficients (L_{ij}) for West Virginia (Table VIII). This is a matrix with 49 rows, including the household row, and 48 columns. There is no household column in the matrix since household purchases of labor in West Virginia are small enough to be ignored.

Direct and indirect labor requirements cannot be obtained by inverting L_{ij}, as was done to obtain the direct and indirect effects upon output of changes in final demand, or $(I - A)^{-1}$. For one thing, L_{ij} is not a square matrix and does not have an inverse. Even if it were square, however, it would not make sense to obtain a "general solution" of the form $(I - L)^{-1}$. The use of an identity matrix would imply that when a sector adds one dollar to final sales, its labor input would increase by one man-hour. This one-to-one relationship between man-hours and deliveries to final demand does not exist. Each sector has a different relationship between its labor inputs and its outputs. Since the $(I - A)^{-1}$ matrix shows the direct and indirect output requirements for a delivery of one dollar to final demand, and the primary labor coefficients show man-hours per dollar of output, the two can be combined to obtain direct and indirect man-hour requirements per dollar of additional sales to final demand.

Table 4.1 Sources of Man–Hour Data
by Sector

West Virginia Sources Only[a]		National Sources Only	National Sources Adjusted after Interviews
2*	22*	14	1
3	23*	15	40
4	24*	18	
5	25*	27	
6	26	30	
7	28	31	
8	29	32	
9*	33	34	
10*	35	37	
11*	36	39	
12*	38	41	
13*	43	42	
16*	44		
17*	45		
19*	46*		
20*	47*		
21*	48*		

[a]Asterisks indicate monthly data.

This is accomplished by calculating $\hat{L}$ $(I - A)^{-1}$, where $\hat{L}$ is the diagonalized matrix of *primary* labor inputs. The 1965 direct and indirect labor coefficients for West Virginia are given in Table IX.

Projecting Labor Coefficients to 1975

Regional labor coefficients are derived from the matrix of input coefficients, the A matrix, and the ratios of man-hours to output in the diagonalized $\hat{L}$ matrix. Thus the labor coefficients will change as the A matrix changes due to technology and shifting trade patterns. They will also be influenced by changes in the ratios of man-hours to output. The method of projecting the elements of the A matrix was discussed in Chapter 3, and will not be repeated here. It will be necessary, however, to discuss the changing ratios of man-hours to output in each sector.

The ratios of man-hours to output will change during the period covered by the forecast because of increases in productivity. Productivity is often defined as total output divided by labor inputs. The designation "labor productivity," however, does not mean that increases in output per man-hour can be imputed solely to improvements in labor efficiency. They are due to a combination of changes, including the substitution of capital for labor, improvements in managerial practices, and improvements in the quality of labor inputs. It might appear that we are double-counting the effects of technological change on labor inputs, but this is not the case.

The *direct* labor coefficients for West Virginia are calculated from what we have called *primary* and *intermediate* labor inputs. The effects of technological change on intermediate labor inputs are reflected in the changing elements of the A matrix, but the A matrix does not include the household row or primary labor inputs. Thus a method had to be devised to adjust the latter for increases in productivity.

The lack of time-series data prevented us from making independent estimates of productivity increases for most West Virginia sectors.[6] National productivity rates were used, and the sources of data by sector are given in Table 4.3. Most of the rates shown were taken directly from two sources. The first is Almon's national projection.[7] The second is a set of exhibits which was used in a lecture given at West Virginia University by John W. Kendrick of George Washington University on March 29, 1968. Adjustments were made in six sectors (indicated by double asterisks in Table 4.3) on the basis of survey data or discussions with representatives of the sector involved.

There are wide variations in the projected increases in productivity by sector. In some cases, such as coal mining, there has been rapid substitution of capital for labor in recent years, and this is expected to continue during the forecast period. The relatively large productivity rates are due to projected increases in output which will be accompanied by modest reductions in employment. In

Table 4.2 Conversion of Average
Weekly Man–Hours to Direct Labor
Coefficients (1965)

		Average Weekly Hours (1)	Employment (2)
1.	Agriculture	44.5	925
2.	Coal mines (underground)	44.7	40,600
3.	Coal mines (strip and auger)	41.2	2,546
4.	Petroleum and natural gas	43.1	4,229
5.	All other mining	44.7	1,421
6.	Building contractors	41.0	6,888
7.	Nonbuilding contractors	40.0	6,441
8.	Special contractors	37.5	8,343
9.	Food products (n. e. c.)	42.6	1,877
10.	Food products (dairies)	42.6	2,244
11.	Food products (bakeries)	42.6	2,347
12.	Food products (beverages)	42.6	1,517
13.	Apparel and accessories	36.8	5,392
14.	Logging and sawmills	41.9	6,707
15.	Furniture and wood fabrication	41.5	1,592
16.	Printing and publishing	39.7	3,674
17.	Chemicals	46.6	25,615

Total Man-hours (1)×(2)×50 (3)	Output (in $1,000) (4)	Primary Labor Coefficients $\frac{(3)}{(4)}$
2,058,382	127,454	0.01615
90,784,727	702,342	0.12926
5,244,837	54,300	0.09659
9,113,775	58,924	0.15467
3,175,784	71,174	0.04462
14,120,060	172,807	0.08171
12,880,335	174,862	0.07366
15,642,043	142,278	0.10994
3,998,111	52,345	0.07638
4,779,731	78,228	0.06110
4,999,144	47,761	0.10467
3,231,323	30,157	0.10715
9,916,555	23,571	0.42071
14,051,047	62,513	0.22477
3,303,298	25,805	0.12801
7,284,757	61,454	0.11854
59,655,011	1,291,234	0.04620

Table 4.2 (continued)

		Average Weekly Hours (1)	Employment (2)
18.	Petroleum products	42.2	712
19.	Glass	38.9	15,485
20.	Stone and clay products	40.0	5,911
21.	Primary metals	40.1	26,664
22.	Fabricated metals	44.3	6,791
23.	Machinery (except electric)	42.8	5,194
24.	Electric machinery	43.4	5,406
25.	Transportation equipment	35.8	5,348
26.	Instruments and products	38.7	547
27.	All other manufacturing	39.9	6,920
28.	Restaurants and bars	36.4	10,901
29.	Wholesale trade	42.0	20,118
30.	Retail food stores	36.6	8,917
31.	Auto service stations	36.6	3,695
32.	All other retail	36.6	41,920
33.	Banking	36.3	4,215
34.	Other finance	37.2	2,074

Total Man-hours (1)$\times$(2)$\times$50 (3)	Output (in \$1,000) (4)	Primary Labor Coefficients $\dfrac{(3)}{(4)}$
1,502,074	69,444	0.02163
30,142,664	268,747	0.11216
11,821,881	132,295	0.08936
53,417,076	969,281	0.05511
15,052,750	120,673	0.12474
11,118,105	112,794	0.09857
11,742,328	118,994	0.09868
9,577,851	177,532	0.05395
1,058,377	8,726	0.12129
13,805,420	126,458	0.10917
19,839,294	115,735	0.17142
42,245,644	309,628	0.13644
16,318,340	119,321	0.13676
6,761,843	38,850	0.17405
76,714,043	394,052	0.19468
7,650,279	99,834	0.07663
3,857,909	56,001	0.06889

Table 4.2 (continued)

		Average Weekly Hours (1)	Employment (2)
35.	Insurance agents	35.3	5,089
36.	Real estate	34.9	2,522
37.	All other FIRE	37.2	1,328
38.	Hotels and lodgings	44.6	4,371
39.	Medical and legal services	36.5	24,118
40.	Educational services	40.0	35,019
41.	All other services	38.8	29,929
42.	Railroads	43.6	12,600
43.	Trucking and warehousing	46.1	7,120
44.	All other transportation	35.8	1,457
45.	Communications	40.5	6,510
46.	Electrical systems	39.4	4,750
47.	Gas systems	40.1	5,703
48.	Water and sanitary services	39.4	1,474

Total Man-hours (1)X(2)X50 (3)	Output (in $1,000) (4)	Primary Labor Coefficients $\frac{(3)}{(4)}$
8,981,177	274,402	0.03273
4,400,513	60,747	0.07244
2,470,285	48,399	0.05104
9,747,197	37,983	0.25662
44,015,004	176,831	0.24891
70,037,328	217,325	0.32227
58,063,895	445,617	0.13030
27,468,641	213,150	0.12887
16,411,590	186,750	0.08788
2,608,708	53,163	0.04907
13,182,209	119,102	0.11068
9,357,066	157,792	0.05930
11,445,584	379,244	0.03018
2,903,822	30,286	0.09588

Table 4.3 Projected Increases in
Productivity (average annual
increases)

1. Agriculture	5.8%*	25. Transportation equipment	3.3%
2. Coal mines (underground)	5.1**	26. Instruments and products	3.6
3. Coal mines (strip and auger)	5.9	27. All other manufacturing	3.9
4. Petroleum and natural gas	4.5*	28. Restaurants and bars	1.4*
5. All other mining	3.1	29. Wholesale trade	3.2
6. Building contractors	1.6*	30. Retail food stores	2.6
7. Nonbuilding contractors	1.6*	31. Auto service stations	2.6
8. Special contractors	1.6*	32. All other retail	2.6
9. Food products (n. e. c.)	4.2*	33. Banking	1.0*
10. Food products (dairies)	2.4*	34. Other finance	1.0*
11. Food products (bakeries)	1.3*	35. Insurance agents	1.0*
12. Food products (beverages)	2.9	36. Real estate	1.0*
13. Apparel and accessories	2.5*	37. All other FIRE	1.0*
14. Logging and sawmills	4.1	38. Hotels and lodgings	2.4*
15. Furniture and wood fabrication	2.0*	39. Medical and legal services	0.2**
16. Printing and publishing	2.7*	40. Educational services	2.4**
17. Chemicals	4.8*	41. All other services	0.8**
18. Petroleum products	3.7*	42. Railroads	5.1
19. Glass	3.6*	43. Trucking and warehousing	3.1
20. Stone and clay products	3.3	44. All other transportation	3.1

Table 4.3 (continued)

21. Primary metals	2.3	45. Communications	3.5**
22. Fabricated metals	2.2	46. Electrical systems	11.2**
23. Machinery (except electric)	2.8	47. Gas systems	7.0*
24. Electric machinery	4.4	48. Water and sanitary services	0

Sources: Data for the sectors with no asterisk are from the Kendrick exhibits; those with a single asterisk are from Almon, *American Economy*, pp. 126–127. A double asterisk indicates that data from either source have been adjusted by the Regional Research Institute.

other sectors, notably those providing financial services, relatively small increases in productivity are expected. In these sectors employment will rise with output. The largest projected increase in productivity is in electric systems, where most of the expansion will be in the capital-intensive activity of generation.

The 1975 labor coefficients were calculated in the same way as the base-year coefficients after primary labor inputs had been adjusted downward for anticipated increases in productivity. The intermediate labor coefficients were calculated by $L_{75}A_{75}$. The row of primary labor coefficients was then added to obtain the complete matrix of projected direct labor coefficients given in Table X. Similarly, direct and indirect man-hour requirements per dollar of delivery to final demand were derived from $L_{75}(I - A)_{75}^{-1}$, and these are given in Table XI.

Projecting Employment to 1975

The table of direct and indirect man-hour requirements was used to project employment by sector to 1975 by reversing the procedure followed to obtain the 1965 labor coefficients. The vector of final demand projected to 1975 was multiplied by the 1975 matrix of direct and indirect labor coefficients. The result is another vector which gives the total man-hour requirements to satisfy projected total output by sector in 1975.

The second step was to convert projected man-hours to employment. This was done by dividing man-hours in each sector by (average hours/week)x50. The results are given in Table 4.4, and comparisons of employment by sector in 1965 and 1975 are given in Table 4.5. This procedure could be followed only in the sectors for which labor coefficients had been calculated. Government employment, exclusive of employment in educational activities, was projected by straightforward time-series extrapolation.

Occupational Projections to 1975

Conventional employment projections are useful since they give an indication of the aggregate demand for labor. But labor is perhaps the least homogeneous of inputs, and it is useful to have as much disaggregation as possible by occupation or occupational group. An important objective of the West Virginia study was to make projections of the sectoral demand for labor by occupation. This should provide broad guidelines for educators and others concerned with labor supply. Before occupational projections to 1975 could be made, however, it was necessary to distribute employment in the base year by occupation.

Occupational data were not collected in the basic survey of purchases and sales conducted in the summer of 1965. Our feeling was that there was a limit to the amount of detailed information that could be requested without reducing

Table 4.4 Projections of Employment
in Processing Sectors to 1975

		Projected man–hours (1)	Average weekly hours (2)	Employment (1) / (2)×50
1.	Agriculture	1,339,450	44.5	602
2.	Coal mines (undg.)	79,827,495	44.7	35,717
3.	Coal (strip and auger)	4,810,100	41.2	2,335
4.	Pet. and nat. gas	10,535,795	43.1	4,889
5.	All other mining	3,003,840	44.7	1,344
6.	Bldg. cont.	20,586,100	41.0	10,042
7.	Nonbldg. cont.	16,110,000	40.0	8,055
8.	Spec. cont.	22,357,500	37.5	11,924
9.	Food prod. (n. e. c.)	3,456,990	42.6	1,623
10.	Dairies	4,781,850	42.6	2,245
11.	Bakeries	5,704,140	42.6	2,678
12.	Beverages	3,152,400	42.6	1,480
13.	Apparel and acc.	12,278,320	36.8	6,673
14.	Logging and sawmills	16,183,875	41.9	7,725
15.	Furn. and wood fab.	4,440,500	41.5	2,140
16.	Print. and pub.	13,366,990	39.7	6,734
17.	Chemicals	55,817,480	46.6	23,956
18.	Pet. prod.	1,755,520	42.2	832
19.	Glass	30,659,035	38.9	15,763

Table 4.4 (continued)

		Projected man–hours (1)	Average weekly hours (2)	Employment (1) / (2)$\times$50
20.	Stone and clay prod.	14,412,000	40.0	7,206
21.	Primary metals	60,310,400	40.1	30,080
22.	Fab. metals	20,346,990	44.3	9,186
23.	Mach. (ex. elec.)	12,640,980	42.8	5,907
24.	Elec. mach.	11,718,000	43.4	5,400
25.	Transp. equip.	9,157,640	35.8	5,116
26.	Ins. and prod.	1,155,195	38.7	597
27.	All other mfg.	14,727,090	39.9	7,382
28.	Rest. and bars	23,614,500	36.4	12,975
29.	Wholesale trade	44,543,100	42.0	21,211
30.	Retail food	16,429,740	36.6	8,978
31.	Auto. serv. sta.	7,879,980	36.6	4,306
32.	All other retail	84,341,040	36.6	46,088
33.	Banking	10,641,345	36.3	5,863
34.	Other finance	4,949,460	37.2	2,661
35.	Ins. agents	11,714,305	35.3	6,637
36.	Real estate	5,659,035	34.9	3,243
37.	All other FIRE	3,240,120	37.2	1,742
38.	Hotels and lodgings	11,395,300	44.6	5,110

Table 4.4 (continued)

		Projected man–hours (1)	Average weekly hours (2)	Employment (1) / (2)✕50
39.	Med. and legal serv.	64,252,775	36.5	35,207
40.	Ed. serv.	110,908,000	40.0	55,454
41.	All other serv.	73,316,480	38.8	37,792
42.	Railroads	23,155,960	43.6	10,622
43.	Truck and warehsg.	19,036,995	46.1	8,259
44.	All other transp.	3,037,630	35.8	1,697
45.	Communications	14,887,800	40.5	7,352
46.	Elec. systems	11,554,050	39.4	5,865
47.	Gas systems	9,750,315	40.1	4,863
48.	Water and san. serv.	4,414,770	39.4	2,241

Table 4.5 West Virginia Employment,
1965, and Projections to 1975

		1965	1975	Percent Change
1.	Agriculture	925	602	−34.9%
2.	Coal mines (undg.)	40,600	35,717	−12.0
3.	Coal (strip and auger)	2,546	2,335	− 8.3
4.	Pet. and nat. gas	4,229	4,889	15.6
5.	All other mining	1,421	1,344	− 5.4
6.	Bldg. cont.	6,888	10,042	45.8
7.	Nonbldg. cont.	6,441	8,055	25.1
8.	Spec. cont.	8,343	11,924	42.9
9.	Food prod. (n. e. c.)	1,877	1,623	−13.5
10.	Dairies	2,244	2,245	0.0
11.	Bakeries	2,347	2,678	14.1
12.	Beverages	1,517	1,480	− 2.4
13.	Apparel and accessories	5,392	6,673	23.8
14.	Logging and sawmills	6,707	7,725	15.2
15.	Furn. and wood fab.	1,592	2,140	34.4
16.	Print. and pub.	3,674	6,734	83.3
17.	Chemicals	25,615	23,956	− 6.5
18.	Pet. prod.	712	832	16.9
19.	Glass	15,485	15,763	1.8

Table 4.5 (continued)

		1965	1975	Percent Change
20.	Stone and clay prod.	5,911	7,206	21.9
21.	Primary metals	26,664	30,080	12.8
22.	Fabricated metals	6,791	9,186	35.3
23.	Mach. (ex. elec.)	5,194	5,907	13.7
24.	Elec. mach.	5,406	5,400	− 0.1
25.	Transp. equip.	5,348	5,116	− 4.3
26.	Ins. and prod.	547	597	9.1
27.	All other mfg.	6,920	7,382	19.0
28.	Rest. and bars	10,901	12,975	19.0
29.	Wholesale trade	20,118	21,211	5.4
30.	Retail food	8,917	8,978	0.7
31.	Auto serv. sta.	3,695	4,306	16.5
32.	All other retail	41,920	46,088	9.9
33.	Banking	4,215	5,863	39.1
34.	Other finance	2,074	2,661	28.3
35.	Ins. agents	5,089	6,637	30.4
36.	Real estate	2,522	3,243	28.6
37.	All other FIRE	1,328	1,742	31.2
38.	Hotels and lodgings	4,371	5,110	16.9

Table 4.5 (continued

		1965	1975	Percent Change
39.	Med. and legal serv.	24,118	35,207	46.0
40.	Ed. serv.	35,019	55,454	58.4
41.	All other serv.	29,929	37,792	26.3
42.	Railroads	12,600	10,662	−15.7
43.	Truck and warehsg.	7,120	8,259	16.0
44.	All other transp.	1,457	1,697	16.5
45.	Communications	6,510	7,352	12.9
46.	Elec. systems	4,750	5,865	23.5
47.	Gas systems	5,703	4,863	−14.7
48.	Water and san. serv.	1,474	2,241	52.0
49.	State and local (n. e. c.)	30,099	50,805	68.8
50.	Federal	12,315	13,310	8.1
51.	Total	477,580	569,912	19.3

the response rate. We also assumed that in a number of sectors, particularly the trades and services, the West Virginia occupational distributions would not differ significantly from the national distribution. There are sectors such as steel, coal, glass and chemicals, however, in which there are *a priori* reasons for believing that there are differences in occupational distributions.

The distribution of employment by occupation in 1965 involved the following steps:

1. The national distribution was applied to all West Virginia sectors to obtain a preliminary distribution for 1965. This was based on unpublished data obtained from the Bureau of Labor Statistics.

2. National distributions were adjusted in 11 sectors using data obtained from the Office of Equal Employment Opportunity.

3. National distributions were completely replaced in seven sectors by distributions based on a survey of sample establishments in each sector. As Table 4.6 shows, national distributions were used in most sectors adjusting only for differences in the degree of aggregation.

The national tables with which we worked gave the distributions of 191 occupations in 154 sectors. The first step was to aggregate the latter to the 48 West Virginia sectors. In a few sectors it was necessary to disaggregate national data to conform to the West Virginia classifications. This was done by weighting the national sectors by the relative importance of employment in the West Virginia sectors. The result was a table of 191 occupations for 48 sectors. Two new employment sectors were added, one for state and local government and the other for federal government employment. These have been numbered sectors 49 and 50 in the occupational tables.

National data were available from the Bureau of Labor Statistics only for 1960 and 1975. It was necessary to project the 1960 data to 1965, and this was done by linear interpolation.

The second step was to aggregate by occupation. Some of the 191 national occupations are not represented in West Virginia, and others in such small numbers that they can be ignored as a separate group. The goal was to retain as much meaningful detail as possible, and the result is a matrix of 58 occupational groups for the 50 West Virginia sectors. These are given in Table XII.

The final step was to project 1975 employment in West Virginia by occupation. The Bureau of Labor Statistics has projected its industry-occupation matrix to 1975. Thus the same steps were followed as those described earlier to obtain the 1975 West Virginia matrix. In the 18 sectors where primary data and data provided by the Equal Employment Opportunity Commission were used to adjust the 1965 West Virginia table, proportional adjustments were made in the 1975 West Virginia industry-occupation matrix (Table XIII). The projections of employment by occupation are summarized in Table 4.7.

Table 4.6 Sources of Occupational
Data by Sector

National data adjusted only by aggregation[a]	National data adjusted by EEO data for West Virginia[b]	Based on West Virginia data[c]
1	2	17
6	3	19
7	4	21
8	5	45
9	16	47
10	20	
11	22	
12	24	
13	39	
14	42	
15	46	
18		
23		
25		
26		
27		
28		
29		
30		
31		
32		
33		
34		
35		
36		
37		
38		
40		
41		
43		
44		
48		
49		
50		

[a] Unpublished occupational table from United States Department of Labor, Bureau of Labor Statistics.

[b] West Virginia data collected by the Equal Employment Opportunity Commission.

[c] Primary data collected by interviews in 1968.

Table 4.7 West Virginia Employment
by Occupation, 1965, and Projections
to 1975

Occupation	1965	1975	Change, 1965–1975 Number	Percent
Professional, Technical, and Managerial				
Chemical Engineers	1,348	1,460	112	8.3%
Industrial Engineers	632	1,070	438	69.3
Mechanical Engineers	993	1,295	302	30.4
Mining Engineers	569	650	81	14.2
Other Engineers	3,132	4,733	1,601	51.1
Chemists	2,012	2,378	366	18.2
Mathematicians	191	309	118	61.8
Physicists	157	294	137	87.3
Other Natural Scientists	644	1,059	415	64.4
Technicians (Excl. Med.–Dent.)	6,645	9,390	2,745	41.3
Med.–Dent. Technicians	1,535	2,602	1,067	69.5
Doctors and Veterinarians	1,725	2,657	932	54.0
Dentists	713	856	143	20.1
Pharmacists	588	674	86	14.6
Professional Nurses	7,553	10,857	3,304	43.7
Elem. and Sec. Teachers	17,855	22,369	4,514	25.3
College Teachers	2,712	4,809	2,097	77.3

Table 4.7 (continued)

Occupation	1965	1975	Change, 1965–1975 Number	Percent
Other Teachers	346	1,840	1,494	431.8
Social Scientists	390	574	184	47.2
Accountants	2,580	3,318	738	28.6
Lawyers	1,766	2,152	386	21.9
Pers. and Labor Rel. Workers	917	1,399	482	52.6
Other Prof. and Technicians	6,771	11,914	5,143	76.0
Managers, Officials, and Prop.	53,593	61,343	7,750	14.5
Clerical and Sales				
Stenos, Typists, and Sec.	15,830	22,041	6,211	39.2
Office Machine Operators	3,305	5,570	2,265	68.5
Accounting Clerks	6,192	6,974	782	12.6
Shipping and Receiving Clerks	1,658	1,517	−141	−8.5
Cashiers	3,498	4,776	1,278	36.5
Telephone Operators	2,763	2,977	214	7.7
Other Clerks	34,326	43,081	8,755	25.5
Sales Workers	28,266	31,767	3,501	12.4
Craftsmen and Foremen				
Brickmasons	1,174	1,466	292	24.9
Carpenters	3,871	4,896	1,025	26.5

111

Table 4.7 (continued)

Occupation	1965	1975	Change, 1965–1975 Number	Percent
Electricians	4,548	4,953	405	8.9
Excavating Machine Operators	4,508	5,314	806	17.9
Plumbers	2,024	2,831	807	39.9
Painters	1,745	2,454	709	40.6
Other Construction Craftsmen	1,608	2,008	400	24.9
Foremen	13,880	15,174	1,294	9.3
Sheet Metal Workers	715	800	85	11.9
Skilled Machine Operators	2,967	3,114	147	5.0
Toolmakers and Diemakers	607	570	−37	−6.1
Other Metalworking Craftsmen	1,671	1,660	−11	−0.7
Motor Vehicle Mechanics	4,750	5,388	638	13.4
Other Mechanics	12,884	18,020	5,136	39.9
Printing Trades Craftsmen	1,100	1,717	617	56.1
Transp. and Pub. Util. Craftsmen	3,904	4,176	272	7.0
Other Craftsmen	9,386	10,340	954	10.2
Operatives and Laborers				
Drivers	18,450	22,502	4,052	22.0
Semiskilled Textile Workers	2,927	3,280	353	12.1
Semiskilled Metalworkers	11,000	12,019	1,019	9.3

Table 4.7 (continued)

Occupation	1965	1975	Change, 1965–1975	
			Number	Percent
Mine Operatives and Laborers	19,230	14,371	–4,859	–25.3
Farmers and Farmworkers	870	559	–311	–35.7
Other Operatives (Semiskilled)	63,450	68,351	4,901	7.7
Laborers	30,254	28,574	–1,680	–5.6
Service				
Waiters, Cooks, and Bartenders	10,497	13,710	3,213	30.6
Other Service Workers	38,355	52,960	14,605	38.1
Total Employment	477,580	569,912	92,332	19.3

Professional and technical requirements will increase considerably by 1975. There will be large gains in the engineering occupations, especially mechanical and industrial. We also expect an increase in the number of mathematicians and scientists, especially physicists. The number of managers and officials will go up at a slower rate.

The number of college teachers is expected to increase by 77% and there will be a fourfold increase in the demand for "other teachers." Most of the latter will be needed to staff vocational training facilities which will have to be expanded to train skilled craftsmen.

The skilled crafts will attract more workers than operatives and laborers. Those unprepared for some type of skilled activity might be jobless by 1975. Mine operatives and laborers will decline, along with farm and other laborers. The service occupations, excluding waiters, cooks and bartenders, show a gain of 38%, or 14,605 additional employees.

The occupational projections are consistent with projected changes in output and employment. Declining occupations are found in sectors where unskilled workers have been and will continue to be displaced by technological change. The expanding occupations are those that require higher education or specialized training. West Virginia is one of the few states to experience a decline in population since 1950; it has not felt the pressures found in other states for the expansion of public schools. The population of West Virginia is expected to show an increase by 1975, however, and this will mean an expansion of its educational system. The effects of technological change will also result in changes in educational emphasis. We turn to some of these matters is the concluding section.

Expansion and Replacement Demand for Labor by Occupation

The projections of employment to 1975, given in Table 4.5, show an increase of more than 92,000 jobs, or a gain of 19% over 1965. This is an estimate of the *net* increase in jobs during the 10-year period; the total demand for labor will be larger since workers will have to be hired to replace those lost to the labor force through death and retirement. This discussion is in terms of jobs and employment rather than hires. This has been done to avoid the complication of labor turnover, which does influence the number of hires, but which does not affect the number of positions in an industry or sector. We have avoided the translation of occupational demand into *strict* educational requirements.[8] This would have involved linking educational attainment to occupation, which is not particularly difficult. But it also would have involved the projection of occupations to be chosen by graduates of West Virginia schools, and the occupations of in-migrants. Such projections are difficult enough to make on a year-to-year basis, and we were unwilling to make long-run projections which would have been little better than guesses. The occupational projections are given in detail in Table 4.8, and have been aggregated to the five broad occupational classes used in this study in Table 4.9.

Table 4.8 Projected Occupational
Demand in West Virginia, 1965—1975

Occupation	Expansion[a]	Replacement	Total Demand[b]
Professional, Technical, and Managerial			
Chemical Engineers	112	127	239
Industrial Engineers	438	95	533
Mechanical Engineers	302	162	464
Mining Engineers	81	78	159
Other Engineers	1,601	521	2,122
Chemists	366	244	610
Mathematicians	118	10	128
Physicists	137	16	153
Other Natural Scientists	415	79	494
Technicians (Exc. Med.–Dent.)	2,745	570	3,315
Med.–Dent. Technicians	1,067	595	1,662
Doctors and Veterinarians	932	490	1,422
Dentists	143	198	341
Pharmacists	86	178	264
Professional Nurses	3,304	4,310	7,614
Elem. and Sec. Teachers	4,514	8,135	12,649
College Teachers	2,097	773	2,870
Other Teachers	1,494	301	1,795

Table 4.8 (continued)

Occupation	Expansion[a]	Replacement	Total Demand[b]
Social Scientists	184	123	307
Accountants	738	627	1,365
Lawyers	386	573	959
Pers. and Labor Rel. Workers	482	177	659
Other Prof. and Technicians	5,143	1,440	6,583
Managers, Officials, and Prop.	7,750	15,621	23,371
Clerical and Sales			
Stenos, Typists, and Sec.	6,211	9,625	15,836
Office Machine Operators	2,265	2,185	4,450
Accounting Clerks	782	1,986	2,768
Shipping and Receiving Clerks	-141	474	333
Cashiers	1,278	1,680	2,958
Telephone Operators	214	1,441	1,655
Other Clerks	8,755	14,874	23,629
Sales Workers	3,501	9,057	12,558
Craftsmen and Foremen			
Brickmasons	292	200	492
Carpenters	1,025	1,020	2,045
Electricians	405	763	1,168

Table 4.8 (continued)

Occupation	Expansion[a]	Replacement	Total Demand[b]
Excavating Machine Operators	806	645	1,451
Plumbers	807	445	1,252
Painters	709	487	1,196
Other Construction Craftsmen	400	366	766
Foremen	1,294	2,918	4,212
Sheet Metal Workers	85	145	230
Skilled Machine Operators	147	610	757
Toolmakers and Diemakers	−37	106	69
Other Metalworking Craftsmen	−11	330	319
Motor Vehicle Mechanics	638	663	1,301
Other Mechanics	5,136	2,513	7,649
Printing Trades Craftsmen	617	259	876
Transp. and Pub. Util. Craftsmen	272	1,013	1,285
Other Craftsmen	954	1,784	2,738

Operatives and Laborers

Drivers	4,052	2,688	6,740
Semiskilled Textile Workers	353	967	1,320
Semiskilled Metal Workers	1,019	1,618	2,637
Mine Operatives and Laborers	−4,859	4,139	−720

Table 4.8 (continued)

Occupation	Expansion[a]	Replacement	Total Demand[b]
Farmers and Farmworkers	−311	120	−191
Other Operatives (Semiskilled)	4,901	13,229	18,130
Laborers	−1,680	4,497	2,817
Service			
Waiters, Cooks, and Bartenders	3,213	4,906	8,119
Other Service Workers	14,605	11,596	26,201
Total Employment	92,332	134,792	227,124

[a] A negative figure indicates contraction.

[b] Total number of jobs to be filled during the projection period.

Table 4.9 Summary of Projected
Occupational Demand, 1965–1975

	Expansion	Replacement	Total
Professional, Technical, and Managerial	34,635	35,443	70,078
Clerical and Sales	22,865	41,322	64,187
Craftsmen and Foremen	13,539	14,267	27,806
Operatives and Laborers	3,475	27,258	30,733
Service	17,818	16,502	34,320
Total	92,332	134,792	227,124

In both tables the total demand for labor by occupation has been divided into its expansion and replacement components. The expansion component, which shows the net change in employment by occupation from 1965 to 1975, has been taken directly from Table 4.7. The replacement component was calculated by applying annual attrition rates to annual employment projections and summing the results for each occupation to give the changes shown in column (2) of Table 4.8. The annual attrition rates by occupation were taken from an unpublished report by the U. S. Department of Labor, Bureau of Labor Statistics. The attrition rates cover death and retirement only.

All negative entries in column (1) of Table 4.8 indicate contracting occupations. In some cases, such as skilled metal workers and laborers, withdrawals from the work force due to death and retirement are larger than the projected reduction in jobs. Thus even where an occupation is declining, some workers will have to be hired over the 10-year period to replace those who leave the labor force. There are two occupational groups, mine operatives and laborers, and farmers and farm laborers, in which replacement employment will not be large enough to offset job contraction. In these occupations there is a net decline in total demand. This is of considerable significance in the case of West Virginia. It indicates that massive job displacements, of the kind that occurred in the coal industry from 1948 through 1963, are not expected to take place during the projection period. Future manpower adjustments in the coal industry will have much less impact than those that created severe dislocations in some parts of the state during the 1950s.

The changing occupational structure of the West Virginia labor force is shown clearly in the aggregated occupational projections of Table 4.9. In all occupational groups except services the number of workers required for replacement is larger than the expansion demand. The largest difference is in the operatives and laborer category. This is partly a function of the age distribution of the present West Virginia work force. Out-migrants tend to be younger than the workers who have remained in the state, and this has raised the average age of the present labor force. The table shows that there will be a substantial demand for unskilled workers, but it will be largely to replace those who leave the labor force through death or retirement.

In the professional, skilled, and white-collar categories the expansion demand is almost as large as that for replacement purposes. This has important implications for educational and training programs in West Virginia. Not all of the workers in these occupational groups will be educated in the state — some will be in-migrants. But the relative distribution of the occupational groups indicates that more than 70% of job openings will be for professional-technical, white-collar, or skilled workers.

Educational planners typically rely on demographic projections to anticipate their long-run needs for facilities and personnel. But demographic techniques rely heavily on past trends, and in a state such as West Virginia, which has experienced severe economic dislocations in recent years, the extrapolation of

Table 4.10 Occupational Trends,
1940–1960, with Projections to 1975

	1940	1950	1960
Professional, Technical, and Managerial	70,650	92,117	96,776
Clerical and Sales	62,655	91,832	99,006
Craftsmen and Foremen	59,996	90,506	80,876
Operatives and Laborers	157,655	194,605	128,794
Service	167,938	159,097	132,762
Total	518,894	628,157	538,214

| 1975 Projections | | Ratio of Input–Output |
Extrapolated	Input–Output	to Extrapolated
132,000	150,002	1.14
110,000	118,703	1.08
60,000	84,881	1.41
105,000	149,656	1.42
70,000	66,670	0.95
477,000	569,912	1.19

Source: 1940–1960 data from U.S. Census of Population, *General Characteristics*, West Virginia.

past trends could give misleading results. This is illustrated by Table 4.10, which compares two projections by occupational group to 1975.

The first set of projections was obtained by simple extrapolation. We are not suggesting that professional demographers would use such a simple technique, but even refined methods which rely on past trends would give essentially the same results. The second column shows the input-output employment projections, which were derived by relating employment to output after adjusting for changes in productivity.

It is interesting to note that the extrapolations understate the demand for both skilled and unskilled workers. In the service category — which includes only waiters, cooks, bartenders, and "other" service workers in our classification — the extrapolation is slightly higher than the input-output projection. In all other occupational classes the input-output projections are from 8 to 42% higher than the extrapolations.

The large decline in operatives and laborers between 1950 and 1960 was highly concentrated in coal mining, and in the sectors that supply inputs to coal. The decline in coal output was reversed in 1963, and we have projected an increase in coal production between 1965 and 1975. There will be a continued decline in coal employment (see Table 4.5), and a continuation of the shift from unskilled to skilled workers. If the levels of output which we have projected are realized by 1975, there will be a net increase in the aggregate demand for operatives and laborers to replace those who withdraw due to death and retirement.

The decline in craftsmen and foremen from 1950 to 1960 was also due to the drop in coal production. Extrapolation of this decline, however, would seriously understate the number of skilled workers who will be needed by 1975. This is not only because of a reversal in the trend of coal output, but because of the shift in skill requirements that is going on in most mining and manufacturing sectors. The input-output projection shows a modest increase over the 1960 level, but a much larger increase than the extrapolation.

Both projections show an increase in professional, technical, and managerial occupations, and the same is true of clerical and sales occupations. In both instances, however, the input-output projections are larger than the extrapolations. Since they are based on fairly conservative assumptions about changes in output during the projection period, the input-output projections should come much closer to realized employment levels in 1975.

Meeting West Virginia's Manpower Requirements

Relatively little can be said about the supply side of the labor market equation in West Virginia. In general, labor supply adapts to changes in the demand for labor, although there can be periods of specific occupational shortages. This is particularly true where a college degree or a long period of training is required for entrance to an occupation. The most rapidly growing occupations in West Virginia, as in the nation, are those which require college degrees or some type of vocational education including on-the-job training.

The number of high school graduates in West Virginia did not change significantly between 1956 and 1963, but it has increased since the latter year. There has also been an increase in college degrees granted, and an even sharper rise in college enrollment in recent years (see Table 4.11). These changes have occurred with a declining population. Once the population trend is reversed, the number of West Virginia residents who complete high school and college will rise at a faster rate.

In terms of sheer numbers there will be more than enough people with the educational requirements for the expanding skilled labor force requirements of the state. As we noted at the outset of this section, however, there is no way of knowing whether they will select the occupations that will present the best job opportunities. There is also cross-migration of high school and college graduates, and it would be hazardous to speculate about the proportions that will move into or out of the state. There should be no problem of labor supply, however, as economic conditions and job opportunities in West Virginia improve.

Recent trends in high school and college graduates, and the occupational projections, are consistent with the projections of capital requirements by educational services given in Table 3.8. More than one billion dollars of capital expenditures, in 1965 prices, will be required by the education sector between 1965 and 1975. Of this amount, about 79% will be expansion capital. Prices have been rising steadily since 1965, and will undoubtedly continue to rise through 1975. In current dollars the capital requirements could be half again as large. Education will require more capital than any other West Virginia sector between now and 1975.

The problem of keeping pace with the growing demand for educational facilities is not a new one in most states, since it is a result of growing population and rising income, but the pressure has been less intense in West Virginia, until recently, because of its declining population. The rate of out-migration has slowed down since 1963, and this is reflected in rising school enrollments. The pressures will become greater for the expansion of schools and colleges after the population curve turns up. The implications of the expansion of the education sector – which is both a cause and a consequence of economic development – will be explored further in Chapter 6.

Table 4.11 High School Graduates and
Degrees Granted in West Virginia
1956—1966

Year	High School Graduates	Degrees Granted by Institutions of Higher Education[a]	Enrollments in Institutions of Higher Education
1956	19,253	3,235	25,718
1957	19,322	na	25,885
1958	19,374	3,788	27,918
1959	20,291	na	28,255
1960	21,758	4,296	33,700
1961	20,637	na	31,610
1962	19,527	4,474	33,700
1963	19,356	4,594	35,231
1964	23,463	5,296	39,095
1965	26,974	na	46,805
1966	26,173	5,857	52,286[b]

[a] na= not available.

[b] Preliminary.

Source: *Statistical Abstract of the United States*, 1956—1968.

5 Simulating Regional Development

The simulation of regional development discussed in this chapter makes use of both the comparative static and dynamic models. It is essentially an impact study, and impact studies are typically conducted within a static framework. The output projections are those derived from the dynamic model, however, since we consider these to be more reliable than the preliminary projections. A modification of the dynamic model also has been used to show the impacts of the simulated sectors on all other sectors, assuming that each new sector will be operating in 1975. If this assumption were realized, some of the investment impacts on other sectors would be felt prior to the target year.

The Rationale Behind the Simulation Model

One of the advantages of interindustry forecasts is that they provide much more detail than that given by aggregative models. Conventional interindustry forecasts, such as those discussed in the last two chapters, are based on a given set of sectors. In this study, the structure of the West Virginia economy has been altered by assuming the development of activities that did not exist in the region in the base year (1965) or at the time of writing. The simulated activities were chosen on the basis of economic feasibility rather than likelihood. There is a chance, however, that one or more of the simulated industries will be operating in the state by 1975. The new sectors were selected on the basis of: (a) recent technological developments, and (b) the anticipated effects of an improved highway transportation system on the location of industry in West Virginia.

The simulated activities were identified during the data-gathering phase of the input-output study. The activities chosen on the basis of new technology are either in the pilot-plant stage or close to a "breakthrough." It was somewhat more difficult to select activities that might become economically feasible in the region as the result of an improved highway system. The industries finally selected are representative of a broader class that could have been included in the study.

The new-technology activities simulated are: (a) the conversion of coal to petroleum, (b) the manufacture of sulfuric acid from pyrites extracted from coal, (c) the production of flyash brick, and (d) the manufacture of "plastic wood." Representing activities that could become economically feasible in West Virginia with an improved highway system are: (a) an electronics-assembly complex, and (b) a book publishing industry serving national or regional rather than purely local markets.

The methods of obtaining data on the input requirements of each sector will be described in the following sections. For the impact analysis the assumption was made that each simulated sector would produce $100 million worth of output for final sale. This was done to permit direct comparisons of the output and employment impacts of each on the regional economy. For the dynamic simulations, however, the assumption of a constant level of final sales was dropped. A "reasonable level" of final deliveries was assumed for each sector on the basis of market potential, and the relative importance of each class of product in the national market. Before turning to the results of the analysis, sources of data and the general characteristics of each of the simulated sectors will be discussed briefly.

Coal Conversion to Petroleum

A pilot plant for the extraction of crude petroleum from coal is currently operating at Cresap, West Virginia. It was established as part of a long-range research project undertaken by the Consolidation Coal Company funded by the U.S. Office of Coal Research. It is now technically possible to produce petroleum from coal. The question of *economic feasibility*, however, hinges on the costs of this method compared with conventional techniques.

At present the cost differential is still slightly in favor of the conventional method, but if the cost of filtration can be reduced, petroleum from coal can be marketed at competitive prices.[1] As earlier technical problems have been solved it has become possible to focus increasingly on the major remaining problem of filtration. With research efforts concentrated on this problem, those in charge of the program are optimistic that it will be solved within a reasonable time. If they are correct, large-scale production could be under way in 10 years or less.

The major physical input required for the production of petroleum from coal is, of course, coal itself. There will also be substantial inputs of natural gas, chemicals, and electricity. The remaining inputs are detailed in Table 5.1, which shows the input coefficients for all simulated sectors.

It has been estimated that about 90% of an operating plant's output would consist of petroleum. Two by-products would account for the remaining 10%. The first is a low-cost boiler fuel which has been called Char. The other is a group of chemicals including phenol, cresols, butane, and ammonia, most of which would probably be purchased by the West Virginia chemical industry.

The input data of Table 5.1 apply to the pilot plant, which purchases

Table 5.1 Input Coefficients for
Simulated Sectors

Sector		Petroleum from Coal (18S)	Sulfuric Acid (17S)
1.	Agriculture	0	0
2.	Coal mining (underground)	0.24211	0.47828
3.	Coal mining (strip and auger)	0	0
4.	Petroleum and natural gas	0	0.00066
5.	All other mining	0	0.00038
6.	General contractors (building)	0	0.00007
7.	General contractors (nonbuilding)	0	0.00014
8.	Special trades contractors	0	0.00059
9.	Food and kindred products (n. e. c.)	0	0.00007
10.	Food and kindred products (dairies)	0	0
11.	Food and kindred products (bakeries)	0	0
12.	Food and kindred products (beverages)	0	0
13.	Apparel and accessories	0	0
14.	Logging and sawmills	0	0
15.	Furniture and other wood fabrications	0	0.00002
15S.	Plastic wood	0	0
16.	Printing and publishing	0.00063	0.00010
16S.	Book printing	0	0
17.	Chemicals	0.09454	0.00435

Flyash Brick (20S)	Plastic Wood (15S)	Electronics Assembly (24S)	Book Printing (16S)
0	0	0	0
0	0	0	0.00002
0	0	0	0.00001
0	0.00079	0	0
0	0	0	0
0	0	0	0.00016
0	0	0	0
0	0	0	0
0	0	0	0
0	0	0	0
0	0	0	0
0	0	0	0
0	0	0	0
0	0.03749	0	0
0	0	0	0
0	0	0	0
0.00105	0.00397	0	0.01088
0	0	0	0
0	0.05471	0.01615	0.00193

Table 5.1 (continued)

Sector	Petroleum from Coal (18S)	Sulfuric Acid (17S)
17S. Sulfuric acid	0	0
18. Petroleum	0	0.00010
18S. Petroleum from coal	0	0
19. Glass	0	0.00005
20. Stone and clay products	0.00210	0.00010
20S. Flyash brick	0	0
21. Primary metal products	0.00012	0.00004
22. Fabricated metal products	0	0.00018
23. Machinery (except electrical)	0.00171	0
24. Electrical machinery and apparatus	0	0.00009
24S. Electronics assembly	0	0
25. Transportation equipment	0	0
26. Instruments and related products	0	0.00022
27. All other manufacturing	0.00167	0.00070
28. Eating and drinking establishments	0.00053	0.00002
29. Wholesale trade	0	0.00070
30. Retail food stores	0	0.00001
31. Retail gasoline stations	0	0

Flyash Brick (20S)	Plastic Wood (15S)	Electronics Assembly (24S)	Book Printing (16S)
0	0	0	0
0	0	0	0
0	0	0	0
0	0	0.00638	0
0	0	0.00747	0
0	0	0	0
0	0	0.05300	0
0	0.00068	0.00889	0.00079
0	0	0.00461	0.00006
0	0	0.02881	0.00001
0	0	0	0
0	0	0	0
0	0.00052	0	0
0	0.00079	0.01796	0.00087
0.00175	0.00039	0	0.00018
0.00040	0.00077	0	0.00057
0	0.00027	0	0
0	0.00091	0	0.00010

Table 5.1 (continued)

Sector	Petroleum from Coal (18S)	Sulfuric Acid (17S)
32. All other retail	0	0.00027
33. Banking	0.01444	0.00647
34. Other finance	0	0
35. Insurance agents and brokerage	0.00595	0.00235
36. Real estate	0.00002	0
37. All other FIRE	0	0.00010
38. Hotels and other lodging places	0	0.00006
39. Medical and legal services	0.00790	0.00012
40. Educational services	0	0.00001
41. All other services	0.01370	0.00065
42. Railroads	0	0.00104
43. Trucking and warehousing	0	0.00233
44. All other transportation	0	0.00031
45. Communications	0.00108	0.00048
46. Electric companies and systems	0.04015	0.02471
47. Gas companies and systems	0.13530	0.00129
48. Water and sanitary services	0.00490	0.01417
49. Households	0.05334	0.13698

Flyash Brick (20S)	Plastic Wood (15S)	Electronics Assembly (24S)	Book Printing (16S)
0	0	0	0.00017
0	0	0	0.00005
0	0	0	0.00837
0.00567	0.01030	0	0.00504
0.01964	0	0	0.00005
0	0	0	0.00018
0.00175	0.00055	0	0.00014
0.00105	0	0	0.00145
0.00070	0	0	0.00032
0.00140	0.00031	0	0.00024
0	0.00661	0	0.00322
0.02727	0.01323	0.01020	0.01343
0	0.00052	0	0.00002
0.00182	0.00066	0	0.00326
0.03836	0.00141	0.00934	0.03105
0.04873	0.00060	0	0.00023
0.00084	0.00038	0	0.00001
0.28175	0.08999	0.46141	0.46610

Table 5.1 (continued)

Sector	Petroleum from Coal (18S)	Sulfuric Acid (17S)
50. Out–of–state (imports)	0.04119	0.08305
51. All other final payments	0.33862	0.23874
52. Total	1.00000	1.00000

Flyash Brick (20S)	Plastic Wood (15S)	Electronics Assembly (24S)	Book Printing (16S)
0.01196	0.64816	0.17235	0.27994
0.55586	0.12599	0.20343	0.17115
1.00000	1.00000	0.99999	1.00000

Note: The numbers in parentheses under the column headings are the numbers assigned to the simulated sectors in the West Virginia transactions table.

electrical energy. An operating establishment would use substantial quantities of electrical energy. Some members of the research team have suggested that, once the scale of an operating establishment has been determined, it might be economical for the coal-conversion plant to generate its own power. In this event, a major generating plant would be constructed in conjunction with the refinery, and surplus electricity would be offered for sale. Since the fuel input for the generation of energy would be Char, this would be a modification of the mine-mouth generating concept. Whether or not it would be economically feasible for a company manufacturing petroleum from coal to also generate electricity is yet to be determined.

The conversion of coal to petroleum is a capital-intensive process, requiring (in 1965 prices) only 5.3 cents of direct labor input per dollar of output. The direct and indirect requirements would, of course, generate additional increases in employment.

Sulfuric Acid

One reason for assuming that the production of sulfuric acid might become feasible in West Virginia is that the enforcement of antipollution legislation will require reduction in the sulfur content of northern West Virginia coal either before or after it is burned. It is now technically possible to remove sulfur pyrites from coal prior to burning, and in simulating a sulfuric acid industry we assumed that this process would be used.

Much of the expansion of coal production in West Virginia by 1975 will take place in the extensive fields of the northern part of the state. This is largely because of their proximity to expanding mine-mouth electrical generating facilities. As a rough estimate, northern West Virginia coal has a sulfur content of 4%. Under federal antipollution standards this will have to be reduced to 2% or less.

There is at present no plant built primarily for the removal of sulfur pyrite from coal. A single plant with daily production of 1000 tons of sulfuric acid was simulated. Data on inputs and costs were obtained from the U.S. Bureau of Mines, consulting firms, and interviews with out-of-state producers of sulfuric acid. At a price of $45 per ton the simulated plant would produce about $12.3 million worth of sulfuric acid per year. To simulate the new sector final sales were expanded to $100 million.

The direct input coefficients for the simulated sulfuric acid industry are given in Table 5.1. The major input is from the coal sectors, but a sulfuric acid industry would purchase some inputs from all but 12 of the West Virginia sectors. The direct and indirect effects of the establishment of this activity in West Virginia would be substantial. Also, compared with petroleum from coal this is a relatively labor-intensive process with a direct labor input of 13.7 cents per dollar of output.

Flyash Brick

The third simulated sector is also tied to West Virginia's expanding coal industry. A flyash brick sector is not only economically feasible, it is one which could move from the pilot-plant to the production stage in a relatively short time.

A unique feature of the flyash brick manufacturing process is that it converts a waste product from coal-burning utilities to a valuable building material. At present, utilities dispose of the flyash that accumulates from the burning of coal at an approximate cost of $2 per ton. Thus the major input of flyash brick would be virtually costless, at least initially. The brick produced from this waste product is considered to be superior to clay brick by the American Society for Testing Material Specifications. It is lighter, stronger, and can be produced in a variety of shapes and colors.[2]

A pilot plant operated by the Coal Research Bureau of West Virginia University is currently producing flyash brick at Morgantown. Data for the simulated sector were obtained from the Plant Coordinator and the Cost Engineer of this plant, and from detailed cost estimates prepared by the Coal Research Bureau. The direct input requirements per dollar of output are given in column 3 of Table 5.1. This industry exhibits relatively little interdependence on the input side. It is more labor-intensive than either of the industries discussed thus far with a direct labor input of more than 28 cents per dollar of output. The entry of almost 56 cents in the "all other final payments" row represents taxes, profits, and depreciation.

It has been estimated by the Coal Research Bureau that flyash brick can be produced at a cost of approximately $22 per thousand. The cost of producing conventional brick is at least twice this high, although there is considerable geographic variation. At the current market price of about $80 per thousand, the estimated return on sales would be in excess of 30%. A plant of the size now operating in Morgantown could produce one-half million bricks per week operating at 100% capacity. The total investment in this plant is slightly less than $578 thousand. Assuming costs and prices unchanged, the annual return on investment of such a plant would be slightly more than 75%. Clearly this rate of profit would not be maintained once the industry began operating on a production basis. The production process is simple and well known. It involves no major innovation in machinery. With the rapid expansion of coal-generated electric energy, the basic raw material will be available in increasing abundance. It is likely, therefore that this process will be adopted. It can be applied at any location close to coal-burning power plants. But, since much of West Virginia's coal will be burned at its source in the future, flyash brick could be produced in this state.

If the present price of flyash brick should fall, as is likely, brick produced in West Virginia could be substituted for building materials currently imported. It also would be substituted to some extent for other stone and clay products currently produced in the state. Because of this, sales to general contractors have been increased in the simulation, and purchases by general contractors from the stone and clay product sector have been reduced.

Plastic Wood

The development of a new product, known popularly as "plastic wood," has involved research by a number of industrial organizations and private research groups. The product discussed in this section, however, was developed at West Virginia University as the result of research started in November 1961.

The process involves impregnating wood with a liquid monomer until the wood is thoroughly saturated. The impregnated wood is then exposed to cobalt rays, and the resulting chain reaction hardens the monomer not only on the surface but throughout the celluar structure of the wood. The physical properties of wood are thus completely changed. It becomes harder, smoother, as well as resistant to fire, abrasion, and most types of chemical reaction. The major advantage of the technique is that it permits the shaping of wood products, by conventional methods, while the wood is soft and easily worked. Plasticizing the product alters the cellular structure of the wood but does not, of course, affect the shape of the product. Virtually anything now made of wood could be converted to plastic wood. Sporting goods, such as skis, boating accessories, and tennis rackets could be made from plastic wood as well as many small items of furniture and household supplies. The wood could also be used to manufacture airplane wingspars, tool handles, and similar industrial or semi-fabricated products. Finally, autobody panels and room paneling are two potential products that could be produced on a large scale.

West Virginia contains a substantial amount of timber, mostly hardwood, but little of this timber is suitable for construction purposes, or for the manufacture of furniture or other products for which there are growing markets. Adoption of the plasticizing technique would, however, permit the production of a number of the products just mentioned.

Shortly before this manuscript went to press, Radiation Machinery Corporation, which operates a nuclear irradiation plant at Hanover, New Jersey, announced that it would construct a new plant near Moorefield, West Virginia. This facility will be used to manufacture plastic wood parquet flooring. Although starting as a relatively small establishment, with an initial investment of \$3.5 million and a work force of 300, this will be the world's largest commercial operation of its type.

Input data for the simulated sector were obtained by interviews with firms doing research on the development of plastic wood, intensive study of the facility at West Virginia University, and a memorandum, *Engineering and Evaluation Study for the Manufacture of Wood Plastic Composite* published by the Atomic Energy Commission.

Wood purchased from Sector 14, logging and sawmills, would amount to 3.7 cents per dollar of output. The West Virginia chemical industry (Sector 17) would provide about 5.5 cents worth of input per dollar of output. Most of the other inputs from processing sectors would come from the trades and services, as indicated by column 4 of Table 5.1. In spite of the relatively small direct impact, a plastic wood sector would add almost as much to gross output as the flyash brick industry because of substantial indirect impacts.

An Electronics Complex

The electronics industry has grown rapidly since the end of World War II. During the early phase of its development this industry was highly localized. By the early 1950s the industry was well represented in the Greater Boston, Great Lakes, and San Francisco—Palo Alto areas. It has continued to grow in these regions, but there also has been dispersion since that time. A number of electronics firms now have plants in the Baltimore-Washington area, and electronics plants are appearing in a growing number of states. The electronics industry is not represented in West Virginia, however. Inclusion of an electronics complex in the simulation of economic activity in West Virginia is based on the assumption that completion of the Interstate Highway System and of the Appalachian Development Highway Corridors will make this a feasible economic activity for the region.

Input data for the simulated sectors discussed thus far were obtained from pilot plants, engineering studies, and other sources which relate directly to the West Virginia economy. This cannot be done, however, in the case of the remaining sectors. The electronics complex assumed for West Virginia is one which would be concerned entirely with manufacturing and assembly operations; such activities as research and development have not been included. In brief, we have assumed that an improved transportation system would permit the manufacture of such items as semiconductors, transistors, rectifiers and similar products in the state. No attempt was made to simulate a specialized branch of the industry. Instead, the activity simulated is of a rather general type now found in many states.

Basic data on direct inputs were obtained from the Philadelphia Region Input-Output Study.[4] The Philadelphia model is highly disaggregated, and it was possible to aggregate direct inputs to conform to the West Virginia sectors. Inputs not produced within the state were assigned to the import sector, and transport inputs were estimated.

This approach to the simulation of a new activity in the region leaves much to be desired, but the sector was included in the simulation model since it indicates the minimal impact of such an activity on the regional economy. It is evident from an examination of column 5 in Table 5.1 that total in-state inputs are understated since no inputs are shown from sectors 28 through 42. It would have been possible to arbitrarily assign relatively small inputs to those sectors where some inputs are obvious. Throughout the study an effort was made to avoid such crude estimation on the assumption that it is better to understate than to overstate direct inputs because the effects of the latter are multiplied when the table of direct coefficients is inverted. In spite of the obvious understatement of direct in-state inputs, an electronics complex would have a substantial direct and indirect impact on the regional economy. The total gross output generated by this activity would be approximately the same as that resulting from the development of an operational flyash brick industry.

Commercial Printing

The final sector simulated, and the second based on the assumption that a new economic activity could become feasible with an improved transportation system, is a commercial printing sector serving an export market. Printing plants that serve national markets must be concerned with transportation costs, but it is not clear that they meet the classic definition of a transport-oriented industry. The printing industry simulated for West Virginia is fairly labor-intensive. It is representative of a class of activities which could be attracted to this state by labor-supply considerations, once the present transportation handicap is overcome.

Data for the simulated printing sector were obtained from an operating plant in a neighboring state. It is a relatively new establishment with modern machinery and processes, and the output of this plant is sold nationally. Input data were obtained from the plant's purchasing department, and the major direct inputs are considered to be highly reliable. Some of the minor inputs were estimated from a percentage distribution provided by the plant's purchasing department. The assumption was made that the entire output of the simulated sector would be sold out of state. The largest direct inputs represent purchases from trucking and warehousing, and from electric utilities. The direct and indirect impact of the export printing industry on the West Virginia economy would be about the same as that of the electronics complex or the flyash brick industry, and only slightly smaller than that of the simulated sulfuric acid industry.

Impact of the Simulated Sectors on the West Virginia Economy

The simulation of the six activities described in the foregoing was accomplished by solving the comparative static equations given in Chapter 2, after the new input columns had been added to the 1975 input coefficient matrix (Table IV). This expanded the original matrix from 48 to 54 sectors, and involved renumbering some sectors in tables 5.1 through 6.2. The simulated sectors are identified by an S after the number. The final demand vector used in the solution was that given in the dynamic model of Chapter 3, with a constant final demand of $100 million assumed for each of the new industries in the impact analysis. In the dynamic analysis, discussed in a later section, the assumption of constant final deliveries was relaxed.

In a few cases, where the simulated activity would provide a substitute for inputs currently produced in the state, offsetting reductions were made in the original input coefficient columns. For example, flyash brick would compete with the West Virginia stone and clay products sector to some extent. It would also substitute for building materials now imported. Purchases per dollar of output by building construction from stone and clay products were reduced by the amount of new purchases from the flyash brick industry. A similar reduction was made in the import of building materials by the construction sector. An adjustment was also made to allow for the substitution of Char for coal in the generation of electricity. Other interindustry transactions, such as sales from sulfuric acid to chemicals, required adjustments only in the import row.

What impact would the addition of the simulated sectors have on the West Virginia economy if each were operating in 1975 with final sales of $100 million? The projected total gross output of the West Virginia economy, in 1965 prices, is $30.7 billion. With $600 million of additional sales to final demand, the simulated sectors would add slightly more than $1.5 billion, or 5%, to West Virginia's TGO. The largest contribution would be made by the sulfuric acid industry, which would add more than $361 million, followed by the coal-based petroleum industry, which would add $297 million. Interestingly, differences between the contributions that would be made by electronics, flyash brick, and plastic wood are negligible, although it must be recalled that the estimate of the impact of the electronics complex is a minimal one. The smallest contribution would be made by the export book sector which, at the simulated scale, would add more than $221 million. A summary of the direct and indirect effects of the simulations is given in Table 5.2.

Since this is basically an impact study each of the simulated sectors has been treated as a separate "industry." We have assumed that each of the simulated sectors purchased the inputs shown in Table 5.1, and that each will sell a single homogeneous product. This was done deliberately to focus attention on the impact of the new *activity;* in other words, the issue of industrial organization has been ignored. It is important to keep this in mind when interpreting the input coefficients of Table 5.1, as well as the direct and indirect impacts given in Tables 5.2 and 5.3. The input coefficients of Table 5.1 should be interpreted, as is customary in input-output analysis, as engineering production functions rather than accounting transactions. The direct inputs from the coal sector by the simulated sulfuric acid industry, for example, represent purchases of sulfur pyrites not coal. Purchases by the coal-based petroleum industry are purchases of coal as such.

If plants for the extraction of sulfur pyrites from coal are established in West Virginia it is likely that they will be financed and operated by the coal industry. It is also reasonable to expect that a coal-based petroleum industry will become part of a more general "energy from coal" sector. The development of new activities which have been simulated in the West Virginia study raise a number of interesting questions concerning industrial organization, but these are largely irrelevant to the main purpose of this study. These matters have been mentioned in passing to clarify the meaning of some of the entries in the table of direct input coefficients. In developing these coefficients every effort was made to think in physical rather than accounting terms.

The assumption that each of the simulated sectors would have equal sales to final demand was necessary for the comparative impact analysis. The *comparative* impact of each of the simulated activities on existing sectors is given in Table 5.3. This table shows, for example, that petroleum from coal would have the largest and flyash brick the smallest impacts on the chemical sector. Similar comparisons can be made for each existing sector by reading down the columns of Table 5.3.

Employment Impacts of the Simulated Sectors

Direct employment in each of the simulated sectors, at the level of operations assumed, is given in column 2 of Table 5.4. It is evident that these activities vary widely in labor-intensity. The sulfuric acid industry, for example, would employ about 3.7 times as many workers as flyash brick. The total employment impact must also take indirect employment into account, however. Direct plus indirect employment in all sectors, as the result of the introduction of the new sectors, is given in column 3 of Table 5.4. Employment multipliers showing the number of indirect jobs per direct job are given in column 4. The coal-based petroleum sector shows the largest employment multiplier, and book printing the smallest. All of the indirect employment figures relate to employment within the region. The details of the employment generated by each new activity, by sector, are given in Table 5.5

We can also relate the gross output generated by each simulated sector to the total employment generated by the same sector. The results of this comparison are given in column 5 of Table 5.4. Flyash brick would generate the largest addition to gross output per worker ($96,444) while the sulfuric acid industry would generate the smallest ($35,742).

Capital Investment, Output and Employment

One ingredient missing from the comparative analysis thus far has been the investment required to develop each of the simulated industries to the scale which would permit final sales of $100 million. This is, of course, a critical variable in development planning.

Capital requirements for the given scale (including interindustry sales in three sectors) were derived from the primary data for five of the sectors. Since data for the electronic complex were "borrowed" from the Philadelphia table, there was no way of directly estimating capital requirements for this sector. An estimate was developed from the National Planning Association's *Capacity Expansion Planning Factors.* The estimated investment requirements are listed in Table 5.6.

Capital/output ratios are given in column 3 of this table, together with capital requirements per worker in the simulated sectors (column 4), and in all sectors (column 5). The employment estimates used to compute capital requirements per worker are the *total* (direct plus indirect) employment that would be generated by each of the simulated sectors.

Table 5.2 Summary of Direct and
Indirect Impacts on the West Virginia
Economy of Simulated Sectors[a]

| Sector | Change in Total Gross Output[b] | |
	Millions of dollars	Percent change
17S. Sulfuric acid	$ 381.8	1.25%
18S. Petroleum from coal	296.9	0.97
24S. Electronics complex	220.3	0.72
20S. Flyash brick	218.9	0.72
15S. Plastic wood	218.9	0.72
16S. Book printing	210.8	0.69
Total change	1,547.7	5.08

[a] Changes in Total Gross Output due to introduction of simulated sectors with assumed sales to final demand of $100 million by each sector.

[b] Detail might not add to total because of rounding.

Table 5.3 Impact on West Virginia
Gross Output of Simulated Sectors[a,b]

		(1) Petroleum from Coal Change in TGO		(2) Sulfuric Acid Change in TGO	
		Thousands of dollars	Percent change	Thousands of dollars	Percent change
1.	Agriculture	$ 35	0.02%	$ 54	0.04%
2.	Coal mines (undgd.)	23,085	2.27	78,106	7.69
3.	Coal (strip and auger)	554	0.63	1,244	1.41
4.	Pet. and nat. gas	1,897	1.79	176	0.17
5.	All other mining	145	0.16	253	0.28
6. '	Bldg. cont.	26	0.01	22	0.01
7.	Nonbldg. cont.	80	0.03	217	0.08
8.	Spec. cont.	257	0.11	516	0.22
9.	Food prod. (n. e. c.)	75	0.11	112	0.16
10.	Dairies	24	0.02	7	0.01
11.	Bakeries	4	0.01	0	0
12.	Beverages	3	0.01	1	*
13.	Apparel and acc.	20	0.01	4	0.01
14.	Logging and sawmills	220	0.20	728	0.68
15.	Furn. and wood fab.	89	0.21	293	0.69
16.	Print. and pub.	338	0.23	243	0.17

(3) Flyash Brick Change in TGO		(4) Plastic Wood Change in TGO		(5) Electronics Change in TGO		(6) Book Printing Change in TGO	
Thousands of dollars	Percent change	Thousands of dollars	Percent change	Thousands of dollars	Percent change	Thousands of dollars	Percent change
$ 8	0.01%	$ 213	0.15%	$ 32	0.02%	$ 5	*%
426	0.04	114	0.01	278	0.03	338	0.03
199	0.23	24	0.03	80	0.09	159	0.18
548	0.52	162	0.15	44	0.04	11	0.01
−22	−0.02	45	0.05	90	0.10	8	0.01
167	0.06	16	0.01	6	*	23	0.01
70	0.03	51	0.02	31	0.01	34	0.01
152	0.06	109	0.05	89	0.04	31	0.01
18	0.03	11	0.02	22	0.03	9	0.01
12	0.01	5	0.01	2	*	6	0.01
8	0.01	1	*	−1	*	0	0
4	0.01	1	*	1	*	1	*
2	0.01	2	0.01	1	*	3	0.01
14	0.01	4,972	4.62	9	0.01	6	0.01
4	0.01	*	*	6	0.01	2	*
365	0.25	597	0.41	95	0.06	1,516	1.103

Table 5.3 (continued)

		(1) Petroleum from Coal Change in TGO		(2) Sulfuric Acid Change in TGO	
		Thousands of dollars	Percent change	Thousands of dollars	Percent change
17.	Chemicals	13,106	0.68	953	0.05
18.	Petroleum	260	0.22	271	0.23
19.	Glass	16	*	19	*
20.	Stone and clay prod.	435	0.19	382	0.17
21.	Primary metals	173	0.01	79	0.01
22.	Fab. metals	168	0.08	242	0.12
23.	Mach. (except elec.)	241	0.14	61	0.04
24.	Elec. mach.	36	0.02	39	0.02
25.	Transp. equip.	3	*	4	*
26.	Instruments and prod.	26	0.19	40	0.30
27.	All other mfg.	378	0.19	248	0.13
28.	Eat. and drink. est.	108	0.07	20	0.01
29.	Wholesale trade	636	0.14	1,062	0.24
30.	Retail food	3	*	2	*
31.	Auto serv. sta.	94	0.16	40	0.07
32.	All other retail	266	0.05	401	0.07
33.	Banking	1,803	1.18	1,093	0.71

(3) Flyash Brick Change in TGO		(4) Plastic Wood Change in TGO		(5) Electronics Change in TGO		(6) Book Printing Change in TGO	
Thousands of dollars	Percent change	Thousands of dollars	Percent change	Thousands of dollars	Percent change	Thousands of dollars	Percent change
7	*	6,423	0.33	2,026	0.11	234	0.01
43	0.04	42	0.04	46	0.04	24	0.02
3	*	7	*	667	0.17	3	*
−782	−0.35	17	0.01	776	0.35	16	0.01
18	*	78	0.01	5,940	0.43	26	*
33	0.02	125	0.06	1,012	0.50	139	0.07
8	*	12	0.01	484	0.29	16	0.01
3	*	7	*	2,896	1.58	6	*
0	0	6	*	3	*	3	*
1	0.01	64	0.47	13	0.10	2	0.01
18	0.01	188	0.10	1,880	0.95	112	0.06
212	0.13	48	0.03	6	*	28	0.02
316	0.07	333	0.07	203	0.05	194	0.04
1	*	28	0.02	0	0	0	0
37	0.06	122	0.21	15	0.03	29	0.05
48	0.01	53	0.01	64	0.01	43	0.01
68	0.04	43	0.03	34	0.02	84	0.05

Table 5.3 (continued)

		(1) Petroleum from Coal Change in TGO		(2) Sulfuric Acid Change in TGO	
		Thousands of dollars	Percent change	Thousands of dollars	Percent change
34.	Other finance	25	0.03	21	0.03
35.	Ins. agents	1,293	0.33	1,714	0.43
36.	Real estate	180	0.21	109	0.13
37.	All other FIRE	230	0.33	379	0.54
38.	Hotels and lodgings	65	0.12	29	0.05
39.	Med. and legal ser.	1,241	0.47	295	0.11
40.	Ed. ser.	8	*	6	*
41.	All other services	2,150	0.35	647	0.11
42.	Railroads	216	0.07	343	0.12
43.	Trucking and warehsg.	483	0.16	727	0.25
44.	All other transp.	314	0.37	123	0.15
45.	Communications	370	0.20	318	0.17
46.	Elec. systems	6,517	1.11	7,235	1.31
47.	Gas systems	16,317	2.57	313	0.05
48.	Water and san. ser.	629	1.36	2,315	4.99
18S.	Pet. from coal	117,740	0	0	0

(3) Flyash Brick Change in TGO		(4) Plastic Wood Change in TGO		(5) Electronics Change in TGO		(6) Book Printing Change in TGO	
Thousands of dollars	Percent change	Thousands of dollars	Percent change	Thousands of dollars	Percent change	Thousands of dollars	Percent change
8	0.01	9	0.01	6	0.01	843	1.06
667	0.17	1,187	0.30	108	0.03	569	0.14
2,177	2.52	124	0.14	27	0.03	35	0.04
70	0.10	140	0.20	23	0.03	81	0.12
204	0.36	69	0.12	12	0.02	23	0.04
200	0.08	115	0.04	49	0.02	224	0.08
74	0.02	4	*	18	*	37	0.01
326	0.05	190	0.03	177	0.03	120	0.02
87	0.03	746	0.25	116	0.04	396	0.13
2,877	0.98	1,511	0.51	1,211	0.41	1,477	0.50
105	0.13	100	0.12	167	0.20	27	0.03
320	0.17	195	0.10	106	0.06	430	0.23
4,195	0.76	323	0.06	1,272	0.23	3,340	0.60
4,996	0.79	197	0.03	149	0.02	56	0.01
107	0.23	55	0.12	25	0.05	7	0.02
0	0	0	0	0	0	0	0

Table 5.3 (continued)

| | | (1) Petroleum from Coal Change in TGO | | (2) Sulfuric Acid Change in TGO | |
		Thousands of dollars	Percent change	Thousands of dollars	Percent change
17S.	Sulfuric acid	0	0	159,887	0
24S.	Electronics	0	0	0	0
20S.	Flyash	0	0	0	0
15S.	Plastic wood	0	0	0	0
16S.	Book printing	0	0	0	0
49.	Households	25,780	0.46	59,995	1.07
50.	Imports	26,502	0.37	-13,987	-0.19
51.	All other value added	52,606	1.28	54,749	1.33
52.	Total	$296,910	0.97%	$381,840	1.25%

(3) Flyash Brick Change in TGO		(4) Plastic Wood Change in TGO		(5) Electronics Change in TGO		(6) Book Printing Change in TGO	
Thousands of dollars	Percent change	Thousands of dollars	Percent change	Thousands of dollars	Percent change	Thousands of dollars	Percent change
0	0	0	0	0	0	0	0
0	0	0	0	100,000	0	0	0
101,294	0	0	0	0	0	0	0
0	0	100,000	0	0	0	0	0
0	0	0	0	0	0	100,000	0
33,290	0.59	14,263	0.03	51,332	0.92	50,058	0.89
5,838	0.08	70,059	0.97	25,217	0.35	30,304	0.42
60,074	1.46	15,679	0.38	23,460	0.57	19,649	0.48
$218,918	0.72%	$218,886	0.72%	$220,325	0.72%	$210,787	0.69%

[a] Changes in Total Gross Output, by sector, due to introduction of simulated sectors with assumed sales to final demand of $100 million by each sector.

[b] Asterisk indicates less than 0.005%.

Table 5.4 Employment Impact of
Simulated Sectors

	Sector	Change in TGO (millions of dollars) (1)	Employment	
			Simulated Sector[a] (2)	All Sectors[b] (3)
15S.	Plastic wood	$218.9	3,653	4,344
16S.	Book printing	210.8	5,548	5,868
17S.	Sulfuric acid	381.8	6,708	10,162
18S.	Petroleum from coal	296.9	2,251	4,183
20S.	Flyash brick	218.9	1,823	2,276
24S.	Electronics complex	220.3	4,729	5,284

Employment Multiplier[c] (4)	TGO per total employment[d] ($ thousands) (5)
1.19	50.4
1.06	35.9
1.51	37.6
1.86	71.0
1.25	96.2
1.12	41.7

[a] Direct and indirect employment in simulated sectors per $100 million sales to final demand.

[b] Direct and indirect employment in all sectors per $100 million sales to final demand.

[c] $(3) \div (2)$.

[d] $(1) \div (3)$.

Table 5.5 Employment Impacts on
all Sectors of Simulated Sectors[a,b]

Sectors	(1) Petroleum from Coal		(2) Sulfuric Acid	
	Number	Percent Change	Number	Percent Change
1. Agriculture	0	0%	0	0%
2. Coal mines (undgd.)	811	2.27	2,746	7.69
3. Coal (strip and auger)	15	0.64	33	1.41
4. Pet. and nat. gas	88	1.80	8	0.16
5. All other mining	2	0.04	4	0.08
6. Bldg. cont.	1	0.01	1	0.01
7. Nonbldg. cont.	3	0.04	7	0.09
8. Spec. cont.	13	0.11	26	0.22
9. Food prod. (n. e. c.)	2	0.12	3	0.18
10. Dairies	1	0.04	0	0
11. Bakeries	0	0	0	0
12. Beverages	0	0	0	0
13. Apparel and acc.	4	0.06	1	0.01
14. Logging and sawmills	16	0.21	52	0.67
15. Furn. and wood fab.	5	0.23	15	0.70
16. Print. and pub.	15	0.22	11	0.16
17. Chemicals	163	0.68	12	0.05

(3) Flyash Brick		(4) Plastic Wood		(5) Electronics		(6) Book Printing	
Number	Percent Change	Number	Percent Change	Number	Percent Change	Number	Percent Change
0	0%	1	0.12%	0	0%	0	0%
15	0.04	4	0.01	10	0.03	12	0.03
5	0.21	1	0.04	2	0.09	4	0.17
25	0.51	7	0.14	2	0.04	1	0.02
0	0	1	0.02	1	0.02	0	0
6	0.06	1	0.01	0	0	1	0.01
2	0.02	2	0.02	1	0.01	1	0.01
8	0.07	5	0.04	4	0.03	2	0.02
0	0	0	0	1	0.06	0	0
0	0	0	0	0	0	0	0
0	0	0	0	0	0	0	0
0	0	0	0	0	0	0	0
0	0	0	0	0	0	1	0.01
1	0.01	357	4.62	1	0.01	0	0
0	0	0	0	0	0	0	0
17	0.25	27	0.40	4	0.06	69	1.02
0	0	80	0.33	25	0.10	3	0.01

156

Table 5.5 (continued)

		(1) Petroleum from Coal		(2) Sulfuric Acid	
	Sectors	Number	Percent Change	Number	Percent Change
18.	Pet. prod.	2	0.24	2	0.24
19.	Glass	1	0.01	1	0.01
20.	Stone and clay prod.	14	0.19	12	0.17
21.	Primary metals	4	0.01	2	0.01
22.	Fab. metals	8	0.09	11	0.12
23.	Mach. (ex. elec.)	8	0.13	2	0.03
24.	Elec. mach.	1	0.02	1	0.02
25.	Transp. equip.	0	0	0	0
26.	Ins. and prod.	1	0.17	2	0.33
27.	All other mfg.	14	0.19	9	0.12
28.	Rest. and bars	9	0.07	2	0.02
29.	Wholesale trade	30	0.14	50	0.24
30.	Retail food stores	0	0	0	0
31.	Auto serv. sta.	7	0.16	3	0.07
32.	All other retail	22	0.05	33	0.07
33.	Banking	69	1.18	42	0.72
34.	Other finance	1	0.04	1	0.04

(3) Flyash Brick		(4) Plastic Wood		(5) Electronics		(6) Book Printing	
Number	Percent Change	Number	Percent Change	Number	Percent Change	Number	Percent Change
0	0	0	0	0	0	0	0
0	0	0	0	27	0.17	0	0
-25	-0.34	1	0.01	25	0.35	1	0.01
0	0	2	0.01	130	0.43	1	*
1	0.01	6	0.07	46	0.50	6	0.07
0	0	0	0	17	0.29	1	0.02
0	0	0	0	86	1.59	0	0
0	0	0	0	0	0	0	0
0	0	3	0.50	1	0.17	0	0
1	0.01	7	0.09	70	0.95	4	0.05
17	0.13	4	0.03	0	0	2	0.02
15	0.07	16	0.08	10	0.05	9	0.04
0	0	2	0.02	0	0	0	0
3	0.07	9	0.21	1	0.02	2	0.05
4	0.01	4	0.01	5	0.01	4	0.01
3	0.05	2	0.03	1	0.02	3	0.05
0	0	0	0	0	0	28	1.05

Table 5.5 (continued)

		(1) Petroleum from Coal		(2) Sulfuric Acid	
	Sectors	Number	Percent Change	Number	Percent Change
35.	Ins. agents	22	0.33	29	0.44
36.	Real estate	7	0.22	4	0.12
37.	All other FIRE	6	0.34	9	0.52
38.	Hotels and lodging	6	0.12	3	0.06
39.	Med. and legal serv.	165	0.47	39	0.11
40.	Ed. serv.	1	*	1	*
41.	All other serv.	133	0.35	40	0.11
42.	Railroads	8	0.08	12	0.11
43.	Trucking and warehsg.	14	0.17	20	0.24
44.	All other transp.	6	0.35	2	0.12
45.	Communications	14	0.19	12	0.16
46.	Elec. systems	65	1.11	77	1.31
47.	Gas systems	125	2.57	2	0.04
48.	Water and san. serv.	30	1.34	112	5.00
18S.	Pet. from coal	2,251	0	0	0
17S.	Sulfuric acid	0	0	6,708	0
24S.	Electronics	0	0	0	0

(3) Flyash Brick Number	Percent Change	(4) Plastic Wood Number	Percent Change	(5) Electronics Number	Percent Change	(6) Book Printing Number	Percent Change
11	0.17	20	0.30	2	0.03	10	0.15
82	2.53	5	0.15	1	0.03	1	0.03
2	0.11	3	0.17	1	0.06	2	0.11
19	0.37	6	0.12	1	0.02	2	0.04
27	0.08	15	0.05	7	0.02	30	0.09
9	0.02	1	*	2	*	5	0.01
20	0.05	12	0.03	11	0.03	7	0.02
3	0.03	27	0.25	4	0.04	14	0.14
81	0.98	42	0.51	34	0.41	41	0.50
2	0.12	2	0.12	3	0.18	1	0.06
12	0.16	8	0.11	4	0.05	17	0.23
44	0.75	3	0.05	13	0.22	35	0.60
38	0.78	2	0.04	1	0.02	0	0
5	0.22	3	0.13	1	0.04	0	0
0	0	0	0	0	0	0	0
0	0	0	0	0	0	0	0
0	0	0	0	4,729	0	0	0

Table 5.5 (continued)

	Sectors	(1) Petroleum from Coal		(2) Sulfuric Acid	
		Number	Percent Change	Number	Percent Change
20S.	Flyash brick	0	0	0	0
15S.	Plastic wood	0	0	0	0
16S.	Book printing	0	0	0	0
49.	Total	4,813	0.83%	10,162	2.01%

(3) Flyash Brick		(4) Plastic Wood		(5) Electronics		(6) Book Printing	
Number	Percent Change	Number	Percent Change	Number	Percent Change	Number	Percent Change
1,823	0	0	0	0	0	0	0
0	0	3,653	0	0	0	0	0
0	0	0	0	0	0	5,548	0
2,276	0.45%	4,344	0.86%	5,284	1.04%	5,868	1.16%

[a]Direct and indirect employment per $100 million sales to final demand by each of the simulated sectors.

[b]Asterisk indicates less than 0.005%.

Table 5.6 Investment Requirements of
Simulated Sectors[a]

Sector	Investment (thousands of dollars) (1)	Output[b] (thousands of dollars) (2)	Capital/ Output Ratio (3)
15S. Plastic wood	$ 49,090	$100,000	0.49
16S. Book printing	103,220	100,000	1.03
17S. Sulfuric acid	46,960	160,000	0.29
18S. Petroleum from coal	157,600	117,000	1.35
20S. Flyash brick	37,308	101,000	0.37
24S. Electronics	26,900[d]	100,000	0.27[d]

Capital requirements per worker[c]	
Simulated Sector (4)	All Sectors (5)
$13,438	$11,303
18,605	17,563
6,991	4,642
70,641	36,147
20,488	16,377
5,688	5,111

[a]Assuming sales by each sector to final demand of $100 million at 100% capacity.

[b]Including interindustry sales of $60 million in 17S; $17 million is 18S; and $1 million in 20S. Total sales of remaining sectors are to final demand.

[c]Column (1) divided by *direct and indirect* employment.

[d]National Planning Association, *Capacity Expansion Planning Factors*, Washington

The lowest capital/output ratio is in the electronics complex. A relatively small investment, about $27 million, would be required to produce an annual output of $100 million. This is not surprising in view of the type of electronics complex simulated. Electronic assembly operations are highly labor-intensive, and they require relatively little sophisticated equipment. Much of the initial investment would be in plant rather than equipment. But an electronics complex would have a relatively low employment multiplier (see Table 5.4), so the capital requirements per worker decline only slightly when the impact on all sectors is taken into account.

The sulfuric acid sector would have only a slightly higher capital/output ratio than the electronics complex. But because it has a considerably larger employment multiplier (Table 5.4) the capital requirement per worker drops significantly when the impact on all sectors is taken into account.

The highest capital/output ratio is in the simulated coal-based petroleum sector, the most capital-intensive of the simulated activities. An initial investment of $157.6 million would be required to produce an output of $117 million, and investment per worker in this sector would be $70.6 thousand. Because of the relatively high employment multiplier of 1.95, however, investment per worker drops to $36 thousand when the impact on all sectors is considered. The significance of these findings for regional development is discussed in the following chapter.

Simulating Dynamic Structural Change

The impact analysis discussed thus far ignores the time staging of the development of new activities. The results are given as though they had occurred instantaneously. In a dynamic setting we can observe how the process of structural change in an economy affects output levels over a period of time. First, there is the creation of capital stocks required by the simulated sectors. Once the new activities are in place production can begin.

During the process of capital accumulation by the new sectors the output of industries supplying the capital can change discontinuously. Industries which are involved, directly or indirectly, in adding to the capital stocks of the new sectors will experience an increase in demand for their products, other things remaining unchanged. To meet the rising demand they will add to their own capital stocks, which will increase the output of other capital goods sectors whose investment requirements will also increase.

After the necessary capital has been accumulated by the simulated sectors, and those which directly or indirectly supply them with current inputs, the output of capital-goods sectors will fall. Temporarily at least, this will result in overcapacity in the capital goods sectors. Some might have overextended their capacity, and those that have will reduce their expenditures for replacement capital. The important point is that peak levels of output will occur in the industries that are major suppliers of capital goods to the simulated sectors before the latter go into production.

The Dynamic Simulation Model

In Equation (3.8) of the dynamic forecasting model the rate of change in output, $\dot{X}$, was approximated by the one-period lag $X_t - X_{t-1}$. For the dynamic simulation, however, $\dot{X}$ is approximated by the one-period lead $X_{t+1} - X_t$. The initial formulation was used in the forecast because it eliminated the need to postulate terminal year conditions. If the same approximation were used in the dynamic simulation, it would go even farther than the static model in showing instantaneous adjustment to change. It would show not only instantaneous production by the simulated sectors, but also instantaneous adjustments in required levels of capital stocks.

The West Virginia dynamic model is a modification of one recently developed by Leontief.[5] Using this model it is possible to start with the postulated beginning of the operation of the simulated sectors, and trace backward the sequence of required changes in output which the new sectors will generate.

The balance equation of the dynamic simulation model is

$$X_t - A_t X_t - D_t X_t - B_t (X_{t+1} - X_t) = Y_t. \tag{5.1}$$

The replacement and expansion capital coefficients, D and B, do not change over time. Time subscripts attached to D and B indicate changes in the dimensions of the capital coefficient matrices only. The matrix of technical coefficients, A_t, is again determined by linear interpolation between A_{65} and A_{75}. Equation (5.1) is solved for X_t to obtain

$$X_t = (I - A_t - D_t + B_t)^{-1} (Y_t + B_{t+1} X_{t+1}). \tag{5.2}$$

For each simulation, the dimensions at t of vectors X and Y are increased from n to $n + 1$, and the dimensions of the matrices I, A_t, D, and B are changed from $(n \times n)$ to $(n + 1 \times n + 1)$. The additional row and column in the matrices represent the simulated activity in each case. For the simulated industries without interindustry sales, the effects on levels of output are obtained by setting the vector X_{t+1} and the first n rows of Y_t, equal to zero. Row $n + 1$ of Y_t is the final demand of the simulated activity. The solution, X_t, represents the *changes* in output levels at time t attributable to the operation of the simulated industry. The changes in output levels at $t - 1$ are determined by

$$X_{t-1} = (I - A_{t-1} - D_{t-1} + B_{t-1})^{-1} (Y_{t-1} + B_t X_t). \tag{5.3}$$

Y_{t-1} is now zero, X_t is the solution to Equation (5.2), and both X_{t-1} and $(I - A_{t-1} - D_{t-1} + B_{t-1})^{-1}$ revert to the n-order dimensions of the year preceding the operation of the simulated activity. B_t and X_t continue to be of order $n + 1$, representing the structure of the economy in the first year of operation of the simulated activity. $B_t X_t$ is therefore a column vector with $n + 1$ rows. Row $n + 1$ is dropped before $B_t X_t$ is multiplied by

$$(I - A_{t-1} - D_{t-1} + B_{t-1})^{-1}.$$

Since none of the simulated activities produced capital goods, the excluded value, $n + 1$, is always zero. Even if a capital-goods producing sector were simulated, however, row $n + 1$ of B_t would still be zero because of the terminal year condition that $X_{t+1} = 0$. It is important that B_t be of order $n + 1$ because column $n + 1$ gives the capital stocks *required by* the simulated activity. Changes in output in period $t - 2$ and all earlier periods are determined in the same manner, except that in these cases all dimensions of the system are of order n.

The procedure is modified slightly for the simulated activities that have interindustry sales, because these sales will vary with total output levels. This is particularly true when the output of the simulated industry is a substitute for the products of other industries. In these cases negative changes in output levels in the terminal year result from both the accelerator effects, which have been discussed in the foregoing, and the substitution effects. If flyash bricks are produced for local construction, for example, conventional brick producers will lose part of their market. They will then fail to maintain earlier levels of replacement investment.

To account for both effects, it was necessary to calculate total output in the terminal year with and without the simulated activity. The difference between the two is the change in output in the terminal year attributable to the simulated sector. After this step, the procedure for deriving changes in output levels in periods $t - 1$, $t - 2$, and earlier periods, is the same as that used in the simulated sectors without interindustry sales.

Results of the Dynamic Simulations

The annual direct and indirect changes in production attributable to the simulated industries exhibit a number of interesting patterns. Some sectors in a regional economy can experience substantial changes in rates of production in a comparatively short period of time. A change in the structure of industry at time t, for example, requires relatively little direct or indirect production during $t - 4$. The necessary adjustments in capital stocks can be made in a short time partly because many capital items are purchased from out-of-state suppliers. At the national level most capital goods are produced domestically, and the impacts on supplying industries can be substantial in earlier time periods.[6]

Toward the end of the period of capital accumulation by the simulated sector, and after the simulated activity is in operation, changes in production in a number of sectors will be negative. The three major patterns of production sequences which were observed are illustrated by Figure 5.1.

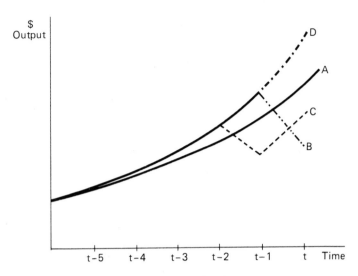

Figure 5-1 Dynamic production sequences

Path *A* represents the trend of output in a typical sector in the absence of the activity simulated. Paths *B*, *C*, and *D* illustrate the three most frequently observed departures from trend *A* resulting from the simulated activity. Path *B* is characteristic of sectors supplying capital goods directly to the simulated sector. It shows increasing production until the capital stocks of the simulated activity are accumulated, then a decline in output below path *A*.

Path *C* is representative of the sectors that sell capital goods to the sectors whose output is described by path *B*. Finally, path *D* is typical of the sectors whose output is affected more, directly or indirectly, by the *operation* of the simulated activity than by its capital accumulation.

The results of the dynamic simulation of the six new sectors in the West Virginia economy are given in Tables 5.7 through 5.12. Each can be interpreted in terms of the hypothetical time paths of Figure 5.1. Each column shows how the introduction of the simulated industries, one at a time, would affect the annual output of existing West Virginia sectors. The total impact each year is the algebraic sum of the sectoral impacts. Because the effects converge rapidly toward zero after $t - 4$, they have been shown separately only for the target year (1975) and the three preceding years.

As one would expect, the capital-goods sectors would have completed their sales to the simulated industries the year before the latter went into operation. The sectors that would sell to the new industries on current account show nominal changes in sales prior to the target year, and the changes that are observed are the indirect effects of the production of capital goods. In the target year, their direct sales to the simulated industries increase sharply. This is particularly noticeable in the two simulated sectors that use coal as their primary input.

The dynamic simulation is a useful supplement to the static impact analysis. It shows that the static analysis overstates output in the target year because it fails to account for accelerator effects. The static analysis understates the *total* impact of new industries on the regional economy, however, since it does not pick up the direct and indirect effects of capital transactions in earlier time periods.

The dynamic analysis has been limited to the six simulated industries that are the central focus of the West Virginia study. It would be possible to analyze all industries in the same manner, however. The result would be a set of 48 tables comparable to Tables 5.7–5.12. It would be a simple matter to have the computer generate such tables. They were not included in this report because it already comes close to being overloaded with data. Regional planners and industrial developers might want to extend the analysis to all industries, however, since it would provide them with highly detailed information on the time-phasing of investment impacts.

Table 5.7 Direct and Indirect Effects
on Output in Target and Preceding
Years of Simulated Coal Conversion to
Petroleum[a] (thousands of dollars)

		Prior to $t-3$	$t-3$	$t-2$	$t-1$	t
1.	Agriculture	3	8	15	16	−8
2.	Coal mines (undgd.)	4	14	56	412	23,149
3.	Coal (strip and auger)	1	3	9	33	514
4.	Petroleum and natural gas	2	6	30	88	1,758
5.	All other mining	46	123	177	−200	20
6.	Building contractors	344	988	3,403	2,502	−6,931
7.	Nonbuilding contractors	69	192	1,217	3,118	−4,430
8.	Special contractors	152	412	2,177	−1,182	−1,227
9.	Food products (n. e. c.)	0	1	4	6	63
10.	Dairies	0	0	1	2	17
11.	Bakeries	0	0	1	1	3
12.	Beverages	0	0	0	1	1
13.	Apparel and accessories	0	0	1	1	17
14.	Logging and sawmills	37	120	153	−364	281
15.	Furn. and wood fabrication	34	116	132	−433	248
16.	Printing and publishing	9	26	67	177	48
17.	Chemicals	5	17	75	289	12,643

Table 5.7 (continued)

		Prior to t-3	t-3	t-2	t-1	t
18.	Petroleum products	15	42	241	481	−515
19.	Glass	1	4	8	0	0
20.	Stone and clay products	68	206	996	−468	−318
21.	Primary metals	94	289	1,203	17,297	−18,643
22.	Fabricated metals	56	158	831	23,679	−24,544
23.	Machinery (except electric)	140	385	1,556	6,437	−7,828
24.	Electric machinery	19	47	131	1,628	−1,758
25.	Transportation equipment	2	4	26	90	−112
26.	Instruments and products	1	1	3	50	−27
27.	All other manufacturing	32	67	200	111	−9
28.	Restaurants and bars	1	5	18	27	53
29.	Wholesale trade	45	122	545	1,797	−1,738
30.	Retail food stores	0	0	0	1	2
31.	Auto service stations	2	7	28	21	35
32.	All other retail	67	178	53	−7	20
33.	Banking	6	20	76	71	1,625
34.	Other finance	1	3	11	35	−25

Table 5.7 (continued)

		Prior to $t-3$	$t-3$	$t-2$	$t-1$	t
35.	Insurance agents	13	37	135	258	862
36.	Real estate	5	17	57	139	⁻48
37.	All other FIRE	2	6	23	69	133
38	Hotels and lodgings	1	2	9	16	35
39.	Medical and legal services	4	13	48	94	1,074
40.	Educational services	0	0	2	16	–13
41.	All other services	16	45	170	453	1,473
42.	Railroads	4	10	37	217	–42
43.	Trucking and warehousing	13	37	156	425	–136
44.	All other transportation	4	12	45	313	–55
45.	Communications	6	18	64	175	106
46.	Electrical systems	11	32	119	545	5,430
47.	Gas systems	6	22	98	332	15,746
48.	Water and sanitary services	14	40	137	177	268
18S.	Petroleum from coal					117,038
49.	Total	1,355	3,855	14,544	58,946	114,255

[a] Assuming final sales of \$105,468 in year t.

Table 5.8 Direct and Indirect Effects
on Output in Target and Preceding
Years of Simulated Sulfuric Acid
Sector[a] (thousands of dollars)

		Prior to $t-3$	$t-3$	$t-2$	$t-1$	t
1.	Agriculture	1	2	8	5	6
2.	Coal mines (undgd.)	1	3	15	45	31,297
3.	Coal (strip and auger)	0	1	3	9	486
4.	Petroleum and natural gas	0	2	6	17	45
5.	All other mining	12	34	167	−216	113
6.	Building contractors	90	250	931	6,689	−7,795
7.	Nonbuilding contractors	17	52	219	252	−433
8.	Special contractors	40	112	391	1,932	−2,231
9.	Food products (n. e. c.)	0	0	1	5	38
10.	Dairies	0	0	0	2	−1
11.	Bakeries	0	0	0	1	−1
12.	Beverages	0	0	0	0	−1
13.	Apparel and accessories	0	0	0	1	0
14.	Logging and sawmills	9	28	114	−22	166
15.	Furn. and wood fabrication	9	24	132	−184	138
16.	Printing and publishing	2	7	25	76	−16

Table 5.8 (continued)

| | | Prior to | | | | |
		$t-3$	$t-3$	$t-2$	$t-1$	t
17.	Chemicals	1	4	19	44	313
18.	Petroleum products	4	11	47	96	−47
19.	Glass	0	1	3	5	−3
20.	Stone and clay products	17	51	203	878	−965
21.	Primary metals	24	67	327	978	−1,337
22.	Fabricated metals	15	42	158	1,091	−1,200
23.	Mach. (except elec.)	36	113	289	1,660	−1,833
24.	Electric machinery	5	13	63	510	−569
25.	Transportation equipment	0	2	3	516	−515
26.	Instruments and products	0	0	2	7	6
27.	All other manufacturing	8	24	50	206	−172
28.	Restaurants and bars	0	1	5	29	−30
29.	Wholesale trade	12	32	133	90	197
30.	Retail food stores	0	0	0	0	1
31.	Auto service stations	0	2	7	21	−14
32.	All other retail	17	49	134	−146	128
33.	Banking	1	5	19	80	335
34.	Other finance	0	1	3	6	−2

Table 5.8 (continued)

		Prior to $t-3$	$t-3$	$t-2$	$t-1$	t
35.	Insurance agents	4	10	36	145	496
36.	Real estate	1	4	16	71	-51
37.	All other FIRE	0	2	6	21	122
38.	Hotels and lodgings	0	1	2	7	1
39.	Medical and legal services	1	3	13	52	47
40.	Educational services	0	0	1	3	-2
41.	All other services	4	12	46	119	82
42.	Railroads	1	3	10	38	90
43.	Trucking and warehousing	3	10	37	106	140
44.	All other transportation	1	3	12	43	-6
45.	Communications	1	5	18	65	37
46.	Electrical systems	3	8	33	126	2,731
47.	Gas systems	1	6	23	73	21
48.	Water and sanitary services	4	10	38	265	619
17S.	Sulfuric acid					64,199
49.	Total	345	1,010	3,768	15,817	84,630

Table 5.9 Direct and Indirect Effects
on Output in Target and Preceding
Years of Simulated Flyash Brick
Sector[a] (thousands of dollars)

		Prior to $t-3$	$t-3$	$t-2$	$t-1$	t
1.	Agriculture	0	1	1	1	1
2.	Coal mines (undgd.)	0	2	9	11	177
3.	Coal (strip and auger)	0	0	1	3	85
4.	Petroleum and natural gas	0	1	3	8	240
5.	All other mining	6	19	1	−15	−1
6.	Building contractors	46	127	668	−110	−620
7.	Nonbuilding contractors	9	32	93	185	−277
8.	Special contractors	20	61	229	−41	−189
9.	Food products (n. e. c.)	0	0	1	1	6
10.	Dairies	0	0	0	0	4
11.	Bakeries	0	0	0	0	4
12.	Beverages	0	0	0	0	2
13.	Apparel and accessories	0	0	0	0	1
14.	Logging and sawmills	5	14	4	−3	−12
15.	Furn. and wood fabrication	5	15	14	−19	−7
16.	Printing and publishing	1	3	11	66	85
17.	Chemicals	1	2	9	55	−62
18.	Petroleum products	1	7	19	32	−21

Table 5.9 (continued)

		Prior to $t-3$	$t-3$	$t-2$	$t-1$	t
19.	Glass	0	0	1	4	−5
20.	Stone and clay products	9	30	65	42	−117
21.	Primary metals	12	40	267	124	−415
22.	Fabricated metals	7	24	51	125	−181
23.	Mach. (except elec.)	20	48	99	6,371	−6,505
24.	Electric machinery	3	6	91	−80	−18
25.	Transportation equipment	0	1	0	14	−14
26.	Instruments and products	0	0	1	715	−715
27.	All other manufacturing	4	9	24	30	−51
28.	Restaurants and bars	0	1	3	3	90
29.	Wholesale trade	5	15	53	331	−237
30.	Retail food stores	0	0	0	0	0
31.	Auto service stations	0	1	3	7	7
32.	All other retail	9	16	44	116	−127
33.	Banking	1	3	10	22	−2
34.	Other finance	0	0	1	3	−2
35.	Insurance agents	1	5	17	76	211
36.	Real estate	1	2	8	3	977
37.	All other FIRE	0	1	3	8	21
38.	Hotels and lodgings	0	0	1	4	87

Table 5.9 (continued)

		Prior to $t-3$	$t-3$	$t-2$	$t-1$	t
39.	Medical and legal services	0	2	6	11	74
40.	Educational services	0	0	1	0	32
41.	All other services	2	6	21	42	88
42.	Railroads	0	1	5	25	13
43.	Trucking and warehousing	1	5	15	120	1,186
44.	All other transportation	0	1	8	57	−16
45.	Communications	1	2	9	20	117
46.	Electrical systems	1	4	16	59	1,843
47.	Gas systems	1	3	10	30	2,246
48.	Water and sanitary services	1	5	27	−2	19
20S.	Flyash brick					46,151
49.	Total	173	515	1,923	8,454	44,173

[a] Assuming final sales of $46,151 in year t.

Table 5.10 Direct and Indirect Effects
on Output in Target and Preceding
Years of Simulated Plastic Wood
Sector[a] (thousands of dollars)

		Prior to $t-3$	$t-3$	$t-2$	$t-1$	t
1.	Agriculture	0	0	2	0	30
2.	Coal mines (undgd.)	0	1	3	6	8
3.	Coal (strip and auger)	0	0	0	2	1
4.	Petroleum and natural gas	0	0	1	11	12
5.	All other mining	2	5	47	-50	4
6.	Building contractors	16	45	126	1,271	-1,443
7.	Nonbuilding contractors	3	9	30	656	-685
8.	Special contractors	6	20	54	357	-422
9.	Food products (n. e. c.)	0	0	0	1	0
10.	Dairies	0	0	0	0	0
11.	Bakeries	0	0	0	0	0
12.	Beverages	0	0	0	0	0
13.	Apparel and accessories	0	0	0	0	0
14.	Logging and sawmills	1	5	29	-30	750
15.	Furn. and wood fabrication	1	3	38	-52	10
16.	Printing and publishing	0	1	5	16	68
17.	Chemicals	0	1	3	26	946
18.	Petroleum products	0	2	7	112	-115

Table 5.10 (continued)

		Prior to $t-3$	$t-3$	$t-2$	$t-1$	t
19.	Glass	0	0	1	1	-1
20.	Stone and clay products	3	9	28	147	-181
21.	Primary metals	4	11	54	-13	-41
22.	Fabricated metals	2	7	28	66	-85
23.	Mach. (except elec.)	6	21	73	-25	-56
24.	Electric machinery	1	3	7	2	-9
25.	Transportation equipment	0	0	0	11	-9
26.	Instruments and products	0	0	0	0	9
27.	All other manufacturing	1	5	5	73	-48
28.	Restaurants and bars	0	0	1	6	0
29.	Wholesale trade	1	6	27	-4	26
30.	Retail food stores	0	0	0	0	4
31.	Auto service stations	0	0	1	4	12
32.	All other retail	3	9	35	19	-43
33.	Banking	0	1	3	18	-15
34.	Other finance	0	0	1	3	-3
35.	Insurance agents	0	2	6	31	140
36.	Real estate	0	1	3	14	0
37.	All other FIRE	0	0	1	4	16
38.	Hotels and lodgings	0	0	0	2	8

Table 5.10 (continued)

		Prior to $t-3$	$t-3$	$t-2$	$t-1$	t
39.	Medical and legal services	0	1	2	12	2
40.	Educational services	0	0	0	0	0
41.	All other services	1	2	8	49	-30
42.	Railroads	0	0	2	6	106
43.	Trucking and warehousing	0	2	7	30	191
44.	All other transportation	0	1	2	3	10
45.	Communications	0	1	3	14	10
46.	Electrical systems	0	1	6	17	23
47.	Gas systems	0	1	4	25	-1
48.	Water and sanitary services	0	2	5	49	-48
15S.	Plastic wood					15,190
49.	Total	51	178	658	2,890	14,341

[a] Assuming final sales of $15,190 in year t.

Table 5.11 Direct and Indirect Effects
on Output in Target and Preceding
Years of Simulated Electronics
Assembly Complex[a] (thousands of
dollars)

		Prior to $t-3$	$t-3$	$t-2$	$t-1$	t
1.	Agriculture	0	2	6	−3	14
2.	Coal mines (undgd.)	1	3	11	35	122
3.	Coal (strip and auger)	0	1	2	9	37
4.	Petroleum and natural gas	0	1	4	39	−19
5.	All other mining	9	29	136	−155	43
6.	Building contractors	72	197	860	3,726	−4,807
7.	Nonbuilding contractors	15	42	131	1,979	−2,134
8.	Special contractors	31	88	312	1,275	−1,637
9.	Food products (n. e. c.)	0	0	1	3	9
10.	Dairies	0	0	0	1	−1
11.	Bakeries	0	0	0	1	−1
12.	Beverages	0	0	0	0	0
13.	Apparel and accessories	0	0	0	1	0
14.	Logging and sawmills	7	23	94	−132	8
15.	Furn. and wood fabrication	6	20	121	−183	41
16.	Printing and publishing	1	6	22	43	−16
17.	Chemicals	1	4	13	147	1,092
18.	Petroleum products	3	9	30	340	−354

Table 5.11 (continued)

	Prior to $t-3$	$t-3$	$t-2$	$t-1$	t
19. Glass	0	1	3	2	407
20. Stone and clay products	14	40	143	477	-180
21. Primary metals	20	54	220	307	3,109
22. Fabricated metals	12	33	121	333	140
23. Mach. (except elec.)	29	87	256	97	-126
24. Electric machinery	4	11	28	2,416	-654
25. Transportation equipment	0	1	11	-13	3
26. Instruments and products	0	0	1	6	-1
27. All other manufacturing	6	20	30	135	985
28. Restaurants and bars	0	1	4	18	-22
29. Wholesale trade	9	26	107	-13	19
30. Retail food stores	0	0	0	0	0
31. Auto service stations	0	1	5	14	-13
32. All other retail	14	38	135	-133	7
33. Banking	1	4	16	57	-56
34. Other finance	0	1	2	9	-9
35. Insurance agents	3	8	30	113	-89
36. Real estate	1	3	14	46	-51
37. All other FIRE	0	1	5	14	-8
38. Hotels and lodgings	0	1	2	7	-5

Table 5.11 (continued)

		Prior to $t-3$	$t-3$	$t-2$	$t-1$	t
39.	Medical and legal services	1	3	11	40	-27
40.	Educational services	0	0	0	11	-1
41.	All other services	3	9	36	176	-114
42.	Railroads	1	2	7	29	33
43.	Trucking and warehousing	3	8	28	118	596
44.	All other transportation	1	2	9	84	8
45.	Communications	1	4	15	64	-21
46.	Electrical systems	2	7	26	137	612
47.	Gas systems	1	4	17	101	-37
48.	Water and sanitary services	3	8	35	157	-185
24S.	Electronics					62,176
49.	Total	275	803	3,060	11,935	59,433

[a] Assuming final sales of $62,176 in year t.

Table 5.12 Direct and Indirect Effects
on Output in Target and Preceding
Years of Simulated Book Printing
Sector[a] (thousands of dollars)

		Prior to $t-3$	$t-3$	$t-2$	$t-1$	t
1.	Agriculture	0	1	2	−1	−1
2.	Coal mines (undgd.)	0	1	5	18	80
3.	Coal (strip and auger)	0	0	1	5	42
4.	Petroleum and natural gas	0	1	2	15	−15
5.	All other mining	4	15	51	−69	3
6.	Building contractors	34	91	485	1,582	−2,168
7.	Nonbuilding contractors	6	20	63	607	−681
8.	Special contractors	15	40	167	457	−670
9.	Food products (n. e. c.)	0	0	0	1	1
10.	Dairies	0	0	0	0	1
11.	Bakeries	0	0	0	0	0
12.	Beverages	0	0	0	0	0
13.	Apparel and accessories	0	0	0	0	0
14.	Logging and sawmills	4	12	35	−43	−7
15.	Furn. and wood fabrication	3	11	45	−67	10
16.	Printing and publishing	1	3	10	16	439
17.	Chemicals	0	2	6	81	−18
18.	Petroleum products	1	4	15	106	−119

Table 5.12 (continued)

		Prior to $t-3$	$t-3$	$t-2$	$t-1$	t
19.	Glass	0	0	1	1	-2
20.	Stone and clay products	6	19	71	151	-239
21.	Primary metals	9	26	93	197	-310
22.	Fabricated metals	5	15	57	70	-106
23.	Mach. (except elec.)	14	39	96	-180	45
24.	Electrical machinery	1	5	11	1,980	-1,996
25.	Transportation equipment	0	1	9	-15	7
26.	Instruments and products	0	0	1	8	-9
27.	All other manufacturing	3	9	18	45	-37
28.	Restaurants and bars	0	0	2	7	-3
29.	Wholesale trade	4	12	47	-27	31
30.	Retail food stores	0	0	0	0	0
31.	Auto service stations	0	1	3	5	0
32.	All other retail	6	18	60	-72	10
33.	Banking	1	2	8	22	-7
34.	Other finance	0	0	1	3	257
35.	Insurance agents	1	4	14	48	107
36.	Real estate	0	2	7	19	-19
37.	All other FIRE	0	1	2	6	16
38.	Hotels and lodgings	0	0	1	4	1

186

Table 5.12 (continued)

		Prior to $t-3$	$t-3$	$t-2$	$t-1$	t
39.	Medical and legal services	0	1	5	17	44
40.	Educational services	0	0	0	9	2
41.	All other services	1	4	17	72	-58
42.	Railroads	0	1	3	14	104
43.	Trucking and warehousing	1	4	13	45	395
44.	All other transportation	0	1	4	61	-59
45.	Communications	0	2	7	33	90
46.	Electrical systems	1	3	12	85	930
47.	Gas systems	1	2	8	44	-40
48.	Water and sanitary services	1	4	19	71	-92
16S.	Book printing					31,035
49.	Total	123	377	1,477	5,431	26,995

[a] Assuming final sales of $31,035 in year t.

6 Input–Output Analysis and the Strategy of Regional Development

Albert Hirschman begins his discussion of economic development with the following comment: "The intensive study of the problem of economic development has had one discouraging result: it has produced an ever lengthening list of factors and conditions, of obstacles and prerequisites. The direction of the inquiry has proceeded from thoroughly objective, tangible and quantitative phenomena to more and more subjective, intangible, and unmeasurable ones."[1] The present study, in light of the foregoing comment, might appear to take a distinct step backward. It is a quantitative investigation based on a rigorous econometric model. We feel, however, that no *apologia* is required. Any comptent observer of the depressed areas of Appalachia, for example, will recognize that not all aspects of the "Appalachian problem" are quantifiable, and that not all of the region's problems can be characterized as economic. It does not follow that there is no further need for reliable measurement, or that purely quantitative models are unable to contribute to a strategy for the development or redevelopment of a region.

The study described in the preceding chapters relies heavily on measurement and estimation. The results must be interpreted within the analytical framework and the assumptions upon which they rest. This project was not designed with the notion that it would lead to the discovery of Hirschman's *primum mobile*, but only with the hope that it would make a meaningful contribution to regional development strategy.[2] Among the requirements of such a strategy are: (1) a clearly defined set of objectives, (2) measurement of the economic effects of alternative policies, and (3) estimates of the costs of the alternative policies. This study has not been concerned with the definition of objectives. Its focus has been on the development of a *method* for evaluating the economic impacts of a limited number of alternative investment opportunities.

Regional development policy in the United States has been primarily concerned with: (1) direct public investment in private establishments, (2) investment in social overhead capital, and (3) investment in human resources. Direct investment has been typically provided by favorable loans to private firms. Investment in social overhead capital (such as highways, sewers, and water systems) has been undertaken on the assumption that it will be followed by private investment. Typically, this type of investment has been supplemented by various forms of technical assistance. Investment in human resources (hospitals, educational facilities, and training), while related to regional programs, is part of a broader effort to "eliminate poverty" in the United States.

The simulations discussed in Chapter 5 represent an effort to evaluate different types of investment in terms of development potential. If a development planner were faced with the problem of allocating a specific amount of public investment in West Virginia, how would he make his choice? Even in a society as affluent as ours there is always a budget constraint on public programs. Development officials are thus interested in allocating limited funds in ways that will maximize incremental employment and income, since regional development policy is concerned with both employment and income effects.

In a hypothetical situation the regional planner might be forced to choose among a specific set of alternative investment proposals. To simplify the illustration assume that these are the six sectors simulated in Chapter 5. Assume further that the economic feasibility of all of the simulated sectors has been established. Once in operation each could compete successfully in the open market. With limited investment funds, the problem is to choose the activity that would have the largest income and employment impacts on the region.

An input-output analysis of the region would be helpful to the planner in making his decision. The comparative analysis indicates clearly that investment in a new sulfuric acid industry would have the maximum payoff. This activity has the lowest capital/output ratio of the six sectors simulated, and the second highest employment multiplier. An investment of $50 million (only part of which would come from public funds under current programs) would result in more than 10,000 new jobs in the state (Table 5.4). The investment per worker, when all direct and indirect effects have been traced, would amount to less than $5,000 per worker (Table 5.6). By way of contrast, a coal-based petroleum plant would require an investment of more than $36,000 per worker, and it would result in only 4,000 new jobs. The decision to invest in a sulfuric acid industry would also result in additional social gains since the elimination of sulfur pyrite from coal would contribute substantially to a reduction in air pollution in coal-burning areas. It is now possible to eliminate virtually all smoke from coal-burning plants; the most serious problem remaining in this regard is that of sulfur pollution.

The conclusion reached in the foregoing is based on the critical assumption that all of the simulated sectors are economically feasible. As a matter of fact, neither the synthetic petroleum nor the sulfuric acid industry could compete in the open market at the present state of their development. Does this mean that development planners should forget about either of these investment opportunities and consider only the remaining four? This is one possibility, and we will return to it in a later section. It does not necessarily follow, however, that development officials would want to eliminate the sulfuric acid industry from consideration. Because of its large potential employment impact they might want to consider a temporary subsidy.

The Costs and Benefits of a Development Subsidy

Is there an economic rationale for the use of a subsidy as part of a development program? Most economists are suspicious of subsidies because they conceal inefficiencies and retard adjustment to disequilibrium. Although many industries in the United States receive subsidies in one form or another, the best-known subsidies are those which have been given to agriculture. There can be little doubt that agricultural subsidies have cushioned adjustments to disequilibrium for many farmers during a long transitional period. But while the costs of agricultural subsidies can be measured, it is difficult to estimate the benefits which this program might have engendered.

Given a set of regional input-output tables, it is possible to calculate the direct, indirect, and induced effects of changes in output by sector. With this and associated cost and discount information it would not be difficult to use the techniques of conventional cost-benefit analysis to evaluate the feasibility of a proposed subsidy to an activity such as the simulated sulfuric acid industry.

The cost of extracting sulfur from coal is presently higher than the market price of raw sulfur obtained from conventional sources. Further engineering research could reduce the cost of extraction and make the sulfur-from-coal process competitive with conventional methods. From a regional point of view, however, the benefits of developing a sulfuric acid industry might be greater than the costs involved even if the latter should include a subsidy to the pyrite extraction process. This is because of the relatively large *indirect* employment and income effects which the industry would have on the regional economy.

The simulated sulfuric acid plant would require $21.52 worth of sulfur to produce one ton of sulfuric acid with a current market price of $45. The delivered price of industrial sulfur varies with market conditions and points of origin and delivery. Only a rough estimate could be obtained of the delivered price of conventional industrial sulfur in Morgantown, West Virginia, assuming this is where the simulated plant would be located. This is currently $61.20 per ton or $12.24 per 400 pounds. (Assuming delivery from Newport News, Virginia, the closest point of origin.) A subsidy of $9.28 per ton of sulfuric acid would be required to make the sulfur-from-coal process competitive. This represents a 20% subsidy, which could only be justified if the regional benefits were greater than this element of cost.

It is doubtful that a subsidy of this size could be justified even by the relatively large indirect effects to be discussed in the next section.[3] Also, there are dangers inherent in any subsidy program since subsidies are easier to establish than to eliminate. A more acceptable approach would be to increase research support for the sulfur pyrite extraction process. If successful, this would accomplish the same objective without need for a continuing subsidy.

If the federal government provided the research support there is no guarantee that the sulfur extraction process would be located in West Virginia. There are coal fields in other states with substantially higher sulfur content than West Virginia coal, and if the extraction of sulfur pyrites is considered alone there are obvious advantages to using coal with the *highest* sulfur content. It is not likely that this would happen, however. The major incentive for extracting sulfur pyrites from coal is that the coal would then meet federal antipollution standards. Only about 60% of the sulfur can be removed from coal by the current process. Coal with very high sulfur content would not meet antipollution standards after the removal of pyrites. Thus if the pyrite-extraction process is to become a reality, plants will be located close to sources of coal with relatively low sulfur content such as that found in the extensive fields of northern West Virginia.

The foregoing discussion indicates that regional input-output analysis could provide useful guidelines to those responsible for allocating federal research funds. Substantial sums have been given in support of the petroleum-from-coal process. To date, there has been little federal support of research on the extraction of sulfur pyrites from coal. The Bureau of Mines has been conducting research on alternative uses of coal for a number of years. This is one reason they have supported research on the synthetic petroleum process. From a regional point of view, however, the pyrite extraction process would have a larger payoff in terms of employment and income.

We do not conclude from this that there should be a reallocation of research funds in the Bureau of Mines. A large investment has been made in the development of a synthetic petroleum industry, and the technical results have been encouraging. Also, our analysis has been conducted strictly within a regional framework, and research programs should be evaluated in a broader context. The only point we want to make is that the *method* we have used lends itself not only to the evaluation of alternative investment opportunities but also to the evaluation of alternative research programs.

The economic feasibility of a sulfuric acid industry using sulfur extracted from coal depends upon future technical developments as well as the extent to which federal antipollution standards are to be enforced. We have not attempted to speculate about what is likely to happen since there are a number of alternatives. In the remainder of our discussion we assume that, for one reason or another, sulfur pyrites will be extracted from coal. If this happens, a sulfuric acid industry could become economically feasible in West Virginia.

Income and Employment Multipliers

Income and employment multipliers for all West Virginia sectors and the six simulated sectors are given in Table 6.1. Two types of multipliers have been calculated. The Type I multipliers show the direct and indirect impacts of an increase in output by each sector. The Type II multipliers add the induced or consumption effects which are calculated by shifting households into the processing matrix.[4]

The components of the two types of multipliers, expressed in terms of requirements per dollar of delivery to final demand, are given in Figures 6.1 and 6.2. In these charts the sectors have been rearranged in declining order of largest *total* impact.

Income and employment multipliers can be useful in regional development planning, but they must be interpreted cautiously. The sector with the largest direct impact is not necessarily one that should be encouraged to expand in a region. The multipliers are ratios in which the direct effects are the denominators. The numerator in the Type I multipliers are the direct plus indirect effects, and in the Type II multipliers induced effects are added. Thus a sector with large direct requirements and small indirect requirements will have a low multiplier. High multipliers are associated with sectors that have relatively large indirect requirements and induced effects.

Sector 13 (apparel and accessories) has relatively low income and employment multipliers. This sector's direct requirements per dollar of delivery to final demand are large. Given the present structure of the industry in West Virginia, however, it would generate relatively little income or employment in other sectors. (Most garment factories in West Virginia are of the "job shop" variety. They do not purchase cloth but receive it on consignment. Thus the primary input is direct labor with only minor interindustry purchases. The cloth comes from out-of-state, but since it is not purchased it does not show up in this sector's import row.) At the other extreme the simulated synthetic petroleum industry, which would use coal as its primary input, has high income multipliers (4.59 and 5.89) and relatively large employment multipliers (1.99 and 2.46). The simulated sulfuric acid industry has relatively high income multipliers, and employment multipliers which fall in the upper middle range.

Multipliers should not be used mechanically in an attempt to evaluate alternative investment opportunities, but they can be useful guides to those concerned with regional development policy. The information that the multipliers provide must be supplemented by additional data, some of which are given in the next section. They are useful, however, because they identify activities that have large indirect and induced effects.

The simulated sectors with the largest income impacts are the sulfuric acid and synthetic petroleum industries, but there are other sectors in the state, such as strip and auger coal mining, and building construction, which also have large income multipliers. The "all other" finance, insurance, and real estate sector also has large indirect income effects. This suggests that development planners might want to consider both the expansion of new industry in the state, and the expansion of supporting services.

Similar conclusions follow from an analysis of the employment multipliers. The simulated sulfuric acid and synthetic petroleum sectors have relatively large employment multipliers. Those for building construction, and "all other" finance, insurance, and real estate are even larger. This supports the conclusion that new industrial activities and supporting services should be encouraged to grow together.

Table 6.1 Income and Employment
Multipliers, West Virginia, 1975

		Income		Employment	
		Type I	Type II	Type I	Type II
1.	Agriculture	1.45	1.86	3.73	7.13
2.	Coal mines (underground)	1.12	1.43	1.14	1.60
3.	Coal mines (strip and auger)	2.24	2.88	2.07	2.73
4.	Petroleum and natural gas	1.54	1.98	1.46	1.79
5.	All other mining	1.40	1.79	1.67	2.44
6.	Building contractors	2.47	3.17	2.15	2.67
7.	Nonbuilding contractors	1.72	2.21	1.61	2.08
8.	Special contractors	1.32	1.70	1.31	1.66
9.	Food products (n. e. c.)	2.33	2.99	1.69	2.14
10.	Food products (dairies)	1.87	2.40	1.44	1.99
11.	Food products (bakeries)	1.31	1.68	1.23	1.55
12.	Food products (beverages)	1.27	1.63	1.23	1.54
13.	Apparel and accessories	1.06	1.36	1.03	1.19
14.	Logging and sawmills	1.58	2.03	1.45	1.74
15.	Furniture and wood fabrication	1.30	1.67	1.30	1.59
15S.	Plastic wood	1.11	1.43	1.12	1.51
16.	Printing and publishing	1.53	1.96	1.53	1.94
16S.	Book printing	1.07	1.38	1.06	1.38
17.	Chemicals	1.64	2.11	1.88	2.63

Table 6.1 (continued)

		Income		Employment	
		Type I	Type II	Type I	Type II
17S.	Sulfuric acid	2.74	3.51	1.51	1.84
18.	Petroleum products	2.12	2.72	2.91	4.10
18S.	Petroleum from coal	4.59	5.89	1.99	2.46
19.	Glass	1.29	1.66	1.26	1.61
20.	Stone and clay products	1.43	1.83	1.44	1.91
20S.	Flyash brick	1.59	2.04	1.19	1.33
21.	Primary metals	1.19	1.52	1.21	1.67
22.	Fabricated metals	1.21	1.55	1.14	1.41
23.	Machinery (except electric)	1.20	1.54	1.17	1.51
24.	Electric machinery	1.38	1.77	1.36	1.81
24S.	Electronics complex	1.18	1.51	1.27	1.93
25.	Transportation equipment	1.17	1.51	1.20	1.70
26.	Instruments and products	1.12	1.44	1.08	1.35
27.	All other manufacturing	1.25	1.60	1.17	1.43
28.	Restaurants and bars	1.30	1.67	1.14	1.36
29.	Wholesale trade	1.11	1.43	1.15	1.66
30.	Retail food stores	1.18	1.52	1.19	1.59
31.	Auto service stations	1.19	1.53	1.16	1.44
32.	All other retail	1.25	1.60	1.18	1.43

Table 6.1 (continued)

	Income		Employment	
	Type I	Type II	Type I	Type II
33. Banking	1.10	1.41	1.19	1.74
34. Other finance	1.13	1.46	1.24	1.95
35. Insurance agents	1.29	1.66	1.47	2.02
36. Real estate	1.30	1.67	1.49	2.09
37. All other FIRE	1.95	2.50	3.70	4.65
38. Hotels and lodgings	1.63	2.09	1.22	1.41
39. Medical and legal services	1.16	1.49	1.11	1.30
40. Educational services	1.22	1.56	1.14	1.35
41. All other services	1.23	1.58	1.20	1.50
42. Railroads	1.13	1.45	1.17	1.65
43. Trucking and warehousing	1.27	1.63	1.36	1.93
44. All other transportation	1.38	1.77	1.57	2.17
45. Communications	1.12	1.44	1.13	1.48
46. Electrical systems	1.50	1.92	1.93	2.98
47. Gas systems	1.95	2.51	2.26	2.90
48. Water and sanitary services	1.44	1.85	1.29	1.59

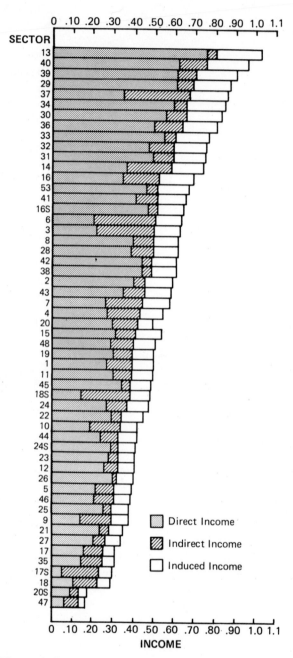

Figure 6-1 Direct, indirect, and induced income per dollar of delivery to final demand, 1975.

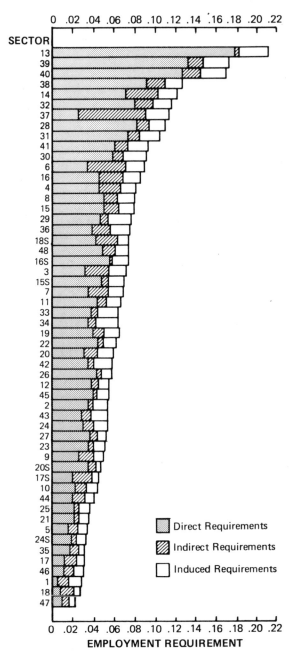

Figure 6-2 Direct, indirect, and induced employment requirements per dollar of delivery to final demand, 1975.

Investment Requirements and Value Added

Some of the information required to supplement the multiplier analysis is provided by Table 6.2, which shows the total investment that would be generated by the expansion of all sectors including those which have been simulated.

The investment requirements in Columns 1 and 2 are not the same as those given for the simulated sectors in Table 5.6. The latter show the *direct* investment requirements for a given scale of operations. The investment figures in Table 6.2 are the *direct and indirect* investment requirements for an additional million dollars worth of final sales. The calculations in Table 6.2 were made to permit comparison of the simulated sectors with existing sectors in West Virginia.

The synthetic petroleum sector would generate the largest amount of investment, both in total terms and in investment per direct and indirect worker. The electronics complex would generate a considerable amount of new investment, most of which would come from the construction sectors. All of the simulated sectors except plastic wood add substantially to value added within the state.

The data in Table 6.2 could be used in conjunction with the multipliers of Table 6.1 in development planning. The simulated plastic wood sector would not be given high priority in West Virginia. More than two-thirds of its inputs would be imported; it would generate relatively little additional investment in the state, and it has relatively low income and employment multipliers. The sulfuric acid industry, however, would purchase more than two-thirds of its primary inputs from West Virginia suppliers; it would generate a considerable amount of additional investment, and it has relatively high income and employment multipliers. The synthetic petroleum industry would also rank high in terms of investment priorities because of its large multipliers, and the additional investment that it would generate in the state.

The purpose of this section is not to evaluate the prospects of the simulated sectors, but rather to illustrate the way in which regional input-output analysis can be used in development planning. Tables 6.1 and 6.2 provide summary measures of the direct, indirect, and induced impacts of existing and simulated sectors. This information as it stands should be useful to those concerned with the economic development of West Virginia. The method could be applied by planners concerned with other regions.

Investment in Human Resources

The detailed employment and occupational projections of Chapter 4, together with the projected investment requirements in educational services, were developed with educational planners in mind. The unique feature of the employment and occupational forecasts is that they focus on demand rather than supply. But if the supply of skilled workers is to be forthcoming, the rate of investment in education in West Virginia will have to be increased

Table 6.2 Total Impact on Selected
Variables of One Million Dollars
Delivered to Final Demand, 1975
(thousands of dollars)

		Total Investment (1)	Investment Per Worker[a] (2)	Imports (3)	Value Added (4)
1.	Agriculture	$1,080	$72	$367	$633
2.	Coal mines (underground)	856	21	377	623
3.	Coal mines (strip and auger)	1,128	21	267	733
4.	Petroleum and natural gas	832	12	196	804
5.	All other mining	567	23	513	487
6.	Building contractors	759	10	293	707
7.	Nonbuilding contractors	905	16	325	675
8.	Special contractors	629	10	275	725
9.	Food products (n. e. c.)	840	21	560	440
10.	Food products (dairies)	740	22	518	482
11.	Food products (bakeries)	595	11	512	488
12.	Food products (beverages)	885	19	381	619
13.	Apparel and accessories	790	4	90	910
14.	Logging and sawmills	1,004	10	219	781
15.	Furniture and wood fabrication	761	12	434	566
15S.	Plastic wood	663	15	701	299
16.	Printing and publishing	1,653	24	230	770

Table 6.2 (continued)

		Total Investment (1)	Investment Per Worker[a] (2)	Imports (3)	Value Added (4)
16S.	Book printing	1,222	21	303	697
17.	Chemicals	1,124	49	507	493
17S.	Sulfuric acid	831	13	283	717
18.	Petroleum products	1,228	58	512	488
18S.	Petroleum from coal	2,055	54	301	699
19.	Glass	686	13	292	708
20.	Stone and clay products	1,212	26	316	684
20S.	Flyash brick	611	27	73	927
21.	Primary metals	837	31	605	395
22.	Fabricated metals	504	10	526	474
23.	Machinery (except electric)	371	9	508	492
24.	Electric machinery	717	18	422	578
24S.	Electronics complex	430	8	252	748
25.	Transportation equipment	731	28	552	448
26.	Instruments and products	377	8	566	434
27.	All other manufacturing	448	10	621	379
28.	Restaurants and bars	514	5	350	650
29.	Wholesale trade	500	19	89	911
30.	Retail food stores	578	8	173	827

Table 6.2 (continued)

		Total Investment (1)	Investment Per Worker[a] (2)	Imports (3)	Value Added (4)
31.	Auto service stations	531	6	150	850
32.	All other retail	584	6	214	786
33.	Banking	531	12	738	262
34.	Other finance	695	17	163	837
35.	Insurance agents	186	7	696	304
36.	Real estate	618	11	144	856
37.	All other FIRE	678	7	237	763
38.	Hotels and lodgings	1,938	17	234	766
39.	Medical and legal services	1,127	8	171	829
40.	Educational services	4,327	30	170	830
41.	All other services	767	10	320	680
42.	Railroads	955	23	288	712
43.	Trucking and warehousing	1,367	36	307	693
44.	All other transportation	938	29	432	568
45.	Communications	3,377	77	192	808
46.	Electrical systems	2,120	106	229	771
47.	Gas systems	1,367	80	699	301
48.	Water and sanitary services	2,919	47	355	645

[a]Direct and indirect investment required per direct and indirect worker.

substantially. This study has concentrated on the capital investments that will be required to replace obsolete educational facilities and to provide for the expansion that will be engendered by a growing population. These are of fundamental importance to long-range educational planning.

The time-horizon for manpower and educational planning should be a relatively long one. The minimum planning period should be perhaps a decade. Adjustments to change in the labor market occur relatively slowly. It requires a minimum of four years, for example, to train engineers, and two or more years to train technicians and supporting craftsmen. The expansion of facilities must be planned even longer in advance.

Public officials concerned with regional development have recognized the need for a general up-grading of education in regions such as Appalachia. Anything that can be done to improve the quality of education should, of course, result in net benefits to the region. The same can be said of programs designed to expand and improve health facilities, and all others that come under the general heading of "investing in human capital." Employment and occupational projections, based on a regional interiudustry model, can be powerful tools for regional planners. It would be unwise to suggest that the specific occupational projections made in this study will be exactly realized by 1975, but the trends indicated, and the changing occupational structure of the labor force, can be used as reliable guides for long-run planning purposes.

Conclusions

This study does not lead to any startling new conclusions about the strategy of regional development. We feel, however, that it demonstrates the versatility and flexibility of the regional input-output model as a *tool* for development planning. The techniques developed and tested in this study required four years to complete, and it cannot be accurately characterized as a "low-budget" study. The application of these techniques to other regions could be accomplished in a much shorter time and at much less expense. A number of the analyses in this study had not been tried before, and this necessarily involved a certain amount of experimentation. The same techniques could be applied to other regions, however, without repeating the trial-and-error experiences of this study.

Finally, at least one conclusion stands out which should be useful to regional planners. As noted at the beginning of this chapter, regional development programs in the United States have generally focused on investment in social overhead capital or direct public investment. There is no doubt that both types of investment have had a positive impact on regional growth.

Relatively little thought has been given, however, to research support as an adjunct of regional development. Four of the sectors simulated in the West Virginia study are based on new technology, and in three of the cases the research received federal support. But research support and regional development have been kept in separate bureaucratic compartments. Research support is always risky since the results cannot be guaranteed in advance; increased support for certain types of applied research could easily become an important part of regional development strategy. The research which led to the development of plastic wood was supported by the Atomic Energy Commission. The parquet flooring plant, discussed briefly in Chapter 5, illustrates how an investment in research can contribute to regional development.

It is not necessary to await the outcome of a research project to determine what its economic impact will be. The analytical framework of this study can be used to estimate impacts in advance, and to compare these impacts with other changes that could take place in the structure of the regional economy. Simulating the income and employment impacts of new activities requires some investment in economic research, but the cost of economic simulations would be a fraction of the amounts that might be spent on scientific and engineering research. It would be helpful to regional planners to know the impacts of new technical developments in advance, and this could help channel research expenditures into activities that would have the largest long-run payoffs.

The regional input-output model used in the analysis of the West Virginia economy does not provide push-button answers to the difficult problems of regional development strategy, but it should minimize some of the guesswork upon which much regional development planning has been based in the past. It provides a flexible framework for the analysis of a wide variety of alternative investment opportunities, and this is essentially what the model was designed to do.

The realization of development objectives requires much more than the detailed analyses and projections that a regional input-output model can supply. The best-laid plans of regional development cannot be realized without strong political leadership and effective community support. But, as Wassily Leontief has noted, development progress "will be faster along a road well mapped in advance and the cost of progress in terms of labor, capital and human sacrifice considerably less" if regional planners use the analytical tools currently available to them.[5]

Appendixes

A

Questionnaire

208

REGIONAL RESEARCH INSTITUTE – WEST VIRGINIA UNIVERSITY

WEST VIRGINIA INTERINDUSTRY

RELATIONS STUDY

BUSINESS QUESTIONNAIRE

Interviewer # _____

Date _____

Sector # _____

SIC # _____

Firm code number _____

1. Name of establishment _____

2. Address _____

3. Respondent and title _____

4. Is this a branch or main office? _____

5. Date of organization in West Virginia _____

6. Legal organization (circle one):

A. Single proprietorship   B. Partnership   C. Corporation   D. Other _____

7. Principal products   1. _____ %   2. _____ %
   (% each of total sales)
                             3. _____ %   4. _____ %

                             5. _____ %   6. _____ %

8. Percent of total sales in 1965 that went to buyers located in West Virginia _____ %

9. How much of these sales were . . . . (in % or $)
   a . . . final consumer goods? _____
   b . . . final investment goods? _____
   c . . . sold to other business establishments to be consumed in current production? _____
   d . . . sold to any branch of government? _____

CONSOLIDATED MANUFACTURING SCHEDULE
AND INCOME STATEMENT
(for year ending Dec. 31, 1965)

1. Total sales (net of returns and discounts)..................... $
2. Finished goods inventory, Jan. 1, 1965 .... $
*3. Goods in process inventory, Jan. 1, 1965 .... $
*4. Raw materials inventory, Jan. 1, 1965 .... $
*5. Raw materials purchases (net of returns and discounts)...... $
6. Freight in .... $
*7. Total cost of raw materials available for use .... $
*8. Less: Raw materials inventory Dec. 31, 1965. .... $
*9. Cost of raw materials consumed. .... $
*10. Direct labor .... $
*11. Manufacturing expenses .... $
*12. Total goods in process during period .... $
*13. Less: goods in process inventory, Dec. 31, 1965. .... $
*14. Cost of goods manufactured. .... $
15. Total cost of finished goods available for sale. .... $
16. Less: Finished goods inventory, Dec. 31, 1965. .... $
17. Cost of goods sold .... $
18. Gross profit on sales. .... $
19. Selling expenses .... $
20. General and administrative expenses .... $
21. Total operating expenses .... $
22. Net profit from operations................................ $
23. Other Income (specify sector and location of origin) 1._____ $
    2._____
    3._____
24. Other expenses (specify sector and location of origin) 1._____ $

2. _____ 3. _____ $

25. Net income before taxes. . . . . $

26. Taxes. . . . .1. Federal $ _____ 2. State $ _____ 3. Local $ _____ . . Total. . . . . $

27. Net income after taxes. . . . . $

1. Amount exported . . . . $

2. Amount retained in W. Va. . . . . $

3. Amount distributed in W. Va. . . . . . (specify sector of recipient) . . . 1. _____ $

2. _____ 3. _____ $

28. Inventories are valued at. . . . . Cost _____ Selling price _____ Other _____

*Applicable to Mfg. & Cont. Const. firms only.

DETAILED TRANSACTIONS—(except Investments)

SALES TO		SECTOR		PURCHASES FROM	
Out-Of-State	In-State	No.	Sector & Description	In-State	Out-Of-State
$	$	1.	Livestock & Livestock Products (Except Dairy Farms)	$	$ R.M. / $ Exp.
$	$	2.	Dairy Farms	$	$ R.M. / $ Exp.
$	$	3.	Field Crops	$	$ R.M. / $ Exp.
$	$	4.	Other Agricultural Products, Forestry, Fisheries & All Agricultural Services	$	$ R.M. / $ Exp.
$	$	5.	Coal Mining (Underground Mines)	$	$ R.M. / $ Exp.
$	$	6.	Coal Mining (Strip & Auger Mines)	$	$ R.M. / $ Exp.
$	$	7.	Crude Petroleum & Natural Gas	$	$ R.M. / $ Exp.
$	$	8.	All Other Mining	$	$ R.M. / $ Exp.

9. General Contractors (Buildings)
   $_____ $_____ R.M.
   $_____ $_____ Exp.

10. General Contractors (Non–Buildings)
   $_____ $_____ R.M.
   $_____ $_____ Exp.

11. Special Trades Contractors
   $_____ $_____ R.M.
   $_____ $_____ Exp.

12. Manufacturers of Food & Kindred Products (Meats & All Other, n.e.c.)
   $_____ $_____ R.M.
   $_____ $_____ Exp.

13. Manufacturers of Food & Kindred Products (Dairy)
   $_____ $_____ R.M.
   $_____ $_____ Exp.

14. Manufacturers of Food & Kindred Products (Bakeries)
   $_____ $_____ R.M.
   $_____ $_____ Exp.

15. Manufacturers of Food & Kindred Products (Beverages)
   $_____ $_____ R.M.
   $_____ $_____ Exp.

16. Manufacturers of Apparel & Accessories
   $_____ $_____ R.M.
   $_____ $_____ Exp.

17. Manufacturing – Logging & Sawmills
   $_____ $_____ R.M.
   $_____ $_____ Exp.

18. Manufacturers of Furniture & Other Wood Products, n.e.c.
   $_____ $_____ R.M.
   $_____ $_____ Exp.

214

19. Manufacturers of Paper & Allied Products — R.M. $ _____ $ _____ | Exp. $ _____ $ _____

20. Manufacturing – Printing & Publishing — R.M. $ _____ $ _____ | Exp. $ _____ $ _____

21. Manufacturers of Basic Chemical Products — R.M. $ _____ $ _____ | Exp. $ _____ $ _____

22. Manufacturers of All Other Chemical Products — R.M. $ _____ $ _____ | Exp. $ _____ $ _____

23. Manufacturers of Petroleum & Coal Products — R.M. $ _____ $ _____ | Exp. $ _____ $ _____

24. Manufacturers of Leather & Leather Products — R.M. $ _____ $ _____ | Exp. $ _____ $ _____

25. Manufacturers of Flat Glass — R.M. $ _____ $ _____ | Exp. $ _____ $ _____

26. Manufacturers of Glass Products (Pressed & Blown) — R.M. $ _____ $ _____ | Exp. $ _____ $ _____

27. Manufacturers of Stone & Clay Products — R.M. $ _____ $ _____ | Exp. $ _____ $ _____

28. Manufacturers of Primary Metals — R.M. $ _____ $ _____ | Exp. $ _____ $ _____

29. Manufacturers of Fabricated Metal Products

R.M. $ _____

Exp. $ _____

30. Manufacturers of Machinery (Except Electrical)

R.M. $ _____

Exp. $ _____

31. Manufacturers of Electrical Machinery & Apparatus

R.M. $ _____

Exp. $ _____

32. Manufacturers of Transportation Equipment

R.M. $ _____

Exp. $ _____

33. Manufacturers of Instruments & Related Products

R.M. $ _____

Exp. $ _____

34. All Other Manufacturing n.e.c.

R.M. $ _____

Exp. $ _____

35. Eating & Drinking Establishments

R.M. $ _____

Exp. $ _____

36. Wholesale Trade

R.M. $ _____

Exp. $ _____

37. Retail Food Stores

R.M. $ _____

Exp. $ _____

38. Retail Gasoline Service Stations

R.M. $ _____

Exp. $ _____

216

39. All Other Retail

$ _____ R.M.
$ _____ Exp.
$ _____

40. Banks

$ _____ R.M.
$ _____ Exp.
$ _____

41. Other Finance

$ _____ R.M.
$ _____ Exp.
$ _____

42. Insurance Agents & Brokerage Firms

$ _____ R.M.
$ _____ Exp.
$ _____

43. Real Estate

$ _____ R.M.
$ _____ Exp.
$ _____

44. All Other F. I. R. E.

$ _____ R.M.
$ _____ Exp.
$ _____

45. Hotels & Other Lodging Places

$ _____ R.M.
$ _____ Exp.
$ _____

46. Medical & Legal Services

$ _____ R.M.
$ _____ Exp.
$ _____

47. Educational Services

$ _____ R.M.
$ _____ Exp.
$ _____

48. All Other Services

$ _____ R.M.
$ _____ Exp.
$ _____

49. Railroads — $ ___ $ ___ R.M. / $ ___ $ ___ Exp.

50. Trucking & Warehousing — $ ___ $ ___ R.M. / $ ___ $ ___ Exp.

51. Water Transportation — $ ___ $ ___ R.M. / $ ___ $ ___ Exp.

52. All Other Transportation — $ ___ $ ___ R.M. / $ ___ $ ___ Exp.

53. Communications — $ ___ $ ___ R.M. / $ ___ $ ___ Exp.

54. Electric Companies & Systems — $ ___ $ ___ R.M. / $ ___ $ ___ Exp.

55. Gas Companies & Systems — $ ___ $ ___ R.M. / $ ___ $ ___ Exp.

56. Water & Sanitary Services — $ ___ $ ___ R.M. / $ ___ $ ___ Exp.

57. Households

1. Salaries & Wages — $ ___
2. Soc. Sec. (employer & employee) — $ ___
3. Supplements to wages — $ ___
4. Unemployment taxes — $ ___
TOTAL GROSS WAGES & SALARIES — $ ___

Sales taxes collected — $ ___

total sales — $ ___

58. Local Government

    1. Property taxes $ _____

    2. Gross Receipts (B&O) $ _____

    3. Sales taxes paid $ _____

    4. Licenses & fees $ _____

    TOTAL LOCAL TAXES & PAYMENTS $ _____

total sales $ _____

59. State Government

    1. Property taxes $ _____

    2. Gross receipts (B&O) $ _____

    3. Sales taxes paid $ _____

    4. Licenses & fees $ _____

    TOTAL STATE TAXES & PAYMENTS $ _____

total sales $ _____

60. Federal Government

    1. Federal income taxes $ _____

    2. Federal excise taxes paid $ _____

Federal excise taxes collected

    3. Any other payments to Fed. govt. $ _____

    TOTAL PAYMENTS TO FEDERAL GOVERNMENT $ _____

PURCHASES OF PLANT AND EQUIPMENT

1965

	AMOUNT	SECTOR PUR-CHASED FROM	LOCATION OF SELLER	AMOUNT	SECTOR PUR-CHASED FROM	LOCATION OF SELLER
1. Construction						
2. Rolling Stock						
3. Other Equipment						
4. Land						

5. Total investment expenditures 1965. $ _____ for expansion _____ % for replacement _____ %.

6. How were these purchases financed? Personal Capital $ _____ Retained earnings $ _____. Borrowing (equity issues) $ _____ Sector & Location Borrowed from _____.

7. What was the depreciated book value of plant and equipment as of January 1, 1965? $ _____.

8. Depreciation expense 1965. $ _____.

9. Have you, or do you plan any plant and equipment acquisitions in 1966 and 1967. Yes _____ No _____ Amount $ _____ for expansion _____ % for replacement _____ %.

10. Estimated annual dollar output potential of plant & equipment as it was Jan. 1, 1965 $ _____.

11. Estimated annual dollar output potential of plant & equipment as it was Dec. 31, 1965 $ _____.

12. Estimated annual dollar output potential of plant & equipment after 1966 and 1967 acquisitions $ _____

1. Total employment 1965 _____

2. Are there any seasonal variations in employment? Yes _____ No _____

3. If yes, explain. _____

INTERVIEWER COMMENTS: _____

_____

_____

B

Input–Output and
Aggregate Income
Accounts

Input–Output and Aggregate Income Accounts

After the final version of the 1965 West Virginia transactions table had been completed it was reconciled with a set of state income and product accounts. These accounts were not mentioned in the text since they were not used in either the forecasts or the simulation of new regional activities, but they provide a concise summary of the sources and uses of funds in the base year of this study, with projections to 1975. Since aggregate accounts of this type are of interest in themselves, the complete details are included in Tables B.1—B.4.

Table B.1 Summary of Receipts and
Expenditures, West Virginia, 1965
(thousands of dollars)

Sectors	Receipts Gross	Net
I. Final Demand (Payments) Sectors		
1. Households	$3,766,000	$3,317,514
2. Local Government	258,638	76,494
3. State Government	478,254	166,455
4. Federal Government	739,690	349,486
5. Saving–Investment	864,255	——
6. Out–of–State	4,734,851	——
II. Processing Sectors	8,816,365	714,370

| Expenditures | | Balance | |
Gross	Net	Gross	Net
$3,621,736	$2,965,352	$144,264	$352,162
273,269	272,227	−14,631	195,733
492,663	333,825	−14,409	−167,370
865,059	348,690	−125,369	796
656,477	——	207,778	——
4,932,484	197,633	−197,633	−197,633
8,816,365	506,592	——	207,778

Table B.1 (continued)

Sectors	Receipts Gross	Net
(Gross State Product)		$4,624,319
Total		
(Total Gross Output)	$19,658,053	

Expenditures		Balance	
Gross	Net	Gross	Net
	4,624,319	0	0
$19,658,053			

Table B.2 Summary of Receipts and
Expenditures, West Virginia, 1975
(thousands of dollars)

		Receipts	
Sectors		Gross	Net
I.	Final Demand (Payments) Sectors		
	1. Households	$5,597,329	$4,843,255
	2. Local Government	487,518	132,471
	3. State Government	842,628	260,979
	4. Federal Government	1,197,346	583,020
	5. Saving–Investment	1,586,702	——
	6. Out–of–State	7,255,278	——
II.	Processing Sectors	13,506,691	1,146,367
	(Gross State Product)		$6,966,092
Total			
	(Total Gross Output)	$30,473,492	

| Expenditures | | Balance | |
Gross	Net	Gross	Net
$5,156,964	$4,094,425	$440,365	$748,830
487,518	485,691	——	-353,220
842,628	574,021	——	-313,042
1,472,977	500,854	-275,631	82,166
1,543,633	——	43,069	——
7,463,081	207,803	-207,803	-207,803
13,506,691	1,103,298	——	43,069
	$6,966,092	0	0
$30,473,492			

Table B.3 Sources and Uses of Funds
in West Virginia—1965 (thousands of
dollars)

Sources		Uses	
(A) Households			
Sources of Earned Income:		Consumption of Goods and Services:	
Processing Sectors	$2,861,203	Processing Sectors	$1,886,088
Households	39,835	Households	39,835
Local Government	53,734	Imports	1,039,429
State Government	89,852	Total Consumption	$2,965,352[b]
Federal Government	75,528	Other Expenditures:	
Investment	27,165	Personal Tax to Local Government	88,944
Out-of-State	170,197		
Total Earned Income	$3,317,514[a]	Personal Tax to State Government	177,440
Other Sources of Income:		Personal Tax to Federal Government	303,000
State Government Transfer	77,782	Social Security Tax to Federal Government	87,000
Federal Government Transfer	370,704	Total Gross Expenditures	$3,621,736
Total Gross Receipts	$3,766,000	Personal Saving	144,264
		Total Gross Outlay	$3,766,000

Table B.3 (continued)

Sources	Uses

(B) Local Government

Receipts from Own Sources:		Expenditures for Goods and Services:	
Processing Sectors	$ 76,494[a]	Processing Sectors	$212,882
Receipts from Other Sources:		Households	53,734
Personal Tax from Households	88,944	Out-of-State	5,611
		Total Expenditures for Goods and Services	$272,227[b]
Transfer from State Government	80,900	Other Expenditures:	
Transfer from Federal Government	12,300	Transfer to State Government	994
Total Gross Receipts	$258,638	Transfer to Federal Government	48
		Total Gross Expenditures	$273,269

(C) State Government

Receipts from Own Sources:		Expenditures for Goods and Services:	
Processing Sectors	$157,147	Processing Sectors	$204,825
Exports	9,308	Households	89,852
Total Earned Income	$166,455[a]	Out-of-State	39,148
Receipts from Other Sources:		Total Expenditures for Goods and Services	$333,825[b]
Personal Tax from Households	177,440	Other Expenditures:	
Transfer from Local Government	994	Transfer to Households	77,782

Table B.3 (continued)

Sources		Uses	
		Transfer to Local Government	80,900
Transfer from Federal Government	133,365		
		Transfer to Federal Government	156
Total Gross Receipts	$478,254		
		Total Gross Expenditures	$492,663

(D) Federal Government

Receipts from Own Sources:		Expenditures for Goods and Services:	
Processing Sectors	$349,486[a]	Processing Sectors	$142,928
Receipts from Other Sources:		Households	75,528
Personal Tax from Households	303,000	Out-of-State	130,234
		Total Expenditures for Goods and Services	$348,690[b]
Social Security Tax from Households	87,000		
		Other Expenditures:	
Transfer from Local Government	48	Transfer to Households	370,704
Transfer from State Government	156	Transfer to Local Government	12,300
Total Gross Receipts	$739,690	Transfer to State Government	133,365
		Total Gross Expenditures	$865,059

(E) Saving–Investment

Business Saving:		Investment Expenditures:	
Depreciation and Retained Profits	$712,370[a]	Processing Sectors	$273,630

Table B.3 (continued)

Sources		Uses	
		Households	27,165
Other Saving:		Imports	211,418
Personal Saving	144,264	Total Gross Expenditures	$512,213
Total Gross Saving	$858,634	Net Inventory Change	(5,621)
		Total Gross Investment	$506,592[b]

(F) Out-of-State

Imports of West Virginia:		Exports of West Virginia:	
Processing Sectors	$2,902,991	Processing Sectors	$4,346,959
Households	1,039,429	Households	170,197
Local Government	5,611	State Government	9,308
State Government	39,148	Imports	406,020
Federal Government	130,234	Total Gross Expenditures	$4,932,484
Gross Private Domestic Investment	211,418	Less Net Imports	197,633[b]
		Total Gross Outlay	$4,734,851
Exports	406,020		
Total Gross Receipts	$4,734,851		

[a]Receipt component of gross state product.

[b]Expenditure component of gross state product.

Table B.4 Sources and Uses of Funds
in West Virginia—1975 (thousands of
dollars)

Sources		Uses	
(A) Households			
Sources of Earned Income:		Consumption of Goods and Services:	
Processing Sectors	$4,146,475	Processing Sectors	$2,428,790
Households	51,903	Households	51,903
Local Government	80,606	Imports	1,613,732
State Government	167,133	Total Consumption	$4,094,425[b]
Federal Government	135,054	Other Expenditures:	
Investment	40,210	Personal Tax to Local Government	153,482
Out-of-State	221,874		
Total Earned Income	$4,843,255[a]	Personal Tax to State Government	295,073
Other Sources of Income:		Personal Tax to Federal Government	485,776
State Government Transfer	89,994	Social Security Tax to Federal Government	128,208
Federal Government Transfer	664,080	Total Gross Expenditures	$5,156,964
Total Gross Receipts	$5,597,329	Personal Saving	440,365
		Total Gross Outlay	$5,597,329

Table B.4 (continued)

Sources		Uses	

(B) Local Government

Receipts from Own Sources:		Expenditures for Goods and Services:	
Processing Sectors	$132,471[a]	Processing Sectors	$395,439
Receipts from Other Sources:		Households	80,606
Personal Tax from Households	153,482	Out-of-State	9,646
Transfer from State Government	178,353	Total Expenditures for Goods and Services	$485,691[b]
Transfer from Federal Government	23,212	Other Expenditures:	
Total Gross Receipts	$487,518	Transfer to State Government	1,745
		Transfer to Federal Government	82
		Total Gross Outlay	$487,518

(C) State Government

Receipts from Own Sources:		Expenditures for Goods & Services:	
Processing Sectors	$246,526	Processing Sectors	$315,528
Exports	14,453	Households	167,133
Total Earned Income	$260,979[a]	Out-of-State	91,360
Receipts from Other Sources:		Total Expenditures for Goods and Services	$574,021[b]
Personal Tax from Households	295,073	Other Expenditures:	
Transfer from Local Government	1,745	Transfer to Households	89,994
Transfer from Federal Government	284,831	Transfer to Local Government	178,353

Table B.4 (continued)

Sources		Uses	
		Transfer to Federal Government	260
Total Gross Receipts	$842,628		
		Total Gross Outlay	$842,628

(D) Federal Government

Receipts from Own Sources:		Expenditures for Goods and Services:	
Processing Sectors	$583,020[a]	Processing Sectors	$213,313
Receipts from Other Sources:		Households	135,054
Personal Tax from Households	485,776	Out-of-State	152,387
		Total Expenditures for Goods and Services	$500,854[b]
Social Security Tax from Households	128,208		
		Other Expenditures:	
Transfer from Local Government	82	Transfer to Households	664,080
Transfer from State Government	260	Transfer to Local Government	23,212
Total Gross Receipts	$1,197,346	Transfer to State Government	284,831
		Total Gross Expenditures	$1,472,977

(E) Saving–Investment

Business Saving:		Investment Expenditures:	
Depreciation and Retained Profits	$1,146,337[a]	Processing Sectors	$494,645
		Households	40,210
Other Saving:		Import	568,413

Table B.4 (continued)

Sources		Uses	
Personal Saving	440,365		
		Total Gross Investment	$1,103,268[b]
Total Gross Saving	$1,586,702		

(F) Out-of-State

Imports of West Virginia:		Exports of West Virginia:	
Processing Sectors	$4,189,087	Processing Sectors	$6,596,201
Households	1,613,732	Households	221,874
Local Government	9,646	State Government	14,453
State Government	91,360	Imports	630,553
Federal Government	152,487	Total Gross Expenditures	$7,463,081
Gross Private Domestic Investment	568,413	Less Net Exports	207,803[b]
		Total Gross Outlay	$7,255,278
Exports	630,553		
Total Gross Receipts	$7,255,278		

[a]Denotes receipt component of gross state product.

Matrix Tables

TABLE I

INTERINDUSTRY FLOW OF GOODS & SERVICES, WEST VIRGINIA, 1965.
(Thousands of Dollars)

SALES TO → PROCESSING SECTORS

← PURCHASES FROM

PROCESSING SECTORS

FINAL PAYMENTS

		1. Agriculture	2. Coal mining (underground)	3. Coal mining (strip & auger)	4. Petroleum & natural gas	5. All other mining	6. General contractors (building)	7. General contractors (non-building)
1.	Agriculture	9,034	0	0	0	396	0	0
2.	Coal mining (underground)	54	5,661	8,413	0	0	45	15
3.	Coal mining (strip & auger)	0	7,661	12,197	0	15	8	6
4.	Petroleum & natural gas	0	0	0	2,174	0	0	0
5.	All other mining	1,229	596	22	166	2,922	1,651	6,102
6.	General contractors (building)	0	0	0	0	0	5,731	0
7.	General contractors (non-building)	0	0	0	0	0	4,873	4,888
8.	Special trades contractors	0	3,087	1	107	342	45,351	5,722
9.	Food & kindred products (meats and n.e.c.)	305	735	0	0	0	0	0
10.	Food & kindred products (dairies)	0	0	0	0	0	0	0
11.	Food & kindred products (bakeries)	0	0	0	0	0	0	0
12.	Food & kindred products (beverages)	0	0	0	0	0	0	0
13.	Apparel & accessories	0	0	0	0	0	0	0
14.	Logging & sawmills	1,158	4,555	35	5	573	521	217
15.	Furniture & other wood fabrication	74	2,566	0	0	89	1,428	238
16.	Printing & publishing	16	548	1	151	31	445	176
17.	Chemicals	12	242	0	0	283	0	4,071
18.	Petroleum	0	1,290	0	3,681	462	384	22,468
19.	Glass	0	0	0	0	0	0	0
20.	Stone & clay products	946	2,670	0	0	8	16,882	10,078
21.	Primary metal products	102	80	0	29	0	3,464	1,639
22.	Fabricated metal products	941	559	113	0	581	7,855	989
23.	Machinery (except electrical)	0	385	39	412	460	50	2,114
24.	Electrical machinery & apparatus	0	0	56	0	0	118	0
25.	Transportation equipment	0	0	0	0	0	0	0
26.	Instruments & related products	0	3	1	0	0	0	8
27.	All other manufacturing	8	679	0	0	149	6,342	56
28.	Eating & drinking establishments	0	0	84	0	0	131	216
29.	Wholesale trade	5,832	8,884	1,043	633	1,602	2,926	2,796
30.	Retail food stores	0	0	0	0	0	0	3
31.	Retail gasoline service stations	256	45	18	77	84	64	125
32.	All other retail	567	2,009	84	496	398	76	321
33.	Banking	2,135	30	588	52	208	1,328	905
34.	Other finance	234	0	121	94	63	53	419
35.	Insurance agents & brokers	2,314	4,913	377	683	738	1,131	2,039
36.	Real estate	1,102	0	853	34	21	1,039	327
37.	All other finance, insurance & real estate	0	1,677	0	0	74	0	38
38.	Hotels & other lodging places	43	0	27	0	20	25	259
39.	Medical & legal services	186	399	275	1,253	138	223	394
40.	Educational services	0	0	0	0	0	0	0
41.	All other services	4,105	2,423	1,458	2,171	346	1,119	7,961
42.	Railroads	65	170	154	130	80	51	796
43.	Trucking & warehousing	431	786	231	86	427	62	4,723
44.	All other transportation	37	62	0	0	0	0	168
45.	Communications	481	697	138	172	107	625	712
46.	Electric companies & systems	713	16,716	100	335	205	206	146
47.	Gas companies & systems	41	29	5	6	0	131	542
48.	Water & sanitary services	0	2	4	20	0	6,348	2
49.	Households	34,514	282,753	13,345	20,153	18,361	37,581	45,941
50.	Local government	3,438	5,217	47	1,090	495	365	1,919
51.	State government	272	9,608	934	2,994	1,208	2,725	3,834
52.	Federal government	366	32,346	1,495	1,083	1,352	2,933	5,995
53.	Gross savings	19,792	57,950	4,213	13,417	5,762	4,802	13,859
54.	Out-of-state (imports)	36,651	244,309	7,828	7,220	33,174	13,715	21,635
55.	Beginning inventory	55,365	602	0	1	284	769	5,579
56.	Total final payments	95,033	634,774	27,862	48,489	60,352	62,121	93,183
57.	Total gross outlay	127,454	702,342	54,300	58,924	71,174	172,807	174,862

	SALES TO →	8. Special trades contractors	9. Food & kindred products (meats and n.e.c.)	10. Food & kindred products (dairies)	11. Food & kindred products (bakeries)	12. Food & kindred products (beverages)	13. Apparel & accessories	14. Logging & sawmills
	TABLE I *(continued)* **INTERINDUSTRY FLOW OF GOODS & SERVICES, WEST VIRGINIA, 1965.** (Thousands of Dollars)							
1.	Agriculture	0	10,726	17,563	320	0	0	3,000
2.	Coal mining (underground)	30	1	0	0	19	10	32
3.	Coal mining (strip & auger)	15	0	0	0	0	0	0
4.	Petroleum & natural gas	0	0	0	0	0	0	0
5.	All other mining	867	8	0	0	0	0	0
6.	General contractors (building)	0	0	0	5	0	0	0
7.	General contractors (non-building)	521	0	22	0	0	0	80
8.	Special trades contractors	2,938	101	58	0	0	479	411
9.	Food & kindred products (meats and n.e.c.)	0	3,930	1,307	31	0	0	0
10.	Food & kindred products (dairies)	0	0	1,498	0	0	0	0
11.	Food & kindred products (bakeries)	0	0	0	50	0	0	0
12.	Food & kindred products (beverages)	0	0	0	0	222	0	0
13.	Apparel & accessories	0	0	0	0	8	0	0
14.	Logging & sawmills	1,405	0	0	0	0	0	9,711
15.	Furniture & other wood fabrication	0	0	0	0	0	0	2
16.	Printing & publishing	72	137	71	70	245	93	20
17.	Chemicals	97	0	0	0	62	0	0
18.	Petroleum	401	0	0	0	0	0	41
19.	Glass	300	0	0	0	338	0	0
20.	Stone & clay products	165	2	0	0	0	0	1
21.	Primary metal products	2,033	0	0	0	0	0	0
22.	Fabricated metal products	8,942	0	0	0	256	0	0
23.	Machinery (except electrical)	356	0	22	0	0	0	64
24.	Electrical machinery & apparatus	64	0	0	0	0	0	10
25.	Transportation equipment	0	0	0	0	0	0	0
26.	Instruments & related products	12	122	0	0	0	0	0
27.	All other manufacturing	1,405	178	254	46	286	97	71
28.	Eating & drinking establishments	91	13	81	2	58	0	4
29.	Wholesale trade	4,198	1,677	473	1,150	380	47	1,223
30.	Retail food stores	0	0	0	0	0	0	0
31.	Retail gasoline service stations	549	84	82	232	238	26	124
32.	All other retail	69	212	265	466	42	0	67
33.	Banking	1,291	217	49	198	11	13	232
34.	Other finance	0	236	0	119	0	0	39
35.	Insurance agents & brokers	2,060	133	469	671	373	9	708
36.	Real estate	551	0	132	0	0	0	424
37.	All other finance, insurance & real estate	254	0	46	14	0	0	563
38.	Hotels & other lodging places	111	19	0	3	58	3	151
39.	Medical & legal services	630	240	157	33	54	5	146
40.	Educational services	0	7	0	0	0	0	0
41.	All other services	1,043	889	1,944	2,006	213	5	728
42.	Railroads	0	0	0	0	0	0	39
43.	Trucking & warehousing	639	118	730	56	335	80	1,202
44.	All other transportation	0	0	5	2	0	8	47
45.	Communications	412	51	160	282	366	410	383
46.	Electric companies & systems	247	625	353	1,131	62	151	605
47.	Gas companies & systems	155	74	80	1,475	33	62	33
48.	Water & sanitary services	121	27	107	134	133	10	22
49.	Households	53,220	7,590	14,387	14,151	7,555	20,171	24,895
50.	Local government	1,538	12	204	78	39	34	201
51.	State government	4,188	296	498	270	4,650	123	577
52.	Federal government	4,705	312	1,530	486	145	39	1,775
53.	Gross savings	19,340	1,345	2,127	1,456	3,579	1,103	6,154
54.	Out-of-state (imports)	27,243	22,963	33,554	22,824	10,397	593	8,728
55.	Beginning inventory	6,011	4,321	1,526	1,191	2,887	22	13,644
56.	Total final payments	110,234	32,518	52,300	39,265	26,365	22,063	42,330
57.	Total gross outlay	142,278	52,345	78,228	47,761	30,157	23,571	62,513

PURCHASES FROM

PROCESSING SECTORS

FINAL PAYMENTS

PROCESSING SECTORS

15. Furniture & other wood fabrication	16. Printing & publishing	17. Chemicals	18. Petroleum	19. Glass	20. Stone & clay products	21. Primary metal products	22. Fabricated metal products	23. Machinery (except electrical)	24. Electrical machinery & apparatus	25. Transportation equipment	
4	0	12	0	0	94	367	3	0	0	0	1
184	40	12,834	1,617	65	840	18,667	60	6	0	0	2
0	16	0	0	15	0	0	0	0	0	0	3
0	0	9,730	4,865	0	0	119	0	0	0	0	4
0	0	5,575	5,129	4,856	8,351	4,472	41	0	0	473	5
19	0	1,087	0	0	0	17	0	0	0	0	6
0	0	2,051	0	0	0	35	0	0	87	0	7
1	0	8,607	0	30	72	1,819	163	16	10	4	8
0	0	1,051	0	0	0	0	0	0	0	0	9
0	0	0	0	0	0	0	0	0	0	0	10
0	0	0	0	0	0	0	0	0	0	0	11
0	0	0	0	0	0	0	0	0	0	0	12
0	0	140	0	0	0	13	0	0	0	0	13
3,462	0	0	55	0	14	13	0	30	0	0	14
185	0	192	0	382	0	0	0	0	25	0	15
54	16,100	1,563	86	122	341	128	326	98	124	49	16
196	9	193,732	3,157	1,177	240	4,960	131	0	2,223	0	17
0	0	1,481	1,745	0	2,938	95	0	0	0	0	18
85	0	832	0	6,784	0	272	3	0	0	0	19
0	-0	1,495	0	823	2,446	0	0	0	0	0	20
0	0	652	0	726	0	3,842	11,471	5,448	22,115	12,580	21
252	1,081	2,628	104	28	2,100	1,428	64	1,716	0	0	22
38	96	3	0	0	27	429	17	5	0	0	23
0	23	1,348	0	0	4	349	7	918	121	0	24
0	0	0	0	0	42	70	0	0	0	0	25
0	0	3,220	0	0	0	0	17	0	103	0	26
8	1,022	10,308	0	11,058	1,126	715	462	859	47	36	27
10	82	408	20	0	0	36	53	43	24	16	28
201	139	10,260	319	2,816	1,426	4,705	1,398	1,010	589	400	29
0	0	152	0	0	0	0	1	0	0	0	30
49	152	81	0	29	145	16	29	50	15	1	31
16	259	3,969	37	738	628	2,449	468	113	406	187	32
63	85	780	409	1,620	316	950	50	424	116	217	33
2	0	0	233	0	0	150	39	0	0	0	34
148	309	4,031	59	2,719	657	1,686	372	1,640	661	321	35
0	78	0	0	68	0	0	373	26	275	0	36
0	280	1,510	0	112	0	569	286	0	0	0	37
6	24	975	0	32	3	185	25	26	25	8	38
61	239	1,815	270	133	291	1,101	87	41	152	213	39
0	9	214	0	15	0	370	4	0	398	0	40
399	319	9,540	258	3,101	688	7,561	759	409	1,060	924	41
13	11	15,201	0	0	666	8,092	24	821	398	3,465	42
327	805	13,173	1,093	983	3,945	8,185	289	1,836	817	129	43
21	39	2,453	1,090	0	13	8,576	2	966	2,340	0	44
102	773	7,075	1,437	1,239	518	2,556	346	280	961	1,437	45
136	187	10,216	492	3,069	1,436	6,619	1,088	655	2,853	1,389	46
106	106	18,791	1,054	7,349	3,267	1,864	596	193	1,033	829	47
9	28	2,372	31	125	89	519	288	19	661	361	48
8,056	22,192	217,745	8,219	99,899	39,002	227,249	39,096	31,884	34,988	45,938	49
57	238	9,125	154	9,698	508	5,901	273	315	882	1,247	50
187	276	5,270	406	2,070	855	4,540	609	490	624	1,162	51
730	2,970	60,456	4,163	13,347	3,090	27,774	3,102	5,663	5,787	9,932	52
1,444	4,571	159,097	6,091	32,422	21,174	58,093	6,474	7,219	9,188	9,820	53
9,174	8,896	477,984	26,851	61,097	34,943	551,725	51,777	49,575	29,886	86,394	54
2,911	1,356	106,248	21,179	40,152	13,157	122,858	13,477	15,688	13,293	21,567	55
19,648	39,143	935,386	45,884	218,533	99,572	875,282	101,355	95,146	81,355	154,493	56
25,805	61,454	1.291,234	69,444	268,747	132,295	969,281	120,673	112,794	118,994	177,532	57

		26. Instruments & related products	27. All other manufacturing	28. Eating & drinking establishments	29. Wholesale trade	30. Retail food stores	31. Retail gasoline service stations	32. All other retail
SALES TO →								
PURCHASES FROM ←	**TABLE I** *(continued)* INTERINDUSTRY FLOW OF GOODS & SERVICES, WEST VIRGINIA, 1965. (Thousands of Dollars)							
PROCESSING SECTORS	1. Agriculture	0	832	643	0	0	0	0
	2. Coal mining (underground)	0	34	55	107	25	15	240
	3. Coal mining (strip & auger)	0	164	20	0	15	10	180
	4. Petroleum & natural gas	0	0	0	0	0	0	0
	5. All other mining	0	0	0	0	0	0	0
	6. General contractors (building)	0	0	0	0	0	0	23
	7. General contractors (non-building)	0	0	0	0	0	0	0
	8. Special trades contractors	0	3,037	0	371	113	5	2,000
	9. Food & kindred products (meats and n.e.c.)	0	1,200	4,573	0	0	0	0
	10. Food & kindred products (dairies)	0	0	3,184	0	0	0	91
	11. Food & kindred products (bakeries)	0	0	3,430	0	0	0	178
	12. Food & kindred products (beverages)	0	0	902	0	0	0	36
	13. Apparel & accessories	0	56	0	0	0	0	0
	14. Logging & sawmills	0	0	0	0	0	0	0
	15. Furniture & other wood fabrication	0	0	0	12	0	0	709
	16. Printing & publishing	4	316	69	257	4,937	93	9,110
	17. Chemicals	375	118	0	352	0	0	0
	18. Petroleum	0	0	0	0	105	846	1,114
	19. Glass	32	0	130	0	20	0	2,838
	20. Stone & clay products	0	1	0	0	0	0	0
	21. Primary metal products	0	0	0	0	0	0	0
	22. Fabricated metal products	0	3,387	0	1	0	0	0
	23. Machinery (except electrical)	0	1,062	0	0	0	0	0
	24. Electrical machinery & apparatus	0	184	0	0	0	0	0
	25. Transportation equipment	0	0	0	96	0	0	37
	26. Instruments & related products	0	0	0	0	0	0	87
	27. All other manufacturing	63	552	0	425	473	0	575
	28. Eating & drinking establishments	0	1	0	403	0	0	263
	29. Wholesale trade	80	196	6,110	5,056	636	429	806
	30. Retail food stores	0	0	532	58	1	0	0
	31. Retail gasoline service stations	0	40	19	2,842	158	33	1,203
	32. All other retail	0	24	173	1,001	71	41	1,148
	33. Banking	13	395	109	842	114	163	3,422
	34. Other finance	0	0	111	1,074	203	0	896
	35. Insurance agents & brokers	15	447	426	2,474	2,050	487	8,903
	36. Real estate	0	54	104	55	5,957	208	8,954
	37. All other finance, insurance & real estate	0	0	8	284	0	0	197
	38. Hotels & other lodging places	0	2	0	222	0	0	828
	39. Medical & legal services	17	128	31	586	161	14	1,721
	40. Educational services	0	0	0	94	0	0	127
	41. All other services	31	881	551	1,977	2,275	4,400	10,401
	42. Railroads	0	1,130	0	1,755	0	29	3,139
	43. Trucking & warehousing	46	409	5	5,333	606	819	3,768
	44. All other transportation	0	41	2	3,155	69	49	1,111
	45. Communications	14	391	827	2,233	1,345	461	1,394
	46. Electric companies & systems	12	762	1,206	5,946	3,616	421	5,112
	47. Gas companies & systems	7	249	1,965	4,667	1,702	238	2,948
	48. Water & sanitary services	2	69	145	165	338	150	1,221
FINAL PAYMENTS	49. Households	2,941	31,161	45,635	187,732	66,302	18,293	192,960
	50. Local government	17	348	551	3,187	1,534	279	7,551
	51. State government	76	649	4,253	36,436	3,818	4,577	7,256
	52. Federal government	463	3,414	5,238	18,923	4,651	461	22,345
	53. Gross savings	134	3,760	1,593	8,986	5,464	3,246	23,987
	54. Out-of-state (imports)	4,384	70,964	33,135	12,521	12,562	3,083	65,173
	55. Beginning inventory	439	20,217	2	131,730	55,935	6,954	421,517
	56. Total final payments	8,015	110,296	90,405	267,785	94,331	29,939	319,272
	57. Total gross outlay	8,726	126,458	115,735	309,628	119,321	38,850	394,052

PROCESSING SECTORS

33. Banking	34. Other finance	35. Insurance agents & brokers	36. Real estate	37. All other finance, insurance & real estate	38. Hotels & other lodging places	39. Medical & legal services	40. Educational services	41. All other services	42. Railroads	43. Trucking & warehousing	
0	0	0	0	0	200	62	0	0	0	0	1
25	0	0	0	0	85	40	422	5	62	35	2
5	0	0	0	516	608	0	225	0	0	0	3
0	0	0	0	0	0	0	0	0	0	0	4
0	0	0	0	0	0	11	0	0	1,805	0	5
0	0	0	0	0	0	0	15,682	0	0	0	6
0	0	0	4,317	0	59	0	6,409	0	2,103	501	7
167	0	0	119	0	261	0	0	0	2,241	539	8
0	0	0	2,048	0	1,169	545	956	227	0	0	9
0	0	14	0	0	0	3,277	21	19	0	0	10
0	0	0	0	0	0	1,226	0	0	0	0	11
0	0	0	0	0	0	133	134	30	0	0	12
0	0	0	0	0	0	67	439	0	0	0	13
0	0	0	0	0	0	810	0	0	0	175	14
0	0	0	0	0	0	4	57	0	0	0	15
546	617	62	1,560	192	56	115	1,027	2,180	16	882	16
0	0	0	0	0	0	680	63	1,072	0	0	17
0	0	51	0	0	0	0	0	423	1,647	198	18
0	0	0	0	0	0	101	113	0	0	0	19
0	0	0	3	0	0	0	157	1,052	0	39	20
0	0	0	0	0	0	0	0	0	1,073	348	21
0	0	0	0	0	0	0	0	715	0	0	22
0	0	0	0	0	0	0	0	0	1,249	0	23
0	215	0	0	0	0	18	0	237	12	0	24
0	0	0	0	0	0	0	0	0	1,482	0	25
0	0	0	0	0	0	228	19	0	0	0	26
0	0	0	0	0	9	1,501	28	1,101	0	0	27
102	70	0	0	0	0	27	739	0	0	159	28
11	43	318	125	19	0	1,670	3,633	7,683	545	9,959	29
46	29	95	499	4	565	205	0	1	0	0	30
0	0	0	0	0	181	132	42	770	2	324	31
9	32	76	36	5	260	1,115	1,601	4,806	109	257	32
286	66	111	401	24	1,383	1,086	145	283	0	568	33
0	3,686	125	430	79	0	499	0	273	0	0	34
85	119	0	0	0	914	1,648	1,366	7,585	4,920	4,490	35
838	31	278	26	75	1,064	405	208	894	0	146	36
521	364	520	3,713	35	0	89	406	177	0	0	37
1,123	0	23,025	20	0	0	165	124	125	42	171	38
6	4	17	234	19	0	4,117	329	1,318	714	488	39
339	441	34	83	20,690	181	140	329	0	77	1,052	40
87	99	0	0	0	0	0	0	0	381	0	41
3,488	729	1,493	984	937	2,731	6,222	2,230	14,195	7,494	550	42
0	0	0	0	0	0	158	71	520	1,525	333	43
12	0	0	0	33	21	376	362	1,432	100	74	44
12	158	56	208	0	252	1,516	2,379	2,338	1,070	385	45
1,218	750	1,415	726	0	1,861	627	1,943	1,545	821	804	46
197	58	229	332	141	1,925	869	1,330	2,526	170	759	47
265	38	235	394	124	612	319	493	461	26	69	48
59	6	50	113	0	317	319	493	461	26	69	49
54,022	32,271	55,800	30,898	16,801	11,704	104,445	142,124	197,925	90,493	77,189	50
702	432	382	1,820	92	639	243	66	1,043	3,023	1,070	51
746	926	7,665	1,537	580	351	1,052	58	12,836	6,446	3,245	52
11,325	2,947	230	1,973	602	2,074	6,822	7,387	4,747	9,819	9,674	53
14,152	3,833	1,552	4,136	729	3,940	11,605	2,887	31,714	26,237	19,946	54
9,440	8,037	180,569	4,012	6,450	4,813	22,458	21,642	143,282	47,523	52,321	55
0	0	0	0	0	1	0	24,739	0	0	0	
90,387	48,446	246,198	44,376	25,254	23,521	146,625	174,164	391,547	183,517	163,445	56
99,834	56,001	274,402	60,747	48,399	37,983	176,831	217,325	445,617	213,150	186,750	57

	SALES TO →	PROCESSING SECTORS				

TABLE I
(continued)

INTERINDUSTRY FLOW
OF GOODS & SERVICES,
WEST VIRGINIA, 1965.
(Thousands of Dollars)

PURCHASES FROM		44. All other transportation	45. Communications	46. Electric companies & systems	47. Gas companies & systems	48. Water & sanitary services
	1. Agriculture	0	0	0	0	0
	2. Coal mining (underground)	0	25	20,792	1,136	35
	3. Coal mining (strip & auger)	0	0	8,500	0	0
	4. Petroleum & natural gas	1,728	0	0	39,467	0
	5. All other mining	0	0	0	0	836
	6. General contractors (building)	0	0	0	0	0
	7. General contractors (non-building)	0	833	0	0	2,130
	8. Special trades contractors	244	0	1	0	0
	9. Food & kindred products (meats and n.e.c.)	0	0	0	0	0
	10. Food & kindred products (dairies)	0	0	0	0	0
	11. Food & kindred products (bakeries)	0	0	0	0	0
	12. Food & kindred products (beverages)	0	0	0	0	0
	13. Apparel & accessories	0	0	0	0	0
	14. Logging & sawmills	0	0	0	0	0
	15. Furniture & other wood fabrication	157	0	10	0	0
	16. Printing & publishing	14	235	449	195	54
PROCESSING SECTORS	17. Chemicals	0	0	0	0	409
	18. Petroleum	222	488	831	91	22
	19. Glass	0	0	0	0	0
	20. Stone & clay products	0	208	411	495	168
	21. Primary metal products	281	34	72	28	3
	22. Fabricated metal products	372	0	985	100	345
	23. Machinery (except electrical)	124	0	0	0	0
	24. Electrical machinery & apparatus	0	178	62	0	205
	25. Transportation equipment	0	0	0	0	0
	26. Instruments & related products	5	0	0	0	0
	27. All other manufacturing	857	0	2	28	0
	28. Eating & drinking establishments	5	83	98	289	7
	29. Wholesale trade	144	42	752	450	383
	30. Retail food stores	0	0	0	0	0
	31. Retail gasoline service stations	69	19	20	336	74
	32. All other retail	23	193	95	176	1,748
	33. Banking	472	112	9	616	3
	34. Other finance	89	0	0	34	0
	35. Insurance agents & brokers	110	85	227	118	89
	36. Real estate	18	140	181	442	0
	37. All other finance, insurance & real estate	0	348	299	241	26
	38. Hotels & other lodging places	5	23	91	208	0
	39. Medical & legal services	20	211	110	100	13
	40. Educational services	0	0	5	9	0
	41. All other services	805	2,683	681	519	23
	42. Railroads	28	2,531	4,180	700	280
	43. Trucking & warehousing	66	830	2,181	1,492	51
	44. All other transportation	4,515	140	683	4,324	5
	45. Communications	389	410	352	246	362
	46. Electric companies & systems	136	391	10,088	394	1,407
	47. Gas companies & systems	75	304	183	1,897	35
	48. Water & sanitary services	12	5	18	43	482
FINAL PAYMENTS	49. Households	13,173	41,891	34,111	36,161	8,286
	50. Local government	305	2,359	6,596	622	558
	51. State government	628	3,501	6,378	4,737	730
	52. Federal government	846	16,956	18,403	8,279	331
	53. Gross savings	7,198	24,328	17,852	22,991	3,608
	54. Out-of-state (imports)	20,028	19,516	22,084	252,280	7,578
	55. Beginning inventory	0	0	6,220	89,700	0
	56. Total final payments	31,346	108,551	105,424	325,070	21,091
	57. Total gross outlay	53,163	119,102	157,792	379,244	30,286

	FINAL DEMAND								
49. Households	50. Local government	51. State government	52. Federal government	53. Gross private state investment	54. Out-of-state (exports)	55. Net inventory change	56. Total final demand	57. Total gross output	
28,630	125	86	3,600	0	54,257	-2,500	84,198	127,454	1
4,981	0	146	271	1,185	624,028	0	630,611	702,342	2
1,348	0	0	0	0	22,776	0	24,124	54,300	3
0	0	0	0	0	841	0	841	58,924	4
8,522	4,525	3,115	0	2,137	7,763	0	26,062	71,174	5
428	1,333	2,356	8,332	123,965	9,517	-64	145,867	172,807	6
1,455	13,687	80,373	13,662	27,219	13,591	-38	149,949	174,862	7
21,657	12,558	9,406	723	9,474	5,665	-187	59,296	142,278	8
30,877	0	0	182	0	5,129	-306	35,882	52,345	9
62,628	0	613	0	9	8,979	0	72,229	78,228	10
25,738	0	0	0	0	18,068	0	43,806	47,761	11
23,276	0	0	0	121	5,500	-406	28,491	30,157	12
5,580	0	0	0	0	16,964	0	22,544	23,571	13
6,633	14	44	238	997	33,935	-1,338	40,523	62,513	14
6,936	0	190	0	3,147	8,825	638	19,736	25,805	15
6,804	674	3,486	610	0	5,850	-23	17,401	61,454	16
4,093	68	361	6,610	0	1,058,989	7,452	1,077,573	1,291,234	17
4,055	680	6,546	161	0	15,727	1,251	28,420	69,444	18
5,684	63	141	0	0	250,321	690	256,899	268,747	19
1,646	5,137	1,633	816	4,457	80,483	73	94,245	132,295	20
517	0	0	0	18,823	895,263	-11,598	903,005	969,281	21
1,346	0	0	3,810	1,340	79,184	-357	85,323	120,673	22
436	0	0	0	54,688	48,999	1,773	105,896	112,794	23
2,982	0	0	4,534	4,958	102,998	-597	114,875	118,994	24
0	0	1,794	74,180	261	99,081	489	175,805	177,532	25
0	0	0	14	569	3,984	61	4,901	8,726	26
273	0	0	0	1,749	67,013	241	85,460	126,458	27
16,457	0	0	0	96	20,117	0	111,773	115,735	28
91,472	36	52	482	5,248	72,614	0	213,689	309,628	29
132,509	1,227	1,609	0	53	6,181	0	118,368	119,321	30
112,134	0	0	21	158	2,199	0	29,857	38,850	31
27,216	179	84	12	9,261	60,382	0	365,981	394,052	32
294,614	778	934	11,450	0	11,866	0	73,492	99,834	33
46,700	1,006	2,470	2,310	0	4,068	0	50,816	56,001	34
42,024	868	1,546	0	0	4,034	0	207,579	274,402	35
202,735	364	446	422	2,480	4,859	0	31,461	60,747	36
23,272	67	361	0	0	6,524	0	16,733	48,399	37
9,880	148	181	56	0	16,922	0	33,669	37,983	38
16,601	18	72	2,009	0	23,247	0	136,449	176,831	39
76,986	12,304	21,903	3,354	0	1,936	0	215,670	217,325	40
4,282	148,834	57,264	869	0	21,074	0	334,519	445,617	41
309,321	1,937	1,318	768	0	137,932	0	160,409	213,150	42
19,861	458	1,390	2,794	0	79,786	0	125,595	186,750	43
38,997	1,054	2,395	58	569	10,017	0	22,588	53,163	44
11,961	150	402	348	0	18,870	0	75,048	119,102	45
54,366	335	1,129	166	0	10,798	-875	69,944	157,792	46
55,513	3,740	602	38	666	289,333	0	319,798	379,244	47
29,449	67	245	28	0	470	0	14,291	30,286	48
13,213	448	132							
39,835	53,734	167,634	446,232	27,165	170,197	0	904,797	3,766,000	49
88,944	0	80,900	12,300	0	0	0	182,144	258,638	50
177,440	994	0	133,365	0	9,308	0	321,107	478,254	51
390,000	48	156	0	0	0	0	390,204	739,690	52
144,264	0	0	0	0	0	5,621	149,885	864,255	53
1,039,429	5,611	39,148	130,234	331,418	406,020	0	1,951,860	4,854,851	54
0	0	0	0	0	0	0	0	1,221,542	55
1,879,912	60,387	287,838	722,131	358,583	585,525	5,621	3,899,997	10,961,688	56
3,766,000	273,269	492,663	865,059	632,213	4,932,484	0	10,961,688	19,778,053	57

TABLE II

DIRECT PURCHASES PER DOLLAR OF OUTPUT, WEST VIRGINIA, 1965*

		1. Agriculture	2. Coal mining (underground)	3. Coal mining (strip & auger)	4. Petroleum & natural gas	5. All other mining	6. General contractors (building)	7. General contractors (non-building)
	1. Agriculture	.07088	0	0	0,	.00556	0	0
	2. Coal mining (underground)	.00042	.00806	.15494	0	0	.00026	.00009
	3. Coal mining (strip & auger)	0	.01091	.22462	0	.00021	.00005	.00003
	4. Petroleum & natural gas	0	0	0	.03689	0	0	0
	5. All other mining	.00964	.00085	.00040	.00282	.04105	.00955	.03490
	6. General contractors (building)	0	0	0	0	0	.03316	0
	7. General contractors (non-building)	0	0	0	0	0	.02820	.02795
	8. Special trades contractors	0	.00439	.00002	.00182	.00480	.26244	.03272
	9. Food & kindred products (meats and n.e.c.)	.00239	.00105	0	0	0	0	0
	10. Food & kindred products (dairies)	0	0	0	0	0	0	0
	11. Food & kindred products (bakeries)	0	0	0	0	0	0	0
	12. Food & kindred products (beverages)	0	0	0	0	0	0	0
	13. Apparel & accessories	0	0	0	0	0	0	0
	14. Logging & sawmills	.00909	.00649	.00064	.00008	.00805	.00302	.00124
	15. Furniture & other wood fabrication	.00058	.00365	0	0	.00125	.00826	.00136
	16. Printing & publishing	.00013	.00078	.00002	.00256	.00044	.00257	.00101
	17. Chemicals	.00009	.00035	0	0	.00398	0	.02328
	18. Petroleum	0	.00184	0	.06247	.00649	.00222	.12849
	19. Glass	0	0	0	0	0	0	0
	20. Stone & clay products	.00742	.00380	0	0	.00011	.09769	.05763
	21. Primary metal products	.00080	.00011	0	.00049	0	.02004	.00937
	22. Fabricated metal products	.00738	.00080	.00208	0	.00816	.04545	.00566
	23. Machinery (except electrical)	0	.00055	.00072	.00699	.00646	.00029	.01209
	24. Electrical machinery & apparatus	0	0	.00103	0	0	.00068	0
	25. Transportation equipment	0	0	0	0	0	0	0
	26. Instruments & related products	0	0	.00002	0	0	0	.00005
	27. All other manufacturing	.00006	.00097	0	0	.00209	.03670	.00032
	28. Eating & drinking establishments	0	0	.00155	0	0	.00076	.00124
	29. Wholesale trade	.04576	.01265	.01921	.01074	.02251	.01693	.01599
	30. Retail food stores	0	0	0	0	0	0	.00002
	31. Retail gasoline service stations	.00201	.00006	.00033	.00131	.00118	.00037	.00072
	32. All other retail	.00445	.00286	.00155	.00842	.00559	.00044	.00184
	33. Banking	.01675	.00004	.01083	.00088	.00292	.00769	.00518
	34. Other finance	.00184	0	.00223	.00159	.00088	.00031	.00240
	35. Insurance agents & brokers	.01816	.00700	.00694	.01159	.01037	.00655	.01166
	36. Real estate	.00865	0	.01571	.00058	.00030	.00601	.00187
	37. All other finance, insurance & real estate	0	.00239	0	0	.00104	0	.00022
	38. Hotels & other lodging places	.00034	0	.00050	0	.00028	.00014	.00148
	39. Medical & legal services	.00146	.00057	.00506	.02127	.00194	.00129	.00225
	40. Educational services	0	0	0	0	0	0	0
	41. All other services	.03221	.00345	.02685	.03684	.00486	.00648	.04553
	42. Railroads	.00051	.00024	.00284	.00221	.00112	.00030	.00455
	43. Trucking & warehousing	.00338	.00112	.00425	.00146	.00600	.00036	.02701
	44. All other transportation	.00029	.00009	0	0	0	0	.00096
	45. Communications	.00377	.00099	.00254	.00292	.00150	.00362	.00407
	46. Electric companies & systems	.00559	.02380	.00184	.00568	.00288	.00119	.00084
	47. Gas companies & systems	.00032	.00004	.00009	.00010	0	.00076	.00310
	48. Water & sanitary services	0	0	.00007	0	0	.03674	.00001
	49. Households	.27079	.40258	.24576	.34202	.25797	.21747	.26273
	50. Out-of-state (imports)	.28756	.34785	.14416	.12254	.46612	.07937	.12373
	51. All other final payments	.18728	.14967	.12320	.31539	.12389	.06263	.14641
	52. Total	1.00000	1.00000	1.00000	1.00000	1.00000	1.00000	1.00000

PROCESSING SECTORS

*Each column shows direct purchases from the sectors at the left per dollar of output by the sector at the top.

PROCESSING SECTORS

	8. Special trades contractors	9. Food & kindred products (meats and n.e.c.)	10. Food & kindred products (dairies)	11. Food & kindred products (bakeries)	12. Food & kindred products (beverages)	13. Apparel & accessories	14. Logging & sawmills	15. Furniture & other wood fabrication	16. Printing & publishing	17. Chemicals	18. Petroleum	
	0	.20491	.22451	.00670	0	0	.04799	.00016	0	.00001	0	1
	.00021	.00002	0	0	.00063	.00042	.00051	.00713	.00065	.00994	.02328	2
	.00011	0	0	0	0	0	0	0	.00026	0	0	3
	0	0	0	0	0	0	0	0	0	.00753	.07006	4
	0	0	0	0	0	0	0	0	0	.00432	.07386	5
	.00609	.00015	0	0	0	0	0	.00074	0	.00084	0	6
	0	0	0	.00010	0	0	.00128	0	0	.00159	0	7
	.00366	0	.00028	0	0	.02032	.00658	.00004	0	.00667	0	8
	.02065	.00193	.00074	0	0	0	0	0	0	.00081	0	9
	0	.07508	.01671	.00065	0	0	0	0	0	0	0	10
	0	0	.01915	0	0	0	0	0	0	0	0	11
	0	0	0	.00105	0	0	0	0	0	0	0	12
	0	0	0	0	.00736	0	0	0	0	.00011	0	13
	0	0	0	0	.00026	0	0	0	0	0	.00079	14
	.00987	0	0	0	0	0	.15534	.13416	0	0	0	15
	0	0	0	0	0	0	.00003	.00717	0	.00015	0	16
	.00051	.00262	.00091	.00147	.00812	.00395	.00032	.00209	.26199	.00121	.00124	17
	.00068	0	0	0	.00206	0	0	.00759	.00015	.15004	.04546	18
	.00282	0	0	0	0	0	.00066	0	0	.00115	.02513	19
	.00211	0	0	0	.01121	0	0	.00329	0	.00064	0	20
	.00116	.00004	0	0	0	0	.00002	0	0	.00116	0	21
	.01429	0	0	0	.00849	0	0	0	0	.00051	0	22
	.06285	0	0	0	0	0	.00102	.00977	.01759	.00204	.00150	23
	.00250	0	.00028	0	0	0	.00016	.00147	.00156	0	0	24
	.00045	0	0	0	0	0	0	0	.00037	.00104	0	25
	0	0	0	0	0	0	0	0	0	.00249	0	26
	.00008	.00233	0	0	0	0	0	0	0	0	0	27
	.00987	.00340	.00325	.00096	.00948	.00412	.00114	.00031	.01663	.00798	0	28
	.00064	.00025	.00103	.00004	.00192	0	.00006	.00039	.00133	.00032	.00029	29
	.02951	.03204	.00605	.02408	.01260	.00199	.01956	.00779	.00226	.00795	.00459	30
	0	0	0	0	0	0.	0	0	0	.00012	0	31
	.00386	.00160	.00105	.00486	.00789	.00110	.00198	.00190	.00247	.00006	0	32
	.00049	.00405	.00339	.00976	.00139	0	.00107	.00062	.00422	.00307	.00053	33
	.00907	.00415	.00063	.00415	.00036	.00055	.00371	.00244	.00138	.00060	.00589	34
	0	.00451	0	.00249	0	0	.00062	.00008	0	0	.00336	35
	.01448	.00254	.00600	.01405	.01237	.00038	.01133	.00574	.00503	.00312	.00085	36
	.00387	0	.00169	0	0	0	.00678	0	.00127	0	0	37
	.00178	0	.00059	.00029	0	0	.00901	0	.00456	.00117	0	38
	.00078	.00036	0	.00006	.00192	.00013	.00242	.00023	.00039	.00076	0	39
	.00443	.00458	.00201	.00069	.00179	.00021	.00234	.00236	.00389	.00141	.00389	40
	0	.00013	0	0	0	0	0	0	0	.00015	.00017	41
	.00733	.01698	.02485	.04200	.00706	.00021	.01165	.01546	.00519	.00739	.00372	42
	0	0	0	0	0	0	.00062	.00050	.00018	.01177	0	43
	.00449	.00225	.00933	.00117	.01111	.00339	.01923	.01267	.01310	.01020	.01574	44
	0	0	.00006	.00004	0	.00034	.00075	.00081	.00063	.00190	.01570	45
	.00290	.00097	.00205	.00590	.01214	.01739	.00613	.00395	.01258	.00548	.02069	46
	.00174	.01194	.00451	.02368	.00206	.00641	.00968	.00527	.00304	.00791	.00708	47
	.00109	.00141	.00102	.03088	.00109	.00263	.00053	.00412	.00172	.01455	.01518	48
	.00085	.00052	.00137	.00281	.00441	.00042	.00035	.00035	.00046	.00184	.00045	49
	.37406	.14500	.18391	.29629	.25052	.85575	.39824	.31219	.36112	.16863	.11835	50
	.19148	.43869	.42892	.47788	.34477	.02516	.13962	.35551	.14476	.37018	.38666	51
	.20924	.03755	.05571	.04795	.27899	.05513	.13927	.09370	.13107	.18117	.15571	52
	1.00000	1.00000	1.00000	1.00000	1.00000	1.00000	1.00000	1.00000	1.00000	1.00000	1.00000	

TABLE II
(continued)

DIRECT PURCHASES PER DOLLAR OF OUTPUT, WEST VIRGINIA, 1965*

PROCESSING SECTORS	19. Glass	20. Stone & clay products	21. Primary metal products	22. Fabricated metal products	23. Machinery (except electrical)	24. Electrical machinery & apparatus	25. Transportation equipment
1. Agriculture	0	.00071	.00038	.00003	0	0	0
2. Coal mining (underground)	.00024	.00635	.01926	.00050	.00005	0	0
3. Coal mining (strip & auger)	.00006	0	0	0	0	0	0
4. Petroleum & natural gas	0	0	.00012	0	0	0	0
5. All other mining	.01807	.06312	.00461	.00034	0	0	.00266
6. General contractors (building)	0	0	.00002	0	0	0	0
7. General contractors (non-building)	0	0	.00004	0	0	.00073	0
8. Special trades contractors	.00011	.00054	.00188	.00135	.00014	.00008	.00002
9. Food & kindred products (meats and n.e.c.)	0	0	0	0	0	0	0
10. Food & kindred products (dairies)	0	0	0	0	0	0	0
11. Food & kindred products (bakeries)	0	0	0	0	0	0	0
12. Food & kindred products (beverages)	0	0	0	0	0	0	0
13. Apparel & accessories	0	0	.00001	0	0	0	0
14. Logging & sawmills	0	.00011	.00001	0	.00027	0	0
15. Furniture & other wood fabrication	.00142	0	0	0	0	.00021	0
16. Printing & publishing	.00045	.00258	.00013	.00270	.00087	.00104	.00028
17. Chemicals	.00438	.00181	.00512	.00109	0	.01868	0
18. Petroleum	0	.02221	.00010	0	0	0	0
19. Glass	.02524	0	.00028	.00003	0	0	0
20. Stone & clay products	.00306	.01849	0	0	0	0	0
21. Primary metal products	.00270	0	.00396	.09506	.04830	.18585	.07086
22. Fabricated metal products	.00010	.01587	.00147	.00053	.01521	0	0
23. Machinery (except electrical)	0	.00020	.00044	.00014	.00004	0	0
24. Electrical machinery & apparatus	0	.00003	.00036	.00006	.00814	.00102	0
25. Transportation equipment	0	.00032	.00007	0	0	0	0
26. Instruments & related products	0	0	0	.00014	0	.00087	0
27. All other manufacturing	.04115	.00851	.00074	.00383	.00762	.00039	.00020
28. Eating & drinking establishments	0	0	.00004	.00044	.00038	.00020	.00009
29. Wholesale trade	.01048	.01078	.00445	.01158	.00895	.00495	.00225
30. Retail food stores	0	0	0	.00001	0	0	0
31. Retail gasoline service stations	.00011	.00110	.00002	.00024	.00044	.00013	.00001
32. All other retail	.00275	.00475	.00253	.00388	.00100	.00341	.00105
33. Banking	.00603	.00239	.00098	.00041	.00376	.00098	.00122
34. Other finance	0	0	.00016	.00032	0	0	0
35. Insurance agents & brokers	.01012	.00497	.00174	.00308	.01454	.00555	.00181
36. Real estate	.00025	0	0	.00309	.00023	.00231	0
37. All other finance, insurance & real estate	.00042	0	.00059	.00237	0	0	0
38. Hotels & other lodging places	.00012	.00002	.00019	.00021	.00023	.00021	.00004
39. Medical & legal services	.00050	.00220	.00114	.00072	.00036	.00128	.00120
40. Educational services	.00006	0	.00038	.00003	0	.00335	0
41. All other services	.01154	.00520	.00780	.00629	.00363	.00891	.00520
42. Railroads	0	.00503	.00835	.00020	.00728	.00335	.01952
43. Trucking & warehousing	.00366	.02982	.00844	.00239	.01628	.00687	.00073
44. All other transportation	0	.00010	.00885	.00002	.00856	.01967	0
45. Communications	.00461	.00392	.00264	.00287	.00248	.00808	.00809
46. Electric companies & systems	.01142	.01086	.00683	.00902	.00581	.02398	.00782
47. Gas companies & systems	.02734	.02469	.00192	.00494	.00171	.00868	.00467
48. Water & sanitary services	.00046	.00068	.00054	.00239	.00017	.00555	.00203
49. Households	.37172	.29481	.23445	.32398	.28267	.29403	.25876
50. Out-of-state (imports)	.22734	.26413	.56921	.42907	.43952	.25114	.48664
51. All other final payments	.21409	.19370	.09935	.08665	.12136	.13850	.12485
52. Total	1.00000	1.00000	1.00000	1.00000	1.00000	1.00000	1.00000

*Each column shows direct purchases from the sectors at the left per dollar of output by the sector at the top.

PROCESSING SECTORS

26. Instruments & related products	27. All other manufacturing	28. Eating & drinking establishments	29. Wholesale trade	30. Retail food stores	31. Retail gasoline service stations	32. All other retail	33. Banking	34. Other finance	35. Insurance agents & brokers	36. Real estate	
0	.00658	.00556	0	0	0	0	0	0	0	0	1
0	.00027	.00048	.00035	.00021	.00039	.00061	.00025	0	0	0	2
0	.00130	.00017	0	.00013	.00026	.00046	.00005	0	0	0	3
0	0	0	0	0	0	0	0	0	0	0	4
0	0	0	0	0	0	0	0	0	0	0	5
0	0	0	0	0	0	.00006	0	0	0	.07106	6
0	0	0	0	0	0	0	0	0	0	.00196	7
0	.02402	0	.00120	.00095	.00013	.00507	.00167	0	0	.03371	8
0	.00949	.03951	0	0	0	0	0	0	.00005	0	9
0	0	.02751	0	0	0	.00023	0	0	0	0	10
0	0	.02964	0	0	0	.00045	0	0	0	0	11
0	0	.00779	0	0	0	.00009	0	0	0	0	12
0	.00044	0	0	0	0	0	0	0	0	0	13
0	0	0	0	0	0	0	0	0	0	0	14
0	0	0	.00004	0	0	.00180	0	0	0	0	15
.00046	.00250	.00060	.00083	.04138	.00239	.02312	.00547	.01102	.00023	.02568	16
.04298	.00093	0	.00114	0	0	0	0	0	0	0	17
0	0	0	0	.00088	.02178	.00283	0	0	.00019	0	18
.00367	0	.00112	0	.00017	0	.00720	0	0	0	0	19
0	.00001	0	0	0	0	0	0	0	0	.00005	20
0	0	0	0	0	0	0	0	0	0	0	21
0	.02678	0	0	0	0	0	0	0	0	0	22
0	.00840	0	0	0	0	0	0	0	0	0	23
0	.00146	0	0	0	0	0	0	.00384	0	0	24
0	0	0	.00031	0	0	.00009	0	0	0	0	25
0	0	0	0	0	0	.00022	0	0	0	0	26
.00722	.00437	0	.00137	.00396	0	.00146	.00102	.00125	0	0	27
0	.00001	0	.00130	0	0	.00067	.00011	.00077	.00116	.00206	28
.00917	.00155	.05279	.01633	.00533	.01104	.00205	.00046	.00052	.00035	.00821	29
0	0	.00460	.00019	.00001	0	0	0	0	0	0	30
0	.00032	.00016	.00918	.00132	.00085	.00305	.00009	.00057	.00028	.00059	31
0	.00019	.00150	.00323	.00059	.00106	.00291	.00286	.00118	.00040	.00660	32
.00149	.00312	.00094	.00272	.00096	.00420	.00868	0	.06582	.00046	.00708	33
0	0	.00096	.00347	.00170	0	.00227	.00085	.00212	0	0	34
.00172	.00353	.00368	.00799	.01718	.01254	.02259	.00839	.00055	.00101	.00043	35
0	.00043	.00090	.00018	.04992	.00535	.02272	.00522	.00650	.00189	.06112	36
0	0	.00007	.00092	0	0	.00050	.01125	0	.08391	.00033	37
0	.00002	0	.00072	0	0	.00210	.00006	.00007	.00006	.00385	38
.00195	.00101	.00027	.00189	.00135	.00036	.00437	.00340	.00788	.00012	.00137	39
0	0	0	.00030	0	0	.00032	.00087	.00177	0	0	40
.00355	.00697	.00476	.00638	.01907	.11326	.02640	.03494	.01302	.00544	.01620	41
0	.00894	0	.00567	0	.00075	.00797	0	0	0	0	42
.00527	.00323	.00004	.01722	.00508	.02108	.00956	.00012	0	0	0	43
0	.00032	.00002	.01019	.00058	.00126	.00282	.00012	.00282	.00020	.00342	44
.00160	.00309	.00715	.00721	.01127	.01187	.00354	.01220	.01339	.00516	.01195	45
.00138	.00603	.01042	.01920	.03031	.01084	.01297	.00197	.00104	.00085	.00546	46
.00080	.00197	.01698	.01507	.01426	.00613	.00748	.00265	.00068	.00086	.00649	47
.00023	.00055	.00125	.00053	.00283	.00386	.00310	.00059	.00011	.00018	.00186	48
.33704	.24641	.39431	.60631	.55566	.47086	.48968	.54112	.57626	.20335	.50863	49
.50241	.56116	.28630	.04044	.10528	.07934	.16539	.09456	.14351	.65804	.06604	50
.07906	.06460	.10052	.21812	.12962	.22040	.15517	.26971	.14531	.03581	.15585	51
1.00000	1.00000	1.00000	1.00000	1.00000	1.00000	1.00000	1.00000	1.00000	1.00000	1.00000	52

TABLE II
(continued)

DIRECT PURCHASES
PER DOLLAR OF
OUTPUT, WEST VIRGINIA,
1965*

PROCESSING SECTORS		37. All other finance, insurance & real estate	38. Hotels & other lodging places	39. Medical & legal services	40. Educational services	41. All other services	42. Railroads
	1. Agriculture	0	.00527	.00035	0	0	0
	2. Coal mining (underground)	0	.00224	.00023	.00194	.00001	.00029
	3. Coal mining (strip & auger)	.01066	.01601	0	.00104	0	0
	4. Petroleum & natural gas	0	0	0	0	0	0
	5. All other mining	0	0	.00006	0	0	.00847
	6. General contractors (building)	0	.00155	0	.07216	0	0
	7. General contractors (non-building)	0	.00687	0	.02949	0	.00987
	8. Special trades contractors	0	.03078	.00308	.00440	.00051	.01051
	9. Food & kindred products (meats and n.e.c.)	0	0	.01853	.00010	.00004	0
	10. Food & kindred products (dairies)	0	0	.00693	0	0	0
	11. Food & kindred products (bakeries)	0	0	.00075	.00062	.00007	0
	12. Food & kindred products (beverages)	0	0	.00038	.00202	0	0
	13. Apparel & accessories	0	0	.00458	0	0	0
	14. Logging & sawmills	0	0	.00002	.00026	0	0
	15. Furniture & other wood fabrication	0	0	0	0	0	0
	16. Printing & publishing	.00397	.00147	.00065	.00473	.00489	.00007
	17. Chemicals	0	0	.00384	.00029	.00241	0
	18. Petroleum	0	0	0	0	.00095	.00773
	19. Glass	0	0	.00057	.00052	0	0
	20. Stone & clay products	0	0	0	.00072	.00236	0
	21. Primary metal products	0	0	0	0	0	.00503
	22. Fabricated metal products	0	0	0	0	.00160	0
	23. Machinery (except electrical)	0	0	0	0	0	.00586
	24. Electrical machinery & apparatus	0	0	.00010	0	.00053	.00006
	25. Transportation equipment	0	0	0	0	0	.00695
	26. Instruments & related products	0	0	.00129	.00009	0	0
	27. All other manufacturing	0	.00024	.00849	.00013	.00247	0
	28. Eating & drinking establishments	.00039	0	.00015	.00340	0	0
	29. Wholesale trade	.00008	.01487	.00944	.01672	.01724	.00256
	30. Retail food stores	0	0	.00116	0	0	0
	31. Retail gasoline service stations	.00010	.00477	.00075	.00019	.00173	.00001
	32. All other retail	.00050	.00684	.00630	.00737	.01079	.00051
	33. Banking	.00163	.03641	.00614	.00067	.00063	0
	34. Other finance	0	0	.00282	0	.00061	0
	35. Insurance agents & brokers	.00155	.02406	.00932	.00629	.01702	.02308
	36. Real estate	.00072	.02801	.00229	.00096	.00201	0
	37. All other finance, insurance & real estate	0	0	.00050	.00187	.00040	0
	38. Hotels & other lodging places	.00039	0	.00093	.00057	.00028	.00020
	39. Medical & legal services	.42749	.00477	.02328	.00151	.00296	.00335
	40. Educational services	0	0	.00079	0	.00017	0
	41. All other services	.01936	.07190	.03519	.01026	.03186	.00179
	42. Railroads	0	0	.00089	.00033	.00117	.03516
	43. Trucking & warehousing	0	.00055	.00213	.00167	.00321	.00715
	44. All other transportation	.00068	0	.00002	.00004	0	.00047
	45. Communications	.00521	.04900	.00857	.01095	.00525	.00502
	46. Electric companies & systems	.00291	.05068	.00355	.00894	.00347	.00385
	47. Gas companies & systems	.00256	.01611	.00491	.00612	.00567	.00080
	48. Water & sanitary services	0	.00835	.00180	.00227	.00104	.00012
	49. Households	.34714	.30814	.59066	.65397	.44416	.42455
	50. Out-of-state (imports)	.13327	.12671	.12702	.09957	.32154	.22295
	51. All other final payments	.04139	.18440	.11154	.04782	.11295	.21359
	52. Total	1.00000	1.00000	1.00000	1.00000	1.00000	1.00000

*Each column shows direct purchases from the sectors at the left per dollar of output by the sector at the top.

PROCESSING SECTORS

43. Trucking & warehousing	44. All other transportation	45. Communications	46. Electric companies & systems	47. Gas companies & systems	48. Water & sanitary services	
0	0	0	0	0	0	1
.00019	0	.00021	.13177	.00299	.00116	2
0	0	0	.05387	0	0	3
0	.03250	0	0	.10407	0	4
0	0	0	0	0	.02760	5
0	0	0	0	0	0	6
.00268	0	.00699	0	0	.07033	7
.00289	.00459	0	.00001	0	0	8
0	0	0	0	0	0	9
0	0	0	0	0	0	10
0	0	0	0	0	0	11
0	0	0	0	0	0	12
0	0	0	0	0	0	13
.00094	0	0	0	0	0	14
0	.00295	0	.00006	0	0	15
.00472	.00026	.00197	.00285	.00051	.00178	16
0	0	0	0	0	.01350	17
.00106	.00418	.00410	.00527	.00024	.00073	18
0	0	0	0	0	0	19
.00021	0	.00175	.00260	.00130	.00555	20
.00186	.00529	.00028	.00046	.00007	.00010	21
0	.00700	0	.00624	.00026	.01139	22
0	.00233	0	0	0	0	23
0	0	.00150	.00039	0	.00677	24
0	0	0	0	0	0	25
0	.00009	0	0	0	0	26
0	.01612	0	.00001	.00007	0	27
.00085	.00009	.00070	.00062	.00076	.00023	28
.05333	.00271	.00035	.00477	.00119	.01265	29
0	0	0	0	0	0	30
.00173	.00130	.00016	.00013	.00089	.00244	31
.00138	.00043	.00162	.00060	.00046	.05772	32
.00304	.00888	.00094	.00006	.00162	.00010	33
0	.00167	0	0	.00009	0	34
.02404	.00207	.00071	.00144	.00031	.00294	35
.00078	.00034	.00118	.00115	.00116	0	36
0	0	.00292	.00189	.00063	.00086	37
.00092	.00009	.00019	.00058	.00055	0	38
.00261	.00038	.00177	.00070	.00026	.00043	39
0	0	0	.00003	.00002	0	40
.00563	.01514	.02253	.00432	.00137	.00076	41
.00294	.00053	.02125	.02649	.00185	.00924	42
.00178	.00124	.00697	.01382	.00393	.00168	43
.00040	.08493	.00118	.00433	.01140	.00016	44
.00206	.00732	.00344	.00223	.00065	.01195	45
.00431	.00256	.00328	.06393	.00104	.04646	46
.00406	.00141	.00255	.00116	.00500	.00116	47
.00037	.00023	.00004	.00011	.00011	.01592	48
.41333	.24779	.35172	.21618	.09537	.27359	49
.28016	.37672	.16386	.13996	.66524	.25021	50
.18173	.16886	.39584	.31197	.09659	.17259	51
1.00000	1.00000	1.00000	1.00000	1.00000	1.00000	52

PROCESSING SECTORS

TABLE III

DIRECT AND INDIRECT REQUIREMENT PER DOLLAR OF DELIVERY TO FINAL DEMAND, WEST VIRGINIA 1965*

		1. Agriculture	2. Coal mining (underground)	3. Coal mining (strip & auger)	4. Petroleum & natural gas	5. All other mining	6. General contractors (building)
1.	Agriculture	1.07762	.00073	.00031	.00023	.00684	.00114
2.	Coal mining (underground)	.00185	1.01431	.20328	.00281	.00099	.00327
3.	Coal mining (strip & auger)	.00067	.01616	1.29323	.00062	.00066	.00081
4.	Petroleum & natural gas	.00029	.00025	.00021	1.04349	.00068	.00143
5.	All other mining	.01149	.00140	.00095	.00835	1.04355	.02248
6.	General contractors (building)	.00078	.00004	.00163	.00009	.00007	1.03494
7.	General contractors (non-building)	.00015	.00007	.00024	.00014	.00011	.03407
8.	Special trades contractors	.00097	.00476	.00241	.00233	.00550	.28042
9.	Food & kindred products (meats and n.e.c.)	.00287	.00121	.00049	.00050	.00012	.00059
10.	Food & kindred products (dairies)	.00003	.00002	.00012	.00017	.00003	.00007
11.	Food & kindred products (bakeries)	.00001	.00001	.00007	.00003	.00001	.00004
12.	Food & kindred products (beverages)	0	0	.00002	.00001	0	.00001
13.	Apparel & accessories	.00001	.00001	.00004	.00011	.00002	.00004
14.	Logging & sawmills	.01184	.00848	.00273	.00031	.01032	.00869
15.	Furniture & other wood fabrication	.00068	.00374	.00077	.00005	.00134	.00872
16.	Printing & publishing	.00143	.00144	.00173	.00456	.00115	.00560
17.	Chemicals	.00045	.00064	.00037	.00391	.00538	.00322
18.	Petroleum	.00054	.00224	.00066	.06717	.00717	.01054
19.	Glass	.00005	.00005	.00004	.00009	.00007	.00069
20.	Stone & clay products	.00838	.00404	.00110	.00018	.00024	.10567
21.	Primary metal products	.00175	.00040	.00077	.00104	.00135	.03211
22.	Fabricated metal products	.00848	.00152	.00331	.00068	.00921	.06873
23.	Machinery (except electrical)	.00011	.00062	.00110	.00740	.00681	.00202
24.	Electrical machinery & apparatus	.00005	.00004	.00139	.00012	.00008	.00123
25.	Transportation equipment	.00003	.00001	.00004	.00003	.00002	.00007
26.	Instruments & related products	.00001	.00001	.00004	.00004	.00002	.00005
27.	All other manufacturing	.00053	.00119	.00059	.00059	.00253	.04252
28.	Eating & drinking establishments	.00015	.00009	.00213	.00010	.00008	.00117
29.	Wholesale trade	.05225	.01430	.02971	.01347	.02553	.03148
30.	Retail food stores	.00001	.00001	.00003	.00003	.00001	.00002
31.	Retail gasoline service stations	.00283	.00029	.00087	.00167	.00159	.00218
32.	All other retail	.00578	.00316	.00346	.00968	.00622	.00444
33.	Banking	.01874	.00048	.01471	.00191	.00364	.01172
34.	Other finance	.00227	.00013	.00307	.00207	.00110	.00065
35.	Insurance agents & brokers	.02161	.00792	.01209	.01396	.01215	.01392
36.	Real estate	.01053	.00053	.02208	.00116	.00081	.00852
37.	All other finance, insurance & real estate	.00228	.00326	.00180	.00132	.00233	.00224
38.	Hotels & other lodging places	.00052	.00008	.00080	.00009	.00039	.00057
39.	Medical & legal services	.00311	.00229	.00802	.02389	.00339	.00453
40.	Educational services	.00005	.00005	.00005	.00004	.00002	.00005
41.	All other services	.03856	.00502	.03880	.04205	.00699	.01465
42.	Railroads	.00145	.00125	.00454	.00311	.00180	.00285
43.	Trucking & warehousing	.00562	.00235	.00685	.00363	.00755	.00799
44.	All other transportation	.00112	.00047	.00059	.00152	.00058	.00116
45.	Communications	.00553	.00155	.00480	.00538	.00244	.00730
46.	Electric companies & systems	.00847	.02649	.00906	.00788	.00446	.00774
47.	Gas companies & systems	.00193	.00058	.00127	.00195	.00087	.00548
48.	Water & sanitary services	.00021	.00006	.00034	.00055	.00012	.03928
49.	Total	1.31407	1.13370	1.68267	1.28049	1.18632	1.83711

*Each column shows the direct and indirect requirements from the sectors at the left to support a delivery of one dollar to final demand by the sector at the top.

PROCESSING SECTORS

	7. General contractors (non-building)	8. Special trades contractors	9. Food & kindred products (meats and n.e.c.)	10. Food & kindred products (dairies)	11. Food & kindred products (bakeries)	12. Food & kindred products (beverages)	13. Apparel & accessories	14. Logging & sawmills	15. Furniture & other wood fabrication	16. Printing & publishing	17. Chemicals
1	.00062	.00085	.23883	.25081	.00742	.00018	.00006	.06133	.00851	.00032	.00043
2	.00516	.00145	.00264	.00129	.00401	.00142	.00151	.00279	.00875	.00190	.01366
3	.00055	.00054	.00125	.00059	.00196	.00035	.00054	.00125	.00077	.00102	.00105
4	.01143	.00059	.00036	.00026	.00354	.00029	.00035	.00033	.00070	.00039	.01145
5	.05270	.00727	.00280	.00278	.00028	.00048	.00020	.00095	.00033	.00012	.00607
6	.00024	.00036	.00021	.00034	.00016	.00003	.00001	.00071	.00089	.00019	.00107
7	1.02924	.00404	.00013	.00051	.00030	.00050	.00026	.00185	.00041	.00027	.00242
8	.03560	1.02217	.00263	.00135	.00030	.00050	.02093	.00889	.00171	.00092	.00906
9	.00023	.00028	1.08198	.01923	.00079	.00025	.00006	.00036	.00016	.00050	.00124
10	.00008	.00007	.00006	1.01958	.00002	.00008	0	.00007	.00004	.00012	.00004
11	.00005	.00003	.00002	.00004	1.00106	.00006	0	.00001	.00002	.00007	.00002
12	.00001	.00001	.00001	.00001	0	1.00743	0	0	.00001	.00002	.00001
13	.00003	.00004	.00003	.00002	.00001	.00028	1.00000	.00004	.00002	.00005	.00015
14	.00290	.01207	.00268	.00279	.00013	.00004	.00027	1.18476	.16020	.00006	.00034
15	.00152	.00003	.00017	.00017	.00005	.00003	.00001	.00011	1.00728	.00003	.00027
16	.00307	.00154	.00474	.00218	.00299	.01150	.00553	.00151	.00347	1.35578	.00251
17	.03633	.00155	.00040	.00027	.00028	.00274	.00007	.00030	.00919	.00043	1.17709
18	.13855	.00380	.00035	.00034	.00068	.00040	.00028	.00137	.00044	.00032	.00285
19	.00014	.00223	.00007	.00005	.00008	.01161	.00005	.00004	.00343	.00006	.00084
20	.06075	.00156	.00202	.00210	.00036	.00017	.00011	.00079	.00033	.00013	.00182
21	.01201	.02117	.00051	.00051	.00012	.00875	.00049	.00054	.00121	.00266	.00152
22	.01026	.06488	.00237	.00229	.00048	.00064	.00160	.00251	.01047	.02466	.00359
23	.01305	.00278	.00008	.00036	.00006	.00013	.00011	.00028	.00156	.00234	.00037
24	.00023	.00054	.00007	.00005	.00008	.00008	.00005	.00005	.00006	.00061	.00129
25	.00007	.00002	.00002	.00001	.00002	.00001	.00001	.00002	.00001	.00001	.00011
26	.00015	.00011	.00253	.00005	.00001	.00001	0	.00001	.00003	.00002	.00295
27	.00213	.01077	.00412	.00369	.00126	.01039	.00447	.00172	.00102	.02293	.00986
28	.00147	.00078	.00039	.00114	.00016	.00202	.00005	.00021	.00048	.00189	.00046
29	.02429	.03302	.04776	.02033	.02635	.01442	.00307	.02888	.01349	.00511	.01167
30	.00004	.00002	.00002	.00001	.00001	.00001	0	.00002	.00001	.00002	.00015
31	.00147	.00438	.00279	.00193	.00531	.00820	.00125	.00291	.00248	.00352	.00035
32	.00375	.00135	.00617	.00538	.01075	.00205	.00015	.00216	.00137	.00618	.00425
33	.00754	.00982	.00927	.00528	.00483	.00078	.00084	.00610	.00352	.00230	.00119
34	.00317	.00022	.00556	.00068	.00269	.00008	.00002	.00102	.00028	.00008	.00012
35	.01647	.01638	.00867	.01221	.01587	.01362	.00099	.01630	.00907	.00811	.00542
36	.00274	.00480	.00268	.00452	.00068	.00029	.00018	.00956	.00151	.00227	.00036
37	.00202	.00367	.00100	.00180	.00185	.00129	.00024	.01224	.00238	.00703	.00200
38	.00171	.00092	.00058	.00018	.00017	.00199	.00016	.00301	.00069	.00060	.00096
39	.00500	.00661	.00628	.00365	.00198	.00266	.00053	.00865	.00414	.00873	.00315
40	.00005	.00004	.00019	.00003	.00003	.00002	0	.00003	.00002	.00022	.00021
41	.05264	.01080	.02897	.03629	.04583	.00970	.00124	.01887	.01982	.00960	.01088
42	.00664	.00086	.00113	.00076	.00133	.00081	.00069	.00173	.00134	.00124	.01523
43	.03408	.00640	.00485	.01137	.00269	.01222	.00395	.02417	.01673	.01852	.01313
44	.00426	.00079	.00081	.00051	.00095	.00036	.00052	.00152	.00138	.00121	.00300
45	.00896	.00429	.00309	.00386	.00694	.01315	.01774	.00867	.00571	.01778	.00724
46	.00496	.00413	.01685	.00772	.02675	.00356	.00721	.01402	.00851	.00552	.01137
47	.00854	.00250	.00282	.00199	.03201	.00208	.00285	.00167	.00507	.00302	.01785
48	.00041	.00118	.00071	.00156	.00301	.00464	.00048	.00060	.00057	.00080	.00234
49	1.60731	1.27369	1.50164	1.43284	1.21664	1.15229	1.07909	1.43491	1.31958	1.51963	1.36340

TABLE III
(continued)

DIRECT AND INDIRECT REQUIREMENT PER DOLLAR OF DELIVERY TO FINAL DEMAND, WEST VIRGINIA 1965*

PROCESSING SECTORS	18. Petroleum	19. Glass	20. Stone & clay products	21. Primary metal products	22. Fabricated metal products	23. Machinery (except electrical)
1. Agriculture	.00067	.00056	.00136	.00049	.00014	.00014
2. Coal mining (underground)	.02643	.00252	.00926	.02085	.00404	.00220
3. Coal mining (strip & auger)	.00113	.00116	.00113	.00090	.00089	.00060
4. Petroleum & natural gas	.07795	.00323	.00469	.00080	.00069	.00064
5. All other mining	.08007	.01970	.06912	.00507	.00098	.00039
6. General contractors (building)	.00008	.00006	.00004	.00007	.00027	.00004
7. General contractors (non-building)	.00039	.00013	.00027	.00026	.00027	.00020
8. Special trades contractors	.00136	.00146	.00152	.00237	.00200	.00075
9. Food & kindred products (meats and n.e.c.)	.00024	.00048	.00019	.00008	.00012	.00013
10. Food & kindred products (dairies)	.00006	.00001	.00003	.00002	.00003	.00002
11. Food & kindred products (bakeries)	.00002	.00001	.00001	.00001	.00002	.00002
12. Food & kindred products (beverages)	.00001	0	0	0	0	0
13. Apparel & accessories	.00004	.00003	.00002	.00002	.00001	.00001
14. Logging & sawmills	.00203	.00048	.00097	.00029	.00008	.00037
15. Furniture & other wood fabrication	.00027	.00151	.00014	.00012	.00003	.00004
16. Printing & publishing	.00271	.00126	.00437	.00053	.00417	.00161
17. Chemicals	.05569	.00558	.00393	.00618	.00199	.00059
18. Petroleum	1.03178	.00060	.02429	.00048	.00025	.00030
19. Glass	.00006	1.02593	.00005	.00032	.00010	.00003
20. Stone & clay products	.00034	.00336	1.01903	.00018	.00014	.00007
21. Primary metal products	.00059	.00305	.00188	1.00444	.09565	.05169
22. Fabricated metal products	.00276	.00176	.01737	.00191	1.00114	.01574
23. Machinery (except electrical)	.00116	.00053	.00083	.00059	.00026	1.00023
24. Electrical machinery & apparatus	.00014	.00010	.00008	.00040	.00014	.00820
25. Transportation equipment	.00002	.00001	.00037	.00014	.00002	.00007
26. Instruments & related products	.00015	.00002	.00002	.00002	.00015	.00001
27. All other manufacturing	.00114	.04266	.00917	.00110	.00414	.00801
28. Eating & drinking establishments	.00040	.00060	.00012	.00008	.00051	.00046
29. Wholesale trade	.00992	.01245	.01557	.00636	.01304	.01091
30. Retail food stores	.00002	0	.00001	0	.00002	.00001
31. Retail gasoline service stations	.00042	.00037	.00150	.00016	.00044	.00063
32. All other retail	.00228	.00335	.00574	.00289	.00454	.00145
33. Banking	.00710	.00663	.00320	.00127	.00077	.00411
34. Other finance	.00378	.00011	.00025	.00022	.00042	.00009
35. Insurance agents & brokers	.00409	.01160	.00756	.00284	.00395	.01576
36. Real estate	.00039	.00060	.00044	.00019	.00353	.00050
37. All other finance, insurance & real estate	.00079	.00161	.00092	.00096	.00286	.00150
38. Hotels & other lodging places	.00014	.00019	.00014	.00024	.00028	.00029
39. Medical & legal services	.00667	.00158	.00334	.00180	.00228	.00131
40. Educational services	.00004	.00008	.00002	.00039	.00008	.00006
41. All other services	.00980	.01389	.00769	.00904	.00819	.00542
42. Railroads	.00198	.00124	.00638	.00922	.00167	.00854
43. Trucking & warehousing	.01827	.00495	.03227	.00909	.00388	.01738
44. All other transportation	.01827	.00067	.00119	.00991	.00127	.01026
45. Communications	.02278	.00547	.00531	.00312	.00361	.00328
46. Electric companies & systems	.01039	.01362	.01356	.00839	.01113	.00758
47. Gas companies & systems	.01708	.02888	.02639	.00235	.00560	.00238
48. Water & sanitary services	.00068	.00059	.00084	.00061	.00255	.00034
49. Total	1.42255	1.22416	1.30256	1.11677	1.18832	1.18433

*Each column shows the direct and indirect requirements from the sectors at the left to support a delivery of one dollar to final demand by the sector at the top.

PROCESSING SECTORS

24. Electrical machinery & apparatus	25. Transportation equipment	26. Instruments & related products	27. All other manufacturing	28. Eating & drinking establishments	29. Wholesale trade	30. Retail food stores	31. Retail gasoline service stations	32. All other retail	33. Banking	34. Other finance	
.00014	.00007	.00011	.00944	.02256	.00008	.00009	.00004	.00019	.00008	.00010	1
.00805	.00278	.00088	.00176	.00272	.00358	.00526	.00296	.00311	.00071	.00033	2
.00211	.00070	.00020	.00224	.00128	.00160	.00265	.00132	.00180	.00044	.00016	3
.00214	.00062	.00063	.00032	.00214	.00217	.00181	.00259	.00130	.00036	.00026	4
.00141	.00344	.00035	.00045	.00038	.00019	.00037	.00198	.00071	.00008	.00007	5
.00049	.00001	.00005	.00007	.00013	.00007	.00394	.00046	.00191	.00050	.00069	6
.00152	.00045	.00015	.00029	.00021	.00025	.00061	.00051	.00057	.00021	.00023	7
.00125	.00049	.00063	.02495	.00037	.00162	.00415	.00075	.00696	.00218	.00070	8
.00010	.00005	.00018	.01038	.04335	.00015	.00013	.00006	.00020	.00021	.00024	9
.00003	.00001	.00002	.00001	.02806	.00006	.00003	.00002	.00031	.00007	.00009	10
.00002	.00001	0	0	.02968	.00005	.00001	.00001	.00049	.00002	.00004	11
.00001	0	0	0	.00785	.00001	0	0	.00010	.00001	.00001	12
.00002	.00001	.00002	.00045	.00001	.00001	.00002	.00001	.00003	.00004	.00004	13
.00017	.00007	.00003	.00042	.00028	.00009	.00013	.00011	.00044	.00004	.00002	14
.00033	.00002	.00002	.00002	.00004	.00010	.00006	.00003	.00187	.00001	.00002	15
.00213	.00060	.00087	.00381	.00185	.00175	.05850	.00472	.03289	.00814	.01599	16
.02343	.00055	.05066	.00130	.00020	.00147	.00027	.00169	.00047	.00019	.00021	17
.00082	.00042	.00017	.00031	.00036	.00070	.00149	.02294	.00343	.00020	.00019	18
.00011	.00004	.00380	.00006	.00127	.00004	.00020	.00003	.00745	.00004	.00002	19
.00037	.00012	.00012	.00020	.00033	.00016	.00066	.00047	.00043	.00020	.00016	20
.18717	.07134	.00013	.00391	.00018	.00026	.00041	.00019	.00043	.00011	.00083	21
.00098	.00030	.00041	.02887	.00040	.00045	.00194	.00057	.00144	.00044	.00048	22
.00024	.00020	.00008	.00858	.00005	.00011	.00019	.00007	.00018	.00004	.00006	23
1.00119	.00007	.00008	.00157	.00004	.00005	.00011	.00013	.00009	.00006	.00390	24
.00006	1.00016	.00001	.00007	.00003	.00036	.00001	.00002	.00016	0	0	25
.00093	0	1.00013	.00004	.00010	.00001	.00001	.00001	.00023	.00001	.00002	26
.00128	.00035	.00790	1.00499	.00061	.00173	.00530	.00051	.00270	.00139	.00181	27
.00031	.00012	.00005	.00008	1.00018	.00140	.00028	.00012	.00085	.00017	.00084	28
.00768	.00321	.01032	.00417	.05777	1.01840	.00750	.00151	.00439	.00151	.00129	29
.00001	0	.00001	0	.00461	.00020	1.00002	.00001	.00001	.00001	.00001	30
.00034	.00008	.00013	.00055	.00112	.00948	.00169	1.00130	.00037	.00023	.00070	31
.00468	.00154	.00033	.00066	.00267	.00362	.00181	.00286	1.00399	.00351	.00183	32
.00165	.00140	.00167	.00374	.00206	.00339	.00184	.00473	.00956	1.00032	.06622	33
.00014	.00005	.00005	.00011	.00151	.00360	.00178	.00023	.00238	.00092	1.00224	34
.00711	.00280	.00237	.00502	.00592	.00939	.01856	.01563	.02450	.00940	.00176	35
.00279	.00012	.00007	.00089	.00169	.00058	.05362	.00621	.02477	.00585	.00750	36
.00091	.00036	.00031	.00064	.00076	.00187	.00202	.00154	.00293	.01216	.00104	37
.00034	.00009	.00006	.00008	.00013	.00079	.00029	.00012	.00228	.00013	.00014	38
.00224	.00165	.00231	.00168	.00123	.00308	.00287	.00177	.00630	.00904	.00896	39
.00343	.00003	.00002	.00002	.00003	.00033	.00002	.00003	.00035	.00089	.00186	40
.01255	.00660	.00459	.00887	.00990	.00921	.02244	.11868	.03013	.03744	.01713	41
.00662	.02140	.00091	.00981	.00105	.00696	.00148	.00187	.00904	.00049	.00049	42
.00968	.00187	.00614	.00412	.00213	.01843	.00689	.02266	.01089	.00062	.00056	43
.02379	.00087	.00027	.00066	.00103	.01173	.00138	.00218	.00355	.00028	.00330	44
.00951	.00864	.00215	.00373	.00843	.00809	.01335	.01365	.00533	.01291	.01490	45
.02832	.00936	.00236	.00747	.01446	.02158	.03374	.01317	.01522	.00263	.00177	46
.00993	.00504	.00192	.00245	.01926	.01585	.01529	.00773	.00858	.00314	.00125	47
.00589	.00213	.00036	.00070	.00155	.00066	.00323	.00414	.00342	.00072	.00027	48
1.37439	1.15021	1.10400	1.15996	1.28195	1.16575	1.27843	1.27590	1.24171	1.11813	1.16067	49

TABLE III
(continued)

DIRECT AND INDIRECT REQUIREMENT PER DOLLAR OF DELIVERY TO FINAL DEMAND, WEST VIRGINIA 1965*

PROCESSING SECTORS		35. Insurance agents & brokers	36. Real estate	37. All other finance, insurance & real estate	38. Hotels & other lodging places	39. Medical & legal services	40. Educational services
1.	Agriculture	.00029	.00022	.00293	.00579	.00682	.00026
2.	Coal mining (underground)	.00042	.00146	.00315	.01389	.00112	.00416
3.	Coal mining (strip & auger)	.00127	.00072	.01423	.02485	.00045	.00226
4.	Petroleum & natural gas	.00019	.00114	.00064	.00213	.00071	.00122
5.	All other mining	.00005	.00220	.00017	.00122	.00033	.00340
6.	General contractors (building)	.00017	.07840	.00021	.00392	.00030	.07479
7.	General contractors (non-building)	.00008	.00517	.00019	.00844	.00032	.03312
8.	Special trades contractors	.00028	.05832	.00183	.03422	.00399	.02603
9.	Food & kindred products (meats and n.e.c.)	.00086	.00021	.00892	.00021	.02080	.00037
10.	Food & kindred products (dairies)	.00030	.00009	.00312	.00006	.00725	.00013
11.	Food & kindred products (bakeries)	.00007	.00008	.00035	.00002	.00078	.00073
12.	Food & kindred products (beverages)	.00002	.00002	.00017	.00001	.00040	.00207
13.	Apparel & accessories	.00017	.00001	.00201	.00003	.00470	.00002
14.	Logging & sawmills	.00001	.00112	.00011	.00065	.00017	.00112
15.	Furniture & other wood fabrication	.00001	.00070	.00003	.00013	.00003	.00071
16.	Printing & publishing	.00101	.03813	.00647	.00479	.00195	.00747
17.	Chemicals	.00022	.00053	.00218	.00085	.00492	.00181
18.	Petroleum	.00027	.00152	.00024	.00223	.00029	.00515
19.	Glass	.00003	.00020	.00030	.00015	.00068	.00069
20.	Stone & clay products	.00007	.00838	.00021	.00154	.00026	.01031
21.	Primary metal products	.00003	.00336	.00014	.00110	.00022	.00286
22.	Fabricated metal products	.00009	.00840	.00053	.00325	.00074	.00585
23.	Machinery (except electrical)	.00001	.00037	.00008	.00028	.00011	.00058
24.	Electrical machinery & apparatus	.00002	.00018	.00012	.00026	.00019	.00015
25.	Transportation equipment	0	.00001	.00001	.00003	.00002	.00002
26.	Instruments & related products	.00005	.00001	.00059	.00002	.00138	.00010
27.	All other manufacturing	.00038	.00443	.00410	.00123	.00918	.00360
28.	Eating & drinking establishments	.00122	.00241	.00054	.00031	.00024	.00361
29.	Wholesale trade	.00110	.01343	.00611	.01996	.01222	.02107
30.	Retail food stores	.00005	.00002	.00051	.00001	.00119	.00003
31.	Retail gasoline service stations	.00036	.00125	.00065	.00540	.00109	.00070
32.	All other retail	.00085	.00810	.00396	.00906	.00736	.00830
33.	Banking	.00091	.00923	.00487	.03783	.00703	.00207
34.	Other finance	.00013	.00016	.00138	.00030	.00311	.00025
35.	Insurance agents & brokers	1.00176	.00325	.00692	.02773	.01117	.00873
36.	Real estate	.00227	1.06645	.00245	.03140	.00309	.00210
37.	All other finance, insurance & real estate	.08412	.00114	1.00097	.00323	.00164	.00285
38.	Hotels & other lodging places	.00015	.00425	.00086	1.00000	.00104	.00073
39.	Medical & legal services	.03703	.00283	.43851	.00738	1.02503	.00343
40.	Educational services	.00003	.00003	.00037	.00007	.00084	1.00002
41.	All other services	.00908	.02129	.03772	.08102	.03955	.01457
42.	Railroads	.00025	.00098	.00103	.00330	.00169	.00155
43.	Trucking & warehousing	.00026	.00201	.00168	.00337	.00314	.00418
44.	All other transportation	.00035	.00443	.00098	.00103	.00035	.00065
45.	Communications	.00611	.01465	.00974	.05159	.00979	.01241
46.	Electric companies & systems	.00149	.00801	.00568	.05672	.00529	.01129
47.	Gas companies & systems	.00142	.00808	.00530	.01787	.00589	.00747
48.	Water & sanitary services	.00029	.00516	.00092	.00894	.00205	.00525
49.	Total	1.15559	1.39252	1.58418	1.47810	1.21087	1.30022

*Each column shows the direct and indirect requirements from the sectors at the left to support a delivery of one dollar to final demand by the sector at the top.

PROCESSING SECTORS

41. All other services	42. Railroads	43. Trucking & warehousing	44. All other transportation	45. Communications	46. Electric companies & systems	47. Gas companies & systems	48. Water & sanitary services	
.00008	.00012	.00012	.00022	.00005	.00017	.00006	.00029	1
.00084	.00140	.00122	.00094	.00100	.15482	.00358	.00954	2
.00039	.00040	.00050	.00033	.00035	.07680	.00023	.00391	3
.00084	.00090	.00073	.03765	.00079	.00088	.10961	.00141	4
.00036	.01050	.00035	.00078	.00107	.00123	.00103	.03381	5
.00021	.00002	.00008	.00005	.00011	.00021	.00011	.00017	6
.00019	.01066	.00289	.00014	.00750	.00042	.00008	.07386	7
.00094	.01166	.00332	.00579	.00067	.00137	.00047	.00350	8
.00017	.00011	.00013	.00023	.00011	.00028	.00011	.00010	9
.00004	.00004	.00006	.00002	.00005	.00004	.00004	.00004	10
.00008	.00001	.00003	.00001	.00003	.00003	.00003	.00004	11
0	0	.00001	0	.00001	.00001	.00001	.00001	12
.00002	.00002	.00002	.00002	.00002	.00001	.00001	.00001	13
.00003	.00029	.00118	.00062	.00006	.00141	.00008	.00062	14
.00003	.00004	.00002	.00326	.00003	.00066	.00006	.00030	15
.00749	.00036	.00675	.00102	.00311	.00474	.00134	.00509	16
.00310	.00097	.00031	.00059	.00064	.00053	.00046	.01925	17
.00131	.00989	.00170	.00727	.00558	.00661	.00746	.01181	18
.00009	.00004	.00003	.00004	.00002	.00002	.00002	.00047	19
.00257	.00069	.00045	.00011	.00232	.00353	.00139	.01036	20
.00036	.00648	.00204	.00691	.00085	.00158	.00032	.00361	21
.00204	.00108	.00044	.00869	.00029	.00733	.00051	.01324	22
.00006	.00632	.00009	.00300	.00037	.00037	.00083	.00124	23
.00059	.00014	.00002	.00009	.00152	.00052	.00002	.00698	24
.00002	.00721	.00004	.00001	.00016	.00021	.00002	.00010	25
.00002	.00001	.00001	.00011	.00001	.00001	.00001	.00008	26
.00286	.00030	.00032	.01794	.00022	.00049	.00039	.00074	27
.00009	.00008	.00099	.00014	.00074	.00085	.00079	.00049	28
.01874	.00431	.05501	.00449	.00168	.01026	.00311	.01701	29
.00001	.00001	.00002	0	.00001	.00001	.00001	.00001	30
.00206	.00016	.00233	.00161	.00027	.00036	.00112	.00301	31
.01149	.00081	.00181	.00120	.00205	.00154	.00159	.05970	32
.00103	.00043	.00344	.01015	.00118	.00124	.00203	.00152	33
.00075	.00011	.00023	.00197	.00023	.00027	.00034	.00048	34
.01841	.02492	.02515	.00362	.00215	.00475	.00212	.00690	35
.00263	.00022	.00110	.00068	.00144	.00278	.00145	.00193	36
.00207	.00218	.00228	.00052	.00290	.00290	.00088	.00183	37
.00036	.00026	.00100	.00014	.00025	.00072	.00058	.00034	38
.00426	.00477	.00396	.00173	.00350	.00285	.00317	.00217	39
.00020	.00001	.00003	.00002	.00002	.00005	.00003	.00006	40
1.03441	.00349	.00751	.01996	.02439	.00854	.00646	.00818	41
.00185	1.03711	.00371	.00133	.02240	.03001	.00236	.01291	42
.00424	.00843	1.00327	.00216	.00783	.01623	.00454	.00677	43
.00043	.00095	.00123	1.09317	.00155	.00543	.01273	.00142	44
.00610	.00594	.00306	.00884	1.00409	.00354	.00149	.01391	45
.00478	.00489	.00613	.00394	.00406	1.07324	.00225	.05308	46
.00656	.00133	.00520	.00209	.00307	.00192	1.00541	.00326	47
.00120	.00020	.00047	.00036	.00012	.00022	.00021	1.01655	48
1.14636	1.17024	1.15077	1.25396	1.11081	1.43195	1.18093	1.41209	49

TABLE IV

DIRECT PURCHASES PER DOLLAR OF OUTPUT, WEST VIRGINIA, PROJECTED TO 1975*

PROCESSING SECTORS

	1. Agriculture	2. Coal mining (underground)	3. Coal mining (strip & auger)	4. Petroleum & natural gas	5. All other mining	6. General contractors (building)
1. Agriculture	.07072	0	0	0	.00556	0
2. Coal mining (underground)	.00018	.00955	.17124	0	0	.00026
3. Coal mining (strip & auger)	0	.00893	.23526	0	.00021	.00005
4. Petroleum & natural gas	0	0	0	.04187	0	0
5. All other mining	.00844	.00084	.00042	.00099	.04105	.00944
6. General contractors (building)	0	0	0	0	0	.03718
7. General contractors (non-building)	0	0	0	0	0	.02420
8. Special trades contractors	0	.00442	.00004	.00181	.02055	.28651
9. Food & kindred products (meats and n.e.c.)	.00298	.00104	0	0	0	0
10. Food & kindred products (dairies)	0	0	0	0	0	0
11. Food & kindred products (bakeries)	0	0	0	0	0	0
12. Food & kindred products (beverages)	0	0	0	0	0	0
13. Apparel & accessories	0	0	0	0	0	0
14. Logging & sawmills	.00911	.00648	.00095	.00008	.00805	.00602
15. Furniture & other wood fabrication	.00058	.00366	0	0	.00125	.01368
16. Printing & publishing	.00013	.00079	.00001	.00417	.00382	.00564
17. Chemicals	.00010	.00034	0	0	.01626	0
18. Petroleum	0	.00184	0	.06243	.00648	.00266
19. Glass	0	0	0	0	0	0
20. Stone & clay products	.00758	.00381	0	0	.00102	.09381
21. Primary metal products	.00080	.00011	0	.00049	0	.02003
22. Fabricated metal products	.00738	.00079	.00059	0	.01016	.05191
23. Machinery (except electrical)	0	.00056	.00036	.00698	.00646	.00063
24. Electrical machinery & apparatus	0	0	.00053	0	0	.00150
25. Transportation equipment	0	0	0	0	0	0
26. Instruments & related products	0	0	.00002	0	0	0
27. All other manufacturing	.00014	.00098	0	0	.00609	.02330
28. Eating & drinking establishments	0	0	.00147	0	0	.00382
29. Wholesale trade	.04424	.00945	.02159	.02448	.01371	.00637
30. Retail food stores	0	0	0	0	0	0
31. Retail gasoline service stations	.00201	.00002	.00017	.01149	.00117	.00013
32. All other retail	.00445	.00286	.00077	.02919	.00713	.00078
33. Banking	.01525	.00004	.01091	.00225	.00384	.00582
34. Other finance	.00177	0	.00333	.00261	.00087	.00069
35. Insurance agents & brokers	.01804	.01539	.00808	.01987	.01737	.01234
36. Real estate	.00866	0	.03734	.00623	.00031	.00601
37. All other finance, insurance & real estate	0	.00237	0	0	.00104	0
38. Hotels & other lodging places	.00066	0	.00023	0	.00012	.00014
39. Medical & legal services	.00166	.00058	.00502	.03553	.00194	.00399
40. Educational services	0	0	0	0	0	0
41. All other services	.03381	.00344	.03850	.05871	.01300	.00552
42. Railroads	.00051	.00024	.00285	.00221	.00112	.00030
43. Trucking & warehousing	.00362	.00115	.00212	.00146	.01550	.00036
44. All other transportation	.00029	.00005	0	0	0	0
45. Communications	.00377	.00102	.00260	.00471	.00129	.00358
46. Electric companies & systems	.00958	.03387	.00262	.00675	.01689	.00319
47. Gas companies & systems	.00048	.00004	.00013	.00011	0	.00102
48. Water & sanitary services	0	0	.00010	.00035	0	.03760
49. Households	.26921	.40191	.21724	.27791	.22398	.20134
50. Out-of-state (imports)	.28868	.33843	.10717	.10285	.42706	.06585
51. All other final payments	.18517	.14500	.12834	.29447	.12670	.06433
52. Total	1.00000	1.00000	1.00000	1.00000	1.00000	1.00000

*Each column shows direct purchases from the sectors at the left per dollar of output by the sector at the top.

PROCESSING SECTORS

7. General contractors (non-building)	8. Special trades contractors	9. Food & kindred products (meats and n.e.c.)	10. Food & kindred products (dairies)	11. Food & kindred products (bakeries)	12. Food & kindred products (beverages)	13. Apparel & accessories	14. Logging & sawmills	15. Furniture & other wood fabrication	16. Printing & publishing	17. Chemicals	18. Petroleum	
0	0	.14294	.29481	.00234	0	0	.03871	.00016	0	.00001	0	1
.00009	.00021	.00001	0	0	.00097	.00043	.00142	.00636	.00065	.01039	.02328	2
.00003	.00009	0	0	0	0	0	0	0	.00026	0	0	3
0	0	0	0	0	0	0	0	0	0	.00753	.06646	4
.02542	.00609	.00015	0	0	0	0	0	0	0	.00432	.07387	5
0	0	0	0	.00010	0	0	0	.00251	0	.00085	0	6
.03423	.00366	0	.00040	0	0	0	.00064	0	0	.00125	0	7
.04006	.02671	.00085	.00106	0	0	.02031	.00658	.00005	.00130	.00575	0	8
0	0	.07509	.00835	.00103	0	0	0	0	0	.00040	0	9
0	0	0	.01427	.00740	0	0	0	0	0	0	0	10
0	0	0	0	.00105	0	0	0	0	0	0	0	11
0	0	0	0	0	.00736	0	0	0	0	0	0	12
0	0	0	0	0	.00224	0	0	0	0	.00007	0	13
.00124	.02117	0	0	0	0	0	.24455	.09337	0	0	.00078	14
.00148	0	0	0	0	0	0	.00001	.00711	0	.00011	0	15
.00093	.00032	.00066	.00133	.00119	.01463	.00396	.00016	.00406	.23744	.00120	.00125	16
.02346	.00106	0	0	0	.00501	0	0	.00762	.00089	.14615	.04546	17
.15225	.00282	0	0	0	0	0	.00235	0	0	.00104	.02765	18
0	.00333	0	0	0	.01356	0	0	.00329	0	.00062	0	19
.06280	.00084	.00004	0	0	0	0	.00002	0	0	.00113	.00613	20
.01141	.01625	0	0	0	.00850	0	0	0	0	.00829	0	21
.00642	.06185	0	0	0	0	0	.00390	.01227	.01991	.00068	.00696	22
.01865	.00666	0	.00040	0	0	0	.00016	.00147	.00376	0	0	23
0	.00085	0	0	0	0	0	0	0	.00014	.00094	0	24
0	0	0	0	0	0	0	0	0	0	0	0	25
.00005	.00008	.01042	0	0	0	0	0	0	0	.00171	0	26
.00152	.02858	.07310	.00172	.00569	.01097	.00413	.00872	.00040	.01004	.00747	0	27
.00036	.00170	.00015	.00150	.00003	.00300	0	.00003	.00035	.00255	.00033	.00030	28
.00747	.01102	.01744	.00667	.02276	.01293	.00180	.00512	.00388	.00168	.01367	.00464	29
.00002	0	0	0	0	0	0	0	0	0	.00010	0	30
.00065	.00720	.00160	.00151	.00571	.00967	.00107	.00240	.00051	.00559	.00004	0	31
.00216	.00024	.00429	.00215	.01126	.00153	0	.00252	.00045	.00356	.00153	.00043	32
.00394	.01641	.00207	.00066	.00655	.00041	.00054	.00265	.00179	.00098	.00040	.00629	33
.00294	0	.02022	0	.00398	0	0	.00062	.00008	0	0	.00120	34
.01174	.01300	.00199	.00416	.02177	.01204	.01334	.01208	.00364	.00441	.00311	.00093	35
.00229	.01029	0	.00243	0	0	0	.01936	0	.00127	0	0	36
.00003	.00283	0	.00086	.00019	0	0	.00700	0	.00545	.00116	0	37
.00096	.00208	.00021	0	.00002	.00300	.00013	.00067	.00021	.00045	.00073	0	38
.00217	.00191	.00654	.00053	.00036	.00277	.00011	.00264	.00104	.00817	.00141	.00389	39
0	0	.00065	0	0	0	0	0	0	0	.00036	.00016	40
.04661	.01263	.01912	.03589	.04537	.01099	.00670	.00901	.01869	.00759	.00272	.00246	41
.00467	0	0	0	0	0	0	.00176	.00051	.00014	.00565	0	42
.02819	.01111	.00113	.00466	.00187	.01730	.01348	.01200	.00636	.02644	.01338	.01574	43
.00118	0	0	.00006	.00003	0	.00035	.00131	.00158	.00080	.00350	.01570	44
.00329	.00392	.04011	.00204	.00532	.01201	.02711	.00640	.00585	.02114	.00370	.02054	45
.00284	.00298	.02340	.00451	.05222	.00519	.00742	.00977	.00700	.00136	.00975	.00747	46
.02292	.00171	.00100	.00102	.02924	.00171	.00539	.00091	.01104	.00098	.01576	.01670	47
.00001	.00051	.00170	.00137	.00187	.00504	.00072	.00079	.00035	.00054	.00112	.00045	48
.25925	.36778	.12818	.18337	.29623	.25775	.74934	.36417	.32341	.34124	.15622	.11045	49
.10393	.16462	.38415	.37483	.43087	.32681	.05368	.11300	.37109	.13076	.37245	.37631	50
.11232	.18749	.04279	.04944	.04555	.25461	.08999	.12037	.10350	.16015	.19320	.16465	51
1.00000	1.00000	1.00000	1.00000	1.00000	1.00000	1.00000	1.00000	1.00000	1.00000	1.00000	1.00000	52

TABLE IV
(continued)

DIRECT PURCHASES PER DOLLAR OF OUTPUT, WEST VIRGINIA, PROJECTED TO 1975*

PROCESSING SECTORS	19. Glass	20. Stone & clay products	21. Primary metal products	22. Fabricated metal products	23. Machinery (except electrical)	24. Electrical machinery & apparatus
1. Agriculture	0	.00249	.00178	.00001	0	0
2. Coal mining (underground)	.00024	.00891	.01930	.00025	.00009	0
3. Coal mining (strip & auger)	.00006	0	0	0	0	0
4. Petroleum & natural gas	0	0	.00020	0	0	0
5. All other mining	.01807	.04156	.00461	.00034	0	0
6. General contractors (building)	0	0	.00002	0	0	0
7. General contractors (non-building)	0	0	.00004	0	0	.00095
8. Special trades contractors	.00011	.00053	.00188	.00151	.00022	.00003
9. Food & kindred products (meats and n.e.c.)	0	0	0	0	0	0
10. Food & kindred products (dairies)	0	0	0	0	0	0
11. Food & kindred products (bakeries)	0	0	0	0	0	0
12. Food & kindred products (beverages)	0	0	0	0	0	0
13. Apparel & accessories	0	.00048	.00001	0	0	0
14. Logging & sawmills	0	.00006	.00001	0	.00009	0
15. Furniture & other wood fabrication	.00632	0	0	0	0	.00023
16. Printing & publishing	.00348	.00634	.00013	.00200	.00687	.00112
17. Chemicals	.00438	.00484	.00380	.00180	0	.02424
18. Petroleum	0	.03765	.00010	0	0	0
19. Glass	.03560	0	.00028	.00002	0	0
20. Stone & clay products	.00306	.02117	0	0	0	0
21. Primary metal products	.00270	0	.00398	.11714	.03830	.15756
22. Fabricated metal products	.00010	.03643	.00153	.00087	.02468	0
23. Machinery (except electrical)	0	.00072	.00046	.00024	.00002	0
24. Electrical machinery & apparatus	0	.00011	.00038	.00003	.01332	.00102
25. Transportation equipment	0	.00112	.00007	0	0	0
26. Instruments & related products	0	0	0	.00024	0	.00288
27. All other manufacturing	.04947	.00450	.00102	.00587	.00375	.00054
28. Eating & drinking establishments	0	0	.00004	.00038	.00024	.00026
29. Wholesale trade	.00648	.01286	.00479	.01124	.00931	.00359
30. Retail food stores	0	0	0	.00001	0	0
31. Retail gasoline service stations	.00009	.00368	0	.00013	.00032	.00011
32. All other retail	.00275	.01825	.00253	.00340	.00060	.00387
33. Banking	.00441	.00061	.00098	.00017	.00246	.00098
34. Other finance	0	0	.00016	.00030	0	0
35. Insurance agents & brokers	.01928	.00823	.00076	.00288	.00954	.00722
36. Real estate	.00025	0	0	.00507	.00013	.00130
37. All other finance, insurance & real estate	.00042	0	.00063	.00137	0	0
38. Hotels & other lodging places	.00012	.00002	.00019	.00012	.00037	.00093
39. Medical & legal services	.00059	.00682	.00116	.00024	.00027	.00166
40. Educational services	.00006	0	.00040	.00003	0	.00434
41. All other services	.02930	.01556	.00794	.00329	.00226	.01107
42. Railroads	0	.00240	.00849	0	.00228	.00334
43. Trucking & warehousing	.00376	.03456	.00824	.00213	.01504	.00768
44. All other transportation	0	.00032	.00915	.00006	.00746	.02800
45. Communications	.00339	.00690	.00256	.00175	.00108	.00849
46. Electric companies & systems	.03884	.03124	.00723	.00962	.00662	.03240
47. Gas companies & systems	.02460	.03506	.00232	.00694	.00231	.00990
48. Water & sanitary services	.00030	.00061	.00057	.00245	.00017	.00456
49. Households	.30342	.29420	.23449	.28960	.27443	.27164
50. Out-of-state (imports)	.17998	.17533	.56789	.43356	.44175	.26742
51. All other final payments	.25837	.18644	.09988	.09494	.13602	.14267
52. Total	1.00000	1.00000	1.00000	1.00000	1.00000	1.00000

*Each column shows direct purchases from the sectors at the left per dollar of output by the sector at the top.

PROCESSING SECTORS

	25. Transportation equipment	26. Instruments & related products	27. All other manufacturing	28. Eating & drinking establishments	29. Wholesale trade	30. Retail food stores	31. Retail gasoline service stations	32. All other retail	33. Banking	34. Other finance	35. Insurance agents & brokers	36. Real estate	
1	0	0	.00658	.00556	0	0	0	0	0	0	0	0	1
2	0	0	.00027	.00049	.00091	.00010	.00039	.00061	.00025	0	0	0	2
3	0	0	.00700	.00016	0	.00010	.00026	.00046	.00045	0	0	0	3
4	0	0	0	0	0	0	0	0	0	0	0	0	4
5	.00265	0	0	0	0	0	0	0	0	0	0	0	5
6	0	0	0	0	0	0	0	.00008	0	0	0	.07105	6
7	0	0	0	0	0	0	0	.00056	0	0	0	.00196	7
8	.00002	0	.02399	0	.00124	.00101	.00005	.00901	.00107	0	0	.03371	8
9	0	0	.00949	.04951	0	0	0	0	0	0	.00005	0	9
10	0	0	0	.03751	0	0	0	.00059	0	0	0	0	10
11	0	0	0	.03964	0	0	0	.00069	0	0	0	0	11
12	0	0	0	.01778	0	0	0	.00023	0	0	0	0	12
13	0	0	.00022	0	0	0	0	0	0	0	0	0	13
14	0	0	0	0	0	0	0	0	0	0	0	0	14
15	0	0	0	0	.00006	0	0	.00180	0	0	0	0	15
16	.00018	.00046	.00718	.00160	.00063	.04166	.00286	.05218	00635	.01710	.00023	.03708	16
17	0	.05993	.00315	0	.00250	0	0	0	0	0	0	0	17
18	0	0	0	0	0	.00044	.00520	.00283	0	0	.00019	0	18
19	0	.00368	0	.00112	0	.00017	0	.01168	0	0	0	0	19
20	0	0	.00001	0	0	0	0	0	0	0	0	.00006	20
21	.07234	0	0	0	0	0	0	0	0	0	0	0	21
22	0	0	.02677	0	0	0	0	0	0	0	0	0	22
23	0	0	.00840	0	0	0	0	0	0	0	0	0	23
24	0	0	.00074	0	0	0	0	0	0	.00407	0	0	24
25	0	0	0	0	.00019	0	0	.00009	0	0	0	0	25
26	0	0	0	0	0	0	0	.00022	0	0	0	0	26
27	.00014	.00821	.00260	0	.00153	.00600	0	.00214	.00088	.00131	0	0	27
28	.00009	0	.00001	0	.00200	0	0	.00169	.00017	.00059	.00118	.00802	28
29	.00231	.01166	.00107	.04504	.01675	.00557	.01120	.00197	.00014	.00047	.00014	.00791	29
30	0	0	0	.00458	.00023	.00001	0	0	0	0	0	0	30
31	.00001	0	.00030	.00014	.00932	.00100	.00036	.00467	.00011	.00030	.00024	.00031	31
32	.00075	0	.00015	.00150	.00373	.00059	.00156	.00431	.00136	.00116	.00030	.00399	32
33	.00102	.00146	.00152	.00094	.00482	.00096	.00260	.01290	0	.06956	.00036	.00540	33
34	0	0	0	.00096	.00689	.00170	0	.00227	.00117	.00223	0	0	34
35	.00173	.00169	.00225	.00368	.01119	.02538	.01029	.01337	.00894	.00054	.00051	.00032	35
36	0	0	.00153	.00090	.00004	.05177	.00534	.00956	.00724	.00650	.00190	.05810	36
37	0	0	0	.00007	.00186	0	0	.00070	.01563	0	.07559	.00033	37
38	.00003	0	0	0	.00124	0	0	.00404	.00008	.00009	.00008	.00200	38
39	.00106	.00192	.00059	.00027	.00293	.00135	.00036	.00701	.00314	.00716	.00012	.00227	39
40	0	0	0	0	.00059	0	0	.00032	.00121	.00187	0	0	40
41	.00514	.00315	.00359	.00476	.00932	.02041	.10237	.04232	.04368	.01196	.00572	.01996	41
42	.01956	0	.00494	0	.00463	0	.00075	.00270	0	0	0	0	42
43	.00065	.00529	.00548	.00124	.01828	.00540	.02108	.01024	.00018	0	0	0	43
44	0	0	.00025	.00003	.01371	.00058	.00211	.00296	.00012	.00301	.00020	.00566	44
45	.00791	.00154	.00209	.00716	.00885	.01135	.01502	.01770	.00212	.01177	.00466	.01036	45
46	.00860	.00161	.00745	.04494	.01935	.03126	.01279	.01641	.00880	.00274	.00074	.00611	46
47	.00501	.00100	.00187	.01698	.01529	.01468	.00608	.00864	.00079	.00038	.00086	.00751	47
48	.00205	.00023	.00025	.00124	.00061	.00303	.00377	.00324	.00078	.00011	.00024	.00312	48
49	.25504	.28959	.21353	.37331	.59899	.54750	.48394	.46315	.53604	.57714	.19795	.48033	49
50	.48988	.52231	.57127	.23836	.03765	.10333	.08453	.14051	.10536	.13448	.67270	.07136	50
51	.12383	.08627	.08546	.10053	.20467	.12465	.22709	.14615	.25394	.14546	.03604	.16308	51
52	1.00000	1.00000	1.00000	1.00000	1.00000	1.00000	1.00000	1.00000	1.00000	1.00000	1.00000	1.00000	52

		37. All other finance, insurance & real estate	38. Hotels & other lodging places	39. Medical & legal services	40. Educational services	41. All other services	42. Railroads
	TABLE IV *(continued)* **DIRECT PURCHASES PER DOLLAR OF OUTPUT, WEST VIRGINIA, PROJECTED TO 1975***						
1.	Agriculture	0	.00527	.00035	0	0	0
2.	Coal mining (underground)	0	.00225	.00023	.00194	.00001	.00029
3.	Coal mining (strip & auger)	.01066	.01714	0	.00104	0	0
4.	Petroleum & natural gas	0	0	0	0	0	0
5.	All other mining	0	0	.00003	0	0	.00847
6.	General contractors (building)	0	.00168	0	.07746	0	0
7.	General contractors (non-building)	0	.00688	0	.02949	0	.00987
8.	Special trades contractors	0	.02866	.00638	.00440	.00722	.01053
9.	Food & kindred products (meats and n.e.c.)	0	0	.02433	.00010	.00004	0
10.	Food & kindred products (dairies)	0	0	.01433	0	0	0
11.	Food & kindred products (bakeries)	0	0	.00075	.00062	.00007	0
12.	Food & kindred products (beverages)	0	0	.00038	.00202	0	0
13.	Apparel & accessories	0	0	.01550	0	0	0
14.	Logging & sawmills	0	0	.00001	.00026	0	0
15.	Furniture & other wood fabrication	0	0	0	0	0	0
16.	Printing & publishing	.00355	.00146	.00051	.01658	.02255	.00008
17.	Chemicals	0	0	.00293	.00029	.00342	0
18.	Petroleum	0	0	0	0	.00187	.00443
19.	Glass	0	0	.00057	.00052	0	0
20.	Stone & clay products	0	0	0	.00072	.01236	0
21.	Primary metal products	0	0	0	0	0	.00505
22.	Fabricated metal products	0	0	0	0	.00659	0
23.	Machinery (except electrical)	0	0	0	0	.00100	.00628
24.	Electrical machinery & apparatus	0	0	.00010	0	.00675	.00006
25.	Transportation equipment	0	0	0	0	0	.00695
26.	Instruments & related products	0	0	.00129	.00009	0	0
27.	All other manufacturing	0	.00027	.00251	.00395	.01033	0
28.	Eating & drinking establishments	.00043	0	.00004	.00260	0	0
29.	Wholesale trade	.00006	.03768	.01178	.01202	.02050	.00173
30.	Retail food stores	0	0	.00102	0	0	0
31.	Retail gasoline service stations	.00006	.00408	.00128	.00007	.00401	.00001
32.	All other retail	.00049	.00561	.00868	.01397	.01603	.00949
33.	Banking	.00170	.03923	.00286	.01665	.00099	0
34.	Other finance	0	0	.00168	0	.00201	0
35.	Insurance agents & brokers	.00165	.02175	.01030	.00314	.02868	.02613
36.	Real estate	.00041	.02800	.00549	.00080	.00150	0
37.	All other finance, insurance & real estate	0	0	.00022	.00191	.00142	0
38.	Hotels & other lodging places	.00043	0	.00050	.00121	.00100	.00020
39.	Medical & legal services	.43359	.00511	.02982	.00281	.00960	.00359
40.	Educational services	0	0	.00031	.00729	.00001	0
41.	All other services	.01851	.07733	.02530	.02708	.01934	.00179
42.	Railroads	0	0	.00089	.00033	.00117	.02484
43.	Trucking & warehousing	0	.00059	.00213	.00167	.00411	.00716
44.	All other transportation	.00067	0	.00034	.00064	.00100	.00047
45.	Communications	.00429	.04101	.00631	.01187	.01289	.00540
46.	Electric companies & systems	.00291	.05229	.00371	.01094	.00825	.00397
47.	Gas companies & systems	.00256	.00780	.00505	.01556	.01345	.00084
48.	Water & sanitary services	0	.00422	.00608	.00225	.00314	.00012
49.	Households	.33880	.29222	.59526	.60599	.41317	.42677
50.	Out-of-state (imports)	.14808	.13355	.10786	.08635	.24129	.23169
51.	All other final payments	.03115	.18592	.10289	.03537	.12423	.20379
52.	Total	1.00000	1.00000	1.00000	1.00000	1.00000	1.00000

PROCESSING SECTORS

*Each column shows direct purchases from the sectors at the left per dollar of output by the sector at the top.

PROCESSING SECTORS

43. Trucking & warehousing	44. All other transportation	45. Communications	46. Electric companies & systems	47. Gas companies & systems	48. Water & sanitary services	
0	0	0	0	0	0	1
.00019	0	.00005	.08937	.00301	.00065	2
0	0	0	.03387	0	0	3
0	.04206	0	0	.10344	0	4
0	0	0	0	0	.02760	5
0	0	0	0	0	0	6
.01536	0	.00698	0	0	.07132	7
.00239	.00460	0	.00001	0	0	8
0	0	0	0	0	0	9
0	0	0	0	0	0	10
0	0	0	0	0	0	11
0	0	0	0	0	0	12
0	0	0	0	0	0	13
.00094	0	0	0	0	0	14
0	.00226	0	.00020	0	0	15
.02047	.00116	.00037	.00395	.00083	.00178	16
0	0	0	0	0	.02348	17
.00106	.00535	.00223	.00527	.00074	.00074	18
0	0	0	0	0	0	19
.00021	0	.00097	.00259	.00129	.00634	20
.00186	.00530	.00028	.00046	.00007	.00089	21
0	.01330	0	.00624	.00089	.01162	22
0	.00442	0	0	0	0	23
0	0	.00150	.00020	0	.00743	24
0	0	0	0	0	0	25
0	.00053	0	0	0	0	26
0	.01430	0	.00001	.00011	0	27
.00033	.00037	.00070	.00062	.00176	.00027	28
.06529	.00681	.00034	.00329	.00097	.01055	29
0	0	0	0	0	0	30
.00326	.00254	.00009	.00008	.00252	.00276	31
.00238	.00162	.00194	.00058	.00170	.03448	32
.00652	.00900	.00298	.00005	.00306	.00011	33
0	.00137	0	0	.00006	0	34
.01330	.00908	.00049	.00090	.00013	.00296	35
.00100	.00035	.00119	.00115	.00507	0	36
0	0	.00292	.00190	.00065	.00087	37
.00045	.00053	.00029	.00115	.00239	0	38
.00471	.00206	.00071	.00127	.00112	.00042	39
0	0	0	.00001	.00002	0	40
.00859	.03226	.02675	.00338	.00087	.00122	41
.00493	.00053	.01075	.01351	.00085	.00873	42
.00163	.00123	.01525	.02082	.00393	.00390	43
.00092	.05278	.00119	.00381	.01243	.00045	44
.01634	.00612	.00243	.00487	.00113	.01204	45
.00536	.00495	.00672	.05563	.00116	.05253	46
.00596	.00359	.00791	.00110	.00500	.00265	47
.00030	.00042	.00004	.00009	.00031	.01592	48
.35361	.24242	.33562	.20619	.07000	.27861	49
.26237	.35651	.16068	.15281	.66137	.25531	50
.20027	.17218	.40863	.38462	.11312	.16437	51
1.00000	1.00000	1.00000	1.00000	1.00000	1.00000	52

		1. Agriculture	2. Coal mining (underground)	3. Coal mining (strip & auger)	4. Petroleum & natural gas	5. All other mining	6. General contractors (building)
TABLE V — DIRECT AND INDIRECT REQUIREMENTS PER DOLLAR OF DELIVERY TO FINAL DEMAND, WEST VIRGINIA, PROJECTED TO 1975*							

PROCESSING SECTORS

	1.	2.	3.	4.	5.	6.
1. Agriculture	1.07734	.00063	.00038	.00047	.00688	.00177
2. Coal mining (underground)	.00182	1.01552	.22807	.00287	.00263	.00405
3. Coal mining (strip & auger)	.00072	.01358	1.31100	.00061	.00136	.00119
4. Petroleum & natural gas	.00040	.00027	.00036	1.04893	.00088	.00190
5. All other mining	.00999	.00132	.00109	.00652	1.04381	.01992
6. General contractors (building)	.00080	.00008	.00389	.00060	.00013	1.03951
7. General contractors (non-building)	.00025	.00011	.00046	.00034	.00049	.03053
8. Special trades contractors	.00153	.00494	.00483	.00386	.02293	.30975
9. Food & kindred products (meats and n.e.c.)	.00361	.00124	.00065	.00113	.00024	.00084
10. Food & kindred products (dairies)	.00007	.00005	.00023	.00063	.00007	.00030
11. Food & kindred products (bakeries)	.00002	.00001	.00011	.00007	.00002	.00020
12. Food & kindred products (beverages)	.00001	0	.00005	.00003	.00001	.00009
13. Apparel & accessories	.00006	.00004	.00014	.00064	.00007	.00018
14. Logging & sawmills	.01326	.00936	.00391	.00042	.01207	.01911
15. Furniture & other wood fabrication	.00068	.00376	.00091	.00010	.00136	.01443
16. Printing & publishing	.00305	.00189	.00529	.01110	.00733	.01166
17. Chemicals	.00081	.00070	.00063	.00435	.02057	.00481
18. Petroleum	.00075	.00240	.00090	.06794	.00750	.01304
19. Glass	.00009	.00007	.00007	.00044	.00020	.00121
20. Stone & clay products	.00902	.00416	.00206	.00145	.00156	.10253
21. Primary metal products	.00207	.00048	.00071	.00129	.00247	.03635
22. Fabricated metal products	.00908	.00176	.00222	.00189	.01307	.07970
23. Machinery (except electrical)	.00017	.00066	.00078	.00756	.00705	.00394
24. Electrical machinery & apparatus	.00031	.00007	.00114	.00062	.00027	.00237
25. Transportation equipment	.00003	.00001	.00004	.00003	.00002	.00014
26. Instruments & related products	.00005	.00002	.00005	.00008	.00005	.00008
27. All other manufacturing	.00135	.00148	.00133	.00144	.00776	.03504
28. Eating & drinking establishments	.00027	.00012	.00251	.00030	.00019	.00479
29. Wholesale trade	.05064	.01085	.03349	.02953	.01765	.01588
30. Retail food stores	.00002	.00001	.00003	.00005	.00001	.00004
31. Retail gasoline service stations	.00300	.00028	.00094	.01297	.00185	.00340
32. All other retail	.00620	.00328	.00324	.03271	.00821	.00554
33. Banking	.01732	.00052	.01547	.00411	.00512	.01226
34. Other finance	.00248	.00018	.00479	.00335	.00115	.00111
35. Insurance agents & brokers	.02221	.01651	.01690	.02487	.02027	.02072
36. Real estate	.01073	.00097	.05259	.00799	.00136	.01149
37. All other finance, insurance & real estate	.00230	.00387	.00235	.00228	.00306	.00316
38. Hotels & other lodging places	.00091	.00011	.00057	.00033	.00033	.00100
39. Medical & legal services	.00385	.00271	.00906	.04100	.00417	.00799
40. Educational services	.00007	.00001	.00006	.00006	.00003	.00006
41. All other services	.04056	.00530	.05573	.06854	.01658	.01733
42. Railroads	.00127	.00096	.00446	.00311	.00199	.00218
43. Trucking & warehousing	.00634	.00275	.00481	.00527	.01851	.01133
44. All other transportation	.00139	.00048	.00109	.00207	.00077	.00140
45. Communications	.00619	.00195	.00602	.00938	.00319	.00861
46. Electric companies & systems	.01388	.03731	.01421	.01102	.02063	.01410
47. Gas companies & systems	.00264	.00072	.00228	.00365	.00154	.00825
48. Water & sanitary services	.00036	.00009	.00077	.00115	.00024	.04044
49. Total	1.32999	1.15361	1.80267	1.42915	1.28765	1.92579

*Each column shows the direct and indirect requirements from the sectors at the left to support a delivery of one dollar to final demand by the sector at the top.

PROCESSING SECTORS

	7. General contractors (non-building)	8. Special trades contractors	9. Food & kindred products (meats and n.e.c.)	10. Food & kindred products (dairies)	11. Food & kindred products (bakeries)	12. Food & kindred products (beverages)	13. Apparel & accessories	14. Logging & sawmills	15. Furniture & other wood fabrication	16. Printing & publishing	17. Chemicals
1	.00077	.00168	.16728	.32371	.00519	.00027	.00009	.05544	.00544	.00037	.00031
2	.00660	.00169	.00340	.00119	.00585	.00214	.00136	.00371	.00790	.00151	.01412
3	.00071	.00086	.00220	.00055	.00273	.00060	.00048	.00105	.00061	.00089	.00093
4	.01553	.00074	.00042	.00037	.00346	.00045	.00071	.00065	.00155	.00039	.01173
5	.04395	.00732	.00191	.00314	.00026	.00058	.00023	.00105	.00035	.00017	.00589
6	.00034	.00095	.00024	.00045	.00017	.00005	.00004	.00210	.00286	.00022	.00109
7	1.03648	.00434	.00065	.00076	.00033	.00085	.00059	.00150	.00045	.00092	.00209
8	.04513	1.02996	.00365	.00220	.00091	.00086	.02120	.01136	.00232	.00275	.00812
9	.00028	.00056	1.08281	.01041	.00136	.00041	.00009	.00058	.00015	.00073	.00074
10	.00012	.00015	.00015	1.01459	.00757	.00018	.00002	.00015	.00006	.00036	.00007
11	.00004	.00008	.00003	.00008	1.00107	.00013	.00001	.00003	.00002	.00015	.00003
12	.00002	.00004	.00001	.00003	.00001	1.00747	0	.00001	.00001	.00007	.00001
13	.00013	.00008	.00016	.00005	.00004	.00232	1.00002	.00015	.00004	.00024	.00014
14	.00394	.02902	.00220	.00405	.00016	.00009	.00063	1.32480	.12473	.00015	.00048
15	.00166	.00007	.00014	.00022	.00007	.00011	.00001	.00011	1.00727	.00003	.00023
16	.00635	.00295	.00422	.00445	.00477	.02086	.00607	.00333	.00681	1.31366	.00312
17	.03913	.00234	.00155	.00055	.00046	.00643	.00018	.00054	.00927	.00172	1.17191
18	.16678	.00407	.00063	.00053	.00087	.00040	.00038	.00380	.00071	.00042	.00271
19	.00027	.00359	.00014	.00007	.00016	.01421	.00008	.00010	.00347	.00009	.00083
20	.06854	.00158	.00197	.00330	.00096	.00039	.00024	.00109	.00074	.00033	.00184
21	.01577	.02510	.00088	.00083	.00030	.00894	.00064	.00125	.00195	.00361	.01051
22	.01498	.06542	.00428	.00336	.00119	.00108	.00173	.00716	.01374	.02704	.00210
23	.02027	.00732	.00079	.00057	.00018	.00024	.00024	.00049	.00163	.00513	.00040
24	.00078	.00115	.00047	.00038	.00041	.00019	.00014	.00018	.00021	.00041	.00120
25	.00013	.00001	.00002	.00001	.00002	.00001	0	.00003	.00001	.00001	.00006
26	.00015	.00011	.01131	.00012	.00002	.00002	0	.00002	.00003	.00004	.00202
27	.00480	.03081	.08017	.00338	.00656	.01234	.00495	.01239	.00234	.01380	.00945
28	.00073	.00197	.00036	.00168	.00027	.00317	.00012	.00040	.00048	.00346	.00052
29	.01626	.01482	.02861	.02372	.02553	.01578	.00344	.01172	.00665	.00601	.01866
30	.00004	.00002	.00002	.00002	.00001	.00002	0	.00001	.00001	.00003	.00013
31	.00218	.00786	.00265	.00277	.00644	.01022	.00142	.00371	.00114	.00768	.00062
32	.00591	.00137	.00652	.00490	.01270	.00239	.00039	.00442	.00152	.00547	.00276
33	.00725	.01767	.00714	.00617	.00758	.00105	.00118	.00526	.00261	.00200	.00119
34	.00363	.00026	.02255	.00109	.00438	.00017	.00005	.00110	.00029	.00015	.00023
35	.01795	.01576	.00733	.01240	.02443	.01387	.01432	.01864	.00669	.00746	.00545
36	.00395	.01274	.00242	.00606	.00090	.00043	.00047	.02832	.00300	.00238	.00053
37	.00202	.00482	.00104	.00213	.00249	.00132	.00133	.01095	.00161	.00794	.00199
38	.00137	.00229	.00051	.00037	.00031	.00313	.00024	.00111	.00042	.00070	.00100
39	.00627	.00488	.00898	.00296	.00258	.00408	.00106	.00920	.00268	.01510	.00347
40	.00005	.00005	.00078	.00004	.00004	.00003	.00001	.00002	.00002	.00049	.00021
41	.05581	.01765	.03084	.05046	.04993	.01466	.00867	.01730	.02204	.01365	.00583
42	.00632	.00085	.00173	.00067	.00124	.00072	.00059	.00304	.00121	.00098	.00747
43	.03794	.01368	.00488	.00743	.00460	.01943	.01476	.01519	.00887	.03613	.01730
44	.00544	.00091	.00092	.00077	.00123	.00055	.00063	.00247	.00231	.00151	.00517
45	.01017	.00594	.04606	.00531	.00748	.01402	.02801	.01040	.00777	.02935	.00559
46	.01059	.00656	.03130	.01022	.05755	.00800	.00866	.01595	.01027	.00376	.01413
47	.03156	.00364	.00298	.00274	.03097	.00321	.00605	.00251	.01232	.00264	.01948
48	.00059	.00100	.00216	.00173	.00223	.00536	.00082	.00143	.00074	.00104	.00149
49	1.71969	1.35676	1.58147	1.52299	1.28801	1.20331	1.13234	1.59623	1.28737	1.52315	1.36538

TABLE V
(continued)

DIRECT AND INDIRECT REQUIRE-MENTS PER DOLLAR OF DELIVERY TO FINAL DEMAND, WEST VIRGINIA, PROJECTED TO 1975*

PROCESSING SECTORS		18. Petroleum	19. Glass	20. Stone & clay products	21. Primary metal products	22. Fabricated metal products	23. Machinery (except electrical)
	1. Agriculture	.00071	.00067	.00322	.00201	.00034	.00015
	2. Coal mining (underground)	.02646	.00511	.01430	.02062	.00385	.00187
	3. Coal mining (strip & auger)	.00096	.00267	.00196	.00069	.00068	.00048
	4. Petroleum & natural gas	.07511	.00306	.00717	.00103	.00098	.00078
	5. All other mining	.08045	.01989	.04771	.00507	.00110	.00031
	6. General contractors (building)	.00014	.00011	.00010	.00008	.00043	.00005
	7. General contractors (non-building)	.00065	.00022	.00086	.00039	.00034	.00037
	8. Special trades contractors	.00284	.00236	.00265	.00257	.00249	.00073
	9. Food & kindred products (meats and n.e.c.)	.00032	.00063	.00035	.00011	.00014	.00010
	10. Food & kindred products (dairies)	.00014	.00005	.00016	.00004	.00004	.00003
	11. Food & kindred products (bakeries)	.00003	.00001	.00003	.00001	.00003	.00002
	12. Food & kindred products (beverages)	.00001	0	.00001	0	.00001	.00001
	13. Apparel & accessories	.00013	.00005	.00064	.00004	.00003	.00002
	14. Logging & sawmills	.00232	.00117	.00094	.00037	.00014	.00019
	15. Furniture & other wood fabrication	.00026	.00666	.00017	.00012	.00004	.00004
	16. Printing & publishing	.00421	.00729	.01251	.00112	.00368	.00995
	17. Chemicals	.05687	.00625	.00928	.00473	.00287	.00076
	18. Petroleum	1.03460	.00092	.04102	.00053	.00029	.00028
	19. Glass	.00010	1.03700	.00027	.00034	.00011	.00003
	20. Stone & clay products	.00703	.00391	1.02254	.00030	.00022	.00013
	21. Primary metal products	.00188	.00336	.00506	1.00457	.11796	.04369
	22. Fabricated metal products	.00913	.00281	.03917	.00215	1.00168	.02536
	23. Machinery (except electrical)	.00123	.00070	.00129	.00066	.00042	1.00020
	24. Electrical machinery & apparatus	.00021	.00031	.00033	.00048	.00016	.01340
	25. Transportation equipment	.00002	.00001	.00118	.00013	.00002	.00003
	26. Instruments & related products	.00012	.00002	.00005	.00002	.00025	.00005
	27. All other manufacturing	.00165	.05225	.00584	.00151	.00630	.00430
	28. Eating & drinking establishments	.00047	.00918	.00028	.00010	.00052	.00035
	29. Wholesale trade	.01120	.00907	.01894	.00642	.01281	.01148
	30. Retail food stores	.00002	.00001	.00002	0	.00002	.00001
	31. Retail gasoline service stations	.00139	.00060	.00463	.00024	.00040	.00062
	32. All other retail	.00410	.00401	.02038	.00309	.00412	.00117
	33. Banking	.00781	.00519	.00214	.00140	.00065	.00289
	34. Other finance	.00169	.00021	.00039	.00027	.00045	.00013
	35. Insurance agents & brokers	.00584	.02220	.01198	.00222	.00369	.01059
	36. Real estate	.00109	.00100	.00115	.00024	.00563	.00050
	37. All other finance, insurance & real estate	.00099	.00249	.00138	.00096	.00185	.00103
	38. Hotels & other lodging places	.00020	.00034	.00035	.00027	.00024	.00046
	39. Medical & legal services	.00813	.00261	.00925	.00200	.00151	.00117
	40. Educational services	.00004	.00009	.00004	.00041	.00009	.00009
	41. All other services	.01136	.03340	.02098	.00951	.00540	.00416
	42. Railroads	.00132	.00123	.00383	.00909	.00142	.00311
	43. Trucking & warehousing	.02005	.00658	.03943	.00912	.00402	.01645
	44. All other transportation	.01797	.00086	.00225	.00997	.00164	.00900
	45. Communications	.02325	.00515	.01046	.00332	.00277	.00228
	46. Electric companies & systems	.01316	.04483	.03782	.00924	.01210	.00880
	47. Gas companies & systems	.01947	.02693	.03847	.00291	.00781	.00323
	48. Water & sanitary services	.00076	.00053	.00104	.00067	.00267	.00039
	49. Total	1.45784	1.32500	1.44400	1.12114	1.21441	1.18120

*Each column shows the direct and indirect requirements from the sectors at the left to support a delivery of one dollar to final demand by the sector at the top.

PROCESSING SECTORS

24. Electrical machinery & apparatus	25. Transportation equipment	26. Instruments & related products	27. All other manufacturing	28. Eating & drinking establishments	29. Wholesale trade	30. Retail food stores	31. Retail gasoline service stations	32. All other retail	33. Banking	34. Other finance	
.00039	.00019	.00012	.00877	.02665	.00014	.00013	.00006	.00044	.00013	.00012	1
.00721	.00249	.00112	.00296	.00600	.00327	.00373	.00225	.00300	.00145	.00052	2
.00181	.00050	.00025	.00967	.00274	.00112	.00185	.00111	.00176	.00132	.00030	3
.00300	.00068	.00088	.00036	.00224	.00252	.00189	.00147	.00158	.00023	.00029	4
.00128	.00343	.00045	.00040	.00044	.00019	.00034	.00072	.00083	.00012	.00007	5
.00053	.00002	.00007	.00020	.00016	.00010	.00411	.00046	.00095	.00069	.00073	6
.00187	.00048	.00026	.00034	.00033	.00056	.00075	.00086	.00141	.00021	.00025	7
.00142	.00061	.00080	.02521	.00065	.00188	.00478	.00148	.01096	.00212	.00090	8
.00015	.00006	.00019	.01039	.05413	.00028	.00022	.00010	.00044	.00034	.00030	9
.00006	.00003	.00004	.00003	.03839	.00016	.00008	.00005	.00083	.00018	.00016	10
.00003	.00001	0	.00001	.03970	.00009	.00004	.00002	.00079	.00003	.00004	11
.00002	0	0	0	.01793	.00004	.00001	0	.00027	.00001	.00002	12
.00005	.00003	.00004	.00024	.00007	.00008	.00006	.00004	.00016	.00018	.00014	13
.00019	.00008	.00005	.00087	.00042	.00013	.00023	.00012	.00062	.00009	.00004	14
.00036	.00002	.00004	.00003	.00007	.00013	.00009	.00004	.00194	.00002	.00003	15
.00323	.00074	.00123	.01028	.00423	.00262	.05886	.00832	.07174	.01053	.02423	16
.02973	.00053	.07036	.00395	.00050	.00316	.00044	.00101	.00083	.00032	.00030	17
.00109	.00037	.00024	.00029	.00063	.00066	.00109	.00607	.00369	.00026	.00020	18
.00015	.00004	.00387	.00010	.00146	.00007	.00022	.00005	.01224	.00004	.00003	19
.00061	.00019	.00020	.00027	.00063	.00034	.00093	.00160	.00099	.00071	.00034	20
.15912	.07286	.00071	.00442	.00040	.00036	.00057	.00043	.00079	.00022	.00084	21
.00140	.00038	.00045	.02913	.00098	.00072	.00240	.00134	.00296	.00085	.00084	22
.00037	.00022	.00011	.00872	.00013	.00019	.00039	.00022	.00052	.00013	.00016	23
1.00129	.00011	.00011	.00094	.00014	.00015	.00026	.00079	.00043	.00034	.00423	24
.00005	1.00015	.00001	.00004	.00002	.00023	.00001	.00002	.00011	0	0	25
.00295	0	1.00013	.00013	.00057	.00003	.00001	.00001	.00024	.00002	.00003	26
.00176	.00037	.00909	1.00455	.00490	.00210	.00720	.00137	.00452	.00163	.00197	27
.00042	.00014	.00007	.00016	1.00035	.00215	.00074	.00018	.00210	.00032	.00077	28
.00685	.00326	.01356	.00343	.05056	1.01944	.00789	.01562	.00527	.00162	.00134	29
.00001	0	.00001	0	.00460	.00025	1.00002	.00001	.00002	.00001	.00001	30
.00051	.00013	.00021	.00069	.00142	.00981	.00169	1.00116	.00559	.00044	.00058	31
.00525	.00145	.00036	.00068	.00315	.00446	.00184	.00381	1.00601	.00241	.00187	32
.00195	.00125	.00171	.00240	.00249	.00602	.00190	.00328	.01413	1.00041	.07003	33
.00020	.00007	.00012	.00031	.00268	.00714	.00185	.00036	.00249	.00131	1.00240	34
.00909	.00282	.00252	.00367	.00709	.01288	.02706	.01427	.01657	.01068	.00207	35
.00184	.00015	.00013	.00267	.00204	.00063	.05558	.00618	.01114	.00804	.00768	36
.00106	.00036	.00036	.00055	.00100	.00311	.00262	.00147	.00282	.01662	.00147	37
.00115	.00010	.00009	.00013	.00030	.00140	.00028	.00022	.00428	.00020	.00017	38
.00306	.00160	.00244	.00133	.00185	.00506	.00374	.00254	.01004	.01133	.00876	39
.00445	.00004	.00002	.00002	.00008	.00064	.00004	.00002	.00038	.00123	.00200	40
.01559	.00661	.00417	.00581	.01247	.01308	.02424	.10650	.04815	.04603	.01683	41
.00585	.02102	.00065	.00545	.00126	.00549	.00088	.00160	.00358	.00030	.00030	42
.01104	.00202	.00679	.00688	.00466	.01994	.00852	.02304	.01391	.00111	.00120	43
.03176	.00092	.00054	.00060	.00135	.01522	.00158	.00298	.00379	.00038	.00350	44
.01042	.00858	.00225	.00342	.01138	.01045	.01435	.01773	.02134	.00347	.01309	45
.03747	.01034	.00320	.00933	.05380	.02215	.03482	.01583	.02022	.01028	.00435	46
.01173	.00553	.00261	.00256	.01977	.01646	.01612	.00846	.01067	.00178	.00110	47
.00494	.00217	.00037	.00044	.00173	.00081	.00359	.00429	.00374	.00110	.00039	48
1.38478	1.15314	1.13302	1.17282	1.38856	1.19791	1.30004	1.25960	1.33130	1.14124	1.17699	49

	TABLE V (continued) DIRECT AND INDIRECT REQUIREMENTS PER DOLLAR OF DELIVERY TO FINAL DEMAND, WEST VIRGINIA, PROJECTED TO 1975*	35. Insurance agents & brokers	36. Real estate	37. All other finance, insurance & real estate	38. Hotels & other lodging places	39. Medical & legal services	40. Educational services
1.	Agriculture	.00036	.00049	.00412	.00587	.00944	.00039
2.	Coal mining (underground)	.00036	.00136	.00326	.01225	.00106	.00424
3.	Coal mining (strip & auger)	.00114	.00061	.01433	.02531	.00041	.00229
4.	Petroleum & natural gas	.00020	.00150	.00072	.00143	.00081	.00254
5.	All other mining	.00006	.00204	.00026	.00101	.00050	.00311
6.	General contractors (building)	.00018	.07849	.00031	.00412	.00053	.08125
7.	General contractors (non-building)	.00010	.00504	.00038	.00822	.00073	.03358
8.	Special trades contractors	.00047	.06086	.00381	.03323	.00814	.03088
9.	Food & kindred products (meats and n.e.c.)	.00103	.00067	.01192	.00033	.02739	.00053
10.	Food & kindred products (dairies)	.00055	.00042	.00654	.00015	.01503	.00022
11.	Food & kindred products (bakeries)	.00008	.00037	.00037	.00004	.00079	.00077
12.	Food & kindred products (beverages)	.00004	.00017	.00019	.00002	.00040	.00211
13.	Apparel & accessories	.00053	.00008	.00695	.00014	.01600	.00010
14.	Logging & sawmills	.00003	.00253	.00022	.00122	.00039	.00216
15.	Furniture & other wood fabrication	.00001	.00113	.00004	.00015	.00005	.00123
16.	Printing & publishing	.00117	.05399	.00682	.00770	.00319	.02556
17.	Chemicals	.00020	.00088	.00190	.00113	.00412	.00227
18.	Petroleum	.00028	.00185	.00031	.00230	.00041	.00648
19.	Glass	.00003	.00030	.00035	.00022	.00077	.00088
20.	Stone & clay products	.00015	.00841	.00058	.00241	.00066	.01132
21.	Primary metal products	.00005	.00397	.00028	.00140	.00044	.00368
22.	Fabricated metal products	.00016	.00989	.00085	.00379	.00120	.00805
23.	Machinery (except electrical)	.00003	.00089	.00014	.00057	.00019	.00115
24.	Electrical machinery & apparatus	.00008	.00045	.00033	.00077	.00040	.00048
25.	Transportation equipment	0	.00002	.00001	.00003	.00001	.00003
26.	Instruments & related products	.00006	.00003	.00071	.00003	.00163	.00012
27.	All other manufacturing	.00030	.00477	.00268	.00259	.00547	.00783
28.	Eating & drinking establishments	.00125	.00916	.00060	.00063	.00025	.00323
29.	Wholesale trade	.00095	.01187	.00740	.04286	.01484	.01571
30.	Retail food stores	.00004	.00005	.00046	.00002	.00106	.00003
31.	Retail gasoline service stations	.00037	.00148	.00103	.00531	.00189	.00104
32.	All other retail	.00085	.00568	.00532	.00809	.01016	.01577
33.	Banking	.00070	.00780	.00368	.04115	.00392	.01865
34.	Other finance	.00011	.00028	.00119	.00069	.00251	.00045
35.	Insurance agents & brokers	1.00135	.00402	.00806	.02685	.01280	.00735
36.	Real estate	.00237	1.06346	.00402	.03216	.00666	.00265
37.	All other finance, insurance & real estate	.07576	.00142	1.00094	.00333	.00145	.00323
38.	Hotels & other lodging places	.00016	.00241	.00078	1.00045	.00069	.00155
39.	Medical & legal services	.03413	.00464	.44808	.00860	1.03222	.00596
40.	Educational services	.00001	.00004	.00016	.00009	.00036	1.00740
41.	All other services	.00865	.02599	.03305	.08705	.03018	.03403
42.	Railroads	.00015	.00065	.00081	.00191	.00143	.00131
43.	Trucking & warehousing	.00034	.00372	.00214	.00507	.00381	.00574
44.	All other transportation	.00036	.00693	.00122	.00151	.00090	.00161
45.	Communications	.00553	.01400	.00895	.04452	.00945	.01482
46.	Electric companies & systems	.00152	.00992	.00654	.05959	.00679	.01507
47.	Gas companies & systems	.00150	.00985	.00581	.01108	.00653	.01857
48.	Water & sanitary services	.00051	.00666	.00299	.00505	.00668	.00575
49.	Total	1.14424	1.43124	1.61158	1.50244	1.25474	1.41321

PROCESSING SECTORS

*Each column shows the direct and indirect requirements from the sectors at the left to support a delivery of one dollar to final demand by the sector at the top.

PROCESSING SECTORS

41. All other services	42. Railroads	43. Trucking & warehousing	44. All other transportation	45. Communications	46. Electric companies & systems	47. Gas companies & systems	48. Water & sanitary services	
.00030	.00015	.00016	.00025	.00007	.00015	.00014	.00033	1
.00159	.00116	.00129	.00122	.00103	.10462	.00363	.00757	2
.00075	.00031	.00044	.00054	.00043	.04842	.00027	.00285	3
.00202	.00070	.00126	.04757	.00131	.00088	.10975	.00205	4
.00104	.01005	.00092	.00091	.00071	.00094	.00086	.03319	5
.00020	.00004	.00012	.00011	.00012	.00026	.00048	.00012	6
.00059	.01075	.01624	.00021	.00766	.00062	.00020	.07555	7
.00855	.01203	.00369	.00607	.00089	.00117	.00098	.00480	8
.00052	.00015	.00022	.00034	.00012	.00026	.00027	.00013	9
.00021	.00008	.00012	.00010	.00007	.00008	.00016	.00008	10
.00011	.00002	.00003	.00003	.00004	.00004	.00008	.00005	11
.00001	.00001	.00001	.00001	.00002	.00002	.00004	.00002	12
.00021	.00008	.00010	.00008	.00004	.00005	.00009	.00005	13
.00029	.00050	.00142	.00051	.00008	.00112	.00011	.00075	14
.00005	.00006	.00005	.00243	.00003	.00062	.00006	.00028	15
.03233	.00143	.02796	.00396	.00220	.00689	.00297	.00642	16
.00490	.00096	.00103	.00095	.00064	.00056	.00057	.03188	17
.00297	.00665	.00399	.00914	.00386	.00643	.00809	.01406	18
.00025	.00017	.00006	.00009	.00004	.00003	.00007	.00049	19
.01311	.00084	.00152	.00064	.00193	.00345	.00160	.01195	20
.00246	.00652	.00237	.00787	.00084	.00162	.00047	.00521	21
.00897	.00130	.00121	.01555	.00055	.00731	.00148	.01420	22
.00137	.00682	.00052	.00526	.00028	.00027	.00088	.00181	23
.00702	.00021	.00014	.00039	.00172	.00031	.00009	.00773	24
.00004	.00713	.00006	.00001	.00008	.00011	.00001	.00010	25
.00006	.00001	.00002	.00057	.00001	.00001	.00002	.00010	26
.01155	.00061	.00078	.01600	.00044	.00049	.00057	.00120	27
.00029	.00011	.00063	.00050	.00077	.00083	.00187	.00052	28
.02298	.00321	.06766	.01024	.00243	.00783	.00491	.01446	29
.00002	.00001	.00003	.00001	.00001	.00001	.00002	.00001	30
.00484	.00029	.00425	.00363	.00038	.00039	.00401	.00345	31
.01747	.01015	.00332	.00407	.00277	.00156	.00536	.03654	32
.00206	.00066	.00735	.01024	.00335	.00107	.00387	.00159	33
.00231	.00012	.00059	.00178	.00013	.00027	.00047	.00050	34
.03092	.02794	.01541	.01246	.00221	.00430	.00330	.00662	35
.00244	.00045	.00156	.00127	.00155	.00347	.00645	.00110	36
.00419	.00224	.00168	.00130	.00324	.00273	.00104	.00181	37
.00125	.00032	.00065	.00068	.00039	.00130	.00248	.00040	38
.01285	.00515	.00645	.00524	.00278	.00340	.00598	.00247	39
.00008	.00001	.00007	.00003	.00002	.00002	.00003	.00007	40
1.02369	.00412	.01261	.03979	.02877	.00740	.00961	.00936	41
.00200	1.02601	.00589	.00119	.01140	.01520	.00132	.01106	42
.00726	.00874	1.00504	.00284	.01629	.02335	.00487	.01045	43
.00214	.00092	.00232	1.05637	.00166	.00465	.01352	.00195	44
.01548	.00657	.01844	.00816	1.00357	.00664	.00271	.01495	45
.01156	.00539	.00805	.00751	.00807	1.06384	.00317	.06042	46
.01554	.00175	.00811	.00515	.00896	.00206	1.00579	.00684	47
.00358	.00026	.00051	.00075	.00020	.00021	.00053	1.01652	48
1.28439	1.17317	1.23633	1.29403	1.12417	1.33725	1.21524	1.42406	49

SALES TO →	PROCESSING SECTORS						
TABLE VI — INTERINDUSTRY FLOW OF GOODS & SERVICES, WEST VIRGINIA, PROJECTED TO 1975 (Thousands of Dollars)	1. Agriculture	2. Coal mining (underground)	3. Coal mining (strip & auger)	4. Petroleum & natural gas	5. All other mining	6. General contractors (building)	7. General contractors (non-building)
1. Agriculture	10,307	0	0	0	508	0	0
2. Coal mining (underground)	26	9,698	15,128	0	0	77	24
3. Coal mining (strip & auger)	0	9,069	20,784	0	19	16	6
4. Petroleum & natural gas	0	0	0	4,429	0	0	0
5. All other mining	1,230	851	37	104	3,750	2,789	6,516
6. General contractors (building)	0	0	0	0	0	10,977	0
7. General contractors (non-building)	0	0	0	0	0	7,145	8,772
8. Special trades contractors	0	4,488	4	191	1,877	84,956	10,266
9. Food & kindred products (meats and n.e.c.)	435	1,058	0	0	0	0	0
10. Food & kindred products (dairies)	0	0	0	0	0	0	0
11. Food & kindred products (bakeries)	0	0	0	0	0	0	0
12. Food & kindred products (beverages)	0	0	0	0	0	0	0
13. Apparel & accessories	0	0	0	0	0	0	0
14. Logging & sawmills	1,328	6,587	84	9	735	1,779	318
15. Furniture & other wood fabrication	84	3,714	0	0	114	4,038	380
16. Printing & publishing	19	799	1	441	349	1,666	239
17. Chemicals	15	343	0	0	1,486	0	6,013
18. Petroleum	0	1,867	0	6,604	592	785	39,022
19. Glass	0	0	0	0	0	0	0
20. Stone & clay products	1,104	3,868	0	0	93	27,697	16,097
21. Primary metal products	116	109	0	52	0	5,915	2,924
22. Fabricated metal products	1,075	803	52	0	928	15,326	1,646
23. Machinery (except electrical)	0	565	32	739	590	186	4,780
24. Electrical machinery & apparatus	0	0	47	0	0	442	0
25. Transportation equipment	0	0	0	0	0	0	0
26. Instruments & related products	0	0	2	0	0	0	14
27. All other manufacturing	20	997	0	0	556	6,880	390
28. Eating & drinking establishments	0	0	130	0	0	1,128	93
29. Wholesale trade	6,448	9,600	1,908	2,589	1,252	1,881	1,915
30. Retail food stores	0	0	0	0	0	0	5
31. Retail gasoline service stations	293	20	15	1,215	107	39	166
32. All other retail	648	2,907	68	3,088	651	230	555
33. Banking	2,223	38	964	238	351	1,718	1,011
34. Other finance	258	0	294	276	79	204	755
35. Insurance agents & brokers	2,630	15,635	714	2,102	1,587	3,642	3,009
36. Real estate	1,262	0	3,298	660	28	1,774	587
37. All other finance, insurance & real estate	0	2,407	0	0	95	0	7
38. Hotels & other lodging places	96	0	20	0	11	41	245
39. Medical & legal services	243	585	444	3,759	177	1,178	556
40. Educational services	0	0	0	0	0	0	0
41. All other services	4,928	3,491	3,402	6,211	1,188	1,631	11,947
42. Railroads	74	244	251	234	102	89	1,196
43. Trucking & warehousing	527	1,167	187	154	1,416	107	7,225
44. All other transportation	42	51	0	0	0	0	302
45. Communications	549	1,031	229	498	118	1,058	843
46. Electric companies & systems	1,397	34,418	231	714	1,542	941	729
47. Gas companies & systems	70	40	11	12	0	301	5,874
48. Water & sanitary services	0	0	9	37	0	11,103	2
49. Households	39,236	408,367	19,192	29,398	20,459	59,448	66,445
50. Local government	3,886	7,305	80	1,685	650	641	2,161
51. State government	312	13,443	1,583	4,628	1,586	4,780	4,308
52. Federal government	412	45,266	2,534	1,676	1,774	5,146	6,738
53. Gross savings	22,377	81,316	7,141	23,159	7,564	8,427	15,580
54. Out-of-state (imports)	42,075	343,920	9,469	10,880	39,014	19,440	26,635
55. Total final payments	108,298	899,617	39,999	71,426	71,047	97,882	121,867
56. Total gross outlay	145,745	1,016,067	88,345	105,782	91,348	295,261	256,296

PURCHASES FROM — PROCESSING SECTORS — FINAL PAYMENTS

	SALES TO →							

TABLE VI *(continued)*

INTERINDUSTRY FLOW OF GOODS & SERVICES, WEST VIRGINIA, PROJECTED TO 1975
(Thousands of Dollars)

PURCHASES FROM

PROCESSING SECTORS / FINAL PAYMENTS

PURCHASES FROM		8. Special trades contractors	9. Food & kindred products (meats and n.e.c.)	10. Food & kindred products (dairies)	11. Food & kindred products (bakeries)	12. Food & kindred products (beverages)	13. Apparel & accessories	14. Logging & sawmills
1.	Agriculture	0	9,760	29,247	145	0	0	4,166
2.	Coal mining (underground)	50	1	0	0	38	16	153
3.	Coal mining (strip & auger)	22	0	0	0	0	0	0
4.	Petroleum & natural gas	0	0	0	0	0	0	0
5.	All other mining	1,452	10	0	0	0	0	.0
6.	General contractors (building)	0	0	0	0	6	0	0
7.	General contractors (non-building)	872	0	40	0	0	0	69
8.	Special trades contractors	6,366	58	105	0	0	758	708
9.	Food & kindred products (meats and n.e.c.)	0	5,127	828	64	0	0	0
10.	Food & kindred products (dairies)	0	0	1,416	459	0	0	0
11.	Food & kindred products (bakeries)	0	0	0	65	0	0	0
12.	Food & kindred products (beverages)	0	0	0	0	288	0	0
13.	Apparel & accessories	0	0	0	0	88	0	0
14.	Logging & sawmills	5,044	0	0	0	0	0	26,316
15.	Furniture & other wood fabrication	0	0	0	0	0	0	1
16.	Printing & publishing	77	45	132	74	573	148	17
17.	Chemicals	252	0	0	0	196	0	0
18.	Petroleum	673	0	0	0	0	0	253
19.	Glass	794	0	0	0	531	0	0
20.	Stone & clay products	200	3	0	0	0	0	2
21.	Primary metal products	3,873	0	0	0	333	0	0
22.	Fabricated metal products	14,741	0	0	0	0	0	420
23.	Machinery (except electrical)	1,587	0	40	0	0	0	17
24.	Electrical machinery & apparatus	203	0	0	0	0	0	0
25.	Transportation equipment	0	0	0	0	0	0	0
26.	Instruments & related products	18	712	0	0	0	0	0
27.	All other manufacturing	6,812	4,991	171	353	430	154	939
28.	Eating & drinking establishments	405	10	149	2	118	0	3
29.	Wholesale trade	2,626	1,191	662	1,411	506	67	551
30.	Retail food stores	0	0	0	0	0	0	0
31.	Retail gasoline service stations	1,716	109	150	354	379	40	258
32.	All other retail	57	293	213	698	60	0	272
33.	Banking	3,910	141	65	406	16	20	285
34.	Other finance	0	1,380	0	247	0	0	67
35.	Insurance agents & brokers	3,099	136	413	1,350	471	498	1,299
36.	Real estate	2,452	0	241	0	0	0	2,083
37.	All other finance, insurance & real estate	675	0	85	12	0	0	753
38.	Hotels & other lodging places	496	14	0	1	118	5	72
39.	Medical & legal services	456	446	53	22	109	4	284
40.	Educational services	0	44	0	0	0	0	0
41.	All other services	3,010	1,305	3,560	2,813	430	250	970
42.	Railroads	0	0	0	0	0	0	189
43.	Trucking & warehousing	2,648	77	462	116	678	503	1,097
44.	All other transportation	0	0	6	2	0	13	141
45.	Communications	935	2,739	202	330	470	1,012	688
46.	Electric companies & systems	711	1,598	447	3,239	203	277	1,051
47.	Gas companies & systems	407	68	101	1,813	67	201	98
48.	Water & sanitary services	122	116	136	116	197	27	85
49.	Households	87,653	8,753	18,192	18,377	10,092	27,980	39,189
50.	Local government	2,312	18	229	96	47	88	299
51.	State government	6,287	440	561	333	5,510	318	859
52.	Federal government	7,059	464	1,721	599	172	101	2,641
53.	Gross savings	29,026	2,001	2,394	1,794	4,241	2,853	9,153
54.	Out-of-state (imports)	39,232	26,233	37,187	26,727	12,795	2,005	12,160
55.	Total final payments	171,569	37,909	60,284	47,921	32,857	33,345	64,301
56.	Total gross outlay	238,330	68,283	99,208	62,019	39,156	37,338	107,608

PROCESSING SECTORS

	15. Furniture & other wood fabrication	16. Printing & publishing	17. Chemicals	18. Petroleum	19. Glass	20. Stone & clay products	21. Primary metal products	22. Fabricated metal products	23. Machinery (except electrical)	24. Electrical machinery & apparatus	25. Transportation equipment	
	7	0	19	0	0	555	2,445	2	0	0	0	1
	269	96	20,056	2,728	93	1,988	26,494	50	15	0	0	2
	0	38	0	0	25	0	0	0	0	0	0	3
	0	0	14,538	7,789	0	0	270	0	0	0	0	4
	0	0	8,339	8,657	7,041	9,273	6,322	69	0	0	624	5
	106	0	1,633	0	0	0	30	0	0	0	0	6
	0	0	2,403	0	0	0	60	0	0	173	0	7
	2	191	11,097	0	42	119	2,585	307	37	6	5	8
	0	0	776	0	0	0	0	0	0	0	0	9
	0	0	0	0	0	0	0	0	0	0	0	10
	0	0	0	0	0	0	0	0	0	0	0	11
	0	0	0	0	0	0	0	0	0	0	0	12
	0	0	141	0	0	107	10	0	0	0	0	13
	3,948	0	0	92	0	13	10	0	16	0	0	14
	301	0	208	2,462	0	0	0	0	0	42	0	15
	172	34,912	2,316	146	1,358	1,415	176	405	1,162	205	43	16
	322	131	282,059	5,328	1,706	1,081	5,220	364	0	4,429	0	17
	0	0	2,013	3,240	0	8,402	140	0	0	0	0	18
	139	0	1,200	0	13,870	0	383	3	0	0	0	19
	0	0	2,185	719	1,192	4,724	0	0	0	0	0	20
	0	0	16,007	0	1,052	0	5,458	23,771	6,475	28,793	16,998	21
	519	2,928	1,307	815	37	8,128	2,096	176	4,173	0	0	22
	62	552	0	0	0	160	627	48	3	0	0	23
	0	20	1,824	0	0	25	552	6	2,252	187	0	24
	0	0	0	0	0	250	93	0	0	0	0	25
	0	0	3,292	0	0	0	0	48	0	525	0	26
	17	1,476	14,409	0	19,276	1,004	1,403	1,192	634	99	32	27
	15	374	631	35	0	0	59	78	41	47	21	28
	164	246	26,374	544	2,525	2,870	6,570	2,280	1,574	656	542	29
	0	0	201	0	0	0	0	2	0	0	0	30
	21	822	73	0	36	822	4	26	53	21	2	31
	19	524	2,947	50	1,073	4,073	3,477	691	101	707	176	32
	76	144	776	737	1,718	136	1,345	35	416	180	239	33
	3	0	0	141	0	0	226	61	0	0	0	34
	154	649	5,994	109	7,513	1,837	1,043	584	1,612	1,320	407	35
	0	187	0	0	96	0	0	1,029	22	237	0	36
	0	801	2,241	0	165	0	869	278	0	0	0	37
	9	66	1,411	0	47	4	259	25	62	170	8	38
	44	1,201	2,715	456	228	1,522	1,598	48	46	304	249	39
	0	52	301	0	25	0	546	6	0	793	0	40
	790	1,116	5,253	289	11,416	3,472	10,898	668	382	2,023	1,207	41
	21	10,896		0	0	535	11,657	0	385	610	4,596	42
	269	3,888	25,828	1,845	1,466	7,712	11,305	431	2,544	1,403	153	43
	67	118	6,762	1,840	0	72	12,563	13	1,261	5,116	0	44
	248	3,109	7,143	2,408	1,321	1,540	3,518	356	182	1,551	1,858	45
	296	200	18,811	876	15,133	6,972	9,926	1,953	1,118	5,921	2,020	46
	467	143	30,421	1,958	9,583	7,824	3,180	1,409	390	1,809	1,177	47
	15	80	2,154	53	115	136	776	498	29	833	481	48
	13,676	50,176	301,491	12,944	118,224	65,647	321,874	58,769	46,398	49,640	59,926	49
	103	694	14,474	274	16,973	823	8,401	505	529	1,396	1,638	50
	338	807	8,376	723	3,628	1,390	6,451	1,122	823	989	1,525	51
	1,321	8,682	95,936	7,429	23,355	5,016	39,546	5,715	9,517	9,154	13,041	52
	2,617	13,364	254,086	10,870	56,716	34,366	82,703	11,924	12,131	14,535	12,893	53
	15,689	19,227	718,796	44,102	70,129	39,126	779,518	87,983	74,689	48,869	115,106	54
	33,744	92,950	1,393,159	76,342	289,025	146,368	1,238,493	166,018	144,087	124,583	204,129	55
	42,286	147,035	1,929,913	117,197	389,639	223,139	1,372,656	202,930	169,072	182,743	234,967	56

	SALES TO →	26. Instruments & related products	27. All other manufacturing	28. Eating & drinking establishments	29. Wholesale trade	30. Retail food stores	31. Retail gasoline service stations	32. All other retail
	TABLE VI (continued) INTERINDUSTRY FLOW OF GOODS & SERVICES, WEST VIRGINIA, PROJECTED TO 1975 (Thousands of Dollars)							
1.	Agriculture	0	1,302	881	0	0	0	0
2.	Coal mining (underground)	0	53	77	409	16	23	342
3.	Coal mining (strip & auger)	0	1,385	26	0	16	15	260
4.	Petroleum & natural gas	0	0	0	0	0	0	0
5.	All other mining	0	0	0	0	0	0	0
6.	General contractors (building)	0	0	0	0	0	0	0
7.	General contractors (non-building)	0	0	0	0	0	0	46
8.	Special trades contractors	0	4,744	0	556	157	3	314
9.	Food & kindred products (meats and n.e.c.)	0	1,877	7,841	0	0	0	5,043
10.	Food & kindred products (dairies)	0	0	5,940	0	0	0	0
11.	Food & kindred products (bakeries)	0	0	6,279	0	0	0	329
12.	Food & kindred products (beverages)	0	0	2,817	0	0	0	385
13.	Apparel & accessories	0	43	0	0	0	0	128
14.	Logging & sawmills	0	0	0	0	0	0	0
15.	Furniture & other wood fabrication	0	0	0	28	0	0	0
16.	Printing & publishing	6	1,420	254	282	6,470	167	1,009
17.	Chemicals	813	622	0	1,120	0	0	29,221
18.	Petroleum	0	0	0	0	68	305	0
19.	Glass	50	0	177	0	27	0	1,587
20.	Stone & clay products	0	2	0	0	0	0	6,540
21.	Primary metal products	0	0	0	0	0	0	0
22.	Fabricated metal products	0	5,296	0	0	0	0	0
23.	Machinery (except electrical)	0	1,662	0	0	0	0	0
24.	Electrical machinery & apparatus	0	146	0	0	0	0	0
25.	Transportation equipment	0	0	0	85	0	0	48
26.	Instruments & related products	0	0	0	0	0	0	122
27.	All other manufacturing	111	515	0	683	931	0	1,199
28.	Eating & drinking establishments	0	2	0	894	0	0	949
29.	Wholesale trade	158	211	7,134	7,497	865	655	1,105
30.	Retail food stores	0	0	726	104	2	0	0
31.	Retail gasoline service stations	0	60	22	4,172	155	21	2,614
32.	All other retail	0	30	238	1,668	91	91	2,412
33.	Banking	20	300	149	2,158	150	152	7,221
34.	Other finance	0	0	152	3,083	264	0	1,269
35.	Insurance agents & brokers	23	444	583	5,008	3,941	602	7,485
36.	Real estate	0	303	143	18	8,040	313	5,352
37.	All other finance, insurance & real estate	0	0	11	834	0	0	392
38.	Hotels & other lodging places	0	1	0	556	0	0	2,261
39.	Medical & legal services	26	116	43	1,309	210	21	3,927
40.	Educational services	0	0	0	266	0	0	178
41.	All other services	43	710	754	4,169	3,170	5,991	23,702
42.	Railroads	0	978	0	2,073	0	44	1,509
43.	Trucking & warehousing	72	1,085	196	8,179	838	1,234	5,733
44.	All other transportation	0	49	4	6,136	90	123	1,658
45.	Communications	21	413	1,133	3,959	1,762	879	9,913
46.	Electric companies & systems	22	1,474	7,118	8,662	4,854	749	9,188
47.	Gas companies & systems	14	370	2,690	6,841	2,280	356	4,838
48.	Water & sanitary services	3	49	197	272	470	220	1,815
49.	Households	3,926	42,236	59,123	268,064	85,023	28,323	259,376
50.	Local government	29	720	755	4,323	1,921	433	10,108
51.	State government	129	1,343	5,819	49,416	4,777	7,104	9,716
52.	Federal government	785	7,063	7,168	25,666	5,820	716	29,915
53.	Gross savings	227	7,777	2,179	12,191	6,839	5,037	32,105
54.	Out-of-state (imports)	7,081	112,997	37,746	16,845	16,046	4,949	78,688
55.	Total final payments	12,177	172,136	112,790	376,505	120,426	46,562	419,908
56.	Total gross outlay	13,559	197,798	158,375	447,526	155,293	58,526	560,002

PROCESSING SECTORS

33. Banking	34. Other finance	35. Insurance agents & brokers	36. Real estate	37. All other finance, insurance & real estate	38. Hotels & other lodging places	39. Medical & legal services	40. Educational services	41. All other services	42. Railroads	43. Trucking & warehousing	
0	0	0	0	0	297	92	0	0	0	0	1
38	0	0	0	0	126	62	847	5	85	57	2
69	0	0	0	748	965	0	457	0	0	0	3
0	0	0	0	0	0	0	0	0	0	0	4
0	0	0	0	0	0	8	0	0	2,503	0	5
0	0	0	6,131	0	94	0	33,872	0	0	0	6
0	0	0	169	0	387	0	12,895	0	2,916	4,514	7
164	0	0	2,909	0	1,613	1,689	1,924	4,416	3,110	702	8
0	0	19	0	0	0	6,442	45	23	0	0	9
0	0	0	0	0	0	3,794	0	0	0	0	10
0	0	0	0	0	0	199	272	44	0	0	11
0	0	0	0	0	0	101	883	0	0	0	12
0	0	0	0	0	0	4,104	0	0	0	0	13
0	0	0	0	0	0	3	113	0	0	277	14
0	0	0	0	0	0	0	0	0	0	0	15
974	25	6,016	98	69	2,188	525	83	13,789	25	6,016	16
0	0	0	0	0	0	777	127	2,088	0	0	17
0	0	76	0	0	0	0	0	1,145	1,309	312	18
0	0	0	0	0	0	150	227	0	0	0	19
0	0	0	5	0	0	0	314	7,558	0	62	20
0	0	0	0	0	0	0	0	0	1,491	546	21
0	0	0	0	0	0	0	0	4,033	0	0	22
0	0	0	0	0	0	0	0	612	1,855	0	23
0	323	0	0	0	0	26	0	4,126	19	0	24
0	0	0	0	0	0	0	0	0	2,052	0	25
0	0	0	0	0	0	342	41	0	0	0	26
135	104	0	0	0	15	665	1,728	6,316	0	0	27
26	47	467	692	30	0	12	1,137	0	0	97	28
21	37	53	683	4	2,121	3,119	5,257	12,536	512	19,193	29
0	0	0	0	0	0	271	0	0	0	0	30
17	24	96	26	4	230	338	29	2,453	3	959	31
208	92	117	345	34	316	2,298	6,110	9,805	2,803	701	32
0	5,521	143	466	120	2,208	757	7,282	602	0	1,916	33
179	177	0	0	0	0	444	0	1,228	0	0	34
1,372	43	202	27	116	1,224	2,728	1,373	17,537	7,721	3,909	35
1,111	516	753	5,013	29	1,576	1,453	349	917	0	293	36
2,398	0	29,882	28	0	0	57	836	870	0	0	37
12	7	31	173	30	0	132	529	612	60	132	38
482	568	46	196	30,426	288	7,896	1,227	5,872	1,060	1,384	39
185	148	0	0	0	0	81	3,187	4	0	0	40
6,701	949	2,261	1,722	1,299	4,353	6,698	11,841	11,828	530	2,524	41
0	0	0	0	0	0	235	146	718	7,339	1,450	42
27	0	0	0	0	33	565	732	2,511	2,117	481	43
18	239	77	488	47	0	91	281	612	139	271	44
325	934	1,843	894	301	2,308	1,670	5,191	7,885	1,595	4,802	45
1,351	217	294	527	204	2,943	983	4,783	5,047	1,172	1,574	46
121	30	341	648	180	439	1,336	6,804	8,225	248	1,751	47
120	9	94	269	0	238	1,609	985	1,923	35	88	48
82,233	45,807	78,253	41,448	23,775	16,449	157,624	264,987	252,665	126,085	103,947	49
1,017	613	553	2,706	100	955	339	96	1,578	3,997	1,855	50
1,157	1,314	11,108	2,285	633	525	1,451	87	19,373	8,527	5,626	51
16,386	4,180	336	2,933	657	3,099	9,424	10,989	7,161	12,988	16,785	52
20,397	5,438	2,249	6,148	798	5,887	16,031	4,294	47,858	34,697	34,605	53
16,165	10,675	265,931	6,160	10,389	7,519	28,568	37,754	147,552	68,454	77,130	54
137,355	68,027	358,430	61,680	36,352	34,434	213,437	318,207	476,187	254,748	239,948	55
153,409	79,369	395,318	86,291	70,173	56,290	264,799	437,279	611,527	295,447	293,959	56

SALES TO →	PROCESSING SECTORS				

TABLE VI (continued)

INTERINDUSTRY FLOW OF GOODS & SERVICES, WEST VIRGINIA, PROJECTED TO 1975 (Thousands of Dollars)

PURCHASES FROM ←

PROCESSING SECTORS / FINAL PAYMENTS

		44. All other transportation	45. Communications	46. Electric companies & systems	47. Gas companies & systems	48. Water & sanitary services
1.	Agriculture	0	0	0	0	0
2.	Coal mining (underground)	0	9	49,450	1,912	30
3.	Coal mining (strip & auger)	0	0	18,742	0	0
4.	Petroleum & natural gas	3,533	0	0	65,786	0
5.	All other mining	0	0	0	0	1,281
6.	General contractors (building)	0	0	0	0	0
7.	General contractors (non-building)	0	1,325	0	0	3,310
8.	Special trades contractors	386	0	6	0	0
9.	Food & kindred products (meats and n.e.c.)	0	0	0	0	0
10.	Food & kindred products (dairies)	0	0	0	0	0
11.	Food & kindred products (bakeries)	0	0	0	0	0
12.	Food & kindred products (beverages)	0	0	0	0	0
13.	Apparel & accessories	0	0	0	0	0
14.	Logging & sawmills	0	0	0	0	0
15.	Furniture & other wood fabrication	190	0	110	0	0
16.	Printing & publishing	98	69	2,188	525	83
17.	Chemicals	0	0	0	0	1,090
18.	Petroleum	450	422	2,918	471	34
19.	Glass	0	0	0	0	0
20.	Stone & clay products	0	184	1,436	824	294
21.	Primary metal products	446	52	257	42	41
22.	Fabricated metal products	1,118	0	3,452	569	539
23.	Machinery (except electrical)	371	0	0	0	0
24.	Electrical machinery & apparatus	0	286	110	0	345
25.	Transportation equipment	0	0	0	0	0
26.	Instruments & related products	44	0	0	0	0
27.	All other manufacturing	1,201	0	4	67	0
28.	Eating & drinking establishments	31	134	343	1,118	12
29.	Wholesale trade	572	65	1,820	616	490
30.	Retail food stores	0	0	0	0	0
31.	Retail gasoline service stations	213	17	46	1,599	128
32.	All other retail	136	368	320	1,079	1,600
33.	Banking	756	565	28	1,943	5
34.	Other finance	115	0	0	38	0
35.	Insurance agents & brokers	762	93	499	82	137
36.	Real estate	29	225	638	3,227	0
37.	All other finance, insurance & real estate	0	554	1,054	410	40
38.	Hotels & other lodging places	44	54	638	1,521	0
39.	Medical & legal services	173	135	704	710	20
40.	Educational services	0	0	4	10	0
41.	All other services	2,710	5,075	1,872	553	57
42.	Railroads	44	2,040	7,474	544	405
43.	Trucking & warehousing	104	2,893	11,520	2,497	181
44.	All other transportation	4,434	225	2,110	7,903	21
45.	Communications	514	460	2,694	719	559
46.	Electric companies & systems	415	1,275	30,780	738	2,438
47.	Gas companies & systems	302	1,500	609	3,178	123
48.	Water & sanitary services	35	7	39	195	739
49.	Households	20,363	63,672	114,090	44,536	12,929
50.	Local government	634	3,878	28,518	1,221	815
51.	State government	1,304	5,759	27,583	9,304	1,066
52.	Federal government	1,756	27,883	79,551	16,261	483
53.	Gross savings	10,766	39,999	77,166	45,153	5,265
54.	Out-of-state (imports)	29,951	30,480	84,550	420,602	11,849
55.	Total final payments	64,774	171,671	411,458	537,077	32,407
56.	Total gross outlay	84,000	189,703	553,323	635,953	46,409

	FINAL DEMAND						
49. Households	50. Local government	51. State government	52. Federal government	53. Gross private state investment	54. Out-of-state (exports)	55. Total final demand	56. Total gross output	
29,885	319	220	3,515	0	52,073	86,012	145,745	1
4,853	0	258	306	0	880,109	885,526	1,016,067	2
1,313	0	0	0	0	34,370	35,683	88,345	3
0	0	0	0	0	9,437	9,437	105,782	4
9,056	5,581	3,842	0	1,136	10,877	30,492	91,348	5
428	3,042	4,284	11,836	208,898	13,877	242,366	295,261	6
1,600	18,537	108,857	19,247	42,146	20,545	210,932	256,296	7
21,657	15,809	12,739	1,036	26,482	9,377	87,100	238,330	8
36,582	0	0	273	0	6,893	43,748	68,283	9
74,200	0	1,005	0	0	12,065	87,270	99,208	10
30,494	0	0	0	0	24,281	54,775	62,019	11
27,577	0	0	0	0	7,362	34,939	39,156	12
7,248	0	0	0	0	25,597	32,845	37,338	13
9,010	14	44	290	4,316	47,262	60,936	107,608	14
8,879	0	244	0	8,493	11,989	29,605	42,286	15
8,541	1,329	6,688	705	0	8,931	26,194	147,035	16
5,544	86	456	17,346	0	1,590,899	1,614,331	1,929,913	17
5,247	1,126	8,756	242	0	29,138	44,509	117,197	18
7,434	63	141	0	0	357,910	365,548	389,639	19
2,130	8,241	2,620	1,298	8,459	131,828	154,576	223,139	20
664	0	0	0	21,973	1,235,268	1,257,905	1,372,656	21
1,718	0	0	4,331	7,671	119,033	132,753	202,930	22
547	0	0	0	90,076	63,961	154,584	169,072	23
4,658	0	0	4,713	15,923	146,540	171,834	182,743	24
0	0	2,392	108,203	2,240	119,604	232,439	234,967	25
386	0	0	16	1,338	6,659	8,399	13,559	26
20,964	0	0	0	5,462	95,463	121,889	197,798	27
117,779	50	75	0	0	31,141	149,045	158,375	28
170,618	1,509	1,762	559	18,095	113,307	305,850	447,526	29
144,383	0	0	0	0	9,599	153,982	155,293	30
35,043	191	104	24	0	3,197	38,599	58,526	31
379,344	1,022	967	20	31,936	92,273	505,562	560,002	32
63,250	1,213	2,668	19,540	0	17,088	103,759	153,409	33
56,917	1,070	1,881	3,743	0	4,818	68,429	79,369	34
274,582	413	539	0	0	6,066	281,600	395,318	35
32,628	95	516	453	0	8,345	42,037	86,291	36
13,381	166	206	0	0	10,666	24,419	70,173	37
20,921	26	125	72	0	25,173	46,317	56,290	38
93,142	19,506	36,438	2,697	0	39,450	191,233	264,799	39
8,241	305,791	106,507	7,035	0	3,875	431,449	437,279	40
391,346	2,349	1,599	1,219	0	32,852	429,365	611,527	41
25,325	790	2,236	895	0	210,102	239,348	295,447	42
49,725	1,757	4,130	2,927	0	121,214	179,753	293,959	43
15,251	259	693	82	0	14,330	30,615	84,000	44
66,597	426	1,437	426	0	36,107	104,993	189,703	45
90,732	3,977	650	175	0	260,257	355,791	533,323	46
40,706	80	272	54	0	484,193	525,305	635,953	47
18,264	602	177	35	0	800	19,878	46,409	48
51,903	80,606	257,127	799,134	40,210	221,874	1,450,854	5,597,329	49
153,482	0	178,353	23,212	0	0	355,047	487,518	50
295,073	1,745	0	284,831	0	14,453	596,102	842,628	51
613,984	82	260	0	0	0	614,326	1,197,346	52
440,365	0	0	0	0	0	440,365	1,586,702	53
1,613,732	9,646	91,360	152,487	568,413	630,553	3,066,191	7,255,278	54
3,168,539	92,079	527,100	1,259,664	608,623	866,880	6,522,885	16,966,801	55
5,597,329	487,518	842,628	1,472,977	1,103,268	7,463,081	16,966,801	30,473,492	56

TABLE VII

WEST VIRGINIA EXPANSION AND REPLACEMENT CAPITAL COEFFICIENTS*

	1. Agriculture	2. Coal mining (underground)	3. Coal mining (strip & auger)	4. Petroleum & natural gas	5. All other mining	6. General contractors (building)	7. General contractors (non-building)
5. All other mining	0 / *0*	0 / *0*	0 / *0*	0 / *0*	.02934 / *.00065*	.02381 / *.00053*	.02479 / *.00055*
6. General contractors (building)	.25161 / *.01007*	.14095 / *.00313*	.02577 / *.00057*	.02484 / *.00055*	.05447 / *.00121*	.00221 / *.00005*	.02301 / *.00051*
7. General contractors (non-building)	.04205 / *.00168*	.00647 / *.00014*	.00861 / *.00019*	.00161 / *.00004*	.00546 / *.00012*	.01107 / *.00025*	0 / *0*
8. Special trades contractors	.04144 / *.00414*	.00159 / *.00016*	.00849 / *.00085*	.00159 / *.00011*	.00538 / *.00054*	.00436 / *.00087*	.00455 / *.00038*
14. Logging & sawmills	.00417 / *.00042*	.00250 / *.00025*	0 / *0*	.00160 / *.00011*	.00541 / *.00054*	.00439 / *.00088*	.00915 / *.00076*
15. Furniture & other wood fabrication	0 / *0*	0 / *0*	0 / *0*	0 / *0*	0 / *0*	.01153 / *.00231*	.02403 / *.00200*
20. Stone & clay products	0 / *0*	.01366 / *.00030*	0 / *0*	.00160 / *.00004*	.00542 / *.00012*	.00440 / *.00010*	.00458 / *.00010*
21. Primary metal products	.02108 / *.00084*	.00373 / *.00008*	0 / *0*	.06077 / *.00135*	0 / *0*	.00959 / *.00021*	.01957 / *.00044*
22. Fabricated metal products	0 / *0*	0 / *0*	.01592 / *.00159*	.00158 / *.00011*	.00537 / *.00054*	.00572 / *.00115*	.00395 / *.00033*
23. Machinery (except electrical)	.02103 / *.00210*	.06909 / *.00691*	.03961 / *.00396*	.15193 / *.01085*	.16340 / *.01634*	.02260 / *.00452*	.06811 / *.00568*
24. Electrical machinery & apparatus	0 / *0*	0 / *0*	0 / *0*	.01575 / *.00112*	.00534 / *.00053*	0 / *0*	0 / *0*
25. Transportation equipment	.02071 / *.00207*	.00148 / *.00015*	0 / *0*	0 / *0*	0 / *0*	0 / *0*	0 / *0*
26. Instruments & related products	0 / *0*	0 / *0*	0 / *0*	0 / *0*	0 / *0*	0 / *0*	0 / *0*
27. All other manufacturing	0 / *0*	0 / *0*	0 / *0*	.00159 / *.00011*	.00539 / *.00054*	.00219 / *.00044*	0 / *0*
29. Wholesale trade	.04104 / *.00410*	.00227 / *.00023*	.02774 / *.00277*	.00786 / *.00056*	.00533 / *.00053*	.00633 / *.00127*	.01288 / *.00107*
32. All other retail	.04121 / *.00412*	.00178 / *.00018*	.01140 / *.00114*	.00309 / *.00022*	.00535 / *.00053*	.00467 / *.00093*	.00737 / *.00061*
50. Out-of-state (imports)	.31157 / *.03116*	.44303 / *.02233*	.41814 / *.04181*	.23437 / *.01674*	.05396 / *.00540*	.03674 / *.00735*	.14662 / *.01222*
51. Total	.79591 / *.06070*	.68655 / *.03386*	.55568 / *.05288*	.50818 / *.03191*	.34962 / *.02759*	.14961 / *.02086*	.34861 / *.02465*

*The coefficients in regular type in each column show the expansion capital purchases from the sectors at the left per dollar of increase in capacity by the sector at the top.

The italicized coefficients in each column show the replacement capital purchases from the sectors at the left per dollar of output by the sector at the top.

8. Special trades contractors	9. Food & kindred products (meats and n.e.c.)	10. Food & kindred products (dairies)	11. Food & kindred products (bakeries)	12. Food & kindred products (beverages)	13. Apparel & accessories	14. Logging & sawmills	15. Furniture & other wood fabrication	16. Printing & publishing	17. Chemicals	18. Petroleum	
0 / 0	0 / 0	0 / 0	0 / 0	0 / 0	0 / 0	0 / 0	0 / 0	0 / 0	0 / 0	0 / 0	5
.17330 / .00385	.09183 / .00153	.15122 / .00252	.13042 / .00217	.04749 / .00079	.11293 / .00251	.04520 / .00452	.15737 / .00350	.20309 / .00451	.26780 / .00595	.18143 / .00403	6
.00521 / .00012	.00575 / .00010	.00948 / .00016	.00218 / .00004	0 / 0	0 / 0	.00848 / .00085	0 / 0	.14167 / .00315	.13856 / .00308	0 / 0	7
0 / 0	.00567 / .00047	.00934 / .00078	.02148 / .00179	.03171 / .00264	.03720 / .00413	0 / 0	.00961 / .00096	0 / 0	0 / 0	.04482 / .00280	8
.02153 / .00179	.01141 / .00095	.00939 / .00078	.01080 / .00090	.03189 / .00266	0 / 0	.00627 / .00105	.01598 / .00160	0 / 0	0 / 0	0 / 0	14
.02012 / .00168	0 / 0	0 / 0	0 / 0	0 / 0	0 / 0	0 / 0	0 / 0	.00583 / .00053	0 / 0	0 / 0	15
.02157 / .00048	.01143 / .00019	.00941 / .00016	.01082 / .00018	.03195 / .00053	0 / 0	.00561 / .00056	.00505 / .00011	.02164 / .00048	.01275 / .00028	0 / 0	20
.02178 / .00048	.01154 / .00019	0 / 0	0 / 0	0 / 0	0 / 0	0 / 0	.00298 / .00007	0 / 0	.02529 / .00056	.00638 / .00014	21
0 / 0	.00566 / .00047	0 / 0	.01071 / .00089	.03163 / .00264	0 / 0	0 / 0	.00917 / .00092	0 / 0	0 / 0	.04113 / .00257	22
.01196 / .00100	0 / 0	0 / 0	0 / 0	0 / 0	.04292 / .00477	.04419 / .00737	.01481 / .00148	.08774 / .00798	.10371 / .00943	0 / 0	23
.00021 / .00002	.00620 / .00052	.00575 / .00048	.00320 / .00027	0 / 0	0 / 0	0 / 0	.00830 / .00083	0 / 0	.01670 / .00152	0 / 0	24
0 / 0	0 / 0	0 / 0	0 / 0	0 / 0	.00260 / .00029	.01113 / .00185	0 / 0	0 / 0	.00040 / .00004	.00448 / .00028	25
0 / 0	0 / 0	0 / 0	0 / 0	0 / 0	0 / 0	0 / 0	0 / 0	0 / 0	0 / 0	0 / 0	26
0 / 0	0 / 0	0 / 0	0 / 0	0 / 0	0 / 0	.04455 / .00743	.02808 / .00281	0 / 0	0 / 0	0 / 0	27
.00021 / .00002	.00562 / .00047	.01850 / .00154	.01063 / .00089	.03140 / .00262	.03684 / .00409	.01831 / .00305	.01021 / .00102	.00115 / .00011	.00154 / .00014	.00976 / .00061	29
.00894 / .00074	.01726 / .00144	.00929 / .00077	.00897 / .00075	.05802 / .00484	.04403 / .00489	.07553 / .01259	.01912 / .00191	.01155 / .00105	.00649 / .00059	.09270 / .00579	32
.12410 / .01034	.14593 / .01216	.09627 / .00802	.10919 / .00910	.38027 / .03169	.28942 / .03216	.25664 / .04277	.22650 / .02265	.55345 / .05031	.17602 / .01479	.42334 / .02646	50
.40893 / .02052	.31830 / .01849	.31865 / .01521	.31840 / .01698	.64436 / .04841	.56594 / .05284	.51591 / .08204	.50718 / .03786	1.02612 / .06812	.74926 / .03638	.80404 / .04268	51

TABLE VII (continued) WEST VIRGINIA EXPANSION AND REPLACEMENT CAPITAL COEFFICIENTS*	19. Glass	20. Stone & clay products	21. Primary metal products	22. Fabricated metal products	23. Machinery (except electrical)	24. Electrical machinery & apparatus	25. Transportation equipment
5. All other mining	0 *0*	0 *0*	0 *0*	0 *0*	0 *0*	0 *0*	0 *0*
6. General contractors (building)	.16642 *.00370*	.08520 *.00189*	.13212 *.00294*	.02568 *.00057*	.09684 *.00215*	.15187 *.00338*	.11766 *.00262*
7. General contractors (non-building)	.06122 *.00136*	.00407 *.00009*	.05107 *.00113*	.00429 *.00010*	.00874 *.00019*	0 *0*	.01475 *.00033*
8. Special trades contractors	.00483 *.00035*	.00401 *.00027*	.05790 *.00362*	.00423 *.00035*	.00431 *.00036*	0 *0*	.01453 *.00242*
14. Logging & sawmills	0 *0*	0 *0*	0 *0*	.00425 *.00036*	0 *0*	0 *0*	0 *0*
15. Furniture & other wood fabrication	.00410 *.00029*	0 *0*	.00199 *.00012*	.00212 *.00018*	.00108 *.00009*	.00211 *.00018*	.01460 *.00243*
20. Stone & clay products	0 *0*	0 *0*	.03245 *.00072*	.00426 *.00010*	0 *0*	0 *0*	.01464 *.00033*
21. Primary metal products	0 *0*	0 *0*	.03624 *.00081*	0 *0*	.03539 *.00079*	0 *0*	.01479 *.00033*
22. Fabricated metal products	.00272 *.00020*	.00020 *.00001*	.02605 *.00163*	0 *0*	.00013 *.00001*	0 *0*	.01450 *.00242*
23. Machinery (except electrical)	.02200 *.00157*	.06605 *.00440*	.08121 *.00508*	.00068 *.00006*	.01511 *.00126*	.00366 *.00031*	.02942 *.00490*
24. Electrical machinery & apparatus	.00291 *.00021*	0 *0*	0 *0*	.00042 *.00004*	.01419 *.00118*	.00167 *.00014*	.01010 *.00168*
25. Transportation equipment	0 *0*	0 *0*	0 *0*	.00068 *.00006*	0 *0*	.00436 *.00036*	0 *0*
26. Instruments & related products	0 *0*	0 *0*	0 *0*	0 *0*	0 *0*	0 *0*	0 *0*
27. All other manufacturing	0 *0*	.00828 *.00055*	.00452 *.00028*	0 *0*	0 *0*	0 *0*	0 *0*
29. Wholesale trade	.00392 *.00028*	.01116 *.00074*	.00784 *.00049*	.00838 *.00070*	.00426 *.00036*	.00541 *.00045*	.02878 *.00480*
32. All other retail	.00224 *.00016*	.08504 *.00567*	.00087 *.00005*	.00177 *.00015*	.00326 *.00027*	.01487 *.00124*	.00289 *.00048*
50. Out-of-state (imports)	.14862 *.01062*	.52025 *.03468*	.25645 *.02154*	.25096 *.02091*	.04628 *.00386*	.14464 *.01205*	.24044 *.04007*
51. Total	.41898 *.01874*	.78426 *.04830*	.68871 *.03841*	.30772 *.02358*	.22959 *.01052*	.32859 *.01811*	.51710 *.06281*

*The coefficients in regular type in each column show the expansion capital purchases from the sectors at the left per dollar of increase in capacity by the sector at the top.

The italicized coefficients in each column show the replacement capital purchases from the sectors at the left per dollar of output by the sector at the top.

	26. Instruments & related products	27. All other manufacturing	28. Eating & drinking establishments	29. Wholesale trade	30. Retail food stores	31. Retail gasoline service stations	32. All other retail	33. Banking	34. Other finance	35. Insurance agents & brokers	36. Real estate	
	0	0	0	0	0	0	0	0	0	0	0	5
	0	*0*	*0*	*0*	*0*	*0*	*0*	*0*	*0*	*0*	*0*	
	.06236	.07692	.01525	.04423	.04380	.07875	.08791	.26518	.05017	.02652	.12014	6
	.00139	*.00171*	*.00038*	*.00074*	*.00088*	*.00158*	*.00176*	*.00530*	*.00100*	*.00059*	*.00267*	
	.00625	.00180	.01153	.00296	.00878	.03948	.00459	.02659	.00419	.00065	.04016	7
	.00014	*.00004*	*.00029*	*.00005*	*.00018*	*.00079*	*.00009*	*.00053*	*.00008*	*.00001*	*.00089*	
	.00616	.02965	.00603	.00428	.00433	.03891	.04306	.02621	.00413	.00064	0	8
	.00077	*.00247*	*.00060*	*.00043*	*.00043*	*.00389*	*.00431*	*.00262*	*.00041*	*.00006*	*0*	
	0	0	.00152	0	0	0	0	0	0	0	0	14
	0	*0*	*.00015*	*0*	*0*	*0*	*0*	*0*	*0*	*0*	*0*	
	.00619	0	0	.00183	.00826	0	.00105	.01316	.00207	.00226	0	15
	.00077	*0*	*0*	*.00018*	*.00083*	*0*	*.00011*	*.00132*	*.00021*	*.00023*	*0*	
	.00621	0	.03262	0	0	0	0	0	0	0	.03987	20
	.00014	*0*	*.00081*	*0*	*0*	*0*	*0*	*0*	*0*	*0*	*.00089*	
	0	0	0	0	0	0	0	0	0	0	0	21
	0	*0*	*0*	*0*	*0*	*0*	*0*	*0*	*0*	*0*	*0*	
	0	.04069	0	.00009	0	.07762	.00018	0	0	0	0	22
	0	*.00339*	*0*	*.00001*	*0*	*.00776*	*.00002*	*0*	*0*	*0*	*0*	
	0	.01039	.00528	.01886	.03855	.00851	.00124	.04323	0	.00235	0	23
	0	*.00087*	*.00053*	*.00189*	*.00385*	*.00085*	*.00012*	*.00432*	*0*	*.00023*	*0*	
	0	.01283	.00121	.00380	.00903	0	.00351	0	0	0	0	24
	0	*.00107*	*.00012*	*.00038*	*.00090*	*0*	*.00035*	*0*	*0*	*0*	*0*	
	0	0	0	0	0	0	0	0	0	0	0	25
	0	*0*	*0*	*0*	*0*	*0*	*0*	*0*	*0*	*0*	*0*	
	0	0	0	0	0	0	.00064	0	0	0	0	26
	0	*0*	*0*	*0*	*0*	*0*	*.00006*	*0*	*0*	*0*	*0*	
	0	0	0	0	0	.00780	.00050	0	0	.01170	0	27
	0	*0*	*0*	*0*	*0*	*.00078*	*.00005*	*0*	*0*	*.00117*	*0*	
	.01220	.01254	.00149	.00189	.02615	.00077	.00112	0	.00164	0	.00784	29
	.00152	*.00104*	*.00015*	*.00019*	*.00262*	*.00008*	*.00011*	*0*	*.00016*	*0*	*.00078*	
	.00613	.00630	.00839	.01141	.00215	.00387	.02562	.00078	.00822	.01653	.01181	32
	.00077	*.00053*	*.00084*	*.00114*	*.00022*	*.00039*	*.00256*	*.00008*	*.00082*	*.00165*	*.00118*	
	.14297	.11660	.11547	.19878	.13714	.02278	.07560	.03468	.42600	.03868	.09920	50
	.01787	*.00972*	*.01155*	*.01988*	*.01372*	*.00228*	*.00756*	*.00347*	*.04260*	*.00387*	*.00992*	
	.24847	.30772	.19879	.28813	.27819	.27849	.24502	.40983	.49642	.09933	.31902	51
	.02337	*.02084*	*.01542*	*.02489*	*.02363*	*.01840*	*.01710*	*.01764*	*.04528*	*.00781*	*.01633*	

TABLE VII (continued) WEST VIRGINIA EXPANSION AND REPLACEMENT CAPITAL COEFFICIENTS*	37. All other finance, insurance & real estate	38. Hotels & other lodging places	39. Medical & legal services	40. Educational services	41. All other services	42. Railroads	43. Trucking & warehousing
5. All other mining	0 *0*	0 *0*	0 *0*	0 *0*	0 *0*	0 *0*	0 *0*
6. General contractors (building)	.02838 *.00063*	.74558 *.01864*	.50842 *.01130*	2.17916 *0*	.08639 *.00192*	.05790 *.00129*	.16229 *.00270*
7. General contractors (non-building)	.00095 *.00002*	.04485 *.00112*	.01639 *.00036*	.10925 *0*	.01733 *.00038*	.02793 *.00062*	.05835 *.00097*
8. Special trades contractors	.00374 *.00037*	.07368 *.00737*	.01616 *.00162*	.05383 *.00218*	.00854 *.00085*	0 *0*	0 *0*
14. Logging & sawmills	0 *0*	.03705 *.00371*	0 *0*	0 *0*	0 *0*	0 *0*	0 *0*
15. Furniture & other wood fabrication	0 *0*	.06025 *.00603*	.00136 *.00014*	.02631 *.00263*	0 *0*	.01771 *.00126*	.01882 *.00235*
20. Stone & clay products	0 *0*	.03711 *.00093*	0 *0*	0 *0*	0 *0*	0 *0*	0 *0*
21. Primary metal products	0 *0*	0 *0*	0 *0*	.00151 *0*	0 *0*	.16106 *.00358*	0 *0*
22. Fabricated metal products	0 *0*	0 *0*	0 *0*	0 *0*	0 *0*	0 *0*	0 *0*
23. Machinery (except electrical)	0 *0*	.02002 *.00200*	.04105 *.00410*	.05520 *.00552*	0 *0*	.03004 *.00215*	.01152 *.00144*
24. Electrical machinery & apparatus	0 *0*	0 *0*	0 *0*	.08709 *.00871*	.02204 *.00220*	0 *0*	0 *0*
25. Transportation equipment	0 *0*	0 *0*	0 *0*	0 *0*	0 *0*	.02610 *.00186*	0 *0*
26. Instruments & related products	0 *0*	0 *0*	.03023 *.00302*	0 *0*	0 *0*	0 *0*	0 *0*
27. All other manufacturing	0 *0*	0 *0*	.00238 *.00024*	.02118 *.00212*	.00856 *.00086*	0 *0*	0 *0*
29. Wholesale trade	.00926 *.00093*	.03648 *.00365*	0 *0*	0 *0*	.00423 *.00042*	0 *0*	0 *0*
32. All other retail	.00186 *.00019*	.01465 *.00146*	.00027 *.00003*	.10117 *.01012*	.01698 *.00170*	0 *0*	.14415 *.01802*
50. Out-of-state (imports)	.07499 *.00750*	.32631 *.03263*	.27211 *.02721*	1.29939 *.03853*	.34242 *.01726*	.38602 *.02757*	.69720 *.05857*
51. Total	.11918 *.00964*	1.39598 *.07754*	.88836 *.04802*	3.93409 *.06981*	.50649 *.02559*	.70676 *.03833*	1.09233 *.08405*

*The coefficients in regular type in each column show the expansion capital purchases from the sectors at the left per dollar of increase in capacity by the sector at the top.

The italicized coefficients in each column show the replacement capital purchases from the sectors at the left per dollar of output by the sector at the top.

44. All other transportation	45. Communications	46. Electric companies & systems	47. Gas companies & systems	48. Water & sanitary services	
0 0	0 0	0 0	0 0	0 0	5
.01076 .00018	.18595 .00413	.47215 .01049	.02990 .00066	.48117 .01069	6
.00539 .00009	.16645 .00370	.05909 .00131	.05288 .00117	.07042 .00156	7
0 0	.03581 .00239	.04402 .00152	0 0	.06940 .00139	8
0 0	.06567 .00438	0 0	0 0	0 0	14
0 0	.00360 .00024	0 0	0 0	0 0	15
0 0	.03124 .00069	.01388 .00031	0 0	0 0	20
.33093 .00552	.01107 .00025	.01528 .00034	.15234 .00338	.27341 .00608	21
0 0	0 0	0 0	0 0	0 0	22
.05407 .00361	.03543 .00236	.04526 .00156	.18993 .00633	.07879 .00158	23
0 0	.02004 .00134	.00363 .00013	0 0	.13352 .00267	24
0 0	0 0	0 0	.00639 .00021	0 0	25
0 0	0 0	.00190 .00007	0 0	0 0	26
.01096 .00073	0 0	0 0	0 0	0 0	27
.00526 .00035	.00220 .00015	.02062 .00071	.12704 .00424	.03436 .00069	29
.01056 .00070	.00015 .00001	.00044 .00001	.00680 .00023	.03450 .00069	32
.28170 .01878	2.52184 .15253	1.07501 .03707	.62833 .02094	1.31219 .02624	50
.70963 .02996	3.07945 .17217	1.75128 .05352	1.19361 .03716	2.48776 .05159	51

TABLE VIII

DIRECT MAN-HOUR REQUIREMENTS PER DOLLAR OF OUTPUT, WEST VIRGINIA, 1965*

PROCESSING SECTORS	1. Agriculture	2. Coal mining (underground)	3. Coal mining (strip & auger)	4. Petroleum & natural gas	5. All other mining	6. General contractors (building)
1. Agriculture	.00114	0	0	0	.00009	0
2. Coal mining (underground)	.00005	.00104	.02003	0	0	.00003
3. Coal mining (strip & auger)	0	.00105	.02170	0	.00002	0
4. Petroleum & natural gas	0	0	0	.00571	0	0
5. All other mining	.00043	.00004	.00002	.00013	.00183	.00043
6. General contractors (building)	0	0	0	0	0	.00271
7. General contractors (non-building)	0	0	0	0	0	.00208
8. Special trades contractors	0	.00048	0	.00020	.00053	.02885
9. Food & kindred products (meats and n.e.c.)	.00018	.00008	0	0	0	0
10. Food & kindred products (dairies)	0	0	0	0	0	0
11. Food & kindred products (bakeries)	0	0	0	0	0	0
12. Food & kindred products (beverages)	0	0	0	0	0	0
13. Apparel & accessories	0	0	0	0	0	0
14. Logging & sawmills	.00204	.00146	.00014	.00002	.00181	.00068
15. Furniture & other wood fabrication	.00007	.00047	0	0	.00016	.00106
16. Printing & publishing	.00001	.00009	0	.00030	.00005	.00031
17. Chemicals	0	.00002	0	0	.00018	0
18. Petroleum	0	.00004	0	.00135	.00014	.00005
19. Glass	0	0	0	0	0	0
20. Stone & clay products	.00066	.00034	0	0	.00001	.00873
21. Primary metal products	.00004	.00001	0	.00003	0	.00110
22. Fabricated metal products	.00092	.00010	.00026	0	.00102	.00567
23. Machinery (except electrical)	0	.00005	.00007	.00069	.00064	.00003
24. Electrical machinery & apparatus	0	0	.00010	0	0	.00007
25. Transportation equipment	0	0	0	0	0	0
26. Instruments & related products	0	0	0	0	0	0
27. All other manufacturing	.00001	.00011	0	0	.00023	.00401
28. Eating & drinking establishments	0	0	.00027	0	0	.00013
29. Wholesale trade	.00624	.00173	.00262	.00147	.00307	.00231
30. Retail food stores	0	0	0	0	0	0
31. Retail gasoline service stations	.00035	.00001	.00006	.00023	.00021	.00006
32. All other retail	.00087	.00056	.00030	.00164	.00109	.00009
33. Banking	.00128	0	.00083	.00007	.00022	.00059
34. Other finance	.00013	0	.00015	.00011	.00006	.00002
35. Insurance agents & brokers	.00059	.00023	.00023	.00038	.00034	.00021
36. Real estate	.00063	0	.00114	.00004	.00002	.00044
37. All other finance, insurance & real estate	0	.00012	0	0	.00005	0
38. Hotels & other lodging places	.00009	0	.00013	0	.00007	.00004
39. Medical & legal services	.00036	.00014	.00126	.00529	.00048	.00032
40. Educational services	0	0	0	0	0	0
41. All other services	.00420	.00045	.00350	.00480	.00063	.00084
42. Railroads	.00007	.00003	.00037	.00028	.00014	.00004
43. Trucking & warehousing	.00030	.00010	.00037	.00013	.00053	.00003
44. All other transportation	.00001	0	0	0	0	0
45. Communications	.00042	.00011	.00028	.00032	.00017	.00040
46. Electric companies & systems	.00033	.00141	.00011	.00034	.00017	.00007
47. Gas companies & systems	.00001	0	0	0	0	.00002
48. Water & sanitary services	0	0	.00001	.00003	0	.00352
49. Households (Primary Labor Inputs)	.01615	.12926	.09659	.15467	.04462	.08171
50. Total	.03761	.13953	.15053	.17823	.05859	.14665

*Each column shows the direct man-hours required by the sectors at the left per dollar of output by the sector at the top.

PROCESSING SECTORS

7. General contractors (non-building)	8. Special trades contractors	9. Food & kindred products (meats and n.e.c.)	10. Food & kindred products (dairies)	11. Food & kindred products (bakeries)	12. Food & kindred products (beverages)	13. Apparel & accessories	14. Logging & sawmills	15. Furniture & other wood fabrication	16. Printing & publishing	17. Chemicals	
0	0	.00331	.00363	.00011	0	0	.00078	0	0	0	1
.00001	.00003	0	0	0	.00008	.00005	.00007	.00092	.00008	.00128	2
0	.00001	0	0	0	0	0	0	0	.00003	0	3
0	0	0	0	0	0	0	0	0	0	.00117	4
.00156	.00027	.00001	0	0	0	0	0	0	0	.00019	5
0	0	0	0	.00001	0	0	0	.00006	0	.00007	6
.00206	.00027	0	.00002	0	0	0	.00009	0	0	.00012	7
.00360	.00227	.00021	.00008	0	0	.00223	.00072	0	0	.00073	8
0	0	.00573	.00128	.00005	0	0	0	0	0	.00006	9
0	0	0	.00117	0	0	0	0	0	0	0	10
0	0	0	0	.00011	0	0	0	0	0	0	11
0	0	0	0	0	.00079	0	0	0	0	0	12
0	0	0	0	0	.00011	0	0	0	0	.00005	13
.00028	.00222	0	0	0	0	0	.03492	.03016	0	0	14
.00017	0	0	0	0	0	0	0	.00092	0	.00002	15
.00012	.00006	.00031	.00011	.00017	.00096	.00047	.00004	.00025	.03106	.00014	16
.00108	.00003	0	0	0	.00009	0	0	.00035	.00001	.00693	17
.00278	.00006	0	0	0	0	0	.00001	0	0	.00002	18
0	.00024	0	0	0	.00126	0	0	.00037	0	.00007	19
.00515	.00010	0	0	0	0	0	0	0	0	.00010	20
.00052	.00079	0	0	0	.00047	0	0	0	0	.00003	21
.00071	.00784	0	0	0	0	0	.00013	.00122	.00219	.00025	22
.00119	.00025	0	.00003	0	0	0	.00002	.00015	.00015	0	23
0	.00004	0	0	0	0	0	0	0	.00004	.00010	24
0	0	0	0	0	0	0	0	0	0	0	25
.00001	.00001	.00028	0	0	0	0	0	0	0	.00030	26
.00003	.00108	.00037	.00035	.00011	.00104	.00045	.00012	.00003	.00182	.00087	27
.00021	.00011	.00004	.00018	.00001	.00033	0	.00001	.00007	.00023	.00005	28
.00218	.00403	.00437	.00082	.00329	.00172	.00027	.00267	.00106	.00031	.00108	29
0	0	0	0	0	0	0	0	0	0	.00002	30
.00012	.00067	.00028	.00018	.00085	.00137	.00019	.00035	.00033	.00043	.00001	31
.00036	.00009	.00079	.00066	.00190	.00027	0	.00021	.00012	.00082	.00060	32
.00040	.00070	.00032	.00005	.00032	.00003	.00004	.00028	.00019	.00011	.00005	33
.00017	0	.00031	0	.00017	0	0	.00004	.00001	0	0	34
.00038	.00047	.00008	.00020	.00046	.00040	.00001	.00037	.00019	.00016	.00010	35
.00014	.00028	0	.00012	0	0	0	.00049	0	.00009	0	36
.00001	.00009	0	.00003	.00001	0	0	.00046	0	.00023	.00006	37
.00038	.00020	.00009	0	.00002	.00049	.00003	.00062	.00006	.00010	.00019	38
.00056	.00110	.00114	.00050	.00017	.00045	.00005	.00058	.00059	.00097	.00035	39
0	0	.00004	0	0	0	0	0	0	.00005	.00005	40
.00593	.00096	.00221	.00324	.00547	.00092	.00003	.00152	.00201	.00068	.00096	41
.00059	0	0	0	0	0	0	.00008	.00006	.00002	.00152	42
.00237	.00039	.00020	.00082	.00010	.00098	.00030	.00169	.00111	.00115	.00090	43
.00005	0	0	0	0	0	.00002	.00004	.00004	.00003	.00009	44
.00045	.00032	.00011	.00023	.00065	.00134	.00193	.00068	.00044	.00139	.00061	45
.00005	.00010	.00071	.00027	.00140	.00012	.00038	.00057	.00031	.00018	.00047	46
.00009	.00003	.00004	.00003	.00093	.00003	.00008	.00002	.00012	.00005	.00044	47
0	.00008	.00005	.00013	.00027	.00042	.00004	.00003	.00003	.00004	.00018	48
.07366	.10994	.07638	.06110	.10467	.10715	.42071	.22477	.12801	.11854	.04620	49
.10736	.13514	.09740	.07522	.12125	.12083	.42729	.27238	.16919	.16096	.06645	50

TABLE VIII
(continued)

DIRECT MAN-HOUR REQUIREMENTS
PER DOLLAR OF OUTPUT,
WEST VIRGINIA, 1965*

PROCESSING SECTORS		18. Petroleum	19. Glass	20. Stone & clay products	21. Primary metal products	22. Fabricated metal products	23. Machinery (except electrical)
1.	Agriculture	0	0	.00001	.00001	0	0
2.	Coal mining (underground)	.00301	.00003	.00082	.00249	.00006	.00001
3.	Coal mining (strip & auger)	0	.00001	0	0	0	0
4.	Petroleum & natural gas	.01084	0	0	.00002	0	0
5.	All other mining	.00330	.00081	.00282	.00021	.00002	0
6.	General contractors (building)	0	0	0	0	0	0
7.	General contractors (non-building)	0	0	0	0	0	0
8.	Special trades contractors	0	.00001	.00006	.00021	.00015	.00002
9.	Food & kindred products (meats and n.e.c.)	0	0	0	0	0	0
10.	Food & kindred products (dairies)	0	0	0	0	0	0
11.	Food & kindred products (bakeries)	0	0	0	0	0	0
12.	Food & kindred products (beverages)	0	0	0	0	0	0
13.	Apparel & accessories	0	0	0	.00001	0	0
14.	Logging & sawmills	.00018	0	.00002	0	0	.00006
15.	Furniture & other wood fabrication	0	.00018	0	0	0	0
16.	Printing & publishing	.00015	.00005	.00031	.00002	.00032	.00010
17.	Chemicals	.00210	.00020	.00008	.00024	.00005	0
18.	Petroleum	.00054	0	.00048	0	0	0
19.	Glass	0	.00283	0	.00003	0	0
20.	Stone & clay products	0	.00027	.00165	0	0	0
21.	Primary metal products	0	.00015	0	.00022	.00524	.00266
22.	Fabricated metal products	.00019	.00001	.00198	.00018	.00007	.00190
23.	Machinery (except electrical)	0	0	.00002	.00004	.00001	0
24.	Electrical machinery & apparatus	0	0	0	.00004	.00001	.00080
25.	Transportation equipment	0	0	.00002	0	0	0
26.	Instruments & related products	0	0	0	0	.00002	0
27.	All other manufacturing	0	.00449	.00093	.00008	.00042	.00083
28.	Eating & drinking establishments	.00005	0	0	.00001	.00008	.00007
29.	Wholesale trade	.00063	.00143	.00147	.00066	.00158	.00122
30.	Retail food stores	0	0	0	0	0	0
31.	Retail gasoline service stations	0	.00002	.00019	0	.00004	.00008
32.	All other retail	.00010	.00053	.00092	.00049	.00075	.00020
33.	Banking	.00045	.00046	.00018	.00008	.00003	.00029
34.	Other finance	.00023	0	0	.00001	.00002	0
35.	Insurance agents & brokers	.00003	.00033	.00016	.00006	.00010	.00048
36.	Real estate	0	.00002	0	0	.00022	.00002
37.	All other finance, insurance & real estate	0	.00002	0	.00003	.00012	0
38.	Hotels & other lodging places	0	.00003	.00001	.00005	.00005	.00006
39.	Medical & legal services	.00097	.00012	.00055	.00028	.00018	.00009
40.	Educational services	0	.00002	0	.00012	.00001	0
41.	All other services	.00048	.00150	.00068	.00102	.00082	.00047
42.	Railroads	0	0	.00065	.00108	.00003	.00094
43.	Trucking & warehousing	.00138	.00032	.00262	.00074	.00021	.00143
44.	All other transportation	.00077	0	0	.00043	0	.00042
45.	Communications	.00229	.00051	.00043	.00029	.00032	.00027
46.	Electric companies & systems	.00042	.00068	.00064	.00040	.00053	.00034
47.	Gas companies & systems	.00046	.00083	.00075	.00006	.00015	.00005
48.	Water & sanitary services	.00004	.00004	.00006	.00005	.00023	.00002
49.	Households (Primary Labor Inputs)	.02163	.11216	.08936	.05511	.12474	.09857
50.	Total	.05023	.12808	.10789	.06477	.13658	.11139

*Each column shows the direct man-hours required by the sectors at the left per dollar of output by the sector at the top.

PROCESSING SECTORS

24. Electrical machinery & apparatus	25. Transportation equipment	26. Instruments & related products	27. All other manufacturing	28. Eating & drinking establishments	29. Wholesale trade	30. Retail food stores	31. Retail gasoline service stations	32. All other retail	33. Banking	34. Other finance	
0	0	0	.00011	.00009	0	0	0	0	0	0	1
0	0	0	.00003	.00006	.00004	.00003	.00005	.00008	.00003	0	2
0	0	0	.00013	.00002	0	.00001	.00002	.00004	0	0	3
0	0	0	0	0	0	0	0	0	0	0	4
0	.00012	0	0	0	0	0	0	0	0	0	5
0	0	0	0	0	0	0	0	0	0	0	6
.00005	0	0	0	0	0	0	0	0	0	0	7
.00001	0	0	.00264	0	.00013	.00010	.00001	.00056	.00018	0	8
0	0	0	.00072	.00302	0	0	0	0	0	0	9
0	0	0	0	.00168	0	0	0	.00001	0	0	10
0	0	0	0	.00310	0	0	0	.00005	0	0	11
0	0	0	0	.00084	0	0	0	.00001	0	0	12
0	0	0	.00019	0	0	0	0	0	0	0	13
0	0	0	0	0	0	0	0	0	0	0	14
.00003	0	0	0	0	0	0	0	.00023	0	0	15
.00012	.00003	.00005	.00030	.00007	.00010	.00490	.00028	.00274	.00065	.00131	16
.00086	0	.00199	.00004	0	.00005	0	0	0	0	0	17
0	0	0	0	0	0	.00002	.00047	.00006	0	0	18
0	0	.00041	0	.00013	0	.00002	0	.00081	0	0	19
0	0	0	0	0	0	0	0	0	0	0	20
.01024	.00391	0	0	0	0	0	0	0	0	0	21
0	0	0	.00334	0	0	0	0	0	0	0	22
0	0	0	.00083	0	0	0	0	0	0	0	23
.00010	0	0	.00014	0	0	0	0	0	0	.00038	24
0	0	0	0	0	.00002	0	0	.00001	0	0	25
.00011	0	0	0	0	0	0	0	.00003	0	0	26
.00004	.00002	.00079	.00048	0	.00015	.00043	0	.00016	.00011	.00014	27
.00003	.00002	0	0	0	.00022	0	0	.00011	.00002	.00013	28
.00068	.00031	.00125	.00021	.00720	.00223	.00073	.00151	.00028	.00006	.00007	29
0	0	0	0	.00063	.00003	0	0	0	0	0	30
.00002	0	0	.00005	.00003	.00160	.00023	.00015	.00053	.00002	.00010	31
.00066	.00020	0	.00004	.00029	.00063	.00012	.00021	.00057	.00056	.00023	32
.00007	.00009	.00011	.00024	.00007	.00021	.00007	.00032	.00067	C	.00504	33
0	0	0	0	.00007	.00024	.00012	0	.00016	.00006	.00015	34
.00018	.00006	.00006	.00012	.00012	.00026	.00056	.00041	.00074	.00027	.00002	35
.00017	0	0	.00003	.00007	.00001	.00362	.00039	.00165	.00038	.00047	36
0	0	0	0	0	.00005	0	0	.00003	.00057	0	37
.00005	.00001	0	0	0	.00018	0	0	.00054	.00002	.00002	38
.00032	.00030	.00048	.00025	.00007	.00047	.00034	.00009	.00109	.00085	.00196	39
.00108	0	0	0	0	.00010	0	0	.00010	.00028	.00057	40
.00116	.00068	.00046	.00091	.00062	.00083	.00248	.01476	.00344	.00455	.00170	41
.00043	.00252	0	.00115	0	.00073	0	.00010	.00103	0	0	42
.00060	.00006	.00046	.00028	0	.00151	.00045	.00185	.00084	.00001	0	43
.00096	0	0	.00002	0	.00050	.00003	.00006	.00014	.00001	.00014	44
.00089	.00090	.00018	.00034	.00079	.00080	.00125	.00131	.00039	.00135	.00148	45
.00142	.00046	.00008	.00036	.00062	.00114	.00180	.00064	.00077	.00012	.00006	46
.00026	.00014	.00002	.00006	.00051	.00045	.00043	.00018	.00023	.00008	.00002	47
.00053	.00019	.00002	.00005	.00012	.00005	.00027	.00037	.00030	.00006	.00001	48
.09868	.05395	.12129	.10917	.17142	.13644	.13676	.17405	.19468	.07663	.06889	49
.11979	.06398	.12767	.12223	.19163	.14918	.15476	.19724	.21305	.08687	.08288	50

TABLE VIII
(continued)

DIRECT MAN-HOUR REQUIREMENTS
PER DOLLAR OF OUTPUT,
WEST VIRGINIA, 1965*

PROCESSING SECTORS

	35. Insurance agents & brokers	36. Real estate	37. All other finance, insurance & real estate	38. Hotels & other lodging places	39. Medical & legal services	40. Educational services
1. Agriculture	0	0	0	.00009	.00001	0
2. Coal mining (underground)	0	0	0	.00029	.00003	.00025
3. Coal mining (strip & auger)	0	0	.00103	.00155	0	.00010
4. Petroleum & natural gas	0	0	0	0	0	0
5. All other mining	0	0	0	0	0	0
6. General contractors (building)	0	.00581	0	.00013	0	.00590
7. General contractors (non-building)	0	.00014	0	.00051	0	.00217
8. Special trades contractors	0	.00371	0	.00338	.00034	.00048
9. Food & kindred products (meats and n.e.c.)	0	0	0	0	.00142	.00001
10. Food & kindred products (dairies)	0	0	0	0	.00042	0
11. Food & kindred products (bakeries)	0	0	0	0	.00008	.00006
12. Food & kindred products (beverages)	0	0	0	0	.00004	.00022
13. Apparel & accessories	0	0	0	0	.00193	0
14. Logging & sawmills	0	0	0	0	.00001	.00006
15. Furniture & other wood fabrication	0	0	0	0	0	0
16. Printing & publishing	.00003	.00304	.00047	.00017	.00008	.00056
17. Chemicals	0	0	0	0	.00018	.00001
18. Petroleum	0	0	0	0	0	0
19. Glass	0	0	0	0	.00006	.00006
20. Stone & clay products	0	0	0	0	0	.00006
21. Primary metal products	0	0	0	0	0	0
22. Fabricated metal products	0	0	0	0	0	0
23. Machinery (except electrical)	0	0	0	0	0	0
24. Electrical machinery & apparatus	0	0	0	0	.00001	0
25. Transportation equipment	0	0	0	0	0	0
26. Instruments & related products	0	0	0	0	.00016	.00001
27. All other manufacturing	0	0	0	.00003	.00093	.00001
28. Eating & drinking establishments	.00020	.00035	.00007	0	.00003	.00058
29. Wholesale trade	.00005	.00112	.00001	.00203	.00129	.00228
30. Retail food stores	0	0	0	0	.00016	0
31. Retail gasoline service stations	.00005	.00010	.00002	.00083	.00013	.00003
32. All other retail	.00008	.00129	.00010	.00133	.00123	.00143
33. Banking	.00003	.00054	.00013	.00279	.00047	.00005
34. Other finance	0	0	0	0	.00019	0
35. Insurance agents & brokers	.00003	.00001	.00005	.00079	.00031	.00021
36. Real estate	.00014	.00443	.00005	.00203	.00017	.00007
37. All other finance, insurance & real estate	.00428	.00002	0	0	.00003	.00010
38. Hotels & other lodging places	.00002	.00099	.00010	0	.00024	.00015
39. Medical & legal services	.00003	.00034	.10641	.00119	.00580	.00038
40. Educational services	0	0	0	0	.00026	0
41. All other services	.00071	.00211	.00252	.00937	.00458	.00134
42. Railroads	0	0	0	0	.00012	.00004
43. Trucking & warehousing	0	0	0	.00005	.00019	.00015
44. All other transportation	.00001	.00017	.00003	0	0	0
45. Communications	.00057	.00132	.00058	.00542	.00095	.00121
46. Electric companies & systems	.00005	.00032	.00017	.00301	.00021	.00053
47. Gas companies & systems	.00003	.00020	.00008	.00049	.00015	.00017
48. Water & sanitary services	.00002	.00018	0	.00080	.00017	.00022
49. Households (Primary Labor Inputs)	.03273	.07244	.05104	.25662	.24891	.32227
50. Total	.03906	.09864	.16285	.29287	.27124	.34119

*Each column shows the direct man-hours required by the sectors at the left per dollar of output by the sector at the top.

PROCESSING SECTORS

41. All other services	42. Railroads	43. Trucking & warehousing	44. All other transportation	45. Communications	46. Electric companies & systems	47. Gas companies & systems	48. Water & sanitary services	
0	0	0	0	0	0	0	0	1
0	.00004	.00002	0	.00003	.01703	.00039	.00015	2
0	0	0	0	0	.00520	0	0	3
0	0	0	.00503	0	0	.01610	0	4
0	.00038	0	0	0	0	0	.00123	5
0	0	0	0	0	0	0	0	6
0	.00073	.00020	0	.00052	0	0	.00518	7
.00006	.00116	.00032	.00050	0	0	0	0	8
0	0	0	0	0	0	0	0	9
0	0	0	0	0	0	0	0	10
.00001	0	0	0	0	0	0	0	11
0	0	0	0	0	0	0	0	12
0	0	0	0	0	0	0	0	13
0	0	.00021	0	0	0	0	0	14
0	0	0	.00038	0	.00001	0	0	15
.00058	.00001	.00056	.00003	.00023	.00034	.00006	.00021	16
.00011	0	0	0	0	0	0	.00062	17
.00002	.00017	.00002	.00009	.00009	.00011	.00001	.00002	18
0	0	0	0	0	0	0	0	19
.00021	0	.00002	0	.00016	.00023	.00012	.00050	20
0	.00028	.00010	.00029	.00002	.00003	0	.00001	21
.00020	0	0	.00087	0	.00078	.00003	.00142	22
0	.00058	0	.00023	0	0	0	0	23
.00005	.00001	0	0	.00015	.00004	0	.00067	24
0	.00038	0	0	0	0	0	0	25
0	0	0	.00001	0	0	0	0	26
.00027	0	0	.00176	0	0	.00001	0	27
0	0	.00015	.00002	.00012	.00011	.00013	.00004	28
.00235	.00035	.00728	.00037	.00005	.00065	.00016	.00173	29
0	0	0	0	0	0	0	0	30
.00030	0	.00030	.00023	.00003	.00002	.00015	.00043	31
.00210	.00010	.00027	.00008	.00032	.00012	.00009	.01124	32
.00005	0	.00023	.00068	.00007	0	.00012	.00001	33
.00004	0	0	.00012	0	0	.00001	0	34
.00056	.00076	.00079	.00007	.00002	.00005	.00001	.00010	35
.00015	0	.00006	.00002	.00009	.00008	.00008	0	36
.00002	0	0	0	.00015	.00010	.00003	.00004	37
.00007	.00005	.00024	.00002	.00005	.00015	.00014	0	38
.00074	.00083	.00065	.00009	.00044	.00017	.00007	.00011	39
.00006	0	0	0	0	.00001	.00001	0	40
.00415	.00023	.00073	.00197	.00294	.00056	.00018	.00010	41
.00015	.00453	.00038	.00007	.00274	.00341	.00024	.00119	42
.00028	.00063	.00016	.00011	.00061	.00121	.00035	.00015	43
0	.00002	.00002	.00417	.00006	.00021	.00056	.00001	44
.00058	.00056	.00023	.00081	.00038	.00025	.00007	.00132	45
.00021	.00023	.00026	.00015	.00019	.00379	.00006	.00275	46
.00017	.00002	.00012	.00004	.00008	.00004	.00015	.00003	47
.00010	.00001	.00004	.00002	0	.00001	.00001	.00153	48
.13030	.12887	.08788	.04907	.11068	.05930	.03018	.09588	49
.14388	.14090	.10122	.06731	.12020	.09402	.04952	.12665	50

TABLE IX

DIRECT AND INDIRECT MAN-HOUR REQUIREMENTS PER DOLLAR OF DELIVERY TO FINAL DEMAND, WEST VIRGINIA, 1965*

PROCESSING SECTORS	1. Agriculture	2. Coal mining (underground)	3. Coal mining (strip & auger)	4. Petroleum & natural gas	5. All other mining	6. General contractors (building)
1. Agriculture	.01740	.00001	.00001	0	.00011	.00002
2. Coal mining (underground)	.00024	.13111	.02628	.00036	.00013	.00042
3. Coal mining (strip & auger)	.00006	.00156	.12491	.00006	.00006	.00008
4. Petroleum & natural gas	.00004	.00004	.00003	.16140	.00010	.00022
5. All other mining	.00051	.00006	.00004	.00037	.04656	.00100
6. General contractors (building)	.00006	0	.00013	.00001	.00001	.08457
7. General contractors (non-building)	.00001	.00001	.00002	.00001	.00001	.00250
8. Special trades contractors	.00011	.00052	.00027	.00026	.00060	.03083
9. Food & kindred products (meats and n.e.c.)	.00022	.00009	.00004	.00004	.00001	.00004
10. Food & kindred products (dairies)	0	0	.00001	.00001	0	0
11. Food & kindred products (bakeries)	0	0	.00001	0	0	0
12. Food & kindred products (beverages)	0	0	0	0	0	0
13. Apparel & accessories	.00001	0	.00002	.00005	.00001	.00002
14. Logging & sawmills	.00266	.00191	.00061	.00007	.00232	.00195
15. Furniture & other wood fabrication	.00009	.00048	.00010	.00001	.00017	.00112
16. Printing & publishing	.00017	.00017	.00020	.00054	.00014	.00066
17. Chemicals	.00002	.00003	.00002	.00018	.00025	.00015
18. Petroleum	.00001	.00005	.00001	.00145	.00016	.00023
19. Glass	.00001	.00001	0	.00001	.00001	.00008
20. Stone & clay products	.00075	.00036	.00010	.00002	.00002	.00944
21. Primary metal products	.00010	.00002	.00004	.00006	.00007	.00177
22. Fabricated metal products	.00106	.00019	.00041	.00009	.00115	.00857
23. Machinery (except electrical)	.00001	.00006	.00011	.00073	.00067	.00020
24. Electrical machinery & apparatus	0	0	.00014	.00001	.00001	.00012
25. Transportation equipment	0	0	0	0	0	0
26. Instruments & related products	0	0	0	.00001	0	.00001
27. All other manufacturing	.00006	.00013	.00006	.00006	.00028	.00464
28. Eating & drinking establishments	.00003	.00001	.00037	.00002	.00001	.00020
29. Wholesale trade	.00713	.00195	.00405	.00184	.00348	.00430
30. Retail food stores	0	0	0	0	0	0
31. Retail gasoline service stations	.00049	.00005	.00015	.00029	.00028	.00038
32. All other retail	.00113	.00061	.00067	.00188	.00121	.00086
33. Banking	.00144	.00004	.00113	.00015	.00028	.00090
34. Other finance	.00016	.00001	.00021	.00014	.00008	.00004
35. Insurance agents & brokers	.00071	.00026	.00040	.00046	.00040	.00046
36. Real estate	.00076	.00004	.00160	.00008	.00006	.00062
37. All other finance, insurance & real estate	.00012	.00017	.00009	.00007	.00012	.00011
38. Hotels & other lodging places	.00013	.00002	.00021	.00002	.00010	.00015
39. Medical & legal services	.00078	.00057	.00200	.00595	.00084	.00113
40. Educational services	.00002	0	.00002	.00001	.00001	.00002
41. All other services	.00502	.00065	.00506	.00548	.00091	.00191
42. Railroads	.00019	.00016	.00058	.00040	.00023	.00037
43. Trucking & warehousing	.00049	.00021	.00060	.00032	.00066	.00070
44. All other transportation	.00005	.00002	.00003	.00007	.00003	.00006
45. Communications	.00061	.00017	.00053	.00060	.00027	.00081
46. Electric companies & systems	.00050	.00157	.00054	.00047	.00026	.00046
47. Gas companies & systems	.00006	.00002	.00004	.00006	.00003	.00017
48. Water & sanitary services	.00002	.00001	.00003	.00005	.00001	.00377
49. Total	.04344	.14337	.17188	.18416	.06212	.16606

*Each column shows the direct and indirect man-hours required by the sectors at the left to support a delivery of one dollar to final demand by the sector at the top.

PROCESSING SECTORS

7. General contractors (non-building)	8. Special trades contractors	9. Food & kindred products (meats and n.e.c.)	10. Food & kindred products (dairies)	11. Food & kindred products (bakeries)	12. Food & kindred products (beverages)	13. Apparel & accessories	14. Logging & sawmills	15. Furniture & other wood fabrication	16. Printing & publishing	17. Chemicals	
.00001	.00001	.00386	.00405	.00012	0	0	.00099	.00014	.00001	.00001	1
.00067	.00019	.00034	.00017	.00052	.00018	.00020	.00036	.00113	.00025	.00177	2
.00005	.00005	.00012	.00006	.00019	.00003	.00005	.00012	.00007	.00010	.00010	3
.00177	.00009	.00006	.00004	.00055	.00004	.00005	.00005	.00011	.00006	.00177	4
.00235	.00032	.00012	.00012	.00001	.00002	.00001	.00004	.00001	.00001	.00027	5
.00002	.00003	.00002	.00003	.00001	0	0	.00006	.00007	.00002	.00009	6
.07581	.00030	.00001	.00004	.00002	.00004	.00002	.00014	.00003	.00002	.00018	7
.00391	.11238	.00029	.00015	.00003	.00005	.00230	.00098	.00019	.00010	.00100	8
.00002	.00002	.08264	.00147	.00006	.00002	0	.00003	.00001	.00004	.00009	9
0	0	0	.06230	0	0	0	0	0	.00001	0	10
.00001	0	0	0	.10478	.00001	0	0	0	.00001	0	11
0	0	0	0	0	.10795	0	0	0	0	0	12
.00001	.00002	.00001	.00001	0	.00012	.42071	.00002	.00001	.00002	.00006	13
.00065	.00271	.00060	.00063	.00003	.00001	.00006	.26630	.03601	.00001	.00008	14
.00020	0	.00002	.00002	.00001	0	0	.00001	.12894	0	.00003	15
.00036	.00018	.00056	.00026	.00035	.00136	.00066	.00018	.00041	.16071	.00030	16
.00168	.00007	.00002	.00001	.00001	.00013	0	.00001	.00042	.00002	.05438	17
.00300	.00008	.00001	.00001	.00001	.00001	.00001	.00003	.00001	.00001	.00006	18
.00002	.00025	.00001	.00001	.00001	.00130	.00001	0	.00038	.00001	.00009	19
.00543	.00014	.00018	.00019	.00003	.00001	.00001	.00007	.00003	.00001	.00016	20
.00066	.00117	.00003	.00003	.00001	.00048	.00003	.00003	.00007	.00015	.00008	21
.00128	.00809	.00030	.00029	.00006	.00008	.00020	.00031	.00131	.00308	.00045	22
.00129	.00027	.00001	.00004	.00001	.00001	.00001	.00003	.00015	.00023	.00004	23
.00002	.00005	.00001	.00001	.00001	.00001	.00001	0	.00001	.00006	.00013	24
0	0	0	0	0	0	0	0	0	0	.00001	25
.00002	.00001	.00031	.00001	0	0	0	0	0	0	.00036	26
.00023	.00118	.00045	.00040	.00014	.00113	.00049	.00019	.00011	.00250	.00108	27
.00025	.00013	.00007	.00020	.00003	.00035	.00001	.00004	.00008	.00032	.00008	28
.00331	.00450	.00652	.00277	.00359	.00197	.00042	.00394	.00184	.00070	.00159	29
.00001	0	0	0	0	0	0	0	0	0	.00002	30
.00026	.00076	.00049	.00034	.00092	.00143	.00022	.00051	.00043	.00061	.00006	31
.00073	.00026	.00120	.00105	.00209	.00040	.00003	.00042	.00027	.00120	.00083	32
.00058	.00075	.00071	.00040	.00037	.00006	.00006	.00047	.00027	.00018	.00009	33
.00022	.00002	.00038	.00005	.00019	.00001	0	.00007	.00002	.00001	.00001	34
.00054	.00054	.00028	.00040	.00052	.00045	.00003	.00053	.00030	.00027	.00018	35
.00020	.00035	.00019	.00033	.00005	.00002	.00001	.00069	.00011	.00016	.00003	36
.00010	.00019	.00005	.00009	.00009	.00007	.00001	.00062	.00012	.00036	.00010	37
.00044	.00024	.00015	.00005	.00004	.00051	.00004	.00077	.00018	.00015	.00025	38
.00125	.00165	.00156	.00091	.00049	.00066	.00013	.00215	.00103	.00217	.00078	39
.00001	.00001	.00006	.00001	.00001	.00001	0	.00001	.00001	.00007	.00007	40
.00686	.00141	.00377	.00473	.00597	.00126	.00016	.00246	.00258	.00125	.00142	41
.00086	.00011	.00015	.00010	.00017	.00010	.00009	.00022	.00017	.00016	.00196	42
.00299	.00056	.00043	.00100	.00024	.00107	.00035	.00212	.00147	.00163	.00115	43
.00021	.00004	.00004	.00003	.00005	.00002	.00003	.00007	.00007	.00006	.00015	44
.00099	.00047	.00034	.00043	.00077	.00146	.00196	.00096	.00063	.00197	.00080	45
.00029	.00024	.00100	.00046	.00159	.00021	.00043	.00083	.00050	.00033	.00067	46
.00026	.00008	.00009	.00006	.00097	.00009	.00009	.00005	.00015	.00009	.00054	47
.00004	.00011	.00007	.00015	.00029	.00044	.00005	.00006	.00005	.00008	.00022	48
.11987	.14006	.10752	.08385	.12542	.12358	.42894	.28697	.17993	.17919	.07359	49

TABLE IX
(continued)

DIRECT AND INDIRECT MAN-HOUR REQUIREMENTS PER DOLLAR OF DELIVERY TO FINAL DEMAND, WEST VIRGINIA, 1965*

PROCESSING SECTORS	18. Petroleum	19. Glass	20. Stone & clay products	21. Primary metal products	22. Fabricated metal products	23. Machinery (except electrical)
1. Agriculture	.00001	.00001	.00002	.00001	0	0
2. Coal mining (underground)	.00342	.00033	.00120	.00270	.00052	.00029
3. Coal mining (strip & auger)	.00011	.00011	.00011	.00009	.00009	.00006
4. Petroleum & natural gas	.01206	.00050	.00073	.00012	.00011	.00010
5. All other mining	.00357	.00088	.00308	.00023	.00004	.00002
6. General contractors (building)	.00001	0	0	.00001	.00002	0
7. General contractors (non-building)	.00003	.00001	.00002	.00002	.00002	.00001
8. Special trades contractors	.00015	.00016	.00017	.00026	.00022	.00008
9. Food & kindred products (meats and n.e.c.)	.00002	.00004	.00001	.00001	.00001	.00001
10. Food & kindred products (dairies)	0	0	0	0	0	0
11. Food & kindred products (bakeries)	0	0	0	0	0	0
12. Food & kindred products (beverages)	0	0	0	0	0	0
13. Apparel & accessories	.00002	.00001	.00001	.00001	.00001	0
14. Logging & sawmills	.00046	.00011	.00022	.00006	.00002	.00008
15. Furniture & other wood fabrication	.00003	.00019	.00002	.00002	0	.00001
16. Printing & publishing	.00032	.00015	.00052	.00006	.00049	.00019
17. Chemicals	.00257	.00026	.00018	.00029	.00009	.00003
18. Petroleum	.02232	.00001	.00053	.00001	.00001	.00001
19. Glass	.00001	.11507	.00001	.00004	.00001	0
20. Stone & clay products	.00003	.00030	.09106	.00002	.00001	.00001
21. Primary metal products	.00003	.00017	.00010	.05535	.00527	.00285
22. Fabricated metal products	.00034	.00022	.00217	.00024	.12488	.00196
23. Machinery (except electrical)	.00011	.00005	.00008	.00006	.00003	.09859
24. Electrical machinery & apparatus	.00001	.00001	.00001	.00004	.00001	.00081
25. Transportation equipment	0	0	.00002	.00001	0	0
26. Instruments & related products	.00002	0	0	0	.00002	0
27. All other manufacturing	.00012	.00466	.00100	.00012	.00045	.00087
28. Eating & drinking establishments	.00007	.00001	.00002	.00001	.00009	.00008
29. Wholesale trade	.00135	.00170	.00212	.00087	.00178	.00149
30. Retail food stores	0	0	0	0	0	0
31. Retail gasoline service stations	.00007	.00006	.00026	.00003	.00008	.00011
32. All other retail	.00044	.00065	.00112	.00056	.00088	.00028
33. Banking	.00054	.00051	.00025	.00010	.00006	.00032
34. Other finance	.00026	.00001	.00002	.00002	.00003	.00001
35. Insurance agents & brokers	.00013	.00038	.00025	.00009	.00013	.00052
36. Real estate	.00003	.00004	.00003	.00001	.00026	.00004
37. All other finance, insurance & real estate	.00004	.00008	.00005	.00005	.00015	.00008
38. Hotels & other lodging places	.00003	.00005	.00004	.00006	.00007	.00007
39. Medical & legal services	.00166	.00039	.00083	.00045	.00057	.00033
40. Educational services	.00001	.00002	.00001	.00013	.00003	.00002
41. All other services	.00128	.00181	.00100	.00118	.00107	.00071
42. Railroads	.00026	.00016	.00082	.00119	.00021	.00110
43. Trucking & warehousing	.00161	.00043	.00284	.00080	.00034	.00153
44. All other transportation	.00090	.00003	.00006	.00049	.00006	.00050
45. Communications	.00252	.00061	.00059	.00034	.00040	.00036
46. Electric companies & systems	.00062	.00081	.00080	.00050	.00066	.00045
47. Gas companies & systems	.00052	.00087	.00080	.00007	.00017	.00007
48. Water & sanitary services	.00006	.00006	.00008	.00006	.00024	.00003
49. Total	.05819	.13195	.11324	.06675	.13962	.11408

*Each column shows the direct and indirect man-hours required by the sectors at the left to support a delivery of one dollar to final demand by the sector at the top.

PROCESSING SECTORS

24. Electrical machinery & apparatus	25. Transportation equipment	26. Instruments & related products	27. All other manufacturing	28. Eating & drinking establishments	29. Wholesale trade	30. Retail food stores	31. Retail gasoline service stations	32. All other retail	33. Banking	34. Other finance	
0	0	0	.00015	.00036	0	0	0	0	0	0	1
.00104	.00036	.00011	.00023	.00035	.00046	.00068	.00038	.00040	.00009	.00004	2
.00020	.00007	.00002	.00022	.00012	.00015	.00026	.00013	.00017	.00004	.00002	3
.00033	.00010	.00010	.00005	.00033	.00034	.00028	.00040	.00020	.00006	.00004	4
.00006	.00015	.00002	.00002	.00002	.00001	.00002	.00009	.00003	0	0	5
.00004	0	0	.00001	.00001	.00001	.00032	.00004	.00016	.00004	.00006	6
.00011	.00003	.00001	.00002	.00002	.00002	.00004	.00004	.00004	.00002	.00002	7
.00014	.00005	.00007	.00274	.00004	.00018	.00046	.00008	.00077	.00024	.00008	8
.00001	0	.00001	.00079	.00331	.00001	.00001	0	.00002	.00002	.00002	9
0	0	0	0	.00171	0	0	0	.00002	0	.00001	10
0	0	0	0	.00311	0	0	0	.00005	0	0	11
0	0	0	0	.00084	0	0	0	.00001	0	0	12
.00001	0	.00001	.00019	0	.00001	.00001	0	.00001	.00002	.00002	13
.00004	.00002	.00001	.00010	.00006	.00002	.00003	.00002	.00010	.00001	0	14
.00004	0	0	0	0	.00001	.00001	0	.00024	0	0	15
.00025	.00007	.00010	.00045	.00022	.00021	.00693	.00056	.00390	.00097	.00190	16
.00108	.00003	.00234	.00006	.00001	.00007	.00001	.00008	.00002	.00001	.00001	17
.00002	.00001	0	.00001	.00001	.00002	.00003	.00050	.00007	0	0	18
.00001	0	.00043	.00001	.00014	0	.00002	0	.00084	0	0	19
.00003	.00001	.00001	.00002	.00003	.00001	.00006	.00004	.00004	.00002	.00001	20
.01032	.00393	.00001	.00022	.00001	.00001	.00002	.00001	.00002	.00001	.00005	21
.00012	.00004	.00005	.00360	.00005	.00006	.00024	.00007	.00018	.00005	.00006	22
.00002	.00002	.00001	.00085	0	.00001	.00002	.00001	.00002	0	.00001	23
.09880	.00001	.00001	.00016	0	.00001	.00001	.00001	.00001	.00001	.00038	24
0	.05396	0	0	0	.00002	0	0	.00001	0	0	25
.00011	0	.12131	0	.00001	0	0	0	.00003	0	0	26
.00014	.00004	.00086	.10971	.00007	.00019	.00058	.00006	.00029	.00015	.00020	27
.00005	.00002	.00001	.00001	.17145	.00024	.00005	.00002	.00015	.00003	.00014	28
.00105	.00044	.00141	.00057	.00788	.13895	.00102	.00206	.00060	.00021	.00018	29
0	0	0	0	.00063	.00003	.13676	0	0	0	0	30
.00006	.00001	.00002	.00010	.00020	.00165	.00029	.17428	.00059	.00004	.00012	31
.00091	.00030	.00006	.00013	.00052	.00070	.00035	.00056	.19546	.00068	.00036	32
.00013	.00011	.00013	.00029	.00016	.00026	.00014	.00036	.00073	.07665	.00507	33
.00001	0	0	.00001	.00010	.00025	.00012	.00002	.00016	.00006	.06904	34
.00023	.00009	.00008	.00016	.00019	.00031	.00061	.00051	.00080	.00031	.00006	35
.00020	.00001	.00001	.00006	.00012	.00004	.00388	.00045	.00179	.00042	.00054	36
.00005	.00002	.00002	.00003	.00004	.00010	.00010	.00008	.00015	.00062	.00005	37
.00009	.00002	.00002	.00002	.00003	.00020	.00008	.00003	.00058	.00003	.00004	38
.00056	.00041	.00057	.00042	.00031	.00077	.00071	.00044	.00157	.00225	.00223	39
.00111	.00001	.00001	.00001	.00001	.00011	.00001	.00001	.00011	.00029	.00060	40
.00164	.00086	.00060	.00116	.00129	.00120	.00292	.01546	.00393	.00488	.00223	41
.00085	.00276	.00012	.00126	.00014	.00090	.00019	.00024	.00117	.00006	.00006	42
.00085	.00016	.00054	.00036	.00019	.00162	.00061	.00199	.00096	.00005	.00005	43
.00117	.00004	.00001	.00003	.00005	.00058	.00007	.00011	.00017	.00001	.00016	44
.00105	.00096	.00024	.00041	.00093	.00089	.00148	.00151	.00059	.00143	.00165	45
.00168	.00056	.00014	.00044	.00086	.00128	.00200	.00078	.00090	.00016	.00010	46
.00030	.00015	.00006	.00007	.00058	.00048	.00046	.00023	.00026	.00009	.00004	47
.00057	.00020	.00003	.00007	.00015	.00006	.00031	.00040	.00033	.00007	.00003	48
.12549	.06604	.12956	.12522	.19669	.15244	.16223	.20207	.21865	.09013	.08569	49

TABLE IX
(continued)

DIRECT AND INDIRECT MAN-HOUR REQUIREMENTS PER DOLLAR OF DELIVERY TO FINAL DEMAND, WEST VIRGINIA, 1965*

PROCESSING SECTORS	35. Insurance agents & brokers	36. Real estate	37. All other finance, insurance & real estate	38. Hotels & other lodging places	39. Medical & legal services	40. Educational services
1. Agriculture	0	0	.00005	.00009	.00011	0
2. Coal mining (underground)	.00005	.00019	.00041	.00179	.00014	.00054
3. Coal mining (strip & auger)	.00012	.00007	.00137	.00240	.00004	.00022
4. Petroleum & natural gas	.00003	.00018	.00010	.00033	.00011	.00019
5. All other mining	0	.00010	.00001	.00005	.00001	.00015
6. General contractors (building)	.00001	.00641	.00002	.00032	.00002	.00611
7. General contractors (non-building)	.00001	.00038	.00001	.00062	.00002	.00244
8. Special trades contractors	.00003	.00641	.00020	.00376	.00044	.00286
9. Food & kindred products (meats and n.e.c.)	.00007	.00002	.00068	.00002	.00159	.00003
10. Food & kindred products (dairies)	.00002	.00001	.00019	0	.00044	.00001
11. Food & kindred products (bakeries)	.00001	.00001	.00004	0	.00008	.00008
12. Food & kindred products (beverages)	0	0	.00002	0	.00004	.00022
13. Apparel & accessories	.00007	.00001	.00085	.00001	.00198	.00001
14. Logging & sawmills	0	.00025	.00002	.00015	.00004	.00025
15. Furniture & other wood fabrication	0	.00009	0	.00002	0	.00009
16. Printing & publishing	.00012	.00452	.00077	.00057	.00023	.00089
17. Chemicals	.00001	.00002	.00010	.00004	.00023	.00008
18. Petroleum	.00001	.00003	.00001	.00005	.00001	.00011
19. Glass	0	.00002	.00003	.00002	.00008	.00008
20. Stone & clay products	.00001	.00075	.00002	.00014	.00002	.00092
21. Primary metal products	0	.00019	.00001	.00006	.00001	.00016
22. Fabricated metal products	.00001	.00105	.00007	.00040	.00009	.00073
23. Machinery (except electrical)	0	.00004	.00001	.00003	.00001	.00006
24. Electrical machinery & apparatus	0	.00002	.00001	.00003	.00002	.00001
25. Transportation equipment	0	0	0	0	0	0
26. Instruments & related products	.00001	0	.00007	0	.00017	.00001
27. All other manufacturing	.00004	.00048	.00045	.00013	.00100	.00039
28. Eating & drinking establishments	.00021	.00041	.00009	.00005	.00004	.00062
29. Wholesale trade	.00015	.00183	.00083	.00272	.00167	.00287
30. Retail food stores	.00001	0	.00007	0	.00016	0
31. Retail gasoline service stations	.00006	.00022	.00011	.00094	.00019	.00012
32. All other retail	.00017	.00158	.00077	.00176	.00143	.00162
33. Banking	.00007	.00071	.00037	.00290	.00054	.00016
34. Other finance	.00001	.00001	.00010	.00002	.00021	.00002
35. Insurance agents & brokers	.03279	.00011	.00023	.00091	.00037	.00029
36. Real estate	.00016	.07725	.00018	.00227	.00022	.00015
37. All other finance, insurance & real estate	.00429	.00006	.05109	.00017	.00008	.00015
38. Hotels & other lodging places	.00004	.00109	.00022	.25670	.00027	.00019
39. Medical & legal services	.00922	.00070	.10915	.00184	.25514	.00085
40. Educational services	.00001	.00001	.00012	.00002	.00027	.32228
41. All other services	.00118	.00277	.00492	.01056	.00515	.00190
42. Railroads	.00003	.00013	.00013	.00042	.00022	.00020
43. Trucking & warehousing	.00002	.00018	.00015	.00030	.00028	.00037
44. All other transportation	.00002	.00022	.00005	.00005	.00002	.00003
45. Communications	.00068	.00162	.00108	.00571	.00108	.00137
46. Electric companies & systems	.00009	.00048	.00034	.00336	.00031	.00067
47. Gas companies & systems	.00004	.00024	.00016	.00054	.00018	.00023
48. Water & sanitary services	.00003	.00049	.00009	.00086	.00020	.00050
49. Total	.04992	.11135	.17575	.30315	.27499	.35122

*Each column shows the direct and indirect man-hours required by the sectors at the left to support a delivery of one dollar to final demand by the sector at the top.

PROCESSING SECTORS

41. All other services	42. Railroads	43. Trucking & warehousing	44. All other transportation	45. Communications	46. Electric companies & systems	47. Gas companies & systems	48. Water & sanitary services	
0	0	0	0	0	0	0	0	1
.00011	.00018	.00016	.00012	.00013	.02001	.00046	.00123	2
.00004	.00004	.00005	.00003	.00003	.00742	.00002	.00038	3
.00013	.00014	.00011	.00582	.00012	.00014	.01695	.00022	4
.00002	.00047	.00002	.00004	.00005	.00005	.00005	.00151	5
.00002	0	.00001	0	.00001	.00002	.00001	.00001	6
.00001	.00078	.00021	.00001	.00055	.00003	.00001	.00544	7
.00010	.00128	.00037	.00064	.00007	.00015	.00005	.00038	8
.00001	.00001	.00001	.00002	.00001	.00002	.00001	.00001	9
0	0	0	0	0	0	0	0	10
.00001	0	0	0	0	0	0	0	11
0	0	0	0	0	0	0	0	12
.00001	.00001	.00001	.00001	.00001	.00001	.00001	.00001	13
.00001	.00007	.00026	.00014	.00001	.00032	.00002	.00014	14
0	0	0	.00042	0	.00008	.00001	.00004	15
.00089	.00004	.00080	.00012	.00037	.00056	.00016	.00060	16
.00014	.00004	.00001	.00003	.00003	.00002	.00002	.00089	17
.00003	.00021	.00004	.00016	.00012	.00014	.00016	.00026	18
.00001	0	0	0	0	0	0	.00005	19
.00023	.00006	.00004	.00001	.00021	.00032	.00012	.00093	20
.00002	.00036	.00011	.00038	.00005	.00009	.00002	.00020	21
.00025	.00013	.00006	.00108	.00004	.00091	.00006	.00165	22
.00001	.00062	.00001	.00030	.00002	.00004	.00008	.00012	23
.00006	.00001	0	.00001	.00015	.00005	0	.00069	24
0	.00039	0	0	.00001	.00001	0	.00001	25
0	0	0	.00001	0	0	0	.00001	26
.00031	.00003	.00004	.00196	.00002	.00005	.00004	.00008	27
.00002	.00001	.00017	.00002	.00013	.00014	.00014	.00008	28
.00256	.00059	.00751	.00061	.00023	.00140	.00042	.00232	29
0	0	0	0	0	0	0	0	30
.00036	.00003	.00041	.00028	.00005	.00006	.00020	.00052	31
.00224	.00016	.00035	.00023	.00040	.00030	.00031	.01162	32
.00008	.00003	.00026	.00078	.00009	.00009	.00016	.00012	33
.00005	.00001	.00002	.00014	.00001	.00002	.00002	.00003	34
.00060	.00082	.00082	.00012	.00007	.00016	.00007	.00023	35
.00019	.00002	.00008	.00005	.00010	.00020	.00010	.00014	36
.00011	.00011	.00012	.00003	.00016	.00015	.00004	.00009	37
.00009	.00007	.00026	.00004	.00006	.00018	.00015	.00009	38
.00106	.00119	.00098	.00043	.00087	.00071	.00079	.00054	39
.00006	0	.00001	.00001	.00001	.00001	.00001	.00002	40
.13478	.00045	.00098	.00260	.00318	.00111	.00084	.00107	41
.00024	.13365	.00048	.00017	.00289	.00387	.00030	.00166	42
.00037	.00074	.08817	.00019	.00069	.00143	.00040	.00060	43
.00002	.00005	.00006	.05364	.00008	.00027	.00062	.00007	44
.00067	.00066	.00034	.00098	.11113	.00039	.00017	.00154	45
.00028	.00029	.00036	.00023	.00024	.06364	.00013	.00315	46
.00020	.00004	.00016	.00006	.00009	.00006	.03034	.00010	47
.00011	.00002	.00005	.00003	.00001	.00002	.00002	.09747	48
.14653	.14384	.10390	.07196	.12251	.10468	.05352	.13632	49

TABLE X

DIRECT MAN-HOUR REQUIREMENTS PER DOLLAR OF OUTPUT, WEST VIRGINIA, PROJECTED TO 1975*

PROCESSING SECTORS	1. Agriculture	2. Coal mining (underground)	3. Coal mining (strip & auger)	4. Petroleum & natural gas	5. All other mining	6. General contractors (building)
1. Agriculture	.00065	0	0	0	.00005	0
2. Coal mining (underground)	.00001	.00075	.01345	0	0	.00002
3. Coal mining (strip & auger)	0	.00049	.01281	0	.00001	0
4. Petroleum & natural gas	0	0	0	.00417	0	0
5. All other mining	.00028	.00003	.00001	.00003	.00135	.00031
6. General contractors (building)	0	0	0	0	0	.00259
7. General contractors (non-building)	0	0	0	0	0	.00152
8. Special trades contractors	0	.00041	0	.00017	.00193	.02688
9. Food & kindred products (meats and n.e.c.)	.00015	.00005	0	0	0	0
10. Food & kindred products (dairies)	0	0	0	0	0	0
11. Food & kindred products (bakeries)	0	0	0	0	0	0
12. Food & kindred products (beverages)	0	0	0	0	0	0
13. Apparel & accessories	0	0	0	0	0	0
14. Logging & sawmills	.00137	.00097	.00014	.00001	.00121	.00091
15. Furniture & other wood fabrication	.00006	.00038	0	0	.00013	.00144
16. Printing & publishing	.00001	.00007	0	.00038	.00035	.00051
17. Chemicals	0	.00001	0	0	.00047	0
18. Petroleum	0	.00003	0	.00094	.00010	.00004
19. Glass	0	0	0	0	0	0
20. Stone & clay products	.00049	.00025	0	0	.00007	.00606
21. Primary metal products	.00004	0	0	.00002	0	.00088
22. Fabricated metal products	.00074	.00008	.00006	0	.00102	.00520
23. Machinery (except electrical)	0	.00004	.00003	.00052	.00048	.00005
24. Electrical machinery & apparatus	0	0	.00003	0	0	.00010
25. Transportation equipment	0	0	0	0	0	0
26. Instruments & related products	0	0	0	0	0	0
27. All other manufacturing	.00001	.00007	0	0	.00045	.00174
28. Eating & drinking establishments	0	0	.00022	0	0	.00057
29. Wholesale trade	.00441	.00094	.00215	.00244	.00137	.00063
30. Retail food stores	0	0	0	0	0	0
31. Retail gasoline service stations	.00027	0	.00002	.00155	.00016	.00002
32. All other retail	.00067	.00043	.00012	.00440	.00107	.00012
33. Banking	.00106	0	.00076	.00016	.00027	.00040
34. Other finance	.00011	0	.00021	.00016	.00005	.00004
35. Insurance agents & brokers	.00053	.00046	.00024	.00059	.00051	.00037
36. Real estate	.00057	0	.00245	.00041	.00002	.00039
37. All other finance, insurance & real estate	0	.00009	0	0	.00004	0
38. Hotels & other lodging places	.00013	0	.00005	0	.00002	.00003
39. Medical & legal services	.00040	.00014	.00122	.00862	.00047	.00097
40. Educational services	0	0	0	0	0	0
41. All other services	.00405	.00041	.00462	.00704	.00156	.00066
42. Railroads	.00004	.00002	.00022	.00017	.00009	.00002
43. Trucking & warehousing	.00023	.00007	.00014	.00009	.00100	.00002
44. All other transportation	.00001	0	0	0	0	0
45. Communications	.00030	.00008	.00020	.00037	.00010	.00028
46. Electric companies & systems	.00020	.00071	.00005	.00014	.00035	.00007
47. Gas companies & systems	.00001	0	0	0	0	.00002
48. Water & sanitary services	0	0	.00001	.00003	0	.00358
49. Households (Primary Labor Inputs)	.00919	.07856	.05445	.09959	.03287	.06972
50. Total	.02600	.08556	.09367	.13201	.04758	.12615

*Each column shows the direct man-hours required by the sectors at the left per dollar of output by the sector at the top.

PROCESSING SECTORS

7. General contractors (non-building)	8. Special trades contractors	9. Food & kindred products (meats and n.e.c.)	10. Food & kindred products (dairies)	11. Food & kindred products (bakeries)	12. Food & kindred products (beverages)	13. Apparel & accessories	14. Logging & sawmills	15. Furniture & other wood fabrication	16. Printing & publishing	17. Chemicals	
0	0	.00131	.00271	.00002	0	0	.00036	0	0	0	1
.00001	.00002	0	0	0	.00008	.00003	.00011	.00050	.00005	.00082	2
0	.00001	0	0	0	0	0	0	0	.00001	0	3
0	0	0	0	0	0	0	0	0	0	.00075	4
0	0	0	0	0	0	0	0	0	0	.00014	5
.00084	.00020	0	0	.00001	0	0	0	.00018	0	.00006	6
.00215	.00023	0	.00003	0	0	0	.00004	0	0	.00008	7
.00376	.00251	.00008	.00010	0	0	.00191	.00062	0	.00012	.00054	8
0	0	.00380	.00042	.00005	0	0	0	0	0	.00002	9
0	0	0	.00069	.00036	0	0	0	0	0	0	10
0	0	0	0	.00010	0	0	0	0	0	0	11
0	0	0	0	0	.00059	0	0	0	0	0	12
0	0	0	0	0	.00074	0	0	0	0	.00002	13
.00019	.00318	0	0	0	0	0	.03678	.01404	0	0	14
.00016	0	0	0	0	0	0	0	.00075	0	.00001	15
.00008	.00003	.00006	.00012	.00011	.00133	.00036	.00001	.00037	.02159	.00011	16
.00068	.00003	0	0	0	.00014	0	0	.00022	.00003	.00423	17
.00229	.00004	0	0	0	0	0	.00004	0	0	.00002	18
0	.00026	0	0	0	.00107	0	0	.00026	0	.00005	19
.00406	.00005	0	0	0	0	0	0	0	0	.00007	20
.00050	.00071	0	0	0	.00037	0	0	0	0	.00036	21
.00064	.00620	0	0	0	0	0	.00039	.00123	.00200	.00007	22
.00139	.00050	0	.00003	0	0	0	.00001	.00011	.00028	0	23
0	.00005	0	0	0	0	0	0	0	.00001	.00006	24
0	0	0	0	0	0	0	0	0	0	0	25
0	.00001	.00089	0	0	0	0	0	0	0	.00015	26
.00011	.00213	.00544	.00013	.00042	.00082	.00031	.00065	.00003	.00075	.00056	27
.00005	.00025	.00002	.00022	0	.00045	0	0	.00005	.00038	.00005	28
.00074	.00110	.00174	.00066	.00227	.00129	.00018	.00051	.00039	.00017	.00136	29
0	0	0	0	0	0	0	0	0	0	.00001	30
.00009	.00097	.00022	.00020	.00077	.00130	.00014	.00032	.00007	.00075	.00001	31
.00033	.00004	.00065	.00032	.00170	.00023	0	.00038	.00007	.00054	.00023	32
.00027	.00114	0	.00005	.00045	.00003	.00004	.00018	.00012	.00007	.00003	33
.00018	0	.00126	0	.00025	0	0	.00004	0	0	0	34
.00035	.00039	.00006	.00012	.00065	.00036	.00040	.00036	.00011	.00013	.00009	35
.00015	.00067	0	.00016	0	0	0	.00127	0	.00008	0	36
0	.00011	0	.00003	.00001	0	0	.00028	0	.00022	.00005	37
.00019	.00042	.00004	0	0	.00061	.00003	.00014	.00004	.00009	.00015	38
.00053	.00046	.00159	.00013	.00009	.00067	.00003	.00064	.00025	.00198	.00034	39
0	0	.00016	0	0	0	0	0	0	.00009	.00004	40
.00559	.00151	.00229	.00430	.00544	.00132	.00080	.00108	.00224	.00091	.00033	41
.00037	0	0	0	0	0	0	.00014	.00004	.00001	.00044	42
.00183	.00072	.00007	.00030	.00012	.00112	.00087	.00066	.00041	.00171	.00087	43
.00004	0	0	0	0	0	.00001	.00005	.00006	.00003	.00013	44
.00026	.00031	.00315	.00016	.00042	.00094	.00213	.00050	.00046	.00166	.00029	45
.00006	.00006	.00049	.00009	.00109	.00011	.00015	.00020	.00015	.00003	.00020	46
.00035	.00003	.00002	.00002	.00045	.00003	.00008	.00001	.00017	.00001	.00024	47
0	.00005	.00016	.00013	.00018	.00048	.00007	.00007	.00003	.00005	.00011	48
.06286	.09381	.05062	.04820	.09199	.08050	.32883	.15039	.10500	.09091	.02892	49
.09111	.11820	.07427	.05934	.10693	.09457	.33637	.19624	.12735	.12466	.04198	50

TABLE X
(continued)

DIRECT MAN-HOUR REQUIREMENTS
PER DOLLAR OF OUTPUT,
WEST VIRGINIA,
PROJECTED TO 1975*

PROCESSING SECTORS	18. Petroleum	19. Glass	20. Stone & clay products	21. Primary metal products	22. Fabricated metal products	23. Machinery (except electrical)
1. Agriculture	0	0	.00002	.00002	0	0
2. Coal mining (underground)	.00183	.00002	.00070	.00152	.00002	.00001
3. Coal mining (strip & auger)	0	0	0	0	0	0
4. Petroleum & natural gas	.00662	0	0	.00002	0	0
5. All other mining	.00243	.00059	.00137	.00015	.00001	0
6. General contractors (building)	0	0	0	0	0	0
7. General contractors (non-building)	0	0	0	0	0	0
8. Special trades contractors	0	.00001	.00005	.00018	.00014	.00002
9. Food & kindred products (meats and n.e.c.)	0	0	0	0	0	0
10. Food & kindred products (dairies)	0	0	0	0	0	0
11. Food & kindred products (bakeries)	0	0	0	0	0	0
12. Food & kindred products (beverages)	0	0	0	0	0	0
13. Apparel & accessories	0	0	.00016	0	0	0
14. Logging & sawmills	.00012	0	.00001	0	0	.00001
15. Furniture & other wood fabrication	0	.00066	0	0	0	0
16. Printing & publishing	.00011	.00032	.00058	.00001	.00018	.00062
17. Chemicals	.00131	.00013	.00014	.00011	.00005	0
18. Petroleum	.00042	0	.00057	0	0	0
19. Glass	0	.00280	0	.00002	0	0
20. Stone & clay products	.00040	.00020	.00137	0	0	0
21. Primary metal products	0	.00012	0	.00017	.00515	.00168
22. Fabricated metal products	.00070	.00001	.00365	.00015	.00009	.00248
23. Machinery (except electrical)	0	0	.00005	.00003	.00002	0
24. Electrical machinery & apparatus	0	0	.00001	.00002	0	.00085
25. Transportation equipment	0	0	.00004	0	0	0
26. Instruments & related products	0	0	0	0	.00002	0
27. All other manufacturing	0	.00368	.00033	.00008	.00044	.00028
28. Eating & drinking establishments	.00004	0	0	.00001	.00006	.00004
29. Wholesale trade	.00046	.00065	.00128	.00048	.00112	.00093
30. Retail food stores	0	0	0	0	0	0
31. Retail gasoline service stations	0	.00001	.00050	0	.00002	.00004
32. All other retail	.00006	.00041	.00275	.00038	.00051	.00009
33. Banking	.00044	.00031	.00004	.00007	.00001	.00017
34. Other finance	.00007	0	0	.00001	.00002	0
35. Insurance agents & brokers	.00003	.00057	.00024	.00002	.00009	.00028
36. Real estate	0	.00002	0	0	.00033	.00001
37. All other finance, insurance & real estate	0	.00002	0	.00003	.00005	0
38. Hotels & other lodging places	0	.00002	0	.00004	.00003	.00007
39. Medical & legal services	.00094	.00014	.00165	.00028	.00006	.00007
40. Educational services	0	.00002	0	.00002	.00001	0
41. All other services	.00030	.00351	.00187	.00095	.00039	.00027
42. Railroads	0	0	.00019	.00067	0	.00018
43. Trucking & warehousing	.00102	.00024	.00224	.00053	.00014	.00097
44. All other transportation	.00057	0	.00001	.00033	0	.00027
45. Communications	.00161	.00027	.00054	.00020	.00014	.00008
46. Electric companies & systems	.00016	.00081	.00065	.00015	.00020	.00014
47. Gas companies & systems	.00026	.00038	.00054	.00004	.00011	.00004
48. Water & sanitary services	.00004	.00003	.00006	.00005	.00023	.00002
49. Households (Primary Labor Inputs)	.01505	.07868	.06459	.04394	.10027	.07477
50. Total	.03499	.09463	.15079	.05077	.10900	.08439

*Each column shows the direct man-hours required by the sectors at the left per dollar of output by the sector at the top.

PROCESSING SECTORS

24. Electrical machinery & apparatus	25. Transportation equipment	26. Instruments & related products	27. All other manufacturing	28. Eating & drinking establishments	29. Wholesale trade	30. Retail food stores	31. Retail gasoline service stations	32. All other retail	33. Banking	34. Other finance	#
0	0	0	.00006	.00005	0	0	0	0	0	0	1
0	0	0	.00002	.00004	.00007	.00001	.00003	.00005	.00002	0	2
0	0	0	.00038	.00001	0	.00001	.00001	.00003	.00002	0	3
0	0	0	0	0	0	0	0	0	0	0	4
0	.00009	0	0	0	0	0	0	0	0	0	5
0	0	0	0	0	0	0	0	.00001	0	0	6
0	0	0	0	0	0	0	0	.00004	0	0	7
.00006	0	0	.00225	0	.00012	.00009	0	.00084	.00010	0	8
0	0	0	.00048	.00251	0	0	0	0	0	0	9
0	0	0	0	.00181	0	0	0	.00003	0	0	10
0	0	0	0	.00365	0	0	0	.00006	0	0	11
0	0	0	0	.00143	0	0	0	.00002	0	0	12
0	0	0	.00007	0	0	0	0	0	0	0	13
0	0	0	0	0	0	0	0	0	0	0	14
.00002	0	0	0	0	.00001	0	0	.00019	0	0	15
.00010	.00002	.00004	.00065	.00015	.00006	.00379	.00026	.00474	.00058	.00155	16
.00070	0	0	.00173	.00009	.00007	0	0	0	0	0	17
0	0	0	0	0	0	.00001	.00008	.00004	0	0	18
0	0	.00029	0	.00009	0	.00001	0	.00092	0	0	19
0	0	0	0	0	0	0	0	0	0	0	20
0	0	0	0	0	0	0	0	0	0	0	21
.00692	.00318	0	.00268	0	0	0	0	0	0	0	22
0	0	0	.00063	0	0	0	0	0	0	0	23
0	0	0	.00005	0	0	0	0	0	0	.00026	24
.00007	0	0	0	0	.00001	0	0	0	0	0	25
0	0	0	0	0	0	0	0	.00002	0	0	26
.00025	0	0	0	0	.00011	.00045	0	.00016	.00007	.00010	27
.00004	.00001	.00061	.00019	0	.00030	0	0	.00025	.00003	.00009	28
.00004	.00001	0	0	0	0	0	0	0	0	0	29
.00036	.00023	.00116	.00011	.00449	.00167	.00055	.00112	.00020	.00001	.00005	30
0	0	0	.00004	.00002	.00126	.00013	.00005	.00063	.00002	.00004	31
.00002	0	0	.00002	.00023	.00056	.00009	.00023	.00065	.00020	.00018	32
.00058	.00011	0	.00011	.00007	.00033	.00007	.00018	.00089	0	.00483	33
.00007	.00007	.00010	.00011	.00007	.00033	.00007	0	.00014	.00007	.00014	34
0	0	0	.00007	.00006	.00043	.00011	0	.00040	.00026	.00002	35
.00021	.00005	.00005	.00007	.00011	.00033	.00075	.00030	.00063	.00048	.00043	36
.00009	0	0	.00010	.00006	0	.00340	.00035	.00003	.00063	0	37
0	0	0	0	0	.00007	0	0	.00082	.00002	.00002	38
.00019	.00001	0	0	0	.00025	0	0	.00170	.00076	.00174	39
.00040	.00026	.00047	.00014	.00007	.00071	.00033	.00009	.00008	.00031	.00047	40
.00110	0	0	0	0	.00112	.00245	.01227	.00507	.00524	.00143	41
.00133	.00062	.00038	.00043	.00057	.00036	0	.00006	.00021	0	0	42
.00026	.00153	0	.00039	0	.00118	.00035	.00136	.00066	.00001	0	43
.00050	.00004	.00034	.00036	.00008	.00050	.00002	.00008	.00011	0	.00011	44
.00101	0	0	.00001	0	.00069	.00089	.00118	.00139	.00017	.00092	45
.00067	.00062	.00012	.00016	.00056	.00069	.00089	.00118	.00139	.00017	.00006	46
.00068	.00018	.00003	.00016	.00094	.00040	.00065	.00027	.00034	.00018	.00006	47
.00015	.00008	.00002	.00003	.00026	.00023	.00023	.00009	.00013	.00001	.00001	48
.06412	.03897	.08523	.07446	.14911	.09958	.10580	.13464	.15061	.06937	.06236	49
.08036	.04627	.09060	.08416	.16694	.11067	.12046	.15302	.17240	.07863	.07480	50

TABLE X
(continued)

DIRECT MAN-HOUR REQUIREMENTS
PER DOLLAR OF OUTPUT,
WEST VIRGINIA,
PROJECTED TO 1975*

PROCESSING SECTORS	35. Insurance agents & brokers	36. Real estate	37. All other finance, insurance & real estate	38. Hotels & other lodging places	39. Medical & legal services	40. Educational services
1. Agriculture	0	0	0	.00005	0	0
2. Coal mining (underground)	0	0	0	.00018	.00002	.00015
3. Coal mining (strip & auger)	0	0	.00058	.00093	0	.00006
4. Petroleum & natural gas	0	0	0	0	0	0
5. All other mining	0	0	0	0	0	0
6. General contractors (building)	0	.00495	0	.00012	0	.00540
7. General contractors (non-building)	0	.00012	0	.00043	0	.00185
8. Special trades contractors	0	.00316	0	.00269	.00060	.00041
9. Food & kindred products (meats and n.e.c.)	0	0	0	0	.00123	.00001
10. Food & kindred products (dairies)	0	0	0	0	.00069	0
11. Food & kindred products (bakeries)	0	0	0	0	.00007	.00006
12. Food & kindred products (beverages)	0	0	0	0	.00003	.00016
13. Apparel & accessories	0	0	0	0	.00510	0
14. Logging & sawmills	0	0	0	0	0	.00004
15. Furniture & other wood fabrication	0	0	0	0	0	0
16. Printing & publishing	.00002	.00337	.00032	.00013	.00005	.00151
17. Chemicals	0	0	0	0	.00008	.00001
18. Petroleum	0	0	0	0	0	0
19. Glass	0	0	0	0	.00004	.00004
20. Stone & clay products	0	0	0	0	0	.00005
21. Primary metal products	0	0	0	0	0	0
22. Fabricated metal products	0	0	0	0	0	0
23. Machinery (except electrical)	0	0	0	0	0	0
24. Electrical machinery & apparatus	0	0	0	0	.00001	0
25. Transportation equipment	0	0	0	0	0	0
26. Instruments & related products	0	0	0	0	.00011	.00001
27. All other manufacturing	0	0	0	.00002	.00019	.00029
28. Eating & drinking establishments	.00018	.00120	.00006	0	.00001	.00039
29. Wholesale trade	.00001	.00079	.00001	.00375	.00117	.00120
30. Retail food stores	0	0	0	0	.00011	0
31. Retail gasoline service stations	.00003	.00004	.00001	.00055	.00017	.00001
32. All other retail	.00004	.00060	.00007	.00085	.00131	.00210
33. Banking	.00003	.00037	.00012	.00272	.00020	.00116
34. Other finance	0	0	0	0	.00010	0
35. Insurance agents & brokers	.00002	.00001	.00005	.00064	.00031	.00009
36. Real estate	.00012	.00381	.00003	.00184	.00036	.00005
37. All other finance, insurance & real estate	.00302	.00001	0	0	.00001	.00008
38. Hotels & other lodging places	.00002	.00041	.00009	0	.00010	.00024
39. Medical & legal services	.00003	.00055	.10521	.00124	.00724	.00068
40. Educational services	0	0	0	0	.00008	.00185
41. All other services	.00069	.00239	.00222	.00927	.00303	.00325
42. Railroads	0	0	0	0	.00007	.00003
43. Trucking & warehousing	0	0	0	.00004	.00014	.00011
44. All other transportation	.00001	.00020	.00002	0	.00001	.00002
45. Communications	.00037	.00081	.00034	.00322	.00049	.00093
46. Electric companies & systems	.00002	.00013	.00006	.00109	.00008	.00023
47. Gas companies & systems	.00001	.00012	.00004	.00012	.00008	.00024
48. Water & sanitary services	.00002	.00030	0	.00040	.00058	.00021
49. Households (Primary Labor Inputs)	.02963	.06558	.04000	.20245	.24264	.25363
50. Total	.03427	.08894	.14922	.23273	.26650	.27654

*Each column shows the direct man-hours required by the sectors at the left per dollar of output by the sector at the top.

PROCESSING SECTORS

41. All other services	42. Railroads	43. Trucking & warehousing	44. All other transportation	45. Communications	46. Electric companies & systems	47. Gas companies & systems	48. Water & sanitary services	
0	0	0	0	0	0	0	0	1
0	.00002	.00002	0	0	.00702	.00024	.00005	2
0	0	0	0	0	.00184	0	0	3
0	0	0	.00419	0	0	.01030	0	4
0	.00028	0	0	0	0	0	.00091	5
0	0	0	0	0	0	0	0	6
0	.00062	.00097	0	.00044	0	0	.00448	7
.00068	.00099	.00022	.00043	0	0	0	0	8
0	0	0	0	0	0	0	0	9
0	0	0	0	0	0	0	0	10
.00001	0	0	0	0	0	0	0	11
0	0	0	0	0	0	0	0	12
0	0	0	0	0	0	0	0	13
0	0	.00014	0	0	0	0	0	14
0	0	0	.00024	0	.00002	0	0	15
.00205	.00001	.00186	.00011	.00003	.00036	.00008	.00016	16
.00010	0	0	0	0	0	0	.00068	17
.00003	.00007	.00002	.00008	.00003	.00008	.00001	.00001	18
0	0	0	0	0	0	0	0	19
.00080	0	.00001	0	.00006	.00017	.00008	.00041	20
0	.00022	.00008	.00023	.00001	.00002	0	.00004	21
.00066	0	0	.00133	0	.00063	.00009	.00117	22
.00007	.00047	0	.00033	0	0	0	0	23
.00043	0	0	0	.00010	.00001	0	.00048	24
0	.00027	0	0	0	0	0	0	25
0	0	0	.00004	0	0	0	0	26
.00077	0	0	.00106	0	0	.00001	0	27
0	0	.00005	.00006	.00011	.00009	.00026	.00004	28
.00204	.00017	.00650	.00068	.00003	.00033	.00010	.00105	29
0	0	0	0	0	0	0	0	30
.00054	0	.00044	.00034	.00001	.00001	.00034	.00037	31
.00241	.00143	.00036	.00024	.00029	.00009	.00026	.00519	32
.00007	0	.00045	.00062	.00021	0	.00021	.00001	33
.00013	0	0	.00009	0	0	0	0	34
.00085	.00077	.00039	.00027	.00001	.00003	0	.00009	35
.00010	0	.00007	.00002	.00008	.00008	.00033	0	36
.00006	0	0	0	.00012	.00008	.00003	.00003	37
.00020	.00004	.00009	.00011	.00006	.00023	.00048	0	38
.00233	.00087	.00114	.00050	.00017	.00031	.00027	.00010	39
0	0	0	0	0	0	0	0	40
.00232	.00021	.00103	.00387	.00321	.00041	.00010	.00015	41
.00009	.00195	.00039	.00004	.00084	.00106	.00007	.00068	42
.00027	.00046	.00011	.00008	.00099	.00135	.00025	.00025	43
.00004	.00002	.00003	.00191	.00004	.00014	.00045	.00002	44
.00101	.00042	.00128	.00048	.00019	.00038	.00009	.00095	45
.00017	.00008	.00011	.00010	.00014	.00116	.00002	.00110	46
.00021	.00001	.00009	.00006	.00012	.00002	.00008	.00004	47
.00030	.00001	.00003	.00004	0	.00001	.00003	.00151	48
.11989	.07837	.06476	.03616	.07848	.02088	.01533	.09511	49
.13862	.08778	.08064	.05371	.08579	.03679	.02952	.11508	50

TABLE XI

DIRECT AND INDIRECT MAN-HOUR REQUIREMENTS PER DOLLAR OF DELIVERY TO FINAL DEMAND, WEST VIRGINIA, PROJECTED TO 1975*

PROCESSING SECTORS	1. Agriculture	2. Coal mining (underground)	3. Coal mining (strip & auger)	4. Petroleum & natural gas	5. All other mining	6. General contractors (building)
1. Agriculture	.00990	.00001	0	0	.00006	.00002
2. Coal mining (underground)	.00014	.07978	.01792	.00023	.00021	.00032
3. Coal mining (strip & auger)	.00004	.00074	.07138	.00003	.00007	.00007
4. Petroleum & natural gas	.00004	.00003	.00004	.10446	.00009	.00019
5. All other mining	.00033	.00004	.00004	.00021	.03431	.00065
6. General contractors (building)	.00006	.00001	.00027	.00004	.00001	.07247
7. General contractors (non-building)	.00002	.00001	.00003	.00002	.00003	.00192
8. Special trades contractors	.00014	.00046	.00045	.00036	.00215	.02906
9. Food & kindred products (meats and n.e.c.)	.00018	.00006	.00003	.00006	.00001	.00004
10. Food & kindred products (dairies)	0	0	.00001	.00003	0	.00001
11. Food & kindred products (bakeries)	0	0	.00001	.00001	0	.00002
12. Food & kindred products (beverages)	0	0	0	0	0	.00001
13. Apparel & accessories	.00002	.00001	.00005	.00021	.00002	.00006
14. Logging & sawmills	.00199	.00141	.00059	.00006	.00182	.00287
15. Furniture & other wood fabrication	.00007	.00039	.00010	.00001	.00014	.00152
16. Printing & publishing	.00028	.00017	.00048	.00101	.00067	.00106
17. Chemicals	.00002	.00002	.00002	.00013	.00059	.00014
18. Petroleum	.00001	.00004	.00001	.00102	.00011	.00020
19. Glass	.00001	.00001	.00001	.00003	.00002	.00010
20. Stone & clay products	.00058	.00027	.00013	.00009	.00010	.00662
21. Primary metal products	.00009	.00002	.00003	.00006	.00011	.00160
22. Fabricated metal products	.00091	.00018	.00022	.00019	.00131	.00799
23. Machinery (except electrical)	.00001	.00005	.00006	.00056	.00053	.00029
24. Electrical machinery & apparatus	.00002	0	.00007	.00004	.00002	.00015
25. Transportation equipment	0	0	0	0	0	.00001
26. Instruments & related products	0	0	0	.00001	0	.00001
27. All other manufacturing	.00010	.00011	.00010	.00011	.00058	.00261
28. Eating & drinking establishments	.00004	.00002	.00037	.00004	.00003	.00071
29. Wholesale trade	.00504	.00108	.00333	.00294	.00176	.00158
30. Retail food stores	0	0	0	.00001	0	0
31. Retail gasoline service stations	.00040	.00004	.00013	.00175	.00025	.00046
32. All other retail	.00093	.00049	.00049	.00493	.00124	.00083
33. Banking	.00120	.00004	.00107	.00029	.00036	.00085
34. Other finance	.00015	.00001	.00030	.00021	.00007	.00007
35. Insurance agents & brokers	.00066	.00049	.00050	.00074	.00060	.00061
36. Real estate	.00070	.00006	.00345	.00052	.00009	.00075
37. All other finance, insurance & real estate	.00009	.00015	.00009	.00009	.00012	.00013
38. Hotels & other lodging places	.00019	.00002	.00011	.00007	.00007	.00020
39. Medical & legal services	.00094	.00066	.00220	.00995	.00101	.00194
40. Educational services	.00002	0	.00002	.00002	.00001	.00002
41. All other services	.00486	.00064	.00668	.00822	.00199	.00208
42. Railroads	.00010	.00008	.00035	.00024	.00016	.00017
43. Trucking & warehousing	.00041	.00018	.00031	.00034	.00120	.00073
44. All other transportation	.00005	.00002	.00004	.00007	.00003	.00005
45. Communications	.00049	.00015	.00047	.00074	.00025	.00068
46. Electric companies & systems	.00029	.00078	.00030	.00023	.00043	.00029
47. Gas companies & systems	.00004	.00001	.00003	.00006	.00002	.00013
48. Water & sanitary services	.00003	.00001	.00007	.00011	.00002	.00385
49. Total	.03163	.08875	.11239	.14055	.05267	.14614

*Each column show the direct and indirect man-hours required by the sectors at the left to support a delivery of one dollar to final demand by the sector at the top.

PROCESSING SECTORS

7. General contractors (non-building)	8. Special trades contractors	9. Food & kindred products (meats and n.e.c.)	10. Food & kindred products (dairies)	11. Food & kindred products (bakeries)	12. Food & kindred products (beverages)	13. Apparel & accessories	14. Logging & sawmills	15. Furniture & other wood fabrication	16. Printing & publishing	17. Chemicals	
.00001	.00002	.00154	.00297	.00005	0	0	.00051	.00005	0	0	1
.00052	.00013	.00027	.00009	.00046	.00017	.00011	.00029	.00062	.00012	.00111	2
.00004	.00005	.00012	.00003	.00015	.00003	.00003	.00006	.00003	.00005	.00005	3
.00155	.00007	.00004	.00004	.00034	.00004	.00007	.00006	.00015	.00004	.00117	4
.00144	.00024	.00006	.00010	.00001	.00002	.00001	.00003	.00001	.00001	.00019	5
.00002	.00007	.00002	.00003	.00001	0	0	.00015	.00020	.00002	.00008	6
.06515	.00027	.00004	.00005	.00002	.00005	.00004	.00009	.00003	.00006	.00013	7
.00423	.09662	.00034	.00021	.00008	.00008	.00199	.00107	.00022	.00026	.00076	8
.00001	.00003	.05481	.00053	.00007	.00002	0	.00003	.00001	.00004	.00004	9
.00001	.00001	.00001	.04890	.00037	.00001	0	.00001	0	.00002	0	10
0	.00001	0	.00001	.09209	.00001	0	0	0	.00001	0	11
0	0	0	0	0	.08110	0	0	0	.00001	0	12
.00004	.00003	.00005	.00002	.00001	.00076	.32884	.00005	.00001	.00008	.00005	13
.00059	.00436	.00033	.00061	.00002	.00001	.00009	.19924	.01876	.00002	.00007	14
.00017	.00001	.00001	.00002	.00001	.00001	0	.00001	.10576	0	.00002	15
.00058	.00027	.00038	.00040	.00043	.00190	.00055	.00030	.00062	.11943	.00028	16
.00113	.00007	.00004	.00002	.00001	.00019	.00001	.00002	.00027	.00005	.03389	17
.00251	.00006	.00001	.00001	.00001	.00001	.00001	.00006	.00001	.00001	.00004	18
.00002	.00028	.00001	.00001	.00001	.00112	.00001	.00001	.00027	.00001	.00007	19
.00443	.00010	.00013	.00021	.00006	.00003	.00002	.00007	.00005	.00002	.00012	20
.00069	.00110	.00004	.00004	.00001	.00039	.00003	.00006	.00009	.00016	.00046	21
.00150	.00656	.00043	.00034	.00012	.00011	.00017	.00072	.00138	.00271	.00021	22
.00152	.00055	.00006	.00004	.00001	.00002	.00002	.00004	.00012	.00038	.00003	23
.00005	.00007	.00003	.00002	.00003	.00001	.00001	.00001	.00001	.00003	.00008	24
0	0	0	0	0	0	0	0	0	0	0	25
0	0	0	0	0	0	0	0	0	0	.00017	26
.00001	.00001	.00096	.00001	0	0	.00037	.00092	.00017	.00103	.00070	27
.00036	.00229	.00597	.00025	.00049	.00092	.00002	.00006	.00007	.00052	.00008	28
.00011	.00029	.00005	.00025	.00004	.00047	0	.00117	.00066	.00060	.00186	29
.00162	.00148	.00285	.00236	.00254	.00157	.00034				.00001	30
0											31
.00029	.00106	.00036	.00037	.00087	.00138	.00019	.00050	.00015	.00103	.00008	32
.00089	.00021	.00098	.00074	.00191	.00036	.00006	.00067	.00023	.00082	.00042	33
.00050	.00123	.00050	.00043	.00053	.00007	.00008	.00036	.00018	.00014	.00008	34
.00023	.00002	.00141	.00007	.00027	.00001	0	.00007	.00002	.00001	.00001	35
.00053	.00047	.00022	.00037	.00072	.00041	.00042	.00055	.00020	.00022	.00016	36
.00026	.00084	.00016	.00040	.00006	.00003	.00003	.00186	.00006	.00032	.00008	37
.00008	.00019	.00004	.00009	.00010	.00005	.00005	.00044	.00006	.00014	.00020	38
.00028	.00046	.00010	.00007	.00006	.00063	.00005	.00022	.00008	.00366	.00084	39
.00152	.00118	.00218	.00072	.00063	.00099	.00026	.00223	.00065	.00012	.00005	40
.00001	.00001	.00020	.00001	.00001	.00001	0	.00001	0	.00164	.00070	41
.00669	.00212	.00370	.00605	.00599	.00176	.00104	.00207	.00264	.00008	.00059	42
.00050	.00007	.00014	.00005	.00010	.00006	.00005	.00024	.00009	.00234	.00112	43
.00246	.00089	.00032	.00048	.00030	.00126	.00096	.00098	.00057	.00005	.00019	44
.00080	.00003	.00003	.00003	.00004	.00002	.00002	.00009	.00061	.00230	.00044	45
.00022	.00047	.00361	.00042	.00059	.00110	.00220	.00082	.00021	.00008	.00029	46
.00022	.00014	.00065	.00021	.00120	.00017	.00118	.00033	.00019	.00004	.00030	47
.00048	.00006	.00005	.00004	.00047	.00005	.00009	.00004	.00007	.00010	.00014	48
.10433	.12458	.08346	.06829	.11154	.09793	.33849	.21665	.13586	.13892	.04743	49

TABLE XI
(continued)

DIRECT AND INDIRECT MAN-HOUR REQUIREMENTS PER DOLLAR OF DELIVERY TO FINAL DEMAND, WEST VIRGINIA, PROJECTED TO 1975*

PROCESSING SECTORS	18. Petroleum	19. Glass	20. Stone & clay products	21. Primary metal products	22. Fabricated metal products	23. Machinery (except electrical)
1. Agriculture	.00001	.00001	.00008	.00002	0	0
2. Coal mining (underground)	.00208	.00040	.00112	.00162	.00030	.00015
3. Coal mining (strip & auger)	.00005	.00015	.00011	.00004	.00004	.00003
4. Petroleum & natural gas	.00748	.00030	.00071	.00010	.00010	.00008
5. All other mining	.00264	.00065	.00157	.00017	.00004	.00001
6. General contractors (building)	.00001	.00001	.00001	.00001	.00003	0
7. General contractors (non-building)	.00004	.00001	.00005	.00002	.00002	.00002
8. Special trades contractors	.00027	.00022	.00025	.00024	.00023	.00007
9. Food & kindred products (meats and n.e.c.)	.00002	.00003	.00002	.00001	.00001	0
10. Food & kindred products (dairies)	.00001	0	.00001	0	0	0
11. Food & kindred products (bakeries)	0	0	0	0	0	0
12. Food & kindred products (beverages)	0	0	0	0	0	0
13. Apparel & accessories	.00004	.00002	.00021	.00001	.00001	.00001
14. Logging & sawmills	.00035	.00018	.00014	.00006	.00002	.00003
15. Furniture & other wood fabrication	.00003	.00070	.00002	.00001	0	0
16. Printing & publishing	.00038	.00066	.00114	.00010	.00033	.00090
17. Chemicals	.00164	.00018	.00027	.00014	.00008	.00002
18. Petroleum	.01557	.00001	.00062	.00001	0	0
19. Glass	.00001	.08159	.00002	.00003	.00001	0
20. Stone & clay products	.00045	.00025	.06605	.00002	.00001	.00001
21. Primary metal products	.00008	.00015	.00022	.04414	.00518	.00192
22. Fabricated metal products	.00092	.00028	.00393	.00022	.10044	.00254
23. Machinery (except electrical)	.00009	.00005	.00010	.00005	.00003	.07479
24. Electrical machinery & apparatus	.00001	.00002	.00002	.00003	.00001	.00086
25. Transportation equipment	0	0	.00005	.00001	0	0
26. Instruments & related products	.00001	0	0	0	.00002	0
27. All other manufacturing	.00012	.00389	.00043	.00011	.00047	.00032
28. Eating & drinking establishments	.00007	.00003	.00004	.00001	.00008	.00005
29. Wholesale trade	.00112	.00090	.00189	.00064	.00128	.00114
30. Retail food stores	0	0	0	0	0	0
31. Retail gasoline service stations	.00019	.00008	.00062	.00003	.00005	.00008
32. All other retail	.00062	.00060	.00307	.00047	.00062	.00018
33. Banking	.00054	.00036	.00015	.00010	.00004	.00020
34. Other finance	.00011	.00001	.00002	.00002	.00003	.00001
35. Insurance agents & brokers	.00017	.00066	.00036	.00007	.00011	.00031
36. Real estate	.00007	.00007	.00008	.00002	.00037	.00003
37. All other finance, insurance & real estate	.00004	.00010	.00006	.00004	.00007	.00004
38. Hotels & other lodging places	.00004	.00007	.00007	.00005	.00005	.00009
39. Medical & legal services	.00197	.00063	.00224	.00048	.00037	.00028
40. Educational services	.00001	.00002	.00001	.00011	.00002	.00002
41. All other services	.00136	.00400	.00252	.00114	.00065	.00050
42. Railroads	.00010	.00010	.00030	.00071	.00011	.00024
43. Trucking & warehousing	.00130	.00043	.00255	.00059	.00026	.00107
44. All other transportation	.00065	.00003	.00008	.00036	.00006	.00033
45. Communications	.00182	.00040	.00082	.00026	.00022	.00018
46. Electric companies & systems	.00027	.00094	.00079	.00019	.00025	.00018
47. Gas companies & systems	.00030	.00041	.00059	.00004	.00012	.00005
48. Water & sanitary services	.00007	.00005	.00010	.00006	.00025	.00004
49. Total	.04315	.09967	.09345	.05255	.11242	.08681

*Each column show the direct and indirect man-hours required by the sectors at the left to support a delivery of one dollar to final demand by the sector at the top.

PROCESSING SECTORS

24. Electrical machinery & apparatus	25. Transportation equipment	26. Instruments & related products	27. All other manufacturing	28. Eating & drinking establishments	29. Wholesale trade	30. Retail food stores	31. Retail gasoline service stations	32. All other retail	33. Banking	34. Other finance	
0	0	0	.00008	.00024	0	0	0	0	0	0	1
.00057	.00020	.00009	.00023	.00047	.00026	.00029	.00018	.00024	.00011	.00004	2
.00010	.00003	.00001	.00053	.00015	.00006	.00010	.00006	.00010	.00007	.00002	3
.00030	.00007	.00009	.00004	.00022	.00025	.00019	.00015	.00016	.00002	.00003	4
.00004	.00011	.00001	.00001	.00001	.00001	.00001	.00002	.00003	0	0	5
.00004	0	.00001	.00001	.00001	.00001	.00029	.00003	.00007	.00005	.00005	6
.00012	.00003	.00002	.00002	.00002	.00003	.00005	.00005	.00009	.00001	.00002	7
.00013	.00006	.00007	.00236	.00006	.00018	.00045	.00014	.00103	.00020	.00008	8
.00001	0	.00001	.00053	.00274	.00001	.00001	.00001	.00002	.00002	.00001	9
0	0	0	0	.00185	.00001	0	0	.00004	.00001	.00001	10
0	0	0	0	.00365	.00001	0	0	.00007	0	0	11
0	0	0	0	.00144	0	0	0	.00002	0	0	12
.00002	.00001	.00001	.00008	.00002	.00003	.00002	.00001	.00005	.00006	.00004	13
.00003	.00001	.00001	.00013	.00006	.00002	.00003	.00002	.00009	.00001	.00001	14
.00004	0	0	0	.00001	.00001	.00001	0	.00020	0	0	15
.00029	.00007	.00011	.00093	.00038	.00024	.00535	.00076	.00652	.00096	.00220	16
.00086	.00002	.00203	.00011	.00001	.00009	.00001	.00003	.00002	.00001	.00001	17
.00002	.00001	0	0	.00001	.00001	.00002	.00009	.00006	0	0	18
.00001	0	.00030	.00001	.00011	.00001	.00002	0	.00096	0	0	19
.00004	.00001	.00001	.00002	.00004	.00002	.00006	.00010	.00006	.00005	.00002	20
.00699	.00320	.00003	.00019	.00002	.00002	.00002	.00002	.00003	.00001	.00004	21
.00014	.00004	.00005	.00292	.00010	.00007	.00024	.00013	.00030	.00008	.00008	22
.00003	.00002	.00001	.00065	.00001	.00001	.00003	.00002	.00004	.00001	.00001	23
.06420	.00001	.00001	.00006	.00001	.00001	.00002	.00005	.00003	.00002	.00027	24
0	.03898	0	0	0	.00001	0	0	0	0	0	25
.00025	0	.08524	.00001	.00005	0	0	0	.00002	0	0	26
.00013	.00003	.00068	.07480	.00037	.00016	.00054	.00010	.00034	.00012	.00015	27
.00006	.00002	.00001	.00002	.14916	.00032	.00011	.00003	.00031	.00005	.00011	28
.00068	.00032	.00135	.00034	.00504	.10152	.00079	.00156	.00052	.00016	.00013	29
0	0	0	0	.00049	.00003	.10580	0	0	0	0	30
.00007	.00002	.00003	.00009	.00019	.00132	.00023	.13480	.00075	.00006	.00008	31
.00079	.00022	.00005	.00010	.00047	.00067	.00028	.00057	.15152	.00036	.00028	32
.00013	.00009	.00012	.00017	.00017	.00042	.00013	.00023	.00098	.06940	.00486	33
.00001	0	.00001	.00002	.00017	.00045	.00012	.00002	.00016	.00008	.06251	34
.00027	.00008	.00007	.00011	.00021	.00038	.00080	.00042	.00049	.00032	.00006	35
.00012	.00001	.00001	.00018	.00013	.00004	.00365	.00041	.00073	.00053	.00050	36
.00004	.00001	.00001	.00002	.00004	.00012	.00010	.00006	.00011	.00066	.00006	37
.00023	.00002	.00002	.00003	.00006	.00028	.00006	.00005	.00087	.00004	.00004	38
.00074	.00039	.00059	.00032	.00045	.00123	.00091	.00062	.00244	.00275	.00213	39
.00113	.00001	.00001	.00001	.00002	.00016	.00001	.00001	.00010	.00031	.00051	40
.00187	.00079	.00050	.00070	.00150	.00157	.00291	.01277	.00577	.00552	.00202	41
.00046	.00165	.00005	.00043	.00010	.00043	.00007	.00013	.00028	.00002	.00002	42
.00071	.00013	.00044	.00045	.00030	.00129	.00055	.00149	.00090	.00007	.00008	43
.00115	.00003	.00002	.00002	.00005	.00055	.00006	.00011	.00014	.00001	.00013	44
.00082	.00067	.00018	.00027	.00089	.00082	.00113	.00139	.00167	.00027	.00103	45
.00078	.00022	.00007	.00019	.00112	.00046	.00073	.00033	.00042	.00021	.00009	46
.00018	.00008	.00004	.00004	.00030	.00025	.00025	.00013	.00016	.00003	.00002	47
.00047	.00021	.00004	.00004	.00016	.00008	.00034	.00041	.00036	.00010	.00004	48
.08510	.04788	.09243	.08729	.17312	.11393	.12677	.15750	.17928	.08281	.07780	49

	TABLE XI (continued) DIRECT AND INDIRECT MAN-HOUR REQUIREMENTS PER DOLLAR OF DELIVERY TO FINAL DEMAND, WEST VIRGINIA, PROJECTED TO 1975*	35. Insurance agents & brokers	36. Real estate	37. All other finance, insurance & real estate	38. Hotels & other lodging places	39. Medical & legal services	40. Educational services
	1. Agriculture	0	0	.00004	.00005	.00009	0
	2. Coal mining (underground)	.00003	.00011	.00026	.00096	.00008	.00033
	3. Coal mining (strip & auger)	.00006	.00003	.00078	.00138	.00002	.00012
	4. Petroleum & natural gas	.00002	.00015	.00007	.00014	.00008	.00025
	5. All other mining	0	.00007	.00001	.00003	.00002	.00010
	6. General contractors (building)	.00001	.00547	.00002	.00029	.00004	.00566
	7. General contractors (non-building)	.00001	.00032	.00002	.00052	.00005	.00211
	8. Special trades contractors	.00004	.00571	.00036	.00312	.00076	.00290
	9. Food & kindred products (meats and n.e.c.)	.00005	.00003	.00060	.00002	.00139	.00003
	10. Food & kindred products (dairies)	.00003	.00002	.00032	.00001	.00072	.00001
	11. Food & kindred products (bakeries)	.00001	.00003	.00003	0	.00007	.00007
	12. Food & kindred products (beverages)	0	.00001	.00001	0	.00003	.00017
	13. Apparel & accessories	.00017	.00003	.00228	.00004	.00526	.00003
	14. Logging & sawmills	0	.00038	.00003	.00018	.00006	.00032
	15. Furniture & other wood fabrication	0	.00012	0	.00002	0	.00013
	16. Printing & publishing	.00011	.00491	.00062	.00070	.00029	.00232
	17. Chemicals	.00001	.00003	.00005	.00003	.00012	.00007
	18. Petroleum	0	.00003	0	.00003	.00001	.00010
	19. Glass	0	.00002	.00003	.00002	.00006	.00007
	20. Stone & clay products	.00001	.00054	.00004	.00016	.00004	.00073
	21. Primary metal products	0	.00017	.00001	.00006	.00002	.00016
	22. Fabricated metal products	.00002	.00099	.00009	.00038	.00012	.00081
	23. Machinery (except electrical)	0	.00007	.00001	.00004	.00001	.00009
	24. Electrical machinery & apparatus	0	.00003	.00002	.00005	.00003	.00003
	25. Transportation equipment	0	0	0	0	0	0
	26. Instruments & related products	0	0	.00006	0	.00014	.00001
	27. All other manufacturing	.00002	.00035	.00020	.00019	.00041	.00058
	28. Eating & drinking establishments	.00019	.00137	.00009	.00009	.00004	.00048
	29. Wholesale trade	.00009	.00118	.00074	.00427	.00148	.00156
	30. Retail food stores	0	.00001	.00005	0	.00011	0
	31. Retail gasoline service stations	.00005	.00020	.00014	.00071	.00025	.00014
	32. All other retail	.00013	.00086	.00080	.00122	.00153	.00238
	33. Banking	.00005	.00054	.00026	.00285	.00027	.00129
	34. Other finance	.00001	.00002	.00007	.00004	.00016	.00003
	35. Insurance agents & brokers	.02967	.00012	.00024	.00080	.00038	.00022
	36. Real estate	.00016	.06974	.00026	.00211	.00044	.00017
	37. All other finance, insurance & real estate	.00303	.00006	.04004	.00013	.00006	.00013
	38. Hotels & other lodging places	.00003	.00049	.00016	.20254	.00014	.00031
	39. Medical & legal services	.00828	.00113	.10872	.00209	.25046	.00145
	40. Educational services	0	.00001	.00004	.00002	.00009	.25551
	41. All other services	.00104	.00312	.00396	.01044	.00362	.00408
	42. Railroads	.00001	.00005	.00006	.00015	.00011	.00010
	43. Trucking & warehousing	.00002	.00024	.00014	.00033	.00025	.00037
	44. All other transportation	.00001	.00025	.00004	.00005	.00003	.00006
	45. Communications	.00043	.00110	.00070	.00349	.00074	.00116
	46. Electric companies & systems	.00003	.00021	.00014	.00124	.00014	.00031
	47. Gas companies & systems	.00002	.00015	.00009	.00117	.00010	.00028
	48. Water & sanitary services	.00005	.00063	.00028	.00048	.00064	.00055
	49. Total	.04394	.10109	.16300	.24168	.27095	.28782

*Each column show the direct and indirect man-hours required by the sectors at the left to support a delivery of one dollar to final demand by the sector at the top.

PROCESSING SECTORS

41. All other services	42. Railroads	43. Trucking & warehousing	44. All other transportation	45. Communications	46. Electric companies & systems	47. Gas companies & systems	48. Water & sanitary services	
0	0	0	0	0	0	0	0	1
.00012	.00009	.00010	.00010	.00008	.00822	.00029	.00059	2
.00004	.00002	.00002	.00003	.00002	.00264	.00001	.00016	3
.00020	.00007	.00013	.00474	.00013	.00009	.01093	.00020	4
.00003	.00033	.00003	.00003	.00002	.00003	.00003	.00109	5
.00001	0	.00001	.00001	.00001	.00002	.00003	.00001	6
.00004	.00068	.00102	.00001	.00048	.00004	.00001	.00475	7
.00080	.00113	.00035	.00057	.00008	.00011	.00009	.00045	8
.00003	.00001	.00001	.00002	.00001	.00001	.00001	.00001	9
.00001	0	.00001	0	0	0	.00001	0	10
.00001	0	0	0	0	0	.00001	0	11
0	0	0	0	0	0	0	0	12
.00007	.00003	.00003	.00003	.00001	.00002	.00003	.00002	13
.00004	.00008	.00021	.00008	.00001	.00017	.00002	.00011	14
.00001	.00001	.00001	.00025	0	.00006	.00001	.00003	15
.00294	.00013	.00254	.00036	.00020	.00063	.00027	.00058	16
.00014	.00003	.00003	.00003	.00002	.00002	.00002	.00092	17
.00004	.00010	.00006	.00014	.00006	.00010	.00012	.00021	18
.00002	.00001	0	.00001	0	0	.00001	.00004	19
.00085	.00005	.00010	.00004	.00012	.00022	.00010	.00077	20
.00011	.00029	.00010	.00035	.00004	.00007	.00002	.00023	21
.00090	.00013	.00012	.00156	.00006	.00073	.00015	.00142	22
.00010	.00051	.00004	.00039	.00002	.00002	.00007	.00014	23
.00045	.00001	.00001	.00002	.00011	.00002	.00001	.00050	24
0	.00028	0	0	0	0	0	0	25
0	0	0	.00005	0	0	0	.00001	26
.00086	.00005	.00006	.00119	.00003	.00004	.00004	.00009	27
.00004	.00002	.00009	.00007	.00012	.00012	.00028	.00008	28
.00229	.00032	.00674	.00102	.00024	.00078	.00049	.00144	29
0	0	0	0	0	0	0	0	30
.00065	.00004	.00057	.00049	.00005	.00005	.00054	.00047	31
.00263	.00153	.00050	.00061	.00042	.00023	.00081	.00550	32
.00014	.00005	.00051	.00071	.00023	.00007	.00027	.00011	33
.00014	.00001	.00004	.00011	.00001	.00002	.00003	.00003	34
.00092	.00083	.00046	.00037	.00007	.00013	.00010	.00020	35
.00016	.00003	.00010	.00008	.00010	.00023	.00042	.00007	36
.00017	.00009	.00007	.00005	.00013	.00011	.00004	.00007	37
.00025	.00007	.00013	.00014	.00008	.00026	.00050	.00008	38
.00312	.00125	.00157	.00127	.00068	.00083	.00145	.00060	39
.00002	0	.00002	.00001	0	.00001	.00001	.00002	40
.12273	.00049	.00151	.00477	.00345	.00089	.00115	.00112	41
.00016	.08041	.00046	.00009	.00089	.00119	.00010	.00087	42
.00047	.00057	.06509	.00018	.00106	.00151	.00032	.00068	43
.00008	.00003	.00008	.03820	.00006	.00017	.00049	.00007	44
.00121	.00052	.00145	.00064	.07876	.00052	.00021	.00117	45
.00024	.00011	.00017	.00016	.00017	.02221	.00007	.00126	46
.00024	.00003	.00012	.00008	.00014	.00003	.01542	.00010	47
.00034	.00002	.00005	.00007	.00002	.00002	.00005	.09668	48
.14385	.09043	.08472	.05914	.08821	.04265	.03503	.12297	49

OCCUPATIONS

PROFESSIONAL, TECHNICAL, AND MANAGERIAL

TABLE XII

WEST VIRGINIA EMPLOYMENT BY SECTOR AND OCCUPATION 1965*

PROCESSING SECTORS	1. Chemical engineers	2. Industrial engineers	3. Mechanical engineers	4. Mining engineers	5. Other engineers	6. Chemists	7. Mathematicians
1. Agriculture	0	0	0	0	0	0	0
2. Coal mining (underground)	4	40	26	409	46	65	0
3. Coal mining (strip & auger)	0	2	2	13	3	4	0
4. Petroleum & natural gas	10	5	5	46	17	4	1
5. All other mining	1	1	1	1	2	1	0
6. General contractors (building)	1	1	5	0	149	1	0
7. General contractors (non-building)	1	1	5	0	140	1	0
8. Special trades contractors	1	2	7	0	181	1	1
9. Food & kindred products (meats and n.e.c.)	0	3	3	0	3	4	0
10. Food & kindred products (dairies)	0	1	3	0	3	2	0
11. Food & kindred products (bakeries)	0	0	1	0	2	0	0
12. Food & kindred products (beverages)	1	1	2	0	2	7	0
13. Apparel & accessories	0	2	0	0	1	1	0
14. Logging & sawmills	0	0	0	0	4	0	0
15. Furniture & other wood fabrication	0	1	0	0	2	0	0
16. Printing & publishing	0	2	1	0	2	1	0
17. Chemicals	1,206	0	238	0	95	1,574	0
18. Petroleum	19	3	7	3	11	15	1
19. Glass	7	22	25	0	42	10	0
20. Stone & clay products	8	6	7	1	28	9	0
21. Primary metal products	12	244	89	2	284	54	9
22. Fabricated metal products	2	13	29	0	35	2	1
23. Machinery (except electrical)	2	31	104	0	73	4	1
24. Electrical machinery & apparatus	1	8	9	0	49	2	1
25. Transportation equipment	4	47	100	0	174	11	8
26. Instruments & related products	1	8	9	0	37	4	1
27. All other manufacturing	4	14	8	0	21	18	1
28. Eating & drinking establishments	0	0	0	0	0	0	0
29. Wholesale trade	3	5	13	4	142	16	6
30. Retail food stores	0	0	3	0	0	1	0
31. Retail gasoline service stations	0	0	0	0	0	0	0
32. All other retail	0	8	2	0	10	0	0
33. Banking	0	0	0	0	0	0	1
34. Other finance	0	0	0	0	0	0	0
35. Insurance agents & brokers	0	5	0	0	2	0	2
36. Real estate	0	0	0	0	1	0	0
37. All other finance, insurance & real estate	0	0	0	0	0	0	0
38. Hotels & other lodging places	0	0	0	0	0	0	0
39. Medical & legal services	0	2	3	0	16	43	1
40. Educational services	10	10	27	26	62	63	67
41. All other services	17	78	112	4	550	32	37
42. Railroads	0	7	20	0	61	10	0
43. Trucking & warehousing	0	1	1	0	2	0	0
44. All other transportation	0	0	1	0	2	0	0
45. Communications	0	0	0	0	18	0	0
46. Electric companies & systems	3	9	27	0	167	4	2
47. Gas companies & systems	3	8	26	0	158	4	2
48. Water & sanitary services	0	1	2	0	35	3	0
49. State and local government	23	26	17	57	242	14	7
50. Federal government	4	14	53	3	258	27	41
51. Total	1,348	632	993	569	3,132	2,012	191

*Each Row Shows the Distribution of Employment by Occupation in Each Sector.

OCCUPATIONS

TABLE XII
(continued)

WEST VIRGINIA EMPLOYMENT
BY SECTOR AND OCCUPATION
1965*

PROCESSING SECTORS	8. Physicists	9. Other natural scientists	10. Technicians (excluding medical and dental)	11. Medical and dental technicians	12. Doctors and veterinarians	13. Dentists	14. Pharmacists
1. Agriculture	0	0	1	0	3	0	0
2. Coal mining (underground)	0	19	155	0	0	0	0
3. Coal mining (strip & auger)	0	1	10	0	0	0	0
4. Petroleum & natural gas	1	61	57	0	0	0	0
5. All other mining	0	1	6	0	0	0	0
6. General contractors (building)	0	1	167	0	0	0	0
7. General contractors (non-building)	0	1	156	0	0	0	0
8. Special trades contractors	0	1	202	0	0	0	0
9. Food & kindred products (meats and n.e.c.)	0	4	14	0	0	0	0
10. Food & kindred products (dairies)	0	4	36	0	0	0	0
11. Food & kindred products (bakeries)	0	0	5	0	0	0	0
12. Food & kindred products (beverages)	0	1	12	0	0	0	0
13. Apparel & accessories	0	0	2	0	0	0	0
14. Logging & sawmills	0	0	3	0	0	0	0
15. Furniture & other wood fabrication	0	1	4	0	0	0	0
16. Printing & publishing	0	0	17	0	0	0	0
17. Chemicals	0	0	2,286	111	0	0	0
18. Petroleum	1	7	35	0	0	0	0
19. Glass	0	0	67	0	0	0	0
20. Stone & clay products	0	1	29	0	0	0	0
21. Primary metal products	9	7	189	2	4	0	0
22. Fabricated metal products	1	0	53	0	0	0	0
23. Machinery (except electrical)	1	1	190	1	1	0	0
24. Electrical machinery & apparatus	3	0	53	0	0	0	0
25. Transportation equipment	6	1	178	0	1	0	0
26. Instruments & related products	2	1	38	3	0	0	0
27. All other manufacturing	0	0	33	0	0	0	0
28. Eating & drinking establishments	0	0	0	5	0	0	0
29. Wholesale trade	0	1	117	2	0	0	10
30. Retail food stores	0	0	3	0	0	0	0
31. Retail gasoline service stations	0	0	0	0	0	0	0
32. All other retail	0	0	43	3	14	0	512
33. Banking	0	0	1	0	0	0	0
34. Other finance	0	0	0	0	0	0	0
35. Insurance agents & brokers	0	0	6	0	2	0	0
36. Real estate	0	0	2	0	0	0	0
37. All other finance, insurance & real estate	0	0	0	0	0	0	0
38. Hotels & other lodging places	0	0	1	1	2	0	0
39. Medical & legal services	2	60	14	1,304	1,484	662	46
40. Educational services	52	151	210	75	63	44	11
41. All other services	37	28	910	7	36	0	1
42. Railroads	0	1	47	0	1	0	0
43. Trucking & warehousing	0	0	2	0	0	0	0
44. All other transportation	0	0	10	0	0	0	0
45. Communications	0	0	11	0	0	0	0
46. Electric companies & systems	3	1	151	0	1	0	0
47. Gas companies & systems	3	1	143	0	1	0	0
48. Water & sanitary services	0	4	30	0	0	0	0
49. State and local government	0	134	513	11	82	5	6
50. Federal government	36	150	433	10	30	2	2
51. Total	157	644	6,645	1,535	1,725	713	588

*Each Row Shows the Distribution of Employment by Occupation in Each Sector.

PROFESSIONAL, TECHNICAL, AND MANAGERIAL

	15. Nurses (professional and student)	16. Elementary and secondary teachers	17. College teachers	18. Other teachers	19. Social scientists	20. Accountants and auditors	21. Lawyers and judges	22. Personnel and labor relations workers	23. Other professional and technical workers	24. Managers, officials, and proprietors
1	0	0	0	0	0	0	0	0	3	4
2	3	0	0	3	4	104	15	22	39	3,869
3	0	0	0	0	0	7	1	1	2	255
4	0	0	0	0	1	32	5	3	9	318
5	0	0	0	0	0	2	0	1	2	112
6	0	0	0	0	1	20	1	3	59	833
7	0	0	0	0	1	19	1	3	55	779
8	0	0	0	1	1	24	2	3	71	1,009
9	1	0	0	0	0	12	1	4	6	145
10	0	0	0	0	0	13	0	3	5	237
11	0	0	0	0	0	6	0	1	2	167
12	1	0	0	0	1	9	0	2	9	167
13	1	0	0	2	1	5	1	4	36	248
14	1	0	0	0	0	10	0	1	40	496
15	0	0	0	0	0	4	0	1	8	110
16	1	0	0	1	2	24	2	4	511	253
17	0	0	0	0	0	0	0	0	0	1,841
18	1	0	0	0	2	21	2	3	9	51
19	7	0	0	0	6	50	4	17	90	958
20	1	0	0	0	0	22	0	4	23	280
21	13	0	0	4	13	244	5	36	90	2,372
22	1	0	0	0	2	12	0	6	27	499
23	4	0	0	0	2	38	1	10	55	375
24	1	0	0	0	1	7	0	2	13	188
25	3	0	0	1	4	48	3	15	85	171
26	0	0	0	0	1	4	1	2	12	34
27	3	0	0	1	2	27	1	11	55	369
28	0	0	0	7	0	6	0	3	68	2,062
29	1	0	0	7	15	168	7	20	97	4,686
30	0	0	0	1	1	15	1	4	4	2,164
31	0	0	0	0	0	3	0	1	0	1,169
32	13	0	0	29	11	108	3	67	206	8,049
33	1	0	0	2	7	56	5	10	27	1,201
34	0	0	0	1	3	28	3	5	13	591
35	1	0	0	1	16	67	21	15	31	698
36	0	0	0	0	0	7	4	0	8	601
37	0	0	0	0	4	22	2	2	81	410
38	0	0	0	1	0	23	0	1	62	991
39	6,305	6	0	19	6	27	1,231	35	286	607
40	1,131	17,846	2,712	94	108	36	4	35	236	992
41	4	0	0	50	28	246	16	77	1,766	3,719
42	2	0	0	0	15	77	13	16	107	592
43	0	0	0	0	0	24	1	4	4	560
44	0	0	0	1	1	7	0	1	15	160
45	0	0	0	1	1	6	0	4	37	1,094
46	1	0	0	1	11	68	5	12	59	612
47	1	0	0	1	10	64	5	12	56	912
48	0	0	0	0	0	8	0	0	3	146
49	39	0	0	75	53	522	328	359	1,929	4,286
50	12	3	0	42	55	228	71	72	360	1,151
51	7,553	17,855	2,712	346	390	2,580	1,766	917	6,771	53,593

OCCUPATIONS

CLERICAL AND SALES

TABLE XII (continued) WEST VIRGINIA EMPLOYMENT BY SECTOR AND OCCUPATION 1965*	25. Stenos, typists, and secretaries	26. Office machine operators	27. Accounting clerks and bookkeepers	28. Shipping and receiving clerks	29. Cashiers	30. Telephone operators
1. Agriculture	1	0	0	0	0	0
2. Coal mining (underground)	144	16	185	29	6	11
3. Coal mining (strip & auger)	9	1	12	2	0	1
4. Petroleum & natural gas	159	14	47	1	0	4
5. All other mining	15	2	14	4	0	0
6. General contractors (building)	96	4	79	1	1	3
7. General contractors (non-building)	90	4	74	1	1	2
8. Special trades contractors	116	5	96	2	1	3
9. Food & kindred products (meats and n.e.c.)	34	18	26	21	1	2
10. Food & kindred products (dairies)	34	36	63	17	6	4
11. Food & kindred products (bakeries)	19	22	17	39	14	2
12. Food & kindred products (beverages)	39	15	27	11	3	2
13. Apparel & accessories	59	26	54	86	1	4
14. Logging & sawmills	11	4	14	1	0	0
15. Furniture & other wood fabrication	25	4	17	13	0	1
16. Printing & publishing	133	21	43	22	2	9
17. Chemicals	906	0	0	95	0	0
18. Petroleum	38	11	10	2	1	2
19. Glass	213	36	58	97	7	16
20. Stone & clay products	41	7	29	18	1	3
21. Primary metal products	534	126	106	227	10	29
22. Fabricated metal products	151	27	20	55	2	7
23. Machinery (except electrical)	176	43	43	55	1	6
24. Electrical machinery & apparatus	43	10	7	9	1	2
25. Transportation equipment	156	33	25	30	2	5
26. Instruments & related products	27	4	5	5	0	1
27. All other manufacturing	160	40	65	76	1	10
28. Eating & drinking establishments	21	11	56	3	240	4
29. Wholesale trade	1,054	433	894	292	28	61
30. Retail food stores	41	58	101	18	1,325	3
31. Retail gasoline service stations	8	4	67	0	4	0
32. All other retail	687	441	1,245	277	929	179
33. Banking	425	280	525	1	107	28
34. Other finance	209	138	259	1	53	14
35. Insurance agents & brokers	922	159	122	3	30	17
36. Real estate	197	5	59	0	4	6
37. All other finance, insurance & real estate	166	48	44	2	24	16
38. Hotels & other lodging places	45	20	33	2	51	63
39. Medical & legal services	989	27	155	6	41	106
40. Educational services	1,619	67	135	6	104	93
41. All other services	1,472	165	472	54	209	140
42. Railroads	185	114	42	25	31	30
43. Trucking & warehousing	132	58	84	13	19	12
44. All other transportation	25	6	10	5	5	4
45. Communications	221	99	90	3	40	1,689
46. Electric companies & systems	170	57	57	3	40	18
47. Gas companies & systems	194	65	65	3	46	21
48. Water & sanitary services	49	17	37	0	12	2
49. State and local government	2,616	375	355	6	82	98
50. Federal government	954	129	149	16	12	30
51. Total	15,830	3,305	6,192	1,658	3,498	2,763

Left margin: PROCESSING SECTORS

*Each Row Shows the Distribution of Employment by Occupation in Each Sector.

		CRAFTSMEN AND FOREMEN									
31. Other clerical workers	32. Sales workers	33. Brick masons, stone, tile setters	34. Carpenters	35. Electricians	36. Excavating, grading machine operators	37. Plumbers and pipefitters	38. Painters and paperhangers	39. Other construction craftsmen	40. Foremen	41. Sheet metal workers (tinsmiths)	42. Skilled machine workers	
3	1	0	1	0	0	0	0	0	1	0	0	1
698	156	125	282	1,994	2,897	127	12	7	3,967	0	513	2
44	10	8	18	125	182	8	1	0	249	0	32	3
154	2	1	3	9	10	6	5	2	161	1	6	4
53	9	1	7	10	75	2	2	1	52	0	7	5
133	22	272	995	231	288	341	450	302	176	62	4	6
124	20	105	329	66	669	69	120	283	164	58	4	7
161	26	380	1,301	330	48	263	445	366	213	75	5	8
93	70	1	4	7	0	3	0	0	78	0	5	9
137	135	1	2	2	0	0	2	0	83	0	1	10
103	205	1	1	3	0	1	0	0	76	0	6	11
71	115	0	4	7	0	2	2	0	67	1	11	12
170	112	0	1	1	0	0	0	0	149	0	1	13
28	14	0	7	3	77	0	0	0	134	0	6	14
48	21	0	32	4	3	1	1	0	59	2	4	15
291	401	1	2	4	0	1	1	0	87	0	10	16
143	419	0	95	334	0	447	0	525	2,147	95	192	17
61	15	1	5	7	1	18	1	1	34	0	9	18
436	39	16	83	115	7	72	5	5	1,032	20	190	19
81	29	25	38	95	62	12	10	11	415	8	55	20
1,711	402	186	98	265	19	70	32	26	715	21	215	21
302	127	2	10	23	1	14	19	17	187	90	187	22
320	70	2	10	33	0	15	2	3	219	33	570	23
58	18	1	5	33	0	7	1	1	203	23	124	24
366	28	2	20	70	0	24	6	5	215	55	189	25
48	8	0	1	4	0	2	0	0	25	2	26	26
376	143	1	16	29	1	16	9	1	313	10	36	27
42	125	2	8	0	0	0	4	0	7	0	0	28
1,657	3,509	4	45	17	0	14	19	6	431	7	2	29
370	2,089	0	9	2	0	1	6	0	50	0	0	30
19	27	0	2	0	0	0	1	0	4	0	0	31
3,300	15,963	8	87	25	2	3	57	0	380	5	0	32
1,254	29	0	1	1	0	0	1	0	5	0	0	33
617	14	0	1	1	0	0	1	0	2	0	0	34
1,122	1,711	0	1	1	0	0	2	0	3	0	0	35
163	802	1	21	2	2	2	32	2	9	0	0	36
225	242	0	0	0	0	0	1	0	1	0	0	37
282	11	0	23	7	0	3	27	2	8	0	0	38
524	12	0	11	11	0	8	15	1	10	1	1	39
1,911	50	7	72	40	4	27	65	11	55	4	13	40
2,498	529	4	77	59	12	14	136	4	245	18	9	41
1,613	25	3	115	282	23	108	69	10	679	56	439	42
548	83	0	3	1	6	1	4	1	105	1	0	43
124	4	0	6	5	1	0	3	1	14	2	2	44
1,075	46	0	2	5	0	0	1	0	30	0	0	45
574	258	1	6	72	12	54	8	2	168	1	9	46
655	80	0	2	31	5	23	3	1	71	1	4	47
187	1	1	3	4	15	29	2	0	71	0	3	48
3,954	29	8	53	69	65	38	103	6	205	3	18	49
5,399	10	3	53	109	21	48	59	5	106	60	59	50
34,326	28,266	1,174	3,871	4,548	4,508	2,024	1,745	1,608	13,880	715	2,967	51

OCCUPATIONS

CRAFTSMEN AND FOREMEN

TABLE XII
(continued)

WEST VIRGINIA EMPLOYMENT
BY SECTOR AND OCCUPATION
1965*

		43. Toolmakers, diemakers, and setters	44. Other metalworking craftsmen	45. Motor vehicle mechanics and repairmen	46. Other mechanics and repairmen	47. Printing trades craftsmen	48. Transportation and public utility craftsmen	49. Other craftsmen
	1. Agriculture	0	0	0	2	0	0	0
	2. Coal mining (underground)	0	98	58	3,275	0	71	1,220
	3. Coal mining (strip & auger)	0	6	4	205	0	4	76
	4. Petroleum & natural gas	1	31	3	97	1	1	302
	5. All other mining	0	4	5	51	0	1	51
	6. General contractors (building)	0	20	10	169	0	17	135
	7. General contractors (non-building)	0	19	9	158	0	15	127
	8. Special trades contractors	0	24	12	205	1	20	164
	9. Food & kindred products (meats and n.e.c.)	0	4	3	50	2	0	18
	10. Food & kindred products (dairies)	0	1	15	57	1	0	22
	11. Food & kindred products (bakeries)	0	1	11	44	1	0	471
	12. Food & kindred products (beverages)	0	1	5	57	1	0	42
	13. Apparel & accessories	0	2	0	40	4	0	38
	14. Logging & sawmills	0	8	13	51	1	1	114
	15. Furniture & other wood fabrication	1	14	1	26	1	0	95
	16. Printing & publishing	0	0	1	36	849	0	71
	17. Chemicals	0	0	0	0	0	0	906
	18. Petroleum	0	7	3	27	1	0	29
	19. Glass	20	105	31	768	28	4	437
	20. Stone & clay products	8	26	34	352	3	2	161
	21. Primary metal products	21	802	14	500	5	31	999
	22. Fabricated metal products	90	82	3	126	9	0	97
	23. Machinery (except electrical)	221	87	5	171	6	1	153
	24. Electrical machinery & apparatus	23	44	1	138	5	19	84
	25. Transportation equipment	112	80	129	194	3	1	110
	26. Instruments & related products	7	2	0	15	2	0	20
	27. All other manufacturing	24	52	2	206	34	1	152
	28. Eating & drinking establishments	0	0	1	32	0	0	49
	29. Wholesale trade	0	8	72	755	14	1	250
	30. Retail food stores	0	0	5	32	2	0	83
	31. Retail gasoline service stations	0	0	334	9	0	1	7
	32. All other retail	0	2	2,517	778	22	1	700
	33. Banking	0	0	0	21	5	0	4
	34. Other finance	0	0	0	10	2	0	2
	35. Insurance agents & brokers	0	0	1	12	5	0	18
	36. Real estate	0	0	1	33	1	0	13
	37. All other finance, insurance & real estate	0	0	0	4	1	1	4
	38. Hotels & other lodging places	0	0	1	87	1	0	42
	39. Medical & legal services	1	0	1	66	1	0	44
	40. Educational services	0	0	20	369	14	0	129
	41. All other services	9	38	864	953	22	7	608
	42. Railroads	56	70	5	755	3	1,352	676
	43. Trucking & warehousing	0	2	262	51	1	0	31
	44. All other transportation	0	1	43	48	0	1	13
	45. Communications	0	0	7	44	1	1,812	30
	46. Electric companies & systems	1	6	20	291	1	353	148
	47. Gas companies & systems	1	3	9	124	1	150	63
	48. Water & sanitary services	0	1	6	177	0	4	116
	49. State and local government	2	5	163	703	20	17	181
	50. Federal government	9	15	47	510	25	15	81
	51. Total	607	1,671	4,750	12,884	1,100	3,904	9,386

PROCESSING SECTORS

*Each Row Shows the Distribution of Employment by Occupation in Each Sector.

	OPERATIVES AND LABORERS						SERVICE		
50. Drivers	51. Semiskilled textile and garment workers	52. Semiskilled metalworkers	53. Mine operatives and laborers	54. Farmers and farm workers	55. Other operatives (semiskilled)	56. Laborers (excluding farm and mine)	57. Waiters, cooks, and bartenders	58. Other service workers	59. Total
11	0	0	0	870	6	15	1	2	925	1
1,604	0	404	15,465	0	2,183	0	6	224	40,600	2
101	0	25	971	0	137	0	0	14	2,546	3
241	0	48	2,236	0	76	0	8	24	4,229	4
232	0	30	558	0	68	0	2	34	1,421	5
283	0	58	0	0	276	1,178	3	37	6,888	6
265	0	54	0	0	258	2,252	3	35	6,441	7
343	0	71	0	0	334	1,477	4	45	8,343	8
97	0	3	0	0	912	180	6	40	1,877	9
743	0	0	0	0	416	125	11	23	2,244	10
533	0	0	0	0	445	74	10	64	2,347	11
270	0	1	0	0	369	150	1	28	1,517	12
19	1,940	2	0	0	2,275	52	2	50	5,392	13
912	0	12	0	0	165	4,557	3	16	6,707	14
73	12	13	0	0	646	318	0	26	1,592	15
76	7	1	0	0	587	66	3	128	3,674	16
0	0	1,192	0	0	10,023	477	0	238	25,615	17
26	0	8	0	0	145	45	1	12	712	18
260	2	75	0	0	8,517	1,295	16	175	15,485	19
815	0	75	0	0	2,120	914	1	41	5,911	20
504	4	2,490	0	0	6,768	5,558	24	470	26,664	21
134	2	1,638	0	0	2,111	502	3	70	6,791	22
35	2	951	0	0	848	142	3	74	5,194	23
47	6	1,858	0	0	2,016	210	5	66	5,406	24
57	19	1,190	0	0	1,115	141	6	100	5,348	25
2	2	67	0	0	99	7	1	7	547	26
66	759	181	0	0	3,159	290	4	119	6,920	27
52	0	0	0	0	64	35	6,283	1,711	10,901	28
2,117	0	86	0	0	1,432	1,373	5	212	20,118	29
256	0	0	0	0	1,338	742	82	107	8,917	30
48	0	0	0	0	1,880	89	2	16	3,695	31
779	51	10	0	0	1,463	1,212	510	1,209	41,920	32
4	0	0	0	0	12	4	7	190	4,215	33
2	0	0	0	0	6	2	3	93	2,074	34
2	0	0	0	0	8	6	7	70	5,089	35
6	0	0	0	0	11	162	2	363	2,522	36
2	0	0	0	0	5	3	1	17	1,328	37
6	0	0	0	0	117	68	546	1,844	4,371	38
141	0	7	0	0	114	149	560	8,957	24,118	39
81	0	4	0	0	207	256	1,659	3,932	35,019	40
882	121	112	0	0	5,320	662	527	5,932	29,929	41
308	0	117	0	0	2,686	1,570	32	152	12,600	42
4,339	0	10	0	0	95	620	1	38	7,120	43
596	0	2	0	0	121	149	14	54	1,457	44
11	0	0	0	0	19	22	13	78	6,510	45
155	0	52	0	0	506	402	3	165	4,750	46
361	0	122	0	0	1,168	935	2	84	5,703	47
78	0	2	0	0	165	238	0	22	1,474	48
355	0	7	0	0	343	902	72	10,518	30,099	49
120	0	22	0	0	296	428	39	429	12,315	50
18,450	2,927	11,000	19,230	870	63,450	30,254	10,497	38,355	477,580	51

	OCCUPATIONS						
TABLE XIII PROJECTED WEST VIRGINIA EMPLOYMENT BY SECTOR AND OCCUPATION 1975*	PROFESSIONAL, TECHNICAL, AND MANAGERIAL						
	1. Chemical engineers	2. Industrial engineers	3. Mechanical engineers	4. Mining engineers	5. Other engineers	6. Chemists	7. Mathematicians
1. Agriculture	0	0	0	0	0	0	0
2. Coal mining (underground)	10	59	30	433	63	105	0
3. Coal mining (strip & auger)	1	4	2	14	4	7	0
4. Petroleum & natural gas	18	10	7	81	26	10	2
5. All other mining	2	1	1	1	4	1	0
6. General contractors (building)	1	2	7	0	247	1	0
7. General contractors (non-building)	1	2	5	0	198	1	0
8. Special trades contractors	1	3	8	0	294	1	0
9. Food & kindred products (meats and n.e.c.)	0	3	3	0	4	4	0
10. Food & kindred products (dairies)	0	2	4	0	4	3	0
11. Food & kindred products (bakeries)	0	1	1	0	4	1	0
12. Food & kindred products (beverages)	1	1	2	0	3	9	0
13. Apparel & accessories	0	3	1	0	1	2	0
14. Logging & sawmills	0	0	0	0	6	0	0
15. Furniture & other wood fabrication	0	2	0	0	3	1	0
16. Printing & publishing	0	5	1	0	5	2	0
17. Chemicals	1,261	30	257	0	127	1,746	6
18. Petroleum	31	3	7	1	13	25	2
19. Glass	9	39	49	0	87	12	0
20. Stone & clay products	7	9	11	2	53	11	0
21. Primary metal products	18	402	125	2	416	70	17
22. Fabricated metal products	5	34	71	0	45	2	0
23. Machinery (except electrical)	2	43	127	0	93	5	1
24. Electrical machinery & apparatus	1	20	14	0	91	5	3
25. Transportation equipment	4	55	114	0	181	12	9
26. Instruments & related products	1	11	10	0	51	5	1
27. All other manufacturing	5	18	9	0	33	22	1
28. Eating & drinking establishments	0	0	0	0	0	0	0
29. Wholesale trade	3	7	14	5	217	21	6
30. Retail food stores	0	0	4	0	0	1	0
31. Retail gasoline service stations	0	0	0	0	0	0	0
32. All other retail	0	10	0	0	12	0	0
33. Banking	0	0	0	0	0	0	2
34. Other finance	0	0	0	0	0	0	1
35. Insurance agents & brokers	0	9	0	0	2	0	4
36. Real estate	0	1	0	0	1	0	0
37. All other finance, insurance & real estate	0	0	0	0	0	0	0
38. Hotels & other lodging places	0	0	1	0	0	0	0
39. Medical & legal services	0	5	3	0	21	74	1
40. Educational services	12	12	32	31	83	88	84
41. All other services	25	155	185	5	930	41	80
42. Railroads	0	12	26	0	66	8	0
43. Trucking & warehousing	0	2	2	0	3	0	0
44. All other transportation	0	1	1	0	3	0	0
45. Communications	0	2	0	0	89	0	0
46. Electric companies & systems	4	11	36	1	232	8	3
47. Gas companies & systems	3	8	24	0	156	6	2
48. Water & sanitary services	0	1	3	0	56	5	1
49. State and local government	27	52	27	70	440	22	16
50. Federal government	7	20	71	4	366	41	67
51. Total	1,460	1,070	1,295	650	4,733	2,378	309

*Each Row Show the Distribution of Employment by Occupation in Each Sector.

OCCUPATIONS

TABLE XIII
(continued)

PROJECTED WEST VIRGINIA EMPLOYMENT BY SECTOR AND OCCUPATION 1975*

PROCESSING SECTORS	8. Physicists	9. Other natural scientists	10. Technicians (excluding medical and dental)	11. Medical and dental technicians	12. Doctors and veterinarians	13. Dentists	14. Pharmacists
1. Agriculture	0	0	1	0	3	0	0
2. Coal mining (underground)	0	18	174	0	0	0	0
3. Coal mining (strip & auger)	0	1	11	0	0	0	0
4. Petroleum & natural gas	2	137	83	0	0	0	0
5. All other mining	0	1	10	0	0	0	0
6. General contractors (building)	0	1	284	0	0	0	0
7. General contractors (non-building)	0	1	227	0	0	0	0
8. Special trades contractors	0	1	337	0	0	0	0
9. Food & kindred products (meats and n.e.c.)	0	4	16	0	0	0	0
10. Food & kindred products (dairies)	0	4	42	0	0	0	0
11. Food & kindred products (bakeries)	0	0	6	0	0	0	0
12. Food & kindred products (beverages)	0	1	13	1	0	0	0
13. Apparel & accessories	0	0	3	0	0	0	0
14. Logging & sawmills	0	0	3	0	0	0	0
15. Furniture & other wood fabrication	0	2	9	0	0	0	0
16. Printing & publishing	0	0	38	0	0	0	0
17. Chemicals	16	28	2,528	108	0	0	0
18. Petroleum	2	10	55	0	1	0	0
19. Glass	0	0	177	0	0	0	0
20. Stone & clay products	1	0	62	0	1	0	0
21. Primary metal products	20	9	312	2	7	0	0
22. Fabricated metal products	1	0	89	1	0	0	0
23. Machinery (except electrical)	1	1	257	2	1	0	0
24. Electrical machinery & apparatus	6	1	162	1	0	0	0
25. Transportation equipment	7	1	195	0	1	0	0
26. Instruments & related products	3	1	54	4	0	0	0
27. All other manufacturing	1	1	57	0	0	0	0
28. Eating & drinking establishments	0	0	0	6	0	0	0
29. Wholesale trade	0	2	172	2	0	0	11
30. Retail food stores	0	0	3	0	0	0	0
31. Retail gasoline service stations	0	0	0	0	0	0	0
32. All other retail	0	0	56	3	14	1	572
33. Banking	0	0	1	1	0	0	0
34. Other finance	0	0	1	0	0	0	0
35. Insurance agents & brokers	0	0	11	1	3	0	0
36. Real estate	0	0	2	0	0	0	0
37. All other finance, insurance & real estate	0	0	1	0	0	0	0
38. Hotels & other lodging places	0	0	1	2	3	0	0
39. Medical & legal services	3	88	21	2,322	2,293	784	64
40. Educational services	90	229	263	101	88	56	14
41. All other services	74	36	1,420	12	43	0	0
42. Railroads	0	1	55	0	1	0	0
43. Trucking & warehousing	0	0	4	0	0	0	0
44. All other transportation	0	0	13	0	0	0	0
45. Communications	0	0	43	0	0	0	0
46. Electric companies & systems	6	0	248	1	1	0	2
47. Gas companies & systems	5	0	173	0	1	0	1
48. Water & sanitary services	0	7	60	0	0	0	0
49. State and local government	0	272	1,086	20	155	12	7
50. Federal government	56	201	551	12	41	3	3
51. Total	294	1,059	9,390	2,602	2,657	856	674

*Each Row Show the Distribution of Employment by Occupation in Each Sector.

PROFESSIONAL, TECHNICAL, AND MANAGERIAL

15. Nurses (professional and student)	16. Elementary and secondary teachers	17. College teachers	18. Other teachers	19. Social scientists	20. Accountants and auditors	21. Lawyers and judges	22. Personnel and labor relations workers	23. Other professional and technical workers	24. Managers, officials, and proprietors	
0	0	0	0	0	0	0	0	2	3	1
3	0	0	3	6	134	19	27	74	3,311	2
0	0	0	0	0	9	1	2	5	230	3
0	0	0	0	1	38	3	6	15	309	4
0	0	0	0	0	3	0	1	5	103	5
0	0	0	0	1	32	2	5	98	1,314	6
0	0	0	0	1	26	1	4	78	1,054	7
0	0	0	0	1	38	2	6	116	1,561	8
1	0	0	0	0	11	1	4	8	128	9
0	0	0	1	0	16	0	4	8	244	10
1	0	0	0	0	7	0	1	2	156	11
1	0	0	0	1	8	0	3	13	156	12
1	0	0	4	1	6	1	8	50	302	13
2	0	0	0	0	14	0	1	62	704	14
0	0	0	0	0	6	0	2	17	128	15
2	0	0	1	4	40	2	8	952	477	16
5	0	0	0	1	0	0	4	53	1,529	17
1	0	0	0	2	25	2	3	20	59	18
15	0	0	0	9	59	5	20	82	980	19
0	0	0	1	0	33	1	5	25	368	20
18	0	0	8	19	296	6	40	130	2,606	21
3	0	0	1	4	14	0	12	63	671	22
6	0	0	0	2	46	1	13	87	479	23
1	0	0	0	0	3	1	1	13	110	24
3	0	0	1	5	43	3	16	93	174	25
0	0	0	0	1	4	1	3	16	33	26
3	0	0	1	2	29	1	14	79	391	27
0	0	0	13	0	8	0	5	87	2,168	28
1	0	0	10	19	175	7	24	138	4,608	29
0	0	0	1	1	14	2	4	6	1,897	30
0	0	0	0	0	1	0	1	1	1,080	31
21	0	0	35	14	90	4	78	282	7,863	32
1	0	0	3	13	52	3	18	48	1,867	33
1	0	0	1	6	24	1	8	22	847	34
2	0	0	1	22	86	25	23	42	918	35
0	0	0	0	0	6	3	1	17	844	36
0	0	0	1	5	23	1	3	146	464	37
1	0	0	1	0	27	0	0	95	1,210	38
8,272	3	0	21	8	35	1,456	52	395	1,063	39
2,401	22,363	4,809	1,486	193	143	5	61	1,337	1,881	40
5	0	0	75	39	324	18	115	2,350	4,132	41
2	0	0	0	15	56	11	18	122	548	42
0	0	0	0	0	27	1	5	7	527	43
0	0	0	1	1	9	0	2	22	185	44
0	0	0	1	0	0	0	17	116	1,321	45
2	0	0	0	16	69	6	18	113	776	46
1	0	0	0	11	43	4	12	81	795	47
0	0	0	0	0	14	0	1	5	201	48
68	0	0	119	84	911	486	639	3,843	7,324	49
13	3	0	50	66	241	66	81	473	1,244	50
10,857	22,369	4,809	1.840	574	3,318	2,152	1,399	11,914	61,343	51

OCCUPATIONS

CLERICAL AND SALES

TABLE XIII
(continued)

PROJECTED WEST VIRGINIA EMPLOYMENT BY SECTOR AND OCCUPATION 1975*

PROCESSING SECTORS	25. Stenos, typists, and secretaries	26. Office machine operators	27. Accounting clerks and bookkeepers	28. Shipping and receiving clerks	29. Cashiers	30. Telephone operators
1. Agriculture	1	0	0	0	0	0
2. Coal mining (underground)	130	35	185	25	5	13
3. Coal mining (strip & auger)	9	2	12	2	0	1
4. Petroleum & natural gas	232	41	52	3	0	3
5. All other mining	14	3	10	5	0	0
6. General contractors (building)	160	9	124	1	1	4
7. General contractors (non-building)	128	8	99	1	1	3
8. Special trades contractors	189	11	147	1	1	4
9. Food & kindred products (meats and n.e.c.)	29	22	21	13	1	2
10. Food & kindred products (dairies)	37	62	62	15	7	4
11. Food & kindred products (bakeries)	20	31	16	40	25	2
12. Food & kindred products (beverages)	35	20	22	6	2	2
13. Apparel & accessories	78	47	59	111	1	6
14. Logging & sawmills	14	8	10	2	0	0
15 Furniture & other wood fabrication	39	8	20	19	0	1
16. Printing & publishing	248	57	50	35	2	16
17. Chemicals	699	96	0	0	0	0
18. Petroleum	46	26	12	2	1	2
19. Glass	171	67	45	70	9	20
20. Stone & clay products	49	22	28	20	0	6
21. Primary metal products	598	209	96	217	11	29
22. Fabricated metal products	200	58	25	61	5	10
23. Machinery (except electrical)	211	65	41	56	1	7
24. Electrical machinery & apparatus	49	39	8	1	1	0
25. Transportation equipment	144	44	24	20	2	4
26. Instruments & related products	27	7	3	2	0	1
27. All other manufacturing	178	63	65	78	1	10
28. Eating & drinking establishments	29	18	75	3	342	5
29. Wholesale trade	1,097	607	943	228	28	73
30. Retail food stores	48	85	102	17	1,694	3
31. Retail gasoline service stations	10	7	69	0	4	0
32. All other retail	653	621	1,224	279	1,308	243
33. Banking	527	467	662	2	200	42
34. Other finance	239	212	301	1	91	19
35. Insurance agents & brokers	1,184	317	136	5	29	21
36. Real estate	280	10	81	0	6	6
37. All other finance, insurance & real estate	196	92	53	3	30	23
38. Hotels & other lodging places	54	31	43	1	66	82
39. Medical & legal services	1,487	56	202	10	63	144
40. Educational services	3,962	138	220	7	181	162
41. All other services	2,018	292	571	68	280	244
42. Railroads	153	176	27	24	28	14
43. Trucking & warehousing	157	97	88	15	21	14
44. All other transportation	31	11	10	8	6	4
45. Communications	252	141	65	4	46	1,528
46. Electric companies & systems	212	87	30	3	57	13
47. Gas companies & systems	167	69	22	2	45	10
48. Water & sanitary services	75	34	60	0	18	1
49. State and local government	4,499	815	595	12	146	166
50. Federal government	976	127	159	19	10	30
51. Total	22,041	5,570	6,974	1,517	4,776	2,977

*Each Row Show the Distribution of Employment by Occupation in Each Sector.

CRAFTSMEN AND FOREMEN

31. Other clerical workers	32. Sales workers	33. Brick masons, stone, tile setters	34. Carpenters	35. Electricians	36. Excavating, grading machine operators	37. Plumbers and pipefitters	38. Painters and paperhangers	39. Other construction craftsmen	40. Foremen	41. Sheet metal workers (tinsmiths)	42. Skilled machine workers	
2	1	0	1	0	0	0	0	0	1	0	0	1
632	190	111	193	1,930	3,107	132	7	5	3,549	0	575	2
41	12	7	13	126	203	9	0	0	232	0	31	3
153	3	2	2	11	12	7	2	2	178	2	4	4
59	8	1	4	7	74	3	2	1	49	0	6	5
223	34	349	1,204	329	457	494	538	449	303	87	5	6
179	28	280	566	164	766	196	132	360	243	70	4	7
265	41	415	1,830	491	142	787	939	533	360	104	6	8
84	63	1	3	7	1	3	0	0	68	0	4	9
187	135	1	1	0	0	0	1	0	83	0	1	10
127	251	1	1	4	0	1	1	0	88	0	7	11
73	101	0	4	7	0	2	2	0	74	1	10	12
241	156	1	2	2	1	1	0	1	208	0	2	13
27	19	0	6	3	128	0	0	0	186	0	5	14
70	32	0	46	5	5	1	1	1	86	2	8	15
558	788	1	2	4	1	2	1	1	169	1	12	16
83	293	0	45	295	16	440	0	494	2,053	86	119	17
67	20	1	5	8	2	20	0	1	40	0	8	18
379	0	13	88	103	7	75	4	7	1,163	17	199	19
120	66	26	47	118	77	14	12	13	513	7	68	20
1,921	544	196	92	311	29	138	27	32	943	13	235	21
414	163	1	10	27	0	18	25	22	282	105	217	22
343	64	2	7	38	0	16	3	3	286	35	745	23
0	12	1	1	29	0	4	0	2	228	27	114	24
335	24	2	19	70	0	25	5	6	204	51	150	25
49	4	0	1	5	0	1	0	0	29	2	24	26
451	166	1	15	33	1	17	10	2	374	10	35	27
42	151	3	14	0	0	0	7	0	8	0	0	28
1,792	3,521	4	52	17	0	14	21	6	540	9	2	29
439	1,825	0	11	3	0	2	6	0	55	0	0	30
20	27	0	2	0	0	0	1	0	4	0	0	31
4,027	17,799	10	111	25	2	2	66	0	463	5	0	32
1,589	49	0	1	1	0	0	1	0	7	0	0	33
721	22	0	0	1	0	0	0	0	3	0	0	34
1,386	2,233	0	2	1	0	0	0	3	4	0	0	35
245	1,105	0	33	2	3	2	54	4	15	0	0	36
267	388	0	0	0	0	0	0	1	2	0	0	37
320	10	1	32	8	0	3	33	3	11	0	0	38
855	10	1	3	17	0	4	4	1	14	1	1	39
4,049	77	12	100	54	6	36	89	23	94	6	12	40
3,391	683	5	126	79	23	17	147	5	325	32	13	41
1,231	30	1	69	288	28	101	51	7	570	52	411	42
687	113	0	3	2	8	1	5	3	133	1	0	43
153	6	0	11	5	1	0	2	1	18	3	2	44
1,144	67	0	2	6	0	0	2	0	39	0	0	45
611	316	2	2	82	22	65	11	2	210	0	4	46
478	65	1	0	18	10	18	4	1	63	0	0	47
291	2	1	3	4	30	42	2	1	117	0	4	48
6,537	39	9	70	94	123	61	169	10	357	6	25	49
5,723	11	3	41	118	29	57	63	6	130	65	46	50
43,081	31,767	1,466	4,896	4,953	5,314	2,831	2,454	2,008	15,174	800	3,114	51

OCCUPATIONS

CRAFTSMEN AND FOREMEN

TABLE XIII
(continued)

PROJECTED WEST VIRGINIA EMPLOYMENT BY SECTOR AND OCCUPATION 1975*

PROCESSING SECTORS	43. Toolmakers, diemakers, and setters	44. Other metalworking craftsmen	45. Motor vehicle mechanics and repairmen	46. Other mechanics and repairmen	47. Printing trades craftsmen	48. Transportation and public utility craftsmen	49. Other craftsmen
1. Agriculture	0	0	0	2	0	0	0
2. Coal mining (underground)	0	63	41	3,955	0	70	967
3. Coal mining (strip & auger)	0	4	3	259	0	5	63
4. Petroleum & natural gas	1	16	4	143	1	1	265
5. All other mining	0	3	5	61	0	1	41
6. General contractors (building)	0	34	14	328	0	31	244
7. General contractors (non-building)	0	27	11	263	0	25	196
8. Special trades contractors	0	41	17	389	0	37	290
9. Food & kindred products (meats and n.e.c.)	0	3	2	53	2	0	14
10. Food & kindred products (dairies)	0	1	17	64	1	0	22
11. Food & kindred products (bakeries)	0	1	13	57	1	0	462
12. Food & kindred products (beverages)	0	1	6	74	1	0	37
13. Apparel & accessories	0	3	0	64	5	0	59
14. Logging & sawmills	0	14	18	83	1	1	169
15. Furniture & other wood fabrication	1	19	1	50	1	0	146
16. Printing & publishing	1	1	1	77	1,405	1	123
17. Chemicals	0	0	0	191	0	0	723
18. Petroleum	0	7	4	36	1	0	27
19. Glass	20	114	33	1,004	28	4	485
20. Stone & clay products	10	26	45	496	4	2	207
21. Primary metal products	15	787	22	905	5	35	1,311
22. Fabricated metal products	124	91	4	218	10	1	162
23. Machinery (except electrical)	219	91	5	219	6	1	175
24. Electrical machinery & apparatus	6	50	1	168	5	22	88
25. Transportation equipment	82	68	118	175	3	1	92
26. Instruments & related products	5	3	0	16	1	0	18
27. All other manufacturing	24	62	2	295	41	1	163
28. Eating & drinking establishments	0	0	1	52	0	0	68
29. Wholesale trade	0	8	83	1,080	16	0	297
30. Retail food stores	0	0	5	46	3	0	67
31. Retail gasoline service stations	0	0	407	10	0	1	9
32. All other retail	0	2	2,739	988	30	1	775
33. Banking	0	0	1	35	8	0	3
34. Other finance	0	0	0	16	3	0	2
35. Insurance agents & brokers	0	0	1	15	3	0	25
36. Real estate	0	0	1	36	1	0	14
37. All other finance, insurance & real estate	0	0	0	7	2	1	5
38. Hotels & other lodging places	0	0	1	117	1	0	50
39. Medical & legal services	1	0	1	134	1	0	26
40. Educational services	0	0	28	645	22	0	176
41. All other services	4	41	970	1,379	29	16	737
42. Railroads	45	38	6	697	2	927	623
43. Trucking & warehousing	0	3	330	76	1	0	40
44. All other transportation	0	1	44	62	0	1	15
45. Communications	0	0	9	61	1	2,245	36
46. Electric companies & systems	2	6	27	441	1	504	199
47. Gas companies & systems	0	1	9	170	0	184	66
48. Water & sanitary services	0	2	11	318	0	8	173
49. State and local government	3	8	288	1,363	35	27	292
50. Federal government	7	20	39	627	36	22	93
51. Total	570	1,660	5,388	18,020	1,717	4,176	10,340

*Each Row Show the Distribution of Employment by Occupation in Each Sector.

50. Drivers	51. Semiskilled textile and garment workers	52. Semiskilled metalworkers	53. Mine operatives and laborers	54. Farmers and farm workers	55. Other operatives (semiskilled)	56. Laborers (excluding farm and mine)	57. Waiters, cooks, and bartenders	58. Other service workers	59. Total	
8	0	0	0	559	5	12	0	1	602	1
1,947	0	552	10,621	0	2,020	0	7	181	35,717	2
127	0	36	694	0	141	0	0	12	2,335	3
286	0	53	2,559	0	63	0	12	28	4,889	4
226	0	30	497	0	70	0	2	29	1,344	5
481	0	98	0	0	478	1,507	5	56	10,042	6
386	0	79	0	0	384	1,808	4	45	8,055	7
572	0	117	0	0	568	1,186	5	67	11,924	8
92	0	2	0	0	808	102	5	31	1,623	9
798	0	0	0	0	324	63	8	18	2,245	10
711	0	0	0	0	503	65	10	60	2,678	11
281	0	1	0	0	374	105	1	25	1,480	12
29	2,372	3	0	0	2,715	60	3	60	6,673	13
1,389	0	18	0	0	275	4,534	3	20	7,725	14
98	16	22	0	0	931	306	1	34	2,140	15
138	8	1	0	0	1,161	108	5	219	6,734	16
0	0	1,119	0	0	9,151	316	7	11	23,956	17
28	0	8	0	0	155	33	2	8	832	18
283	2	70	0	0	8,679	911	17	133	15,763	19
1,159	0	99	0	0	2,492	829	2	39	7,206	20
620	1	2,807	0	0	7,655	5,302	26	425	30,080	21
191	3	2,148	0	0	2,920	589	7	59	9,186	22
40	1	1,022	0	0	831	134	3	70	5,907	23
47	5	1,803	0	0	2,019	177	7	53	5,400	24
59	15	1,084	0	0	1,201	87	6	79	5,116	25
3	2	71	0	0	111	6	1	6	597	26
80	655	191	0	0	3,357	235	4	95	7,382	27
83	0	0	0	0	98	39	7,645	2,005	12,975	28
2,280	0	90	0	0	1,496	1,264	6	195	21,211	29
217	0	0	0	0	1,475	748	88	106	8,978	30
57	0	0	0	0	2,502	76	2	15	4,306	31
884	62	11	0	0	1,618	1,280	624	1,181	46,088	32
8	0	0	0	0	14	2	10	225	5,863	33
4	0	0	0	0	6	1	5	101	2,661	34
3	0	0	0	0	8	7	9	96	6,637	35
8	0	0	0	0	11	211	1	239	3,243	36
3	0	0	0	0	4	2	1	18	1,742	37
6	0	1	0	0	162	81	637	2,015	5,110	38
179	0	10	0	0	418	443	651	13,486	35,207	39
126	0	6	0	0	291	347	2,881	5,842	55,454	40
1,027	138	135	0	0	5,535	822	788	7,808	37,792	41
323	0	114	0	0	2,531	1,092	0	22	10,622	42
5,121	0	11	0	0	136	574	1	40	8,259	43
708	0	2	0	0	129	148	15	62	1,697	44
14	0	0	0	0	13	6	12	70	7,352	45
202	0	66	0	0	552	400	3	180	5,865	46
317	0	105	0	0	940	716	1	55	4,863	47
144	0	2	0	0	226	292	0	26	2,241	48
578	0	7	0	0	538	1,168	130	16,955	50,805	49
131	0	25	0	0	237	380	47	353	13,310	50
22,502	3,280	12,019	14,371	559	68,351	28,574	13,710	52,960	569,912	51

Selected Bibliography

Selected Bibliography

Selected Bibliography

Books

Almon, Clopper, Jr., *The American Economy to 1975* (New York: Harper & Row, 1966).

Baumol, William J., *Business Behavior, Value, and Growth* (New York: The Macmillan Company, 1959).

Chapman, John H., Jr., and Shellhammer, Kenneth L., *The Structure of the West Virginia Economy, 1965: A Preliminary Report* (Morgantown, W. Va.: Regional Research Institute, November 1967).

Chenery, Hollis B., and Clark, Paul G., *Interindustry Economics* (New York: John Wiley & Sons, Inc., 1959).

Creamer, Daniel, *Capital Expansion and Capacity in Postwar Manufacturing*, National Industrial Conference Board, Studies in Business Economics, No. 72 (New York, 1961).

Hirschman, Albert O., *The Strategy of Economic Development* (New Haven: Yale University Press, 1958).

Isard, Walter, *Methods of Regional Analysis: An Introduction to Regional Science* (Cambridge, Mass.: The M. I. T. Press, 1960).

Isard, Walter, Langford, Thomas W., Jr., and Romanoff, Eliah, *Philadelphia Region Input-Output Study* (Philadelphia: Regional Science Research Institute, n.d.

Lange, Oskar, *Introduction to Econometrics* (New York: The Macmillan Company, 1963).

Leontief, Wassily, *Input-Output Economics* (New York: Oxford University Press, 1966).

————. *The Structure of the American Economy 1919–1939* (New York: Oxford University Press, 1951).

Miernyk, William H., *The Elements of Input-Output Analysis* (New York: Random House, 1965).

Miernyk, William H., Bonner, Ernest R., Chapman, John H., Jr., and Shellhammer, Kenneth L., *Impact of the Space Program on a Local Economy* (Morgantown, W. Va.: West Virginia University Library, 1967).

Miernyk, William H., and Shellhammer, Kenneth L., *The Structure of the West Virginia Economy in 1975: A Preliminary Forecast* (Morgantown, W.Va.: Regional Research Institute, 1967).

National Planning Association, *Capacity Expansion Planning Factors* (Washington, 1966).

National Bureau of Economic Research, "The Measurement of Capital Coefficients and Productive Capacity," *Problems of Capital Formation*, Vol. 19 (Princeton: Princeton University Press, 1957), pp. 287–468.

Parnes, H. S., *Planning Education for Economic and Social Development* (Paris: OECD, 1964).

Schuchman, Abe, *Scientific Decision Making in Business* (New York: Holt, Rinehart & Winston, Inc., 1963).

Shaffer, H. E., et al., *Report on Bricks from Flyash* (Morgantown, W. Va.: Coal Research Bureau, West Virginia University, Report No. 29 (March 1967).

Stone, Richard, *Input-Output and National Accounts* (Paris: OECD, 1961).
Tilanus, C. B., *Input-Output Experiments* (Rotterdam: Rotterdam University Press, 1966).

Articles

Carter, Anne P., "Changes in the Structure of American Economy, 1947–1958 and 1962," *The Review of Economics and Statistics* (May 1967), pp. 209–224.

——— . "Incremental Flow Coefficients for a Dynamic Input-Output with Changing Technology," in *Structural Interdependence and Economic Development,* Tibor Barna (ed.) (New York: St. Martin's Press, 1963), pp. 277–302.

——— . "The Economics of Technological Change," *Scientific American* (April 1966), pp. 25–31.

Evans, Duane W., and Hoffenberg, Marvin, "The Interindustry Relation Study for 1947," *The Review of Economics and Statistics* (May 1952), p. 100.

Horowitz, M. A., and Herrnstadt, I. L., "More Doubts About Average Training Times Computed from CED and SUP Levels," *Review of Economics and Statistics* (November 1967), pp. 638–640.

Kain, John F., and Meyer, John R., "Computer Simulations, Physio-Economic Systems, and Intraregional Models," *American Economic Review* (May 1968), pp. 171–181.

Klein, Lawrence, "Some Theoretical Issues in the Measurement of Capacity," *Econometrica* (April 1960), pp. 272–386.

Leontief, Wassily, "Dynamic Analysis," in Leontief *et al., Studies in the Structure of the American Economy* (New York: Oxford University Press, 1953), pp. 53–90.

——— . "The Dynamic Inverse" in *Contributions to Input-Output Analysis* (Amsterdam: North-Holland Publishing Company, 1970).

——— . "The Structure of Development," *Scientific American* (September 1963), pp. 148–166.

McFadden, C. R., and Leonard, J. W., "West Virginia Improves Coal Outlook with a Research Program," *Appalachia* (March 1968), pp. 12–13.

Marks, Jerome A., and Ziegler, Martin, "Recent Developments in Productivity and Unit Labor Costs," *Monthly Labor Review* (May 1967), pp. 26–29.

Miernyk, William H., "The Dynamic Model," *Growth and Change*, Vol. I, No. 2 (1970).

——— . "Long-Range Forecasting with a Regional Input-Output Model," *Western Economic Journal*, VI (June 1968): 165–176.

——— . "Sampling Techniques in Making Regional Industry Forecasts," *Applications of Input-Output Analysis* (Amsterdam: North-Holland Publishing Company, 1970).

Philips, Almarin, "An Appraisal of Measures of Capacity," *American Economic Review* (May 1963), pp. 275–292.

Sevaldson, Per, "Changes in Input-Output Coefficients," in *Structural Interdependence and Economic Development*, Tibor Barna (ed.) (New York: St. Martin's Press, 1963), pp. 308–328.

Tiebout, Charles M., "Regional and Interregional Input-Output Models: An Appraisal," *The Southern Economic Journal* (November 1957), pp. 140–147.

Weirtele, Zivia S., "A Note on Some Stability Properties of Leontief's Dynamic Models," *Econometrica* (October 1959), pp. 672–675.

Government Publications

Area Development Committee of the Public Utilities Association of the Virginias, *Gas for Industry in Virginia and West Virginia* (1961).

Area Development Committee of the Public Utilities Association of the Virginias, *Power for Industry in Virginia and West Virginia* (1961).

Council of Economic Advisers, *Economic Report of the President, 1969.*

Internal Revenue Service, *Depreciation Guidelines* (Revised, August 1964).

Joint Economic Committee, *Economic Analysis of Public Investment Decisions: Interest Rate Policy and Discounting Analysis* (Washington, D. C.: Government Printing Office, 1968).

The National Underwriters Company, *Underwriters Handbook of West Virginia* (May 1964).

State of West Virginia, Department of Mines, *Annual Report, 1964.*

State Road Commission of West Virginia, Construction Division, Contract Department, *Prequalified Contractors as of July 8, 1966.*

U. S. Bureau of Labor Statistics, *Employment and Earnings* (July 1966).

U. S. Department of Agriculture, *Agricultural Statistics* (1965).

U. S. Department of Agriculture, *Farm Income Situation* (July 1965).

U. S. Department of Commerce, Bureau of the Census, *Annual Survey of Manufacturers, 1964 and 1965* (1968).

U. S. Department of Commerce, Bureau of the Census, *Area Statistics* (1967).

U. S. Department of Commerce, Bureau of the Census, *Census of Mineral Industries 1963*, Vol. II.

U. S. Department of Commerce, Bureau of the Census, *Statistical Abstract of the United States* (1967, 88th ed.).

U. S. Department of Labor, Bureau of Labor Statistics, *Employment and Earnings Statistics for States and Areas, 1939–67* (August 1968).

U. S. Department of Labor, Bureau of Labor Statistics, *Handbook of Labor Statistics* (1967).

U. S. Department of Labor, Bureau of Labor Statistics, *Projections 1970, Interindustry Relationships, Potential Demand, Employment,* BLS Report No. 1536 (December 1966).

U. S. Department of Labor, Bureau of Labor Statistics, *1970 Input-Output Coefficients* BLS Report N. 326 (n.d.).

West Virginia Department of Commerce, Planning and Research Division, *West Virginia Manufacturing Directory,* 1965 (Beckley, W. Va.: Biggs, Johnston and Withrow, 1966).

West Virginia Department of Mines, Oil and Gas Division, *List of Oil and Gas Operators* (1965).

West Virginia Hospital Association, *Directory of Hospitals* (1966).

West Virginia Real Estate Commission, *Directory of Licenses to Real Estate Brokers and Salesmen* (September 1965).

West Virginia State Medical Association, *Roster of Members* (1966).

West Virginia State Tax Commission, *Consumer Listing by Class, and Retail Master File.*

Notes

Notes

Chapter 1
The 1965 Transactions Table

1. John H. Chapman, Jr., and Kenneth L. Shellhammer, *The Structure of the West Virginia Economy, 1965: A Preliminary Report* (Morgantown, W. Va.: Regional Research Institute, West Virginia University, November 1967).

2. William H. Miernyk and Kenneth L. Shellhammer, *Simulating Regional Development with an Input-Output Model* (Morgantown, W. Va.: Regional Research Institute, West Virginia University, July 1968), p. 6.

3. The basic sources for compiling these lists were: State of West Virginia, Department of Mines, *Annual Report* (1964); State Road Commission of West Virginia, Construction Division, Contract Department, *Prequalified Contractors as of July 8, 1966*; West Virginia Department of Commerce, Planning and Research Division, *West Virginia Manufacturing Directory, 1965,* (Beckley, W. Va.: Biggs, Johnston and Withrow, 1966); *The Southern Bankers Directory* (Atlanta, Ga., 1966); *Underwriters Handbook of West Virginia,* the National Underwriters Company (May 1964); *Directory of Licenses to Real Estate Brokers and Salesmen,* West Virginia Real Estate Commission (September 1965); West Virginia State Medical Association, *Roster of Members* (1966); West Virginia Hospital Association, *Directory of Hospitals* (1966); *Power for Industry in Virginia and West Virginia,* Area Development Committee of the Public Utilities Association of the Virginias (1961); *Gas for Industry in Virginia and West Virginia,* Area Development Committee of the Public Utilities Association of the Virginias (1961); West Virginia Department of Mines, Oil and Gas Division, *List of Oil and Gas Operators* (1965).

Lists from these sources were supplemented by cross checks with the 13 telephone directories issued by the C. & P. Telephone Company of West Virginia published between May 1965 and June 1966. The lists were finally checked against West Virginia State Tax Commission, *Consumer Listing by Class, and Retail Master File.*

Data obtained from the Economic Research Service were supplemented by information from U. S. Department of Agriculture, *Farm Income Situation* (July 1966), and *Agricultural Statistics* (1965).

4. For an illustration of a recapitulation sheet see William H. Miernyk, Ernest R. Bonner, John H. Chapman, Jr., and Kenneth L. Shellhammer, *Impact of the Space Program on a Local Economy* (Morgantown, W. Va.: West Virginia University Library, 1967), pp. 64–73, and Appendix V. Many of the procedures used in the West Virginia study are refinements of techniques developed in this earlier impact study.

Chapter 2
Comparative Static Projections to 1975

1. W. Duane Evans and Marvin Hoffenberg. "The Interindustry Relation Study for 1947," *The Review of Economics and Statistics* (May 1952), p. 100.

2. See Anne P. Carter, "Incremental Flow Coefficients for a Dynamic Input-Output Model with Changing Technology," in *Structural Interdependence and Economic Development,* Tibor Barna (ed.) (New York. St. Martin's Press, 1963), pp. 277–302; and Per Sevaldson, "Changes in Input-Output Coefficients," *ibid.,* pp. 308–328. See also the comments on Sevaldson's paper by Tsunehiko Watanabe, *ibid.,* pp. 328–332.

3. The results are reported in Anne P. Carter, "The Economics of Technological Change." *Scientific American* (April 1966), pp. 25–31; and "Changes in the Structure of American Economy, 1947–1958 and 1962," *The Review of Economics and Statistics* (May 1967), pp. 209–224. In the Netherlands, input-output tables were published on an annual basis between 1948 and 1961. For an analysis of the technical coefficients see C. B. Tilanus, *Input-Output Experiments,* (Rotterdam: Rotterdam University Press, 1966), especially pp. 36–51.

4. Carter, "Structure of American Economy," p. 223.

5. Carter, "Economics of Technological Change," p. 27; and *The Review of Economics and Statistics,* p. 224.

6. For a general discussion of this problem see William H. Miernyk, *The Elements of Input-Output Analysis,* (New York: Random House, 1965), pp. 71–72.

7. For a discussion of the logic behind this method see Miernyk, *Elements of Input-Output Analysis,* pp. 117–125. Additional details are given by the following articles by Miernyk: "Long-Range Forecasting with a Regional Input-Output Model," *Western Economic Journal,* VI (June 1968), pp. 165–176: and "Sampling Techniques in Making Regional Industry Forecasts," in *Applications of Input-Output Analysis* (Amsterdam: North-Holland Publishing Company, 1970).

8. Trends in national coefficients were obtained from *Survey of Current Business* (September 1965), pp. 40–44; and U. S. Department of Labor, Bureau of Labor Statistics, *1970 Input-Output Coefficients,* BLS Report No. 326 (n. d.).

9. This has been discussed in Miernyk, "Long-Range Forecasting," and "Sampling Techniques."

10. Miernyk and Shellhammer, *Simulating Regional Development.*

11. *Projections 1970, Interindustry Relationships, Potential Demand, Employment,* U. S. Department of Labor, Bureau of Labor Statistics, Bulletin No. 1536 (December 1966).

Chapter 3
Final Forecasts to 1975

1. Wassily Leontief, "Dynamic Analysis," in Leontief *et al., Studies in the Structure of the American Economy* (New York: Oxford University Press, 1953), pp. 53–90. For a clear and concise statement of the theory of dynamic

input-output systems see also Leontief, *Input-Output Economics* (New York: Oxford University Press, 1966), pp. 145—151. For a discussion of dynamic models of capital formation illustrated by a simple numerical example, see Hollis B. Chenery and Paul G. Clark, *Interindustry Economics* (New York: John Wiley & Sons Inc., 1959), pp. 71—80. An interesting discussion within the framework of a planned economy is given by Oskar Lange in *Introduction to Econometrics*, 2nd ed. (New York: The Macmillan Company, 1963), pp. 259—293.

2. Clopper Almon, Jr., *The American Economy to 1975* (New York: Harper & Row, 1966).

3. For a review of some of the problems encountered in these efforts, see the articles and comments under Part II, "The Measurement of Capital Coefficients and Productive Capacity," in National Bureau of Economic Research, *Problems of Capital Formation*, Vol. 19 (Princeton: Princeton University Press, 1957), pp. 287—468. Fixed capital coefficients for the U. S. economy in 1939 are given in Robert N. Grosse, "The Structure of Capital," in Leontief *et al.*, *Studies in the Structure of American Economy*, Table 1, Chap. 6.

4. For a general discussion of capacity and capital coefficients see Chenery and Clark, *Interindustry Economics*, pp. 149—153; and Richard Stone, *Input-Output and National Accounts* (Paris: OECD, 1961), pp. 64—72.

5. William J. Baumol, *Business Behavior, Value, and Growth* (New York: The Macmillian Company, 1959), Chaps. 6—8.

6. For a review of these measures see Almarin Phillips, "An appraisal of Measures of Capacity," *American Economic Review* (May 1963), pp. 275—92.

7. Only the NICB approach will be discussed since the FRB uses NICB data. A more detailed discussion of the NICB approach is found in Daniel Creamer, *Capital Expansion and Capacity in Postwar Manufacturing*, National Industrial Conference Board, Studies in Business Economics, No. 72 (New York, 1961).

8. See the statement by Daniel Creamer in Joint Economic Committee, *Measures of Productive Capacity*, Report of the Subcommittee on Economic Statistics (Washington: Government Printing Office, July 24, 1962), pp. 36—41.

9. For further discussion of this method, which has been used by the Wharton School Econometric group, see Lawrence Klein, "Some Theoretical Issues in the Measurement of Capacity," *Econometrica* (April 1960), pp. 272—386.

10. *West Virginia Manufacturing Directory*, West Virginia Department of Commerce, Planning and Research Division (1965).

11. Miernyk and Shellhammer, *Simulating Regional Economic Development with an Input-Output Model*, pp. 48—66.

12. Internal Revenue Service, *Depreciation Guidelines* (Revised, August 1964).

13. Anne Carter, "Capital Coefficients as Economic Parameters: The Problem of Instability," in *Problems of Capital Formation*, Vol. 19 (Princeton: Princeton University Press, 1957), pp. 287—310.

14. Carter, "Capital Coefficients as Economic Parameters," pp. 308—310.

15. Zivia S. Weirtele, "A Note on Some Stability Properties of Leontief's Dynamic Models," *Econometrica* (October 1959), pp. 672—675.

336

Chapter 4
Projecting Labor Requirements

1. Wassily Leontief, *The Structure of the American Economy 1919–1939* (New York: Oxford University Press, 1951), p. 143.
2. Leontief, *Structure of American Economy.*
3. Leontief, *Structure of American Economy*, p. 144.
4. U. S. Department of Labor, Bureau of Labor Statistics, *Employment and Earnings Statistics for States and Areas, 1939–67* (August 1968) pp. 469–471; *Handbook of Labor Statistics* (1967), pp. 97–106. U. S. Department of Commerce, Bureau of the Census, *Statistical Abstract of the United States* (1967, 88th ed.), pp. 237–241; *Annual Survey of Manufacturers, 1964 and 1965* (1968), pp. 318–319; *Census of Mineral Industries 1963*, Vol. II, *Area Statistics* (1967), p. 47; Council of Economic Advisers, *Economic Report of the President, 1969*, pp. 260–263; Interviews with Ralph Halsted, West Virginia Department of Employment Security (October 16, 1968), and with representatives of personnel departments in selected West Virginia business establishments (September–October 1968).
5. U. S. Bureau of Labor Statistics, *Employment and Earnings* (July 1966), pp. 112–113.
6. Cross-sectional data on productivity cannot be used to estimate long-run trends because of the significant effects on the ratios of short-term fluctuations in output. On this see Jerome A. Marks and Martin Ziegler, "Recent Developments in Productivity and Unit Labor Costs," *Monthly Labor Review* (May 1967), pp. 26–29.
7. Almon, *American Economy to 1975*, pp. 126–127.
8. The hazards of such an exercise have been covered in a number of manpower studies. See, for example, H. S. Parnes, *Planning Education for Economic and Social Development* (Paris:OECD, 1964), pp. 147–157; and M. A. Horowitz and I. L. Herrnstadt, "More Doubts About Average Training Times Computed from CED and SVP Levels," *Review of Economics and Statistics* (November 1967), pp. 638–640.

Chapter 5
Simulating Regional Development

1. Another possibility which cannot be overlooked is that oil-from-coal will also have to compete with oil-from-shale, and some estimates place the cost of shale oil at about 50% of the present price of high-grade crude at the wellhead. For a recent discussion see *Business Week* (July 13, 1968), pp. 115–117.
2. For details see C. R. McFadden and J. W. Leonard, "West Virginia Improves Coal Outlook with a Research Program," *Appalachia*, (March 1968), pp. 12–13. See also H. E. Shaffer, Jr., *et al., Report on Bricks from Flyash*, Report No. 29 (Morgantown, W. Va.: Coal Research Bureau, West Virginia University, March 1967).
3. McFadden and Leonard, "West Virginia Improves Coal Outlook," p. 13.
4. Walter Isard, Thomas W. Langford, Jr., and Eliah Romanoff, *Philadelphia Region Input-Output Study*, preliminary working papers, Vols. I and II, and accompanying tables, (Philadelphia: Regional Science Research Institute, n. d.).

5. Wassily Leontief, "The Dynamic Inverse," in *Contributions to Input-Output Analysis* (Amsterdam: North-Holland Publishing Company, 1970).

6. For illustration see Leontief, "Dynamic Inverse."

Chapter 6
Input-Output Analysis and
the Strategy of Regional Development

1. Albert O. Hirschman, *The Strategy of Economic Development* (New Haven: Yale University Press, 1958), p. 1.

2. Hirschman, *Strategy of Economic Development*, p. 2.

3. We did not calculate a benefit-cost ratio for the simulated sulfuric acid industry for two reasons. First, we do not want to leave the impression that we favor a subsidy. Second, the outcome would depend largely on the discount rate employed, and we were unwilling to estimate the present opportunity cost of capital in West Virginia which is one basis for selecting the discount rate. Development officials would presumably be in a position to make such an estimate. For further discussion of this issue see Joint Economic Committee. *Economic Analysis of Public Investment Decisions: Interest Rate Policy and Discounting Analysis* (Washington, D. C.: Government Printing Office, 1968).

4. For the steps involved in calculating both types of multipliers see Miernyk, *Input-Output Analysis*, pp. 42—55.

5. Wassily Leontief, *Input-Output Economics* (New York: Oxford University Press, 1966), p. 67.

About the Authors

About the Authors

William H. Miernyk is Benedum Professor of Economics and Director, Regional Research Institute, West Virginia University. He received his B. A. from the University of Colorado, and an M. A. and Ph. D. from Harvard University. He has taught at Northeastern University and the University of Colorado, and has been visiting professor of economics at Harvard and M. I. T. His earlier books include *The Economic State of New England* (co-author, 1954); *Inter-Industry Labor Mobility* (1955); *Trade Unions in the Age of Affluence* (1962); *The Economics of Labor and Collective Bargaining* (1965); *The Elements of Input-Output Analysis* (1965); and (with others) *Impact of the Space Program on a Local Economy* (1967).

Kenneth L. Shellhammer is Assistant Professor of Economics, West Virginia University. He received his undergraduate and graduate education in economics at the University of Colorado. He is a co-author of *Impact of the Space Program on a Local Economy* (1967).

Douglas M. Brown is Assistant Professor of Economics, Northeastern University. He received his B. A. from Wittenberg College, an M. A. degree from The Ohio State University, and his Ph. D. in economics from West Virginia University.

Ronald L. Coccari holds B. S. and MBA degrees from West Virginia University, where he is a candidate for the Ph. D. in economics.

Charles J. Gallagher is Assistant Professor of Economics at the University of Georgia. He received a B. S. from Rider College, and is a candidate for the Ph. D. in economics at West Virginia University.

Wesley H. Wineman was awarded his B. A. by West Virginia University, where he is continuing his work as a graduate student and research assistant in the Regional Research Institute.